The Macroeconomics of Fiscal Policy

The Macroeconomics of Fiscal Policy

edited by

Richard W. Kopcke

Geoffrey M. B. Tootell

Robert K. Triest

The MIT Press
Cambridge, Massachusetts
London, England

MIT Press books may be purchased at special quantity discount for business or sale promotional use. For information, please email special_sales@mitpress.mit.edu or write to Special Sales Department, The MIT Press, 55 Hayward Street, Cambridge, MA 02142

This book was set in Sabon by Sztrecska Publishing and was printed and bound in the United States of America.

Library of Congress Cataloging-in-Publication Data

The macroeconomics of fiscal policy / edited by Richard W. Kopcke, Geoffrey M.B. Tootell, Robert K. Triest.
      p. cm.
   Includes bibliographical references and indexes.
   ISBN 0-262-11295-7 (alk. paper)
      1. Fiscal policy —United States. 2. Fiscal policy. 3. Macroeconomics. I. Kopcke, Richard W. II. Tootell, Geoffrey M.B. (Geoffrey Matthew Bemis) III. Triest, Robert K.

HJ257.2.M33 2006
339.5'2—dc22   2005054537

10 9 8 7 6 5 4 3 2 1

Contents

Acknowledgments

The Federal Reserve Bank of Boston and the three editors served as the principal organizers of this volume. They would like to thank all the persons who contributed to their efforts. At the risk of omitting some, we thank in particular Susan Rodburg and Patricia Geagan, who managed the arrangements with the able assistance of Tom DeCoff, Donna Dulski, Nancy Gillespie, Radoslav Raykov, and Matthew S. Rutledge; as well as Ann Eggleston, Heidi Furse, Brad Hershbein, Sally Sztrecska, Linda Walsh, and Julie Weinstein, who helped in the preparation of the volume. Special mention must be accorded Elizabeth Murry of MIT Press, who worked with the editors in defining the concept of the volume, and Suzanne Lorant, who had primary responsibility for shepherding the book from manuscript review to final copy.

1
Introduction

Introduction: The Macroeconomics of Fiscal Policy

Richard W. Kopcke, Geoffrey M. B. Tootell, and Robert K. Triest

It is hard to imagine a more opportune time for a volume on the macroeconomics of fiscal policy, since the last few years have seen government spending, taxation, and deficit financing move to the forefront of policy debates worldwide. In Japan in the 1990s, deflation and short-term interest rates that hovered near zero forced policymakers to turn to fiscal policy to stimulate the country's sluggish economy. For somewhat similar reasons, fiscal policy also played an important role in fostering the U.S. economy's recovery after the 2001 recession. Members of the European Monetary Union are also reconsidering the merits of maintaining the fiscal restraint required by their "Pact for Stability and Growth" as they seek ways to foster expansion after years of weak growth. At the same time, the discussion of fiscal policies has renewed attention to the effects of large sustained fiscal deficits on national savings, investment, interest rates, and the current account.

The effect of government expenditures, taxation, and debt on the aggregate economy is of immense importance, and therefore great controversy, in economics. A broad range of essential services is provided by governments, requiring the collection of taxes and fees. This book, however, covers only a subset of these issues, those associated with the macroeconomic aspects of fiscal policy. The authors of the chapters and commentaries included in this volume address questions such as: Should fiscal policy be used to help stabilize the economy and smooth business-cycle fluctuations? Do large government deficits harm economic activity? Has recent U.S. fiscal policy contributed to overconsumption by American consumers? And, how is U.S. fiscal policy related to the current account and international capital flows?

In this chapter, we provide a brief introduction to the important topics addressed by the subsequent chapters. We start with a general discussion of fiscal policy's potential effects on economic activity, in order to outline the main concerns and controversies related to the macroeconomics of fiscal policy. Following this discussion, we provide a brief description of how the chapters in this volume address the important issues pertaining to fiscal policy today.

1.   How Does Fiscal Policy Affect the Macro Economy?

Fiscal policy affects aggregate demand, the distribution of wealth, and the economy's capacity to produce goods and services. In the short run, changes in spending or taxing can alter both the magnitude and the pattern of demand for goods and services. With time, this aggregate demand affects the allocation of resources and the productive capacity of an economy through its influence on the returns to factors of production, the development of human capital, the allocation of capital spending, and investment in technological innovations. Tax rates, through their effects on the net returns to labor, saving, and investment, also influence both the magnitude and the allocation of productive capacity.

Macroeconomics has long featured two general views of the economy and the ability of fiscal policy to stabilize or even affect economic activity. The equilibrium view sees the economy quickly returning to full capacity whenever disturbances displace it from full employment. Accordingly, changes in fiscal policy, or even in monetary policy for that matter, have little potential for stabilizing the economy. Instead, inevitable delays in recognizing economic disturbances, in enacting a fiscal response, and in the economy's reacting to the change in policy can aggravate, rather than diminish, business-cycle fluctuations. An alternative view sees critical market failures causing the economy to adjust with more difficulty to these disturbances. If, for example, consumers were to reduce their current spending in order to consume more in the future, producers, who would not know the consumers' future plans for want of the appropriate futures markets for goods and services, would see only an indefinite drop in demand, and this might encourage them, in turn, to reduce their hiring and capital spending. In this world, changes in fiscal and monetary policy have greater potential for stabilizing aggregate demand and economic activity. How the economy reacts to fiscal policy depends on whether it is at full employment or operating below its full capacity.

Effects of a Tax Cut on Consumer Spending

To illustrate the importance of the difference in these two views for fiscal-policy stabilization, consider the effects of a cut in personal taxes—a classic countercyclical fiscal-policy action. Lower taxes, everything else being constant, increase households' disposable income, allowing consumers to increase their spending. The consequences of the cut—how much is spent or saved, and the response of economic activity—depend on the way households make their decisions and on prevailing macroeconomic conditions.

For example, whether the tax cut is perceived to be temporary or permanent will influence how much consumers save. A temporary cut when the economy is at full employment will alter households' lifetime disposable income relatively little, and so might have little effect on consumption. If the cut is, instead, perceived to be permanent, then households will perceive a larger increase in their lifetime disposable income and so will likely increase their desired consumption by much more than they would if they thought the cut were temporary.

So far, we have been considering the effect of a tax cut on households' consumption expenditures with everything else held constant. However, lower taxes will increase the government's fiscal deficit. Suppose that the economy tends to remain near full employment and that households do not expect their disposable income to rise any higher than it would have risen without the change in fiscal policy. Even if the tax cut is long-lasting, many will conclude that future taxes will need to be higher than they otherwise would have been in order to retire the extra public debt resulting from the tax cut. In the extreme case, households will not feel that their disposable income has risen, because they have completely internalized the increase in the public debt arising from the tax cut, treating it as though it were equivalent to personal debt.

Yet even in the full-employment view, consumption might increase as a result of the tax cut if capital markets are imperfect. Consumers who are liquidity constrained, living from paycheck to paycheck, will likely increase their spending even if they internalize the public debt. So the effect of the tax cut will depend on its incidence over different types of taxpayers. Consumption will also increase if the government can borrow at a lower rate of interest than the consumer.

However, consumption can increase more significantly when the economy is not at full employment and if the tax cut is seen as an instance of a continuing fiscal policy that stabilizes economic activity, or if the tax cut otherwise raises households' expected income by increasing the economy's future productive capacity. Although the tax cut entails an increase in public debt, higher current and future income diminishes the burden of servicing or repaying this debt. In this case, the tax cut is essentially an investment in a public good that redounds to the benefit of households.

Effects on Interest Rates, Capital Formation, and International Capital Flows

Over time, an increase in the budget deficit resulting from a tax cut will increase the public debt. That increase raises important issues concerning the long-run effects of the tax cut on interest rates, capital investment, and future economic welfare. The rich range of possible consequences makes this a very controversial and interesting topic.

Fiscal policies that increase the deficit will result in future taxes being higher than they otherwise would have been, but, depending on the policies' effects on incentives for investing in human or physical capital, they might also raise future living standards. Policies that absorb slack resources or foster investment might reduce government saving, as reflected in the greater budget deficit, while they increase total saving, as reflected in the greater rate of capital formation. This additional saving might be supplied by the increase in national income, or it might come from foreign sources. Policies that fail to raise income and investment not only reduce government saving, but also reduce total saving.

When the economy is at full employment and a tax cut today is expected to be offset by a tax increase in the future, as discussed above, lower taxes do not necessarily increase consumption spending. In this extreme case, the increase in the government's deficit will be matched by an increase in private saving. As a result, national saving, interest rates, and investment spending will be much the same as if there had been no change in fiscal policy. If, instead, consumers spend much of their additional disposable income while the economy is already at full employment, personal saving will not rise sufficiently to offset the drop in public saving, interest rates will rise, and investment spending will decline, unless business saving (resulting from the additional consumption spending) or capital inflows from abroad increase sufficiently to make up the difference. If the economy is not at full employment, national income might expand as a result of the cut, providing additional income-tax receipts and saving, and thereby preventing a drop in national saving. In either case, a tax cut that increases the return on capital can increase business saving and attract, for a time, an inflow of foreign saving sufficient to maintain total saving and investment. If, however, fiscal policy depresses investment, then both the capital stock and economic output will be lower in the future than they otherwise would have been. The lower capital stock will tend to be accompanied by real interest rates that are higher than they otherwise would have been.

If capital inflows from abroad increase sufficiently to offset any drop in national saving resulting from a change in fiscal policy, then investment need not fall. In this case, the current account deficit, which is equal to the quantity of capital inflows from abroad, will increase at least enough to offset the increase in the budget deficit less the induced increase in private saving. The future levels of the capital stock and real output will not fall, but future domestic consumption will be reduced because an increased share of the return to capital will accrue to foreign nationals—unless the fiscal policy fosters a greater utilization of the stock of capital, greater capital formation, or greater net returns on capital to compensate for the outflow. The concurrent large budget and current account deficits that occurred in the early 1980s and again in the last few years have led many to believe that increases in the current account deficit would generally accompany large increases in the budget deficit, and gave rise to the term "twin deficits."

Tension Between Short-Term Stabilization and Long-Term Goals

In the discussion so far, it is apparent that there is a potential conflict between the use of fiscal policy to stimulate aggregate demand when the economy is operating below potential in the short run and the use of policy to promote longer-run goals for national saving and capital formation to improve future living standards. When there are underutilized economic resources, fiscal stimulus can increase investment. But when the economy is operating near potential, an increase in the public debt might eventually depress private investment, unless the fiscal stimulus is reversed as the economy approaches full employment or the policy fosters capital formation and increases the supply of labor.

This tension between short-run stabilization and longer-run growth is prominent in the rest of this volume. The volume begins with a reconsideration of the role of fiscal policy in macroeconomic stabilization before turning to an analysis of longer-term concerns.

2.   Overview of the Volume

This volume does not examine what the theory should say about the data, but rather explores what the data say about the theory. As is clear, different economic theories can justify almost any policy. The chapters in this book revisit the empirical evidence concerning the effect of fiscal policy on the economy. Is there evidence that fiscal policy can help to stabilize the economy? Has it done so in the past? And, finally, has it accomplished the long-run goals it should? Before the latter two questions can be answered, the first should be addressed.

Can Fiscal Policy Improve Macro Stabilization?
Countercyclical Fiscal Policy in Theory
Through the 1980s and 1990s, the predominant answer in the profession was a resounding "no." Alan Blinder takes issue with that conclusion in "The Case Against the Case Against Discretionary Fiscal Policy." Blinder reminds the reader that views on the use of discretionary fiscal policy as a tool for macroeconomic stabilization have undergone a sea change since the early 1960s, when the prevailing wisdom was that discretionary stabilization policy was effective and desirable for taming the business cycle, and that fiscal policy was the most important tool with which to conduct stabilization policy. Then, beginning in the late 1960s, theoretical and empirical work raised serious doubts about fiscal policy's abil-

ity to accomplish countercyclical stabilization, while large deficits in the 1980s made it unlikely any would be attempted.

Blinder begins by reviewing the intellectual and policy developments that led to the diminished role of fiscal policy, and then turns his attention to a critical analysis of the arguments against the use of discretionary fiscal policy as a stabilization tool. After discussing the theoretical assumptions underlying Ricardian equivalence[1], Blinder evaluates the empirical research on this topic. He concludes that the weight of the evidence supports the view that both temporary and permanent tax changes do affect consumption spending.

Overall, Blinder finds the practical arguments against the use of discretionary fiscal policy to be more compelling than the theoretical arguments. Long lags in the formulation and implementation of appropriate stabilization policies are likely to be especially severe when the policy instrument is government purchases, leading Blinder to conclude that changes in taxes and transfers are more effective fiscal instruments for stabilization. Blinder suggests that institutional changes, such as placing short-run tax policy in the hands of a board of technical experts modeled after the Federal Reserve Board, might alleviate some of the practical aspects of using tax policy for stabilization.

Another suggestion Blinder makes is to improve the targeting of changes in taxes and transfers. If tax and transfer changes were better targeted at those households that are most likely to change their consumption spending in response to temporary changes in their disposable income, then fiscal policy would be more effective at influencing aggregate demand. Blinder cites the expansion of unemployment insurance benefits as an example of a fiscal policy that is well targeted for increasing consumption.

Blinder also suggests that future fiscal stabilization make greater use of opportunities to exploit intertemporal substitution. Examples of policies that exploit intertemporal substitution to temporarily stimulate aggregate demand are a temporary cut in sales-tax rates, which creates an incentive for consumers to purchase durable goods earlier than they otherwise would in order to avoid paying the tax, and a temporary investment tax credit, which provides an incentive for firms to accelerate the timing of new investment projects.

In the final analysis, Blinder concludes that monetary policy should be relied upon as the primary policy tool for macroeconomic stabilization, but that discretionary fiscal policy can play an important stabilization role under unusual circumstances. When a recession is unusually long or deep, or when short-term nominal interest rates approach zero, then it is appropriate to supplement monetary policy with fiscal stimulus.

In his comments, Olivier Blanchard agrees with Blinder that fiscal policy can be effective in stimulating aggregate demand and output in the short run. However, he offers the caveat that recent empirical evidence examining the effect of fiscal stimulus on output is mixed, and he believes that caution is warranted. Blanchard agrees with Blinder on the virtue of exploiting intertemporal substitution in formulating a fiscal stimulus, and, like Blinder, believes that temporary investment tax credits and temporary decreases in consumption tax rates deserve further attention and development.

Christopher Sims points to what he sees as an important omission in Blinder's evaluation of fiscal stabilization: that fiscal stimulus may exacerbate "intergenerationally unfair crowding out." Fiscal stimulus increases the budget deficit and public debt, and Sims notes that if the public believes that any tax increases needed to finance the debt will occur only in the distant future, then savings will fall *now* and the tax burden will be pushed onto future generations. Of course, if one wishes to increase aggregate demand, then a short-run increase in consumption is desirable. However, Sims believes it is important to pay attention to the consequences for intergenerational equity of using fiscal policy for stabilization purposes.

Sims adds a number of other caveats to Blinder's analysis. Sims thinks that one reason that countercyclical fiscal policy went out of fashion is the growing popularity of the view that at least a portion of the fluctuation in economic activity associated with the business cycle is part of a necessary reallocation of resources. However, the fluctuation also partly reflects market failure, and Sims believes that fiscal policy may be useful in offsetting the inefficient aspects of the fluctuation. As an example, he cites a policy also supported by Blinder: recession-related extensions of unemployment insurance benefits.

Blanchard, Blinder, and Sims agree that judicious use of countercyclical fiscal policy can be effective in some circumstances, particularly when monetary policy is less flexible, as when interest rates are already very low. The obvious next question is whether fiscal policy has been used in such a prudent manner.

American Fiscal Policy in Reality

Alan Auerbach attempts to answer this question by analyzing the evolution of American fiscal policy over the post-World War II era. Over this period, Auerbach notes that federal spending net of interest has been a relatively constant fraction of GDP since 1962, whereas there have been substantial shifts in the composition of spending, with entitlement spending growing and defense spending shrinking relative to GDP. Similarly, the composition of tax revenue has changed, with payroll taxes growing in relative importance. In discussing the behavior of the budget deficit, Auerbach highlights the sharp increase in the deficit that has occurred since 2000, but he emphasizes that it is still smaller in relation to GDP than the deficit of the mid-1980s.

Auerbach next illustrates how fiscal policy has helped to stabilize the economy over this period. He presents econometric results that indicate that both tax and expenditure policies respond countercyclically, with tax revenue decreasing and expenditures increasing in response to an increase in the gap between actual and potential GDP. Auerbach's measures of policy change are constructed to be independent of the automatic stabilizing effects of the fiscal system, and are designed to capture only the revenue and expenditure changes associated with explicit policy actions. The empirical analysis also shows that fiscal policy responds to budget conditions, with an increase in the budget surplus leading to a reduction in revenue and an increase in expenditures.

Auerbach links deviations from the estimated econometric relationships with specific historical events. For example, the 1993 Clinton tax increase is associated with a larger increase in revenue than the econometric results would predict, and the 2001 and 2003 tax cuts are associated with larger-than-predicted drops in revenue.

Auerbach attempts to put the recent fiscal deficit into historical context and then attempts to project the previous stabilization propensities into the future. Once the implications of the increasing importance of spending on Social Security, Medicare, and Medicaid are included, the picture becomes fairly grim, with a large gap between spending and tax revenue looming in coming decades. While the long-run fiscal problem is familiar to many, more surprising is Auerbach's finding that the change in the nature of the public sector will result in decreased responsiveness of future spending to changes in economic and budget conditions than has been the case in the past. Auerbach's econometric results indicate that discretionary spending responds more strongly to economic and budget conditions than does spending on social insurance. So, overall spending will become less responsive as social insurance benefit payments come to constitute a larger proportion of total spending.

Auerbach notes that the official budget deficit does not capture changes in future liabilities associated with social insurance programs and that this could make a difference in policy decisions. The econometric results show that fiscal-policy decisions are responsive to the budget deficit, and, therefore, the way the deficit is defined may well influence which policy proposals are adopted. The 2000 budget would have shown a substantial deficit, rather than a surplus, if the incremental liabilities associated with the social insurance programs had been incorporated into the official deficit measure, and Auerbach speculates that Congress would have been less likely to pass the 2001 tax cut if the official deficit had been defined in this way.

In reviewing the history of the major fiscal-policy changes of the past four decades, James Duesenberry finds that actual fiscal policy generally has not been good stabilization policy. Duesenberry advocates adoption of fiscal policies that avoid the potential conflict between long-term objectives and short-term stabilization that has proven to be problematic in the past. To address this problem, he would like to see greater use of semiautomatic fiscal stabilizers, such as an extension of unemployment benefits when a prespecified trigger point is reached, along with a goal of balancing the budget at full employment.

Douglas Elmendorf agrees with Auerbach's overall conclusions, but he believes that fiscal policy in recent decades is best described as consisting of two major episodes of dramatic deficit increases, the tax cuts early in the Reagan administration and the tax cuts in the George W. Bush administration, along with a period between these episodes of incremental adjustments toward restoring balance to the budget. Elmendorf agrees with Auerbach regarding the importance of the way in which we frame choices about fiscal policy. He advocates balancing the budget excluding Social Security and Medicare on average over the business cycle, and reforming the social insurance programs to achieve long-term solvency.

Fiscal Policy and Long-Run Financing
The Early Reagan Era: A Sea Change

So far, the discussion of fiscal policy has concentrated on stabilization policy. However, fiscal policy since the 1980s has been dominated by concerns about long-run financing. As Elmendorf points out, the deficits that resulted from the tax cuts early in the Reagan administration were a major factor driving fiscal policy for many years afterwards. C. Eugene Steuerle, W. Elliot Brownlee, Rudolph Penner, and Van Doorn Ooms provide four perspectives on fiscal policy in the early part of the Reagan era.

Steuerle's essay sets the stage with a review of post-war fiscal policy, with an emphasis on the three major tax cuts of the period: those of the Kennedy-Johnson, Reagan, and G.W. Bush administrations. Of these three sets of tax cuts, the Kennedy-Johnson cuts are the smallest, and the G.W. Bush cuts are the largest. After evaluating and applying a variety of measures, Steuerle concludes that the G.W. Bush tax cuts are the largest fiscal stimulus in the nation's history, excluding those accompanying world wars.

Turning to the question of the sustainability of the three tax cuts, Steuerle notes that sustainability was not really an issue when the Kennedy tax cuts were passed. The tax system was not yet indexed to inflation, so revenue grew as long as there was nominal income growth. And, with Social Security not yet mature, and Medicare and Medicaid not yet enacted, expenditures were largely discretionary and relatively easy to adjust. By the 1980s, the situation had changed. Tax brackets were inflation indexed starting in 1985, and a larger proportion of federal expenditure was devoted to entitlements. As a result, the deficits resulting from the 1982 Tax Act were quite persistent, and several rounds of legislated policy changes were required to restore fiscal balance. The

fiscal environment had changed still more by 2001 because of the growing share of federal expenditures devoted to entitlements and other
mandatory spending. This factor, along with a likely slowdown of tax-
revenue growth as the baby boomers retire, makes the recent tax cuts
unsustainable.

Brownlee, Ooms, and Penner each examine the fiscal policymaking
process in the early Reagan years that produced these unsustainable tax
cuts. Although the three authors approach this subject from different
perspectives, several common themes are evident. One is that the tax cuts
embedded in the 1981 Economic Recovery Tax Act (ERTA) turned out
to be larger in real terms than originally intended. All three authors note
that fiscal policymakers did not anticipate that monetary policy would be
as effective in quickly lowering the rate of price inflation as it turned out
to be. Because indexing of tax brackets and exemption amounts was not
implemented until 1985, the "bracket creep" that accompanied inflation
tended to increase tax revenue as a share of GDP. The ERTA tax cuts
were formulated, in part, to compensate for the "bracket creep" that was
expected to accompany inflation in the 1981-to-1985 period. Because
"bracket creep" was much smaller in magnitude than had been anticipated, some of the reduction in real tax revenue resulting from ERTA was
essentially accidental.

Brownlee, Ooms, and Penner also highlight that the larger-than-
expected deficits following ERTA produced a bipartisan effort to craft
new policy measures to reduce future deficits. At the same time, fiscal
policy was largely abandoned in favor of monetary policy as the primary tool of countercyclical stabilization. The initial round of new tax
increases was passed while the economy was still in the midst of a deep
recession, but the perceived problems associated with the budget deficits
outweighed any concerns about the effects of the tax increases on aggregate demand.

Government Financing in the Long Run

The deficits that emerged in the 1980s were unprecedented in a peacetime economy. These deficits raised serious concerns about the long-run
financing of government spending. Benjamin Friedman focuses on the
long-run implications of fiscal-policy choices. Friedman notes that the

economic implications of a budget deficit depend critically on whether it is transitory or persistent. Although fiscal stimulus might be beneficial in the short run when resources are underutilized, the long-term effects of persistent deficits are undesirable. Friedman presents econometric evidence, based on data from 1959 to 2003, indicating that increases in the deficit exhibit considerable persistence, but fade over time. Deficits (measured relative to GDP) tend to start decreasing a year after their initial increase, with the reversion half complete after three years (although the half-life is a little longer than four years when the data are restricted to the post-1980 period). Controlling for prior movements in economic output and inflation, which might be associated with either automatic stabilizers or discretionary fiscal stabilization, shortens the half-life of the persistence in the deficit to a little under two years. The persistence of increased deficits cumulates into an increase in the ratio of public debt to GDP. Friedman's estimates indicate that an increase in the debt-to-GDP ratio also decays over time, but with a half-life of over 20 years.

Because fiscal policy exhibits considerable persistence, it has the potential for inducing substantial long-run economic effects. And this brings us, once again, to the Ricardian equivalence controversy. Although Friedman acknowledges the difficulty of resolving this controversy econometrically, he points to a sign of consensus in two recent studies that find that a one-percentage-point increase in the expected debt-to-GDP ratio increases expected future real interest rates by about 3 to 5.8 basis points. This is sizable, and Friedman points out that if interest rates increase by 4 basis points per percentage-point increase in the debt-to-GDP ratio, then the increase in government debt between 1981 and 1993 would have increased real interest rates by nearly a full percentage point. He notes that an increase in real interest rates of that magnitude implies a substantial decrease in the economy's equilibrium capital-output ratio.

Friedman questions why public discussion of fiscal policy focuses on the economic effects of deficits, while economic theory implies that it is the debt-to-GDP ratio that matters. Given the identity that investment must equal the sum of private saving plus government saving plus financial inflows from abroad, a change in the deficit (government saving) may require substantial changes in investment or capital inflows from abroad unless private saving offsets the change in government saving.

Friedman presents econometric evidence that, after controlling for the effects of GDP growth and inflation, an increase in the budget deficit leads to a decrease in the rate of private investment that lasts for five quarters. Although he acknowledges that it is hard to distinguish econometrically between the effects of deficits and the effects of expected increases in the debt-to-GDP ratio resulting from persistent deficits, Friedman also notes that because portfolio adjustment is costly, it is theoretically plausible that budget deficits will have crowding out effects on investment that are independent of the deficit-induced increase in the debt-to-GDP ratio.

Barry Bosworth provides a different interpretation of deficit persistence. In his view, the deficits of the 1980s and early 1990s were reversed mainly by good luck rather than by intentional policy. Absent the run of good luck in the 1990s, especially the high rates of productivity growth and the low unemployment rate, the 1980s' deficits might have proven to be even more persistent.

Bosworth sides with those who emphasize deficits over the debt-to-GDP ratio as the more important area of concern. He believes that the impact of the public debt needs to be evaluated in the context of how it arose. Public debt that is accumulated during a period of economic slack has a lower economic cost than debt accumulated when resources are fully employed. But when deficits run during recessions are combined with those run during a boom into a single measure of the stock of public debt, that context is lost.

Deficits can be viewed as a transfer of income between generations. Susanto Basu offers a known framework for making decisions about such transfers. Basu notes that underlying the concerns of Friedman and many others regarding the long-term economic consequences of persistent budget deficits is an implicit moral judgment that it is unethical to promote current living standards at the expense of the economic welfare of future generations. Basu believes we should base our normative analysis of fiscal policy on rigorous thinking, rather than just on implicit judgments regarding which policies are desirable. Application of Rawls's theory of distributive justice might lead one to accept deficits that reduce the welfare of future generations if the future generations were certain to be better off than we are at present. But the same principles that lead one to favor redistribution toward relatively poor generations would also lead one to favor redistribution toward those who are disadvantaged within any given generation. So, distributive justice does not seem to provide justification for policies that reduce taxes on those currently wealthy, with the consequence of creating persistent deficits that reduce the economic welfare of future generations.

Why Has the United States Suffered Persistent Deficits Since 1980?

Another way to put Basu's question may be to ask whether the United States is, in some sense, overconsuming? Deficits are equivalent to government dis-saving, and so an increase in the deficit will result in decreased national saving, unless private saving increases enough to offset the drop in government saving. The combination of a personal saving rate that fell precipitously during the 1990s and the reemergence of large U.S. federal budget deficits in the early 2000s brings up the question of whether the United States is prone to saving too little and consuming too much.

Jean-Philippe Cotis, Jonathan Coppel, and Luiz de Mello tackle this question in their chapter. As Basu made clear in his comments on Friedman's chapter, the answer to this question depends on the normative criteria that one adopts. Cotis, Coppel, and de Mello take as their normative benchmark the notion from economic growth theory that, in the steady state, aggregate consumption should grow at the "natural rate," the sum of the rate of technical progress and the growth rate of the labor force. An example of an economy that is prone to overconsumption in this context would be one where private saving does not increase by an amount sufficient to return consumption growth to the natural rate following a shift into persistently larger fiscal deficits.

Cotis, Coppel, and de Mello present econometric evidence that the high rate of consumption growth in the United States in recent years can be explained as the result of increases in wealth and income, as well as decreases in interest rates. So, in this sense, households do not seem to have been overconsuming relative to normal behavior.

Capital inflows from abroad allowed the high rate of consumption growth and the declining rate of personal saving in the United States during the late 1990s to be accompanied by a high rate of investment. The rate of investment fell sharply in the early 2000s at the same time that the federal budget position went from a substantial surplus to a large and seemingly persistent deficit. Capital inflows have continued, but Cotis, Coppel, and de Mello caution that it will be difficult to return investment to its steady-state rate without an increase in the national saving rate. Econometric results they present suggest that private saving in the United States generally does not increase to offset the effects of increased budget deficits. Combined with the prospect of even larger budget deficits in the relatively near future as spending on social insurance benefits increases, this suggests the need for changes in public policy aimed at increasing national saving.

Willem Buiter points to the difficulty of answering the question of whether the United States consumes too much and saves too little. Insufficient understanding of the need to provide for their retirement consumption, and overestimation of how much of their retirement needs will be provided by government programs, may lead U.S. households to save at suboptimally low rates. On the other hand, the high rate of productivity growth in the United States simultaneously makes saving for the future less compelling and increases the attractiveness of the United States as a destination for foreign investment, arguably the driver of the large U.S. current account deficit. Buiter believes that the United States is in a relatively advantageous position regarding its external liabilities, which are mostly either real liabilities, such as equity and real estate, for which there is essentially no default risk, or dollar-denominated debt, the value of which can be reduced by inflation.

The Twin Deficits

Buiter raises the question of the ultimate cause of the capital inflow: Was it high returns to investment in the United States relative to the rest of the world, or low saving in the United States? In an attempt to answer this question, the volume concludes with a section considering the relationship between the current account deficit and the government budget deficit. Edwin Truman's essay provides an overview of the relationship between the two deficits, along with a discussion of their economic implications. Truman observes that, although the current account and fiscal deficits are linked through the saving-investment identity, they are not analytical or behavioral twins. The concurrence of large fiscal and current account deficits in the early 1980s gave rise to the "twin deficits" label, but Truman notes that the deficits do not generally move in the same direction.

Truman cites a consensus that neither deficit is sustainable at its current size relative to national output. Noting that the fiscal deficit is more directly controlled by policy than is the external deficit, and that it is also likely to have more serious adverse consequences for national economic welfare, Truman advocates efforts to reduce the fiscal deficit.

Jeffrey Frankel compares the two twin-deficit periods, the early 1980s and the early 2000s, with a focus on how increases in the budget deficit are split between reductions in investment and increases in the current account deficit. Confirming the results of earlier research by Martin Feldstein and Charles Horioka [Feldstein and Horioka (1980)] that there is a strong correlation between national saving and investment, Frankel presents regression estimates that suggest that roughly half of the changes in national saving are financed by changes in the current account, with the rest financed by changes in investment.

Catherine Mann highlights the point that the composition of fiscal deficits matters. A large portion of the fiscal deficits of recent years is due to tax cuts that have boosted consumer spending, which, in turn, has contributed to widening the trade and current account deficits. Mann also stresses that there is a negative feedback loop relating the two deficits. Continued foreign purchases of the Treasury securities issued to finance the fiscal deficit will increase the interest income flowing to the foreign holders, thereby increasing the current account deficit.

Alice Rivlin agrees that the twin deficits of the 1980s were related. She also believes that the only politically feasible way to reduce today's current account deficit is to solve the fiscal imbalance. Rivlin reviews options that she and Isabel Sawhill recently developed for closing the fiscal deficit. Rivlin emphasizes that it is possible to balance the federal budget over a 10-year period, but that the only politically feasible way to do so entails both expenditure limitations and tax increases. Political agreement about exactly how to reduce expenditures and increase taxes will be difficult and may require budget rules similar to those used in the late 1980s and early 1990s.

3. Concluding Comments

Although there is clearly a diversity of opinion regarding what constitutes appropriate fiscal policy evident among the contributors to this volume, several common themes emerge. There is widespread agreement that, although monetary policy is the primary instrument for macroeconomic stabilization, fiscal policy can potentially play a stabilizing role, particularly in relatively severe downturns and in periods when inflation is very low. Concern about lags and political motives in fiscal-policy decision-making is evident, and there is considerable interest in the further development of semiautomatic or rule-based fiscal stabilizers that might help to circumvent some of the practical problems associated with using fiscal policy for stabilization purposes.[2]

There is a clear tension between using fiscal policy for short-term stabilization and pursuing fiscal policy conducive to long-term growth. Deficits tend to be persistent over time, indicating that a fiscal expansion initially adopted with a stated stabilization goal may eventually crowd out private investment. Again, semiautomatic, rule-based fiscal stabilization policies would help to address this problem.

Several of the contributors expressed concern about current U.S. fiscal policy. The looming increases in social insurance benefit payouts will amplify the magnitude of the deficits in the relatively near future, and the increasingly dominant position of entitlements in the composition of federal expenditures has reduced policymakers' latitude to make short-run budget adjustments. The large current account deficits and rapidly deteriorating net international investment position of the United States may also limit the ability of the United States to accommodate future deficit increases without a higher degree of crowding out of private investment. Although there is significant support for the limited use of fiscal stimulus for stabilization purposes under appropriate circumstances, the consensus seems to be that this is a time for fiscal tightening.

Endnotes

1. Ricardian equivalence is described by Blinder in the following way: On the assumption that the pure permanent income hypothesis with perfect foresight holds, so that only the present value budget constraints matter, consumer spending will be unaffected by what amounts to a pure shift in timing.

2. The recent volume by Seidman (2003) is devoted to this topic.

References

Blinder, Alan, J. 2006. The case against the case against discretionary fiscal policy. In *The macroeconomics of fiscal policy.* Cambridge: MIT Press.

Feldstein, Martin and Charles Horioka. 1980. "Domestic savings and international capital flows," The 1979 W. A. Mackintosh Lecture at Queen's University. *Economic Journal* 90(358). June: 314–329.

Seidman, Laurence S. 2003. *Automatic fiscal policies to combat recessions.* Armonk, NY: M.E. Sharpe.

2

Can Fiscal Policy Improve
Macro Stabilization?

The Case Against the Case Against Discretionary Fiscal Policy

Alan S. Blinder

Serious discussion of fiscal policy has almost disappeared.
— Robert M. Solow (2002)

Times change. When I was introduced to macroeconomics as a Princeton University freshman in 1963, fiscal policy—and by that I mean *discretionary* fiscal *stabilization* policy—was all the rage.[1] The policy idea that eventually would become the Kennedy–Johnson tax cuts was the new, new thing. In those days, discussions of monetary policy often fell into the "Oh, by the way" category, with a number of serious economists and others apparently believing that monetary policy was not a particularly useful tool for stabilization policy.[2] The appropriate role for central bank policy was often said to be "accommodating" fiscal policy, which was cast in the lead role.[3] Thus, many people, probably including President John F. Kennedy, thought that Walter Heller, who was then chairman of the Council of Economic Advisers, was more instrumental to stabilization policy than William McChesney Martin, who was then chairman of the Federal Reserve Board. Indeed, it was said that Kennedy remembered that *Martin* was in charge of *monetary* policy only by the fact that both words began with the letter "M."[4]

Multiply by –1, and you have a capsule summary of the conventional wisdom today. As the opening quotation suggests, virtually every contemporary discussion of stabilization policy by economists—whether the discussion is abstract or concrete, theoretical or practical—is about monetary policy, not fiscal policy. It never crosses anyone's mind that Greg Mankiw might be more influential in formulating stabilization policy than Alan Greenspan. And President George W. Bush, I trust, does not need a mnemonic to remember what Greenspan does for a living. This paper explores whether this complete about-face in conventional wisdom was well justified.

Don't be alarmed by the title.[5] It speaks only of "the case against the case against" fiscal policy, not "the case for." I have no intention, at a Federal Reserve conference or anywhere else, of challenging the now-standard view that the central bank *should* and *does* have a dominant role in stabilization policy. This paper agrees that a sharp revision of the fiscalist views held by some economists *circa* 1966 was called for, but it also suggests that the pendulum may have swung just a bit too far, that the case against fiscal policy may have been taken to extremes. Yes, monetary policy merits the preeminent role in stabilization policy that it now holds. It is perfectly appropriate for there to be 10 to 20 conferences on monetary policy for every one on fiscal policy. My modest suggestion is only that the idea of using fiscal policy to help stabilize demand should not be relegated to the dustbin of history. There are circumstances under which the lessons of Lord Keynes are best not forgotten.

1.   The Issues

The prevailing view today is that stabilization policy is about filling in troughs and shaving off peaks, that is, reducing the variance of output around a mean trend that is itself unaffected by monetary or fiscal policy.[6] For the most part, I will adhere to this canon. But note that contemporary conventional wisdom makes two assumptions that are at least debatable:

Assumption 1: The macroeconomy is not subject to hysteresis. In a system with a unit root, any shock to aggregate demand—whether it be from fiscal policy or anything else—will leave a permanent impact on output. There are many possible rationales for hysteresis in a macroeconomic setting. One example is insider–outsider models [Lindbeck and Snower (1988)], in which workers who become unemployed cease having any effect on wage settlements. Another example is based on endogenous human capital formation. If a boom brings more people into the labor market, the new workers may acquire skills on the job that naturally augment the supply of labor for the future. Conversely, skills may atrophy during lengthy spells of unemployment. Hysteresis can also come from technology shocks, if faster (slower) technological progress is induced by a booming (slumping) economy.

But theorizing is cheap. The more important question is whether any of these theories of hysteresis capture the essence of macroeconomic reality. To begin with, does output actually have a unit root?

Unfortunately, that question is difficult to answer statistically. In a well-known and provocative paper written nearly two decades ago, Campbell and Mankiw (1987) argued that it does. More recent work, however, has emphasized how difficult it is to discriminate between a model with a unit root and a trend stationary model with a root close to, but below, unity—especially with relatively short time series. For example, Stock and Watson (1999, p. 55) estimate that the 90-percent confidence interval for the largest autoregressive root in the time series for log real gross domestic product (GDP) in the United States runs from 0.96 to 1.10.[7] For analyzing and describing *very long-run* behavior, it makes a world of difference whether the largest root is, say, 0.98 or 1.00. But, in the *short run*, these two time-series models are virtually indistinguishable. Believers in mean reversion have taken solace from this point, but it also means that hysteresis cannot be dismissed easily.

Assumption 2: The conventional, though much-disputed, effects of fiscal deficits on interest rates, and thus on the capital stock, leave no lasting imprint on GDP. The old "crowding-out" argument holds that deficit finance, while expansionary in the short run, is contractionary in the long run. A larger accumulated public debt leads to higher real interest rates, and thus to less business investment, and thus to a smaller capital stock and lower potential output in the future. Indeed, this chain of logic is one of the ideas behind several of the models that the Congressional Budget Office (2003) recently used for the "dynamic scoring" of tax cuts. Therefore, in several of those models, the estimated long-run effect of the 2003 Bush tax cut was to reduce real GDP, not to increase it.

Furthermore, in most of what follows, I will adhere to the consensus view by assuming that:

Assumption 3: Due to some sort of nominal rigidities, real output does respond in the short run to aggregate demand shocks, such as monetary and fiscal policy; and:

Assumption 4: The macroeconomy has the natural-rate property, by which I mean (a) that output returns to potential, and (b) that the path of potential output is unaffected by either monetary or fiscal policy.[8]

Assumptions 3 and 4 imply that both fiscal and monetary multiplier paths—which, these days, are often identified with impulse-response functions—have characteristic "hump" shapes, rising to a peak and then falling back to zero. Two examples of such paths for fiscal policy are displayed in Figure 2.1. Each requires some explanation, for standard impulse-response functions and multipliers are really two different animals.

Figure 2.1(a) illustrates the results of a vector autoregression (VAR) analysis of fiscal policy by Blanchard and Perotti (2002). When interpreting this graph (which includes standard-error bands), recall that, in any VAR, a shock sets in motion complex dynamic reactions that move *all* the variables. In particular, an initial fiscal shock in the three-variable Blanchard–Perotti model leads to subsequent changes not just in real GDP, but also in both government spending and taxes. Because of this fact, interpreting the impulse-response functions in their paper as traditional "fiscal multipliers" is somewhat problematic; and many of them do not have the familiar hump shape. Instead, I have chosen to display the reaction of real GDP to their dummy variable for 1975:2—because that was the quarter when a large, unanticipated, and nonrepeated income-tax rebate occurred. The dummy, of course, does not change subsequently; and the dynamic responses of government spending and taxes to this shock shown in Blanchard and Perotti's paper (but not repeated here) are very small. So Figure 2.1(a) comes close to showing the pure effect of a one-time, nonrepeated fiscal stimulus.[9]

Figure 2.1(b) shows the dynamic multiplier path generated by a simulation of the Federal Reserve Board's FRB/US model—a large, structural, macroeconometric model with forward-looking expectations, developed and used by the Fed staff. It simulates the effect of a sustained rise in government spending, allowing for the partially offsetting *monetary* policy reaction implied by a Taylor rule. Unlike the case with a VAR, however, there are no further (endogenous) responses of other *fiscal* variables. Thus, although panels (a) and (b) look similar, the comparison between them is not clean. That being said, both display the characteristic hump shape.

Percent

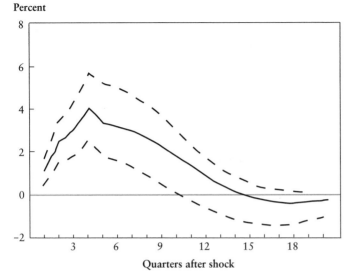

Quarters after shock

Figure 2.1(a)
Response of real GDP to a one-shot tax reduction.   *Source:* Blanchard and
Perotti (2002, Figure IV).

Multiplier

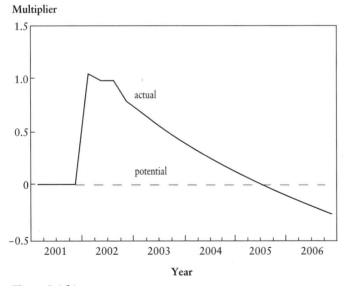

Year

Figure 2.1(b)
Response of real GDP to a sustained rise in government purchases.   *Source*
Elmendorf and Reifschneider (2002, Figure 11).

The two panels of Figure 2.1 should remind one of an important but oft-ignored point about fiscal policy: "Transitory" does not necessarily mean "fleeting." In Figure 2.1(a), the peak effect on GDP comes after five or six quarters, but notable effects still exist three or more *years* later. In Figure 2.1(b), the peak multiplier (of about 1) is reached immediately, and then it recedes gradually; but there are still sizable effects one and two years after the fiscal shock. With real effects lasting that long, well-designed fiscal policy can indeed be used to "fill in troughs and shave off peaks"—which would appear to make fiscal policy a viable candidate for the role of macroeconomic stabilizer. Indeed, in the early post-Keynesian period, fiscal policy was expected to play precisely that role.

So why, then, did educated opinion converge on the proposition that fiscal policy is, to a first approximation, useless? There appear to be two very different sets of arguments.

Practical/Political Arguments

The lags depicted in Figure 2.1 are called *outside lags*, the time that elapses between a fiscal policy shock and its effects on the economy. Most evidence from VARs and large-scale econometric models suggests that these outside lags are substantially shorter than the corresponding outside lags for monetary policy.

But fiscal policy is also subject to potentially long *inside lags*, the delays between recognition of the need for fiscal stimulus or restraint and the promulgation of the appropriate policies. Some of these inside lags occur for compelling administrative reasons. For example, if Congress decides to stimulate economic activity by building more public infrastructure, the natural spend-out rate of such programs will probably be very slow. Artificially speeding up the process for stabilization purposes would be wasteful. Similarly, when tax changes are made, the Internal Revenue Service needs some time to change withholding schedules, send out rebate checks, issue new tax forms, and so on.

Other inside lags occur for political reasons. Even when there is a modicum of bipartisanship and goodwill, Congress may need (or take) a long time to reach a decision on whether and how to change taxes or spending. After all, they don't call the United States Senate "the world's greatest deliberative body" for nothing. Beyond that, political wrangling can delay Congressional decisions for many months, especially in a presidential system with weak party discipline like ours, rather than in a more disciplined parliamentary system like the United Kingdom's. Delays from this source are especially likely when different parties control the White House and Congress. Thus, at least in the United States, long political lags may be the most cogent argument against discretionary fiscal policy.

Theoretical/Economic Arguments

As noted earlier, nominal rigidities are sufficient to imbue aggregate demand shocks with short-run effects on real output. But some well-known theoretical arguments imply that fiscal policy cannot even affect aggregate *demand*. During the long-running monetarist-Keynesian debate, monetarists argued that fiscal policy was powerless to move aggregate demand, which was controlled instead by monetary policy—presumably because the LM curve (equating the demand for and supply of money) was vertical. That old debate has a slightly (and deservedly) archaic ring to it today. For decades, the most-discussed argument for why fiscal policy might be impotent was the badly named "Ricardian equivalence" proposition.[10]

Suppose the pure permanent income hypothesis (PIH) with perfect foresight holds, so that only present-value budget constraints matter. [11] Then, a bond-financed tax cut simply defers tax payments until some future time when the interest and principal payments come due. *It does not change the present value of those tax payments,* because the present value of the future payments to the bondholders must be exactly equal to the market value of the bonds, and hence of the tax cut. On the assumption that only present-value budget constraints matter to consumers, spending will be unaffected by what amounts to a pure shift in timing.[12] As Barro (1974) and, before him, Patinkin (1956) pointed out long ago, consumers will simply save their tax cuts so as to be able to make the interest and principal payments when they come due.

Finally, even if fiscal policy can influence aggregate demand, so can monetary policy. And many contemporary macroeconomists would argue that, because the central bank always gets to "play last," monetary policy always can and will offset the effects of fiscal policy on aggregate demand. In subsequent sections, I will evaluate both the practical/

political and the theoretical/economic arguments for the futility of fiscal policy. But first, it may be useful to review briefly the interplay of events and ideas that led to such dramatic changes in the conventional view of the feasibility of conducting a stabilizing fiscal policy. The roles of both sets of arguments will be apparent.

2.   Changing Views: A Brief History of Events and Ideas on Fiscal Policy

The history of thought on fiscal policy since its birth in 1936 divides naturally into four episodes.

The Triumph of Keynesianism: 1936–1966

The first three decades following publication of *The General Theory of Employment, Interest, and Money* (1936) were the years of what Stein (1969) called "the fiscal revolution in America." Keynes's ideas, which emphasized fiscal over monetary policy,[13] spread like wildfire. Lerner (1943) wrote of the importance of using well-timed budgetary changes for "functional finance"—his term for what we now call "fiscal stabilization policy." The early editions of Samuelson's pathbreaking textbook, *Economics: An Introductory Analysis* (first edition: 1948), explained the use of both fiscal and monetary policy, but clearly emphasized the former. One notable section of that estimable text (pp. 353–354) was entitled, "The Inadequacies of Monetary Control of the Business Cycle"; it emphasized the (now) old saw that a central bank can "lead a horse to water but cannot make him drink." Mindful of potential political delays, Musgrave (1959) later promoted the idea of "formula flexibility," whereby Congress would pre-legislate both the form and the trigger (say, a drop in GDP) for future tax or expenditure changes for stabilization purposes—thereby converting discretionary policy into automatic stabilization.[14] Others advocated maintaining a backlog of spending projects "on the shelf," for use when cyclical conditions warranted.

The Kennedy–Johnson tax cuts of 1964–1965 marked the first *deliberate* use of fiscal policy in U.S. history, and they were judged to be a great success. From a modern perspective, one can only marvel at the unabashed optimism about activism exuded by Walter Heller (1966) in his memoir on the New Frontier. Heller wrote that both monetary and fiscal policy had "to be put on constant, rather than intermittent, alert" in order "to provide the essential stability at high levels of employment and growth that the market mechanism, left alone, cannot deliver." To do so, fiscal policy must become "more activist and bolder," and "has to rely less on the automatic stabilizers and more on discretionary action."[15] In brief, fine tuning was "in."

The Consensus Crumbles: 1967–1977

However, fine tuning would soon be "out." A series of adverse events first shook and then destroyed faith, not only in fiscal policy, but in stabilization policy more broadly. In the space of a scant decade, the old consensus utterly collapsed.

The first blow was the Vietnam War, which piled heavy government spending atop an economy that was already fully employed. President Lyndon B. Johnson overrode the counsel of his Keynesian advisors by insisting on prosecuting the war without either trimming Great Society spending or raising taxes.[16] The predictable—and, in fact, predicted—result was an overheated economy. Soon, inflation was on the rise, and Keynesian economics was being accused, unjustly, of being inherently inflationary.

That charge received apparent support from both the world of ideas and real-world events. On the intellectual front, Friedman (1968) and Phelps (1968) challenged, and eventually demolished, the notion that the Phillips curve represented an exploitable, long-run tradeoff. Aiming to keep unemployment below the natural rate, they argued, would drive inflation ever higher.

On the policy front, what Gordon (1980, p. 136) aptly called "the Waterloo of activist fiscal stabilization" came about when the 1968 tax surcharge failed to curb Vietnam-induced inflation.[17] The failure of the 1968 surtax greatly damaged the idea of using fiscal policy for stabilization purposes—in two distinct ways. First, the 2½-year delay in getting the tax hike enacted illustrated just how painfully long the inside lags in fiscal policy could be.[18] In a world in which recessions typically last less than a year, and an entire business cycle was thought to take about four years, an inside lag of over a year made fiscal stabilization a dubious proposition, at best. Second, Eisner (1969) raised an intellectual conundrum. The activist use of tax policy for stabilization purposes would seem to call for *temporary*, and perhaps even frequent, changes in income taxes. But the PIH implies that such tax changes, if believed to be temporary, should have only small effects on consumer spending.[19] So repetitive use of the income-tax weapon for stabilization purposes should severely undermine its efficacy.

These dual failures seemed to be replicated in the deep recession of 1974–1975, when first President Richard M. Nixon and then President Gerald R. Ford failed to recommend antirecessionary policies until it was too late.[20] Then, the temporary nature of the 1975 tax cut undermined its effectiveness. My study of the 1968 and 1975 episodes together [Blinder (1981)] concluded that the two temporary taxes had about half as much short-run impact on aggregate demand as equally-sized permanent tax changes would have had.

Lengthy inside lags, weak tax effects due to the PIH, and the vertical long-run Phillips curve have precious little to do with the monetarist claim of fiscal impotence owing to a vertical LM curve. When all these problems with fiscal policy seemed to become conflated in the anti-Keynesian backlash, fiscal stabilization fell deeply out of favor. Its nadir may have come in 1977 when President Jimmy Carter's call for a short-term fiscal stimulus was swiftly rejected by Congress—an event that was to be repeated 16 years later for President Bill Clinton.

Huge Deficits Crowd Out Stabilization Policy: 1981–2001

President Ronald Reagan's massive tax cuts proved to be another landmark in the history of fiscal policy. Despite the Reaganite attack on the weak Carter economy, the 1981 tax cuts were justified not by Keynesian aggregate demand considerations—which were denigrated—but by a new doctrine called "supply-side economics." This is not the place to discuss that ill-fated (and, some would say, silly) doctrine, other than to observe that it helped pave the way for a huge multiyear tax cut that ushered in an era of chronically large federal budget deficits.

The Reagan legacy of huge deficits "as far as the eye can see" fostered a dramatic repositioning of fiscal policy—away from cyclical stabilization policy and toward secular deficit reduction. The newfound devotion to fiscal prudence grew to be so extreme that, in 1985, Congress passed the Gramm–Rudman–Hollings Act, which, had it actually been followed, would have short-circuited even the automatic stabilizers by requiring strict adherence to annual targets for the federal budget deficit (an endogenous variable). Five years later, when the economy slipped into recession, fiscal stimulus was considered out of the question. Instead, taxes were *increased* as part of the 1990 deficit-reduction package. By then, even Keynesian economists were so desperate for deficit reduction that they accepted this procyclical tax hike without protest.

After the election of 1992, things went quite a bit further. President Clinton's original budget proposal combined substantial long-run fiscal consolidation with a small, short-run fiscal stimulus—a strategy of one step backward, five steps forward. But this two-pronged strategy proved to be too clever by half, and the stimulus part was quickly rejected by Congress. Instead, a deficit-reduction package, even larger than the one Clinton had proposed, barely passed. So Clintonomics turned out to be about fiscal prudence: first reducing the deficit, then balancing the budget, and finally building a sizable budget surplus. (There are worse policies, and we now have them.)

The new political realities of the 1980s and 1990s were reflected rapidly in academic thinking. Scores of papers appeared on the effects (or lack thereof) and the sustainability (or lack thereof) of budget deficits. Tellingly, the 1986 NBER conference volume, *The American Business Cycle: Continuity and Change* [Gordon (1986)], did not even include a chapter on fiscal policy—despite the avowedly cyclical focus of its title. In its place was a long essay by Barro (1986) on "The Behavior of United States Deficits," which focused on the tax-smoothing hypothesis [Barro (1979)].

The fact that the Clinton boom started shortly after Congress passed a budget *reduction* package gave rise to some serious (and some muddled) rethinking of even the *sign* of the fiscal-policy multiplier. Among politicians and media types, the notion that raising taxes and/or cutting spending would expand (rather than contract) the economy took hold rapidly and uncritically—with seemingly little thought about exactly *how* this was supposed to happen. Faster than you can say "Robert Rubin," the idea that *reducing* the budget deficit (or increasing the surplus) is the way to "grow" the U.S. economy—even in the short run—came to dominate thinking in Washington and in the media. This thinking was, of course, profoundly anti-Keynesian.

In the academic world, some earlier theoretical research by Turnovsky and Miller (1984) and Blanchard (1984) was dusted off and used to explain how a *credible* reduction in *expected future* budget deficits could, in fact, increase aggregate demand by lowering long-term interest rates today. Those models, of course, did not claim that a reduction in the *current* budget deficit would be expansionary. Still, the Turnovsky–Miller–Blanchard thesis offered one theoretically coherent explanation of the Clinton boom. (There were also many incoherent ones.) However, few people asked whether the lessons of those glory years could be generalized.[21]

The New Era Since 2001

It is hard to know how to characterize the fiscal policy of the current President George W. Bush. The ideas that eventually morphed into the tax cuts of 2001–2003 began as campaign promises in 1999. Given what has happened since, the original argument sounds like a bad joke: The federal government should "give back" the money to the people rather than run excessive budget surpluses. The tax cuts were most emphatically *not* recommended for short-run stabilization-policy purposes.[22] In fact, the Federal Reserve was worried at the time that the U.S. economy might be overheating. But when the economy slowed in 2000, and then sagged in 2001, the Bush administration quickly changed its rationale for the tax cuts to the more traditional Keynesian one: The economy needed stimulus. However, the basic policy remained the same: large, permanent tax cuts tilted toward the upper-income brackets.

In terms of our brief history of events and ideas, three remarkable phenomena have already transpired during the presidency of George W. Bush. First, consistency proved to be the hobgoblin of small minds. Without skipping a beat, both political parties and most of the press jettisoned the Clinton-era view that deficit *reduction* was the way to stimulate the economy and returned to the older Keynesian notion that deficit *expansion* would do the trick—apparently, without noticing the inconsistency.

Second, a political consensus in favor of fiscal stimulus formed quickly and decisively in 2001—so quickly that both the 2001 and 2003 tax cuts were enacted in a matter of months, thereby demonstrating that the inside lags in fiscal policy could really be quite short, even in a narrowly divided Congress.

Third, yet another old Keynesian idea—the liquidity trap—rose like Lazarus from the tomb of discarded doctrines.[23] As the Fed lowered the federal funds rate toward 1 percent, and the economy still did not revive, economists began to express concern about the zero bound on nominal interest rates—a trap that had already ensnared the Bank of Japan and, on that account, had engaged the interest of a number of academic and Federal Reserve economists.[24]

Briefly, the problem is this: Once the central bank lowers the overnight interest rate to zero, it is left with only "unconventional" monetary tools because base money and short-term debt become perfect substitutes. But these unconventional weapons are weaker than the conventional weapon: lowering the short-term interest rate by purchasing short-term government paper.

For example, the central bank can always expand the monetary base by purchasing long-term bonds rather than short-term issues.[25] But that is equivalent to a two-part policy in which the central bank first purchases short-term debt in the open market (thereby creating bank reserves) and then turns around and sells this debt to purchase an equivalent amount (at market value) of long-term debt. The first part of this operation is a conventional open-market purchase, which has no effect when the nominal interest rate is zero. The second part is a dose of "Operation Twist" which, we have been conditioned to believe, does not accomplish much. If that is what monetary policy comes down to at zero nominal interest rates,[26] then fiscal policy, for all its flaws, starts to look like a viable option after all. Indeed, some of the most compelling suggestions for ending Japan's deflationary slump combine expansionary monetary and fiscal policy in monetized deficit spending (or tax cutting).[27]

Were it not for the fact that the ink is not yet dry on this fourth episode in U.S. fiscal-policy history, it would be tempting to say that we have come full circle. Just think about what, in addition to mammoth budget deficits, has been restored since George W. Bush took office: belief in fiscal stimulus, belief that the inside lags in fiscal policy are short, and skepticism about the efficacy of monetary policy. This is a world in which Walter Heller would feel at home.

With this as background, I now turn to some of the economic/theoretical arguments that have been made *against* the efficacy of fiscal stabilization policy.

3.   Temporary Income Taxes and Present-Value Budget Constraints Theory

The structure of the basic argument against the use of temporary *income*-tax changes as stabilization devices is straightforward—far simpler than much of the literature, with its emphasis on intergenerational transfers, transversality conditions, and the like. Here is the simplest nonstochastic version of the Ricardian-equivalence argument.

Suppose a representative consumer's current spending depends *only* on the present discounted value of her lifetime resources:

$$W_t = A_t + \Sigma_t \, \delta^i y_{t+i} \, ,$$

where A_t is current net worth, y_{t+i} is future after-tax earnings, and δ^i is the appropriate discount factor for cash flows at date t+i. This is the central assumption. As Hillel said, although in an admittedly different context, all the rest is commentary.

Now, consider a tax cut of Δy financed by issuing bonds. Current receipts rise to $y_t + \Delta y$. But future taxes must rise by just enough to meet the interest and principal payments on the bonds—meaning that the *present value* of these future taxes must rise by exactly Δy. Thus, W_t is not changed by this fiscal operation, which alters only the *timing* of receipts and *not* its discounted present value. As a result, consumption is also unchanged.

This basic argument can be, and has been, gussied up in many ways. In essence, all the fancier variants come down to the same simple argument I just made. What can go wrong with this argument? Many things; but since most of the objections to Ricardian equivalence are so familiar, I will list them very briefly.

1. *Bequests*: Suppose some of the future tax burden falls on generations yet unborn. Of course, that part cannot affect *their* spending *today*, as they are not alive yet. But Barro (1974) pointed out long ago that, under one particular specification of intergenerational altruism, today's con-

sumers will essentially act as farsighted agents for their heirs—and will adjust their bequests so as to make debt and taxes equivalent. Of course, Barro's model is not the only possible model of the bequest motive. Much ink has been spilled over this issue, but, in my view, most of that debate is beside the point. In the real world, the bonds that will be issued to cover deficits will almost always mature in 10 years or less—a time frame within which most of today's taxpayers will still be around to pay the bills. So intergenerational aspects of present-value budget constraints are of secondary importance, at best.

2. *Liquidity constraints*: Current consumption may not depend only, or even mostly, on the present-value budget constraint. If liquidity constraints are binding, for example, current income will matter more than future income because it loosens liquidity constraints. In that case, a debt-financed tax cut will raise spending. Even if only a portion of the population is liquidity constrained, as the evidence suggests, Ricardian equivalence will fail. Because liquidity restraints are so important to the central questions of this paper, I will return to them later.

3. *Different discount rates*: The simple present-value argument assumes that taxpayers and bondholders discount future cash flows at the same rate. But if taxpayers discount the future at an interest rate higher than the government bond rate, the present value of the *current* purchasing power gained will exceed the present value of the *future* purchasing power lost—and consumption will rise as a result. A variant of this objection is:

4. *Myopia*: *Homo sapiens* may not be as farsighted as *homo economicus*. Real people, it appears, give insufficient weight to the future or (what comes to the same thing) discount future flows at extraordinarily high rates or have short planning horizons. For such (real) people, the rise in current income is a stronger influence on current consumption than is the fall in future income.[28]

5. *Precautionary saving*: Precisely this last sort of behavior can even be rationalized (for many reasonable utility functions), on optimizing grounds, by the theory of precautionary saving.[29] Receiving more income today and *expecting* to receive less income in the future reduces income uncertainty, which, in turn, reduces the need for precautionary saving. So long as tax payments rise with income, such a swap of present for future income can lead to higher spending today.

6. *Consumer spending may react more than consumption*: Current tax receipts that are not spent must be saved. One way to "save," by economists' definition, is to purchase a consumer durable that yields a flow of consumption services into the future. But that part of saving actually adds to current aggregate demand.

While each of the six objections summarized above is familiar, a seventh one seems not to be:

7. *The present-value government budget constraint is irrelevant in practice*: Modern economic models lean heavily on the so-called present-value government budget constraint (PV-GBC)—which ensures, for example, that any additional deficit run today must be balanced by surpluses *eventually* because the debt cannot explode upward forever. It is the PV-GBC that makes every income-tax change, in a sense, temporary. Let's grant this point. But note that the transversality condition from which the PV-GBC is derived holds only asymptotically.[30] As Ronald Reagan proved in the 1980s, and as George W. Bush may be proving again today, the government budget can traverse an explosive debt path for a decade or two without any cataclysmic consequences. Thus, the PV-GBC is a theoretical nicety that, in most circumstances, places no meaningful constraint on policy today, next year, or for the next decade or two.

Evidence

Okun (1971) was the first to study the temporary tax issue empirically. His context was the explicitly temporary income-tax surcharge enacted in 1968. Using the consumption equations of four different econometric models, he compared the "full effect" view (that the surcharge reduced spending by as much as a permanent tax increase would have) to the "zero effect" view (that the surcharge did not affect spending at all). He concluded that the "full effect" view explained the data better. However, Solow and I (1974, pp. 107–109) subsequently showed that an intermediate "50-percent effect view" fit Okun's data better than either extreme.

Modigliani and Steindel (1977) and Eckstein (1978) conducted similar studies of the effects of the 1975 tax rebate, using the consumption equations of two large-scale econometric models. Like Okun, each found sizable effects on spending—although Modigliani and Steindel (1977) expressed skepticism about the model's predictions. Some years later, I reexamined the 1968 and 1975 episodes together [Blinder (1981)], using a more complex specification that treated a temporary tax change as a weighted average of a permanent tax change and a pure windfall.[31] The point estimate of the weighting parameter was exactly 0.50, although its standard error was a large 0.32. However, when Deaton and I (1985) reexamined this question with a different model and, perhaps more important, revised data, we found something closer to the "zero effect" view.

This older, time-series literature tested the PIH by asking whether consumers' responses to *explicitly temporary* income changes are greater than predicted by theory. The answer seemed to be: "Yes, probably." But, as Deaton and I (1985, p. 498) concluded, the time-series data offer so few observations on temporary taxes that the "results are probably not precise enough to persuade anyone to abandon strongly held *a priori* views." A newer strand of research, influenced profoundly by Hall's (1978) rational expectations approach to the consumption function, poses a different, though related, question: Is the response of consumers to *easily predictable* income changes greater than theory suggests? Furthermore, it seeks answers mainly in cross-sectional data.

Some of this research takes advantage of what might be called "natural experiments." It began with a clever paper by Shapiro and Slemrod (1995), who noted that President George H.W. Bush conducted a rather curious tax experiment in 1992: He reduced withholding rates by executive order beginning in March of that year, even though Congress had not cut income-tax rates. Thus, over the last 10 months of 1992, American taxpayers were treated to higher cash flow, but not to higher accrued after-tax income. In return, they owed larger tax payments in their April 15, 1993, settlements. The Bush experiment, therefore, amounted to a *very temporary* increase in disposable income that was quickly reversed. According to the PIH, consumers should ignore such a change in the timing of receipts, exactly as in the Barro (1974) model.[32] Yet, nearly half of the respondents told the University of Michigan's survey takers that they would spend "most" of their (very temporary) increases in take-home pay. A similar subsequent study of the so-called income-tax "rebate" of 2001 by the same authors [Shapiro and Slemrod (2003)] found that only 22 percent of respondents said they would spend "most" of it.

Parker (1999) exploited the fact that, for a minority of workers each year, the payroll tax for Social Security falls abruptly to zero when their earnings rise above the Social Security maximum, and then suddenly jumps back to normal again on January 1 of the following year. Under the pure PIH, such predictable, seasonal fluctuations in after-tax income should have no effect on spending. But Parker (1999) found that they do; in fact, he estimated a marginal propensity to consume (MPC) of about 0.5 over a three-month period.

Similarly, when Souleles (1999) studied consumer responses to income-tax refunds—another predictable source of after-tax income—he found an MPC of around 0.6. And, in a subsequent study, Souleles (2002) found that, even though the phased-in Reagan tax cuts were preannounced and predictable, people did not spend their additional after-tax income until they had the money in hand.[33] The estimated MPC for nondurables was 0.6 or greater when the taxes were actually cut.

Hsieh (2003) reported some puzzling findings for Alaskan families. Their spending apparently did not react to the Alaskan Permanent Fund's relatively large and predictable annual payments, which come from oil revenues, but did react strongly to relatively small and predictable income-tax refunds—just as Souleles (1999) had found.

Most recently, Johnson, Parker, and Souleles (2004) assessed spending from the so-called 2001 tax rebate. This episode was interesting for two reasons. First, while widely described as a "rebate," the 2001 tax cut was actually an early installment payment on a permanent tax-rate reduction. Second, for administrative reasons, the checks were sent out on a randomized basis, which enabled Johnson *et al.* to estimate, with some precision, sizable initial-quarter spending responses.

While these two strands of consumption literature pose different questions, their respective answers display a certain consistency: Both point strongly toward the importance of binding liquidity constraints. In the time-series literature, it is presumably liquidity constraints that make consumers react much *more strongly* to current cash income than the PIH says they should. In the cross-section literature, liquidity constraints are the presumptive reason why households react much *less strongly* to anticipated future income—even when the future is not very far off.

Instead, consumers wait until they have their hands on the money, just as the time-series evidence suggests.

The lesson for stabilization policy, therefore, seems clear: Even *temporary* income-tax changes can pack substantial punch, though perhaps not quite as much as a permanent tax cut. Deaton (1992, pp. 101–102) had it about right a dozen years ago, when he wrote in his survey of consumption that "if macroeconomic policymakers wish to use taxes to fine-tune the economy...then the empirical failures of the [permanent income] theory [with rational expectations] are certainly large enough to make a big difference." Perhaps we economists have taken the PIH too much to heart.

4. Temporary Tax Changes and Intertemporal Substitution

Making an *income*-tax change temporary probably undermines its effectiveness, at least somewhat. Other sorts of tax changes, however, become *more* powerful when they are made temporary. I refer, of course, to taxes that create incentives for intertemporal substitution, such as investment tax credits, value-added taxes, sales and excise taxes, and the like.

The idea is simple enough. Consider a one-year reduction in a consumption tax from τ_0 to $\tau_1 < \tau_0$, reverting back to τ_0 next year. The relative price of goods next year versus goods this year will rise from $P_{t+1}/[(1 + r_t)P_t] \equiv \lambda_t$ when the tax rate is the same in both periods to:

$$[P_{t+1}(1 + \tau_0)]/[(1 + r_t)P_t(1 + \tau_1)] = [(1 + \tau_0)/(1 + \tau_1)]\lambda_t > \lambda_t,$$

when the tax rate is τ_1 this year and τ_0 next year. In theory, this change in relative prices should redirect spending from next year to this year.

Can intertemporal tax incentives like this be used effectively as instruments of fiscal policy? Sumner (1979) found little evidence that temporary changes in Ontario's retail sales tax had an extra-large impact on consumer spending due to intertemporal substitution. In general, the econometric evidence suggests rather little intertemporal substitution in consumption [see Hall (1988)].

In the United States, there is no value-added tax, and sales taxes are the province of the states. So the main intertemporal tax policy that has actually been utilized as part of fiscal policy is the *investment tax credit (ITC)*. The credit was invented by President Kennedy's Council of Economic Advisers and was introduced in 1962—for Keynesian reasons, by the way—at a 7-percent rate. Between then and its abolition as part of the Tax Reform Act of 1986, the ITC was suspended or repealed twice and had its rates readjusted twice—often for cyclical reasons.[34] ITCs have also been implemented in a number of other industrialized countries, often under a different name.[35]

Economic theory strongly suggests that the credit should be more powerful when it is enacted on a temporary basis. In his famous paper on econometric policy evaluation, Lucas (1976, p. 30) observed that: "The whole point, after all, of the investment tax credit is that it be viewed as temporary, so that it can serve as an inducement to firms to reschedule their investment projects." Yet, when the ITC was made "permanent" in 1979, two years after what I labeled "the nadir of fiscal policy," the U.S. Department of the Treasury (1979, p. 365) stated emphatically that "changes in the investment tax credit rate should not be considered in terms of short-run stabilization objectives."

Econometric appraisals of the "bang for the buck" effectiveness of the ITC have given the credit mediocre reviews.[36] One reason may be that the credit has never been made *marginal*—rather, it has always been applied to all qualified investments. In the 1992 Clinton campaign, economists had persuaded the candidate to propose a marginal ITC as a low-cost way to provide some fiscal stimulus, but the idea was quickly scrapped in 1993 for lack of support in Congress. I still think the idea is a good one.

The 2002 tax-cut bill included a provision that offered accelerated (called "bonus") depreciation for about 18 months. A year later, the "bonus" was increased and the period was extended slightly (to the end of 2004) as part of the 2003 tax cut. The idea, of course, was exactly the same as that behind the ITC: to put investment goods "on sale" for a while, thereby encouraging intertemporal substitution. Nonetheless, a controversy arose at the time, with economists in the Bush administration claiming that the bonus depreciation provision would be more powerful if enacted for a *longer* period! It is, of course, too early for there to have been any econometric studies of this most recent episode.

5. Countercyclical Variations in Government Purchases

As mentioned earlier, one stabilization policy idea that dates back to the early Keynesian period is the use of timely variations in expenditures on "public works" in order to smooth cyclical fluctuations. While the roots of this idea are thoroughly practical and atheoretical, it makes good theoretical sense on allocative grounds—at least in principle. After all, periods of slack resource utilization are times in which the shadow values of factor inputs are presumably low in the private sector. What better time to put those resources to use for public purposes?

Barro (1981) found that federal government defense purchases have a significant positive impact on real output, with temporary changes (mainly associated with wars) having larger effects than permanent ones. He argued that this finding provides support for a theoretical model in which temporarily higher government purchases raise the real rate of return, thereby inducing intertemporal substitution in both consumption (less today, more tomorrow) and labor supply (more today, less tomorrow). But Barro's theoretical rationale (intertemporal substitution) and his empirical results (wars boost real output) are sufficiently disconnected that one can accept the latter without buying into the former.

The major objections to using public expenditures as a countercyclical weapon seem to be more practical than theoretical, but I think they are powerful nonetheless.

To begin with, wars do not seem like particularly promising devices for stabilization policy! More seriously, there are normally quite lengthy lags in the political process before Congress authorizes new spending projects. Then, since authorizing committees and appropriating committees are different legislative bodies, still more time elapses between legal *authorization* and the actual *appropriation* of funds. These legislative lags could conceivably be short-circuited by having a queue of projects preauthorized, preappropriated, and sitting "on the shelf" ready to go if the cyclical need arose. But I, for one, have a hard time imagining the U.S. Congress doing anything like that. And even if the lags in the authorizing and appropriating processes could be eliminated completely, the slow natural spend-out rates of most public infrastructure projects remain a serious handicap. For example, out of each dollar appropriated for highway expenditures, less than one-third is likely to be spent within a year. Accelerating the pace of spending on public works for stabilization purposes would be inefficient and wasteful.

To my mind, this all adds up to a recognition that the inside lags for many sorts of government purchases are lengthy enough to vitiate their usefulness for stabilization policy. The idea works in theory but not in practice. If fiscal policy is to be used for stabilization purposes, taxes (and transfers) are probably the instrument of choice.

6.   Is There a Case for Streamlining Fiscal Policy Institutions?

This discussion points to long inside lags as perhaps the most critical element of the case against discretionary fiscal policy, but these lags are not immutable. The sources of many, if not most, of them lie in policymaking institutions that can be changed—at least in principle. Over the years, a number of suggestions for doing just that have been proposed.

One such idea, formula flexibility in setting income-tax rates or public expenditures, was mentioned earlier. Its main virtue is both obvious and substantial. If what we now think of as *discretionary* policy changes for stabilization purposes could somehow be made *automatic*, then the lengthy inside lags in fiscal policy could be reduced dramatically. Since the outside lag for most garden-variety fiscal policy changes is relatively short (as depicted in Figure 2.1), the feasibility of conducting a stabilizing fiscal policy would thereby be greatly enhanced.

What is the down side? For good reasons elucidated earlier, most discussions of formulaic fiscal responses have focused on taxes rather than on government spending. But, as noted above, temporary changes in income-tax rates are believed to elicit muted spending responses. Perhaps more important, Congress has not shown the slightest inclination to relinquish any of its ability to bestow gifts upon taxpayers when the economy is weak. And symmetry does not rescue us when the economy is strong. While it is true that members of Congress are eager to avoid the blame for raising taxes at times of peak demand, they already have a straightforward way of accomplishing that: Following the old Nancy Reagan motto, they "just say no." The last time Congress enacted a tax *increase* aimed squarely at reducing aggregate demand for stabilization purposes was in 1968.[37] Instead, Congress lets the Fed do all the dirty work by raising interest rates. So, it is hardly surprising that Congress has shown no interest whatsoever in formula flexibility.

A related ivory-tower idea should be mentioned in this context. In a paper published eight years ago [Blinder (1997)], I asked why some economic decisions are delegated to unelected technocrats, while others are reserved for politicians. One important specific example of this question is: Why do just about all countries put monetary policy in the hands of independent central bankers, and yet leave tax policy in the hands of elected politicians? I went on to speculate about whether technocratic decision-making on tax policy might produce better outcomes than political decision-making, suggesting that the answer might indeed be yes.

In broaching the idea of transferring some aspects of tax policy from the political sphere to the technocratic sphere, I was not thinking about stabilization policy, but rather about getting the details of the tax code—with their complex allocative and distributive effects—right. However, the same point applies to getting the *timing* right in a business-cycle context, as advocates of formula flexibility realized many decades ago.

Suppose a group of technocrats, modeled on the Federal Reserve Board, were empowered to make decisions on the *level* of taxation, subject to (potentially numerous) constraints laid down by Congress. Under that institutional structure, the possibility of conducting a timely and rational fiscal policy would be greatly enhanced. Of course, the probability that Congress would delegate such authority is probably roughly equal to the probability that the Red Sox will win the World Series. But fans can dream.[38]

Subsequently, the Business Council of Australia (1999) picked up on this idea and advocated the establishment of an independent fiscal-policy agency for Australia, along the lines just suggested.[39] In one version of their proposal, a new agency as independent as the Reserve Bank of Australia would actually be given the *power* to make small, across-the-board adjustments in personal and/or corporate tax rates for stabilization purposes—unless its order was publicly and explicitly countermanded by the government. In a softer version of their proposal, the new agency would be merely *advisory*, making public recommendations to the government.

A series of related proposals has been made for the euro zone, although the focus there has been on secular budget discipline, rather than on cyclical stabilization. The much-maligned—and, one might say, much-ignored—Stability and Growth Pact (SGP) requires member governments to limit budget deficits to no more than 3 percent of GDP. Even before the pact was agreed upon, critics noted that the 3-percent limit could, in principle, interfere with the workings of the automatic stabilizers because it was phrased in terms of *actual* budget deficits rather than *cyclically adjusted* deficits. So, if weak economic performance lowered tax revenue and raised social welfare expenditures sufficiently, even a "responsible" fiscal policy could produce a deficit in excess of the 3-percent limit— thereby requiring offsetting fiscal actions that are procyclical.[40] In practice, European governments have shown themselves unwilling to take such actions, preferring to violate the pact instead. Consequently, the pact has become something of an embarrassment.[41]

Notice the analogy to the old formula flexibility discussions in the United States. In principle, the SGP requires *discretionary* responses to (certain) changes in economic activity. But those changes have proven difficult or impossible to sustain politically, and they may not make good economic sense anyway (for example, if they are procyclical). Instead, some economists have proposed institutional changes that would make long-run fiscal discipline somewhat closer to *automatic,* while still allowing for cyclical responses. For example, von Hagen and Harden (1995), Wyplosz (2002), and others have called for replacing the SGP's excessive-deficit procedure with a council of experts not unlike the softer version of the Australian proposal.[42] This group of technocrats would report and opine—quite publicly—on the sustainability of the fiscal programs of the euro-zone governments. The idea would be to bring public and market pressure to bear on governments that insist upon pursuing unsustainable policies.

7.   Out of the Detritus: Creative Ideas for Fiscal Stabilization

A short summary of the conclusions so far might run something like this. The *theoretical* arguments against the efficacy of fiscal policy as a stabilization tool turn out to be pretty thin gruel, but the *practical* arguments seem to be more substantive. Timely variations in government purchases (say, public works) for stabilization policy, though fine in theory, do not appear to be either sensible or workable. Changes in taxes and/or transfer programs are far more suitable for stabilization purposes, but current institutional arrangements make the prospects for success slim. Nor do any of the institutional changes that would make successful fiscal stabilization more achievable seem likely to be adopted. So maybe the current conventional wisdom is right after all.

Before giving up, however, let us consider some creative suggestions for stabilizing fiscal policy that have been made in recent years. Each is designed to address the main perceived weakness of using temporary income-tax changes to alter consumer spending: Elementary theory says that temporary changes in income taxes should yield less aggregate-demand "bang" for each income-loss "buck" than permanent tax changes. Yet, the rhythm of the business cycle virtually dictates that tax-transfer changes for stabilization purposes should be temporary. What can be done?

Better Targeting of Tax-Transfer Payments

One response suggested by the empirical literature would be to target tax-transfer changes made for stabilization purposes on those people who are most likely to be liquidity constrained, and therefore to have MPCs (marginal propensities to consume) at or near 1. To some extent, that means targeting income-tax changes on lower-income households, which are more likely to be living hand to mouth. There are two drawbacks to this approach.

First, the suggested remedy is strikingly asymmetric. When the economy needs stimulus, targeting income-tax *reductions* and *increases* in transfer payments disproportionately on the poor seems right; it admirably serves both stabilization and distributional objectives. On the other hand, the idea of targeting income-tax *hikes* or *cuts* in transfers on the poor when the economy needs restraint is repugnant to most people. But, as noted earlier, Congress never uses fiscal policy to "shave off peaks" anyway. So, if discretionary fiscal policy is used only when stimulus is called for, maybe this problem is not important in practice.

Second, since income is an imperfect indicator of who is—and who is not—liquidity constrained, the ratio of assets to income may make more sense on theoretical grounds.[43] In principle, large negative *transitory* income should be a better indicator of who is constrained, since a sizable negative income shock suggests a strong likelihood of a binding liquidity constraint. And since transitory income and current income are highly correlated,[44] current income may be a decent statistical proxy. However, it would be helpful if we could do better. Two suggestions have been made in that regard.

One idea is to use receipt of unemployment insurance (UI) benefits as a proxy for being liquidity constrained. After all, most people who are collecting UI have recently suffered a severe drop in earnings (about 50 percent on average), making their transitory incomes negative and large. If these people are striving to maintain their previous consumption levels, they are probably liquidity constrained.

Indeed, extending UI benefits during times of high unemployment has become almost standard practice in the United States.[45] An additional 13 weeks of coverage, beyond the usual 26 weeks, is triggered *automatically* in a particular state once the level of insured unemployment breaches certain levels.[46] And Congress often enacts additional *discretionary* increases in UI coverage that become effective during, and especially after, recessions. Data on payments under the Extended Benefits program display sharp spikes in 1976, 1983, 1992–1993, and 2002–2003[47]—all years following recessions.

During the Congressional debate over the 2001 stimulus package, a number of Democrats and liberal economists argued that UI benefits should be extended in time and broadened in coverage—for example, by making part-time workers eligible.[48] The main problem with this idea appears to be magnitudes. Feasible policy changes in UI benefits are simply not big enough to combat a recession. Or are they? Let's look at some numbers.

Between the years 2000 (when the unemployment rate averaged 4.0 percent) and 2002 (when the unemployment rate averaged 5.8 percent), total UI benefits increased from $20.5 billion to $42.1 billion.[49] Let's imagine that aggressive policy changes might have boosted that $21.6 billion *increase* by 50 percent—that is, by another $10.8 billion—which seems a high-end estimate of what Congress might actually have done. Assuming an MPC of 1 (which is probably too high) and no multiplier effects (which is probably too low), those additional UI payments would have raised GDP by $10.8 billion. By comparison, the peak-to-trough decline in real GDP actually experienced between the fourth quarter of 2000 and the third quarter of 2001 (expressed in 2002 dollars) was $55.2 billion—and the 2001 recession was very mild by historical standards. Thus, no conceivable expansion of UI benefits can make a big dent in a deep recession.

Nonetheless, in designing stabilization policies, we should be thinking about *mitigating* recessions, not *eliminating* them. In that context, discretionary variations in UI benefits may deserve a more prominent role than they have been given to date. By like reasoning, a more generous UI program would be a better *automatic* stabilizer.

A second idea along these same lines, which was suggested by several Democratic politicians in 2001, is temporarily rebating the "first part" of the payroll tax. Here, the numbers are potentially much larger. The Social Security Administration reports 144.8 million wage and salary workers in 2002. Of these, 103.5 million workers earned $10,000 or more, and hence would have been eligible for the full $620 tax cut—for a total expenditure of $64.2 billion. A rough estimate of the value of the 6.2-percent tax cut to the 41.3 million workers with covered earnings below $10,000 adds another $10.7 billion[50]—raising the total cost to about $75 billion. That is more than enough to "fill in a trough." The problem in this case is targeting.[51] Under this particular payroll-tax rebate plan, even middle- and upper-income households will receive temporary tax cuts. Many of them—perhaps the majority, weighted by income—will not be liquidity constrained.

Exploiting Intertemporal Substitution

Two other recent fiscal policy suggestions seek to exploit the idea that, unlike income taxes, variations in sales taxes are likely to be made *more* powerful by enacting them on an explicitly temporary basis.

As a way to bring incentives for intertemporal substitution to bear on stimulating consumer spending, Martin Feldstein (2001) suggested temporarily suspending Japan's 5-percent value-added tax (VAT), and following that by an increase two years later. He subsequently offered a more complicated version of this idea [Feldstein (2002)]: The government of Japan should embark on a multiyear plan of simultaneously *raising* the consumption tax and *reducing* the income tax, in a balanced-budget way. The idea is the same in each case: to create incentives for consumers to buy *now*, rather than in the future.

That was the same idea behind a suggestion I made during the debate over the 2001 stimulus package in the United States [Blinder (2001)]. The federal government in the United States has neither a VAT nor a general sales tax, but 45 of the 50 states have the latter. Therefore, I suggested that the federal government offer to replace the lost tax revenue of any state that would agree to cut its sales tax (up to some limit) for the next 12 months. Of course, I would not want to exaggerate the impact of such a policy, given the low rates of sales taxation in the United States and the modest degree of intertemporal substitution suggested by econometric studies. A *temporary* and *marginal* ITC might be a more potent option.

8.   Wrapping Up: Is There Anything New Under the Sun?

Today's conventional wisdom holds that discretionary changes in fiscal policy are unlikely to do much good, and might even do harm. Why is that? First, the lags in fiscal policy, especially the inside lags, are long—perhaps longer than the duration of a typical recession. Second, the effects of the most plausible fiscal policy weapon, changes in personal income taxes (or transfer payments), are likely to be weakened by deploying it on a temporary basis. And third, an obviously superior stabilization weapon—namely, monetary policy—is readily available.[52]

When might that argument go wrong? Occasionally, there will be times and places—such as Japan in the 1990s—where the need to boost aggregate demand is extremely large and lasts a very long time, longer than any conceivable lags in fiscal policy. Models with hysteresis offer extreme examples of this possibility, but a model with a maximum root of 0.98 or so will do almost as well. And remember, Stock and Watson (1999) estimated the maximum root for real GDP in the United States to be between 0.96 and 1.10.

Second, there are institutional structures that can make the inside lags in fiscal policy quite short. The United Kingdom's parliamentary system legislates fiscal changes very quickly, and even the U.S. Congress has shown itself capable of moving within a few months—on occasion. It may be that we generalized too quickly from the terribly long inside lags witnessed in 1968 and 1974; economists generally insist on more than two data points. Furthermore, if we really want to speed up fiscal policy decision-making, there are a variety of institutional changes that could help.

Third, to the extent that we are worried that low MPCs out of temporary income-tax changes will undermine the effectiveness of fiscal policy, there are non-income-tax options that can induce intertemporal substitution by reducing current prices relative to future prices—for both consumer goods and investment goods.

Fourth, these more exotic options may not even be needed, for a fascinating body of recent econometric evidence suggests that a sizable fraction of the U.S. population (even weighted by income) is, or acts as if it is, subject to binding liquidity constraints. Thus, even explicitly temporary changes in income taxes may pack significant spending punch. Furthermore, with a little ingenuity, we can target tax cuts on people who are more likely to be living hand to mouth, such as poor people and the unemployed.

Fifth, occasionally there will be extraordinary circumstances—contemporary Japan is again the outstanding example—where the zero bound on nominal interest rates makes monetary policy a less powerful stabilizer than it usually is. In such a situation, monetary policy *alone* may be too weak to do the job, and a combined monetary-fiscal effort—deficit spending or tax cuts financed by printing money—may do the job better. Indeed, fiscal policy might well be the senior member of such a partnership, since a liquidity trap not only reduces the power of monetary policy, but also increases the power of fiscal policy (because there is little or no "crowding out" from higher interest rates). Precisely this sort of two-pronged stabilization policy is what many economists long urged on Japan.

Sixth, in certain rare emergencies—for example, in the United States during the aftermath of the 9/11 attacks—the monetary policy medicine may simply be too slow acting to provide a timely cure. The inside lags in monetary policy would probably be negligible in a clear emergency.[53] But the outside lags remain quite long—a year or more for real GDP, and two years or more for inflation—and there is not much the Federal Reserve can do about it. With monetary policy lags as long as that, fiscal policy may be the only cyclical medicine that can work in time—provided the inside lags can be kept short. In fact, in the end, I am inclined to conclude that the long inside lags (with the concomitant politics) constitute the most important count in the indictment against fiscal policy.

So my overall conclusion runs something like this. Under *normal* circumstances, monetary policy is a far better candidate than fiscal policy for the stabilization job. It should, therefore, take first chair. Nothing in this paper is intended to dispute this piece of conventional wisdom. That being said, however, there will be occasional *abnormal* circumstances in which monetary policy can use a little (or maybe a lot) of help in stimulating the economy—for example, when recessions are extremely long and/or extremely deep, when nominal interest rates approach zero, or when significant weakness in aggregate demand arises abruptly.[54] To be prepared for such contingencies, it makes sense to keep one or more fiscal policy vehicles tuned up and parked in the garage—and perhaps even to adopt institutional structures that make it easier to pull them out and take them for a spin when needed.

■ *I am grateful to Susanto Basu, Richard Berner, Olivier Blanchard, Willem Buiter, Christopher Sims, and especially Lars Svensson for helpful comments on an earlier draft. I also thank Luke Willard for excellent research assistance, Kathleen Hurley for handling the manuscript superbly, and Princeton University's Center for Economic Policy Studies for financial support.*

Notes

1. As my assignment was to discuss *discretionary* fiscal policy, automatic stabilization is barely touched upon in this paper. That is not because it is unimportant.

2. See, among others, Stein (1969, chs. 15–17).

3. Curiously, this phrase has survived into current Federal Reserve jargon. Even though the Fed is clearly in the driver's seat when it comes to stabilization policy, it routinely refers to increasing or reducing the degree of "monetary accommodation."

4. Stein (1969, p. 4). In researching this paper, I was astonished to find that the index of Heller (1966) does not contain a single reference to Martin.

5. Old-timers may note that I have adapted the title from Solow (1966), and for much the same reasons that he chose it.

6. This is not meant to deny that some types of fiscal policy—for example, changes in marginal tax rates—may have incentive effects that change behavior and thus change potential GDP.

7. Multivariate analyses, however, do not always agree with univariate analyses of the unit root issue.

8. However, see Assumption 2 above.

9. Blanchard and Perotti (2002, p. 1346) present VAR results with both deterministic and stochastic trends. Figure 2.1(a) corresponds to their deterministic trend case. In his discussion of this paper, Blanchard notes that results like these are not necessarily obtained with data from other countries.

10. It is badly named because Ricardo did not believe in it. See O'Driscoll (1977).

11. Perfect foresight is not necessary. Rational expectations will do.

12. As is well known, this assumes, among other things, that consumers discount future flows at the government bond rate. More on this below.

13. This probably was due to interest rates being so low during the Great Depression. I will return to this point later.

14. Seidman (2003) and Solow (2002) have recently tried to revive this idea. Seidman's book is a particularly useful reference on many of the points touched upon in this paper.

15. Heller (1966). The quotations come from pages 9, 68, and 69, respectively.

16. See Okun (1970), especially Chapter 3.

17. See Eisner (1969) and Okun (1971).

18. Johnson's advisors urged a tax hike on him as early as late 1965. See Okun (1970). LBJ resisted until the middle of 1967, when he recommended a temporary income-tax surcharge. Congress then took about 18 months to enact one.

19. This very point resurfaced recently in the context of the Bush tax cuts in 2001.

20. But Congress acted speedily this time, demonstrating that the inside lag could be short.

21. For more on this subject, see Blinder and Yellen (2001, Chapter 4.)

22. Nor was it ever argued, even by opponents, that lower taxes that led to a deficit would slow down economic growth.

23. See Krugman (1998).

24. For example, it was the subject of a Federal Reserve conference in October 1999. See the November 2000 special issue of the *Journal of Money, Credit and Banking.*

25. Krugman (1998) actually argued that the central bank should commit itself to future actions that would engender inflationary expectations—so as to make the zero nominal interest rate negative in real terms. The problem, of course, is how to accomplish that credibly—which is where the "unconventional" policies come in.

26. Svensson (2001) has argued that combining currency depreciation with price-level targeting is a better (even "foolproof") policy option.

27. Among the many sources that could be cited, see Bernanke (2000).

28. Gruen (2001) has suggested another departure from full rationality. He shows that "near rational" consumers will lose very little by ignoring the link between bonds and future taxes.

29. See, for example, Barsky, Mankiw, and Zeldes (1986).

30. The PV-GBC is derived from the government's flow budget constraint and the transversality condition of the household's maximization problem. See, for example, Canzoneri, Cumby, and Diba (2002, footnotes 22 and 23).

31. Note that a windfall does not have "zero effect" on spending under the permanent income hypothesis.

32. Well, not quite *exactly*. Since the government gave taxpayers *interest-free* loans, the present value of lifetime resources was raised slightly.

33. This last finding echoed what Deaton and I (1985) had found years earlier in studying consumer responses to the Reagan tax cuts.

34. See Chirinko (1999), a particularly useful source of information on the investment tax credit.

35. For example, see Jorgenson and Landau (1993).

36. See Auerbach and Hassett (1991) and Chirinko (1993) for a survey.

37. Congress did raise taxes in 1982, 1983, 1990, and 1993. But in none of those cases was cyclical restraint the main reason. In fact, the economy was very weak in the first three instances, and grew only modestly in the fourth case.

38. These words were written in the spring of 2004. That fall, the Red Sox won their first World Series since 1918. An omen?

39. Nicholas Gruen was the intellectual force behind this proposal.

40. Qualitatively, the analogy to the central problem with the Gramm–Rudman–Hollings Act in the United States is almost perfect. However, marginal tax-and-transfer rates are much higher in the euro zone than in the United States, making the quantitative dimensions of the problem more severe in Europe. See Canzoneri, Cumby, and Diba (2002), pp. 340–343.

41. At the time of the Boston Fed conference, the European Union was considering changes in the SGP, partly for the reasons enunciated here. It has now made those changes, considerably weakening the pact.

42. For a summary of and the rationale for such proposals, see Fatás *et al.* (2003).

43. This is Zeldes's (1989) view. However, Jappelli (1990) finds that people with lower incomes are, indeed, more likely to be liquidity constrained.

44. For example, Hall and Mishkin (1982) estimate that the variance of the innovation to transitory income is more than twice as large as the variance to the innovation of permanent income.

45. However, the Bush administration and the Republican-controlled Congress refused to do so in late 2003, despite objections from Democrats.

46. Some states add an additional seven weeks.

47. See http://workforcesecurity.doleta.gov/unemploy/content/chartbook/images/chtb1.gif on the Department of Labor website.

48. See, for example, Krueger (2001).

49. *Economic Report of the President, 2004*, Table B-45, p. 337.

50. See http://www.ssa.gov/policy/docs/statcomps/supplement/2003/4b.html#table4.b7. That source divides the 41.3 million sub-$10,000 workers into three ranges:

Income range	Workers (millions)
0–$999	8.24
$1,000–$4,999	17.62
$5,000–$9,999	15.44

The calculation in the text assumes that the average earnings in each of these three brackets is the midpoint of the bracket.

51. Another problem is that the Social Security Trust Fund cannot spare the revenue. But this problem can be overcome by using general revenue to replace any payroll-tax receipts that the Trust Fund loses.

52. In summarizing the case against fiscal stabilization, Feldstein (2002) added one further item to this list: the possibility that tax cuts or expenditure increases can depress demand by raising long-term interest rates. But he did not suggest that tax *increases* or expenditure *cuts* can stimulate the economy by lowering interest rates.

53. For example, the Federal Reserve cut interest rates within days of the 9/11 attacks.

54. As previously noted, I see little hope that fiscal policy can be used effectively for restraint. Using discretionary fiscal policy only for stimulus would, of course, impart a bit of a bias toward higher levels of public debt and higher real interest rates. But, realistically, that tendency would probably be small enough to be counterbalanced by the normal "bracket creep" from real growth.

References

Auerbach, Alan J. and Kevin A. Hassett. 1991. Recent U.S. investment behavior and the Tax Reform Act of 1986. *Carnegie-Rochester Conference Series on Public Policy* 35:185–215.

Barro, Robert J. 1974. Are government bonds net wealth? *Journal of Political Economy* 82(6): 1095–1117.

Barro, Robert J. 1979. On the determination of the public debt. *Journal of Political Economy* 87(5): 940–971.

Barro, Robert J. 1981. Output effects of government purchases. *Journal of Political Economy* 89(6): 1086–1121.

Barro, Robert J. 1986. The behavior of United States deficits. In *The American business cycle: Continuity and change*, ed. Robert J. Gordon, 361–387. Chicago: University of Chicago Press.

Barsky, Robert B., N. Gregory Mankiw, and Stephen P. Zeldes. 1986. Ricardian consumers with Keynesian propensities. *American Economic Review* 76(4) September: 676–691.

Bernanke, Ben S. 2000. Comment on America's historical experience with low inflation. *Journal of Money, Credit and Banking* 32(4) November: 994–997.

Blanchard, Olivier J. 1984. Current and anticipated deficits, interest rates, and economic activity. *European Economic Review* 20(1) June: 7–27.

Blanchard, Olivier J., and Roberto Perotti. 2002. An empirical characterization of the dynamic effects of changes in government spending and taxes on output. *Quarterly Journal of Economics* 117(4) November: 1329–1368.

Blinder, Alan S. 1981. Temporary income taxes and consumer spending. *Journal of Political Economy* 89(1) February: 26–53.

Blinder, Alan S. 1997. Is government too political? *Foreign Affairs* 76(6) November/December: 115–126.

Blinder, Alan S. 2001. The economic stimulus we need. *New York Times*, September 28.

Blinder, Alan S., and Angus Deaton. 1985. The time-series consumption function revisited. *Brookings Papers on Economic Activity* 2:465–511.

Blinder, Alan S., and Robert M. Solow. 1974. Analytical foundations of fiscal policy. In *The economics of public finance*, eds. Alan S. Blinder *et al*. Washington, D.C.: Brookings Institution.

Blinder Alan S., and Janet L. Yellen. 2001. *The fabulous decade: Macroeconomic lessons from the 1990s*. New York: Century Foundation Press.

Business Council of Australia. 1999. Avoiding boom/bust: Macroeconomic reform in a globalised economy. New Directions discussion paper 2.

Campbell, John Y., and N. Gregory Mankiw. 1987. Are output fluctuations transitory? *Quarterly Journal of Economics* 102(4) November: 857–880.

Canzoneri, Matthew B., Robert E. Cumby, and Behzad T. Diba. 2002. Should the European Central Bank be concerned about fiscal policy? In *Rethinking stabilization policy: A symposium sponsored by the Federal Reserve Bank of Kansas City*, 333–389. Kansas City: Federal Reserve Bank of Kansas City.

Chirinko, Robert S. 1993. Econometric models and empirical findings for business investment. Salomon Brothers Center Series: Financial markets, institutions, and instruments monograph. New York: Basil Blackwell.

Chirinko, Robert S. 1999. Investment tax credits. In *Encyclopedia of taxation and tax policy*, eds. Joseph J. Cordes, Robert D. Ebel, and Jane G. Gravelle, 211–215. New York: Urban Institute Press (for the National Tax Association).

Congressional Budget Office. 2003. *How CBO analyzed the macroeconomic effects of the President's budget*. Washington, D.C.: Government Printing Office.

Deaton, Angus. 1992. *Understanding consumption*. New York: Oxford University Press.

Eckstein, Otto. 1978. *The great recession, with a postscript on stagflation*. Amsterdam: North-Holland.

Eisner, Robert. 1969. Fiscal and monetary policy reconsidered. *American Economic Review* 59(5) December: 897–905.

Elmendorf, Douglas W., and David L. Reifschneider. 2002. Short-run effects of fiscal policy with forward-looking financial markets. *National Tax Journal* 55 September: 357–386.

Fatás, Antonio, Jurgen von Hagen, Andrew Hughes Hallett, Anne Sibert, and Rolf R. Strauch. 2003. *Stability and growth in Europe: Towards a better pact*. Monitoring European Integration 13. London: Centre for Economic Policy Research.

Feldstein, Martin S. 2001. Japan needs to stimulate spending. *Wall Street Journal*, July 16.

Feldstein, Martin S. 2002. Commentary: Is there a role for discretionary fiscal policy? In *Rethinking stabilization policy*, 151–162. Kansas City: Federal Reserve Bank of Kansas City.

Friedman, Milton. 1968. The role of monetary policy. *American Economic Review* 58(1) March: 1–17.

Gordon, Robert J., ed. 1986. *The American business cycle: Continuity and change*. Chicago: University of Chicago Press.

Gordon, Robert J. 1980. Postwar macroeconomics: The evolution of events and ideas. In *The American economy in transition*, ed. Martin S. Feldstein, 101–162. The National Bureau of Economic Research Monograph. Chicago: University of Chicago Press.

Gruen, David. 2001. Ignorance and Ricardian equivalence. *Economic Record* 73(220): 35–44.

Hall, Robert E. 1978. Stochastic implications of the life-cycle permanent income hypothesis: Theory and evidence. *Journal of Political Economy* 86(6): 971–987.

Hall, Robert E. 1988. Intertemporal substitution in consumption. *Journal of Political Economy* 96(2): 339–357.

Hall, Robert E., and Frederic S. Mishkin. 1982. The sensitivity of consumption to transitory income: Estimates from panel data on households. *Econometrica* 50(2) March: 461–481.

Heller, Walter W. 1966. *New dimensions of political economy.* Cambridge: Harvard University Press.

Hsieh, Chang-Tai. 2003. Do consumers react to anticipated income changes? Evidence from the Alaska Permanent Fund. *American Economic Review* 93(1): 397–405.

Jappelli, Tullio. 1990. Who is credit constrained in the U.S. economy? *Quarterly Journal of Economics* 105(1): 219–234.

Johnson, David S., Jonathan A. Parker, and Nicholas S. Souleles. 2004. The response of consumer spending to the randomized income-tax rebates of 2001. Princeton University Working Paper. February.

Keynes, John M. 1936. *The general theory of employment, interest, and money.* New York: Harcourt, Brace.

Krueger, Alan B. 2001. Temporary stimulus needed. *New York Times*, October 13.

Krugman, Paul R. 1998. It's baaack: Japan's slump and the return of the liquidity trap. *Brookings Papers on Economic Activity* 2:137–187.

Lerner, Abba P. 1943. Functional finance and the federal debt. *Social Research* 10: 38–51.

Lindbeck, Assar, and Dennis J. Snower. 1988. *The insider-outsider theory of employment and unemployment.* Cambridge: MIT Press.

Lucas, Robert E. 1976. Econometric policy evaluation: A critique. *Carnegie-Rochester Conference Series on Public Policy* 1: 19–46.

Modigliani, Franco, and Charles Steindel. 1977. Is a tax rebate an effective tool for stabilization policy? *Brookings Papers on Economic Activity* 1: 175–203.

Musgrave, Richard A. 1959. *The theory of public finance.* New York: McGraw-Hill.

O'Driscoll, Gerald P. Jr. 1977. The Ricardian nonequivalence theorem. *Journal of Political Economy* 85(1) February: 207–210.

Okun, Arthur M. 1970. *The political economy of prosperity.* New York: W.W. Norton for the Brookings Institution.

Okun, Arthur M. 1971. The personal tax surcharge and consumer demand 1968–70. *Brookings Papers on Economic Activity* 1: 167–211.

Parker, Jonathan A. 1999. The reaction of household consumption to predictable changes in Social Security taxes. *American Economic Review* 89(4) September: 959–973.

Patinkin, Don. 1956. *Money, interest, and prices: An integration of monetary and value theory.* New York: Harper & Row.

Phelps, Edmund S. 1968. Money-wage dynamics and labor market equilibrium. *Journal of Political Economy* 76(4) July: 678–711.

Samuelson, Paul A. 1948. *Economics: An introductory analysis.* New York: McGraw-Hill.

Seidman, Laurence S. 2003. *Automatic fiscal policies to combat recessions.* Armonk: M.E. Sharpe.

Shapiro, Matthew D., and Joel Slemrod. 1995. Consumer response to the timing of income: Evidence from the change in tax withholding. *American Economic Review* 85(1) March: 274–283.

Shapiro, Matthew D., and Joel Slemrod. 2003. Consumer response to tax rebates. *American Economic Review* 93(1) March: 381–396.

Solow, Robert M. 1966. The case against the case against the guideposts. In *Guidelines, informal controls and the marketplace*, eds. George Shultz and Robert Aliber, 41–54. Chicago: University of Chicago Press.

Solow, Robert M. 2002. Is fiscal policy possible? Is it desirable? Presidential address to the XIII World Congress of the International Economic Association, Lisbon, September.

Souleles, Nicholas S. 1999. The response of household consumption to income-tax refunds. *American Economic Review* 89(4) September: 947–958.

Souleles, Nicholas S. 2002. Consumer response to the Reagan tax cuts. *Journal of Public Economics* 85(1) July: 99–120.

Stein, Herbert. 1969. *The fiscal revolution in America.* Chicago: University of Chicago Press.

Stock, James H., and Mark Watson. 1999. Business cycle fluctuations in U.S. macroeconomic time series. In *Handbook of macroeconomics*, vol. 1A, eds. John B. Taylor and Michael Woodford, 3–64. Amsterdam: North-Holland.

Sumner, M.T. 1979. A skeptical note on the efficacy of temporary sales tax reductions. *Canadian Public Policy* 5(1) Winter: 97–101.

Svensson, Lars E.O. 2001. The foolproof way of escaping from a liquidity trap: Is it really, and can it help Japan? The Frank D. Graham Memorial Lecture, Princeton University, April 5.

Turnovsky, Stephen J., and Marcus H. Miller. 1984. The effects of government expenditure on the term structure of interest rates. *Journal of Money, Credit and Banking* 16(1) February: 16–33.

U.S. Department of the Treasury. 1979. *The annual report of the Secretary of the Treasury on the state of the finances.* Washington, D.C.: Government Printing Office.

von Hagen, Jurgen, and Ian J. Harden. 1995. Budget processes and commitment to fiscal discipline. *European Economic Review* 39(3–4) April: 771–779.

Wyplosz, Charles. 2002. Fiscal discipline in EMU: Rules or institutions? Working Paper prepared for the Group of Economic Analysis of the European Commission.

Zeldes, Stephen P. 1989. Consumption and liquidity constraints: An empirical investigation. *Journal of Political Economy* 97(2) April: 305–346.

Comments on Blinder's "The Case Against the Case Against Discretionary Fiscal Policy"

Olivier J. Blanchard

I agree with everything that Alan Blinder wrote, and these comments will focus on just two points.

The first is the empirical evidence. Like Blinder, I have a very strong prior that fiscal policy can work to increase or decrease output. If one believes that aggregate demand determines output in the short run, which most of us do; that aggregate demand is C + I + G + NX, which most of us do; that Ricardian equivalence does not hold, which most of us do; and that we stay away from high deficits and high debt environments in which many things can go wrong, then, it is very difficult to see how a decrease in taxes or an increase in spending would not lead to an increase in output. This led Roberto Perotti and me [Blanchard and Perotti (2002)] to look at the effects of tax shocks, defined as the changes in taxes that cannot be predicted either from the past or from the automatic response of taxes to economic activity; and trace through the effect of these tax changes and the spending changes on output, without imposing our prior, namely, that it should work through aggregate demand.

As Blinder points out, we found that when taxes are decreased in the United States, GDP goes up for a while, then turns around and falls back. The data look just as in the textbook.

On the basis of these results, Roberto Perotti (2002) performed the same exercise for a number of Organisation for Economic Cooperation and Development (OECD) countries. When he attempted to identify the tax changes and follow the effects on GDP and other variables for OECD countries, the results were much less conclusive—and this is a euphemism. I would like to highlight several of Perotti's results.

First, when he looked at the effect of spending changes, say, spending increases, he found that there was a positive effect on GDP, but the multiplier was much less than 1. However, he did not find the response of interest rates that would naturally explain that effect. Then, on the tax changes, he found a set of results that can, at best, be called disappointing. Table 2.1 below (Table 9 from the paper) shows impulse responses for each of the five countries he examined: the United States, Germany, Great Britain, Canada, and Australia.

The table shows the effect of a 1-percent-of-GDP decrease in taxes after two quarters, four quarters, eight quarters, 12 quarters, and 20 quarters, respectively. The sample covers 1960 to 2000, and it is split into two sub-periods, one from 1960 to 1980, and the other from 1980 to 2000. One would expect that a decrease in taxes would increase GDP and that the effect would go away. Looking at the first line, corresponding to the United States, this is exactly what one finds, replicating what Perotti and I (2002) found earlier. The table also shows, however, that there are an unusual number of negative signs. In roughly half the cases, Perotti did not find the predicted effect of tax cuts on GDP. Interestingly, he also found that the effect was always weaker or more likely to be wrongly signed in the second period, from 1980 to 2000, than in the earlier period. This may tell us something about the weaknesses of structural VARs (vector autoregressions), as well as something about fiscal policy. I think it would be wrong to say that the fault is entirely with the structural VARs. The results may be the effects of the methodology, but they may also reflect something real.

The second point concerns automatic stabilizers. There, we suffer from enormous schizophrenia, in that we basically accept the automatic stabilization we have: We neither want to reduce it, nor to increase it. There is absolutely no reason, however, why history would have given us the optimal automatic stabilizers. A country that has a more progressive income tax has more automatic stabilization. While that may be very good for some countries, it is not necessarily the way to go for all countries. We should think about whether we could do better. Basically, very little work has been done on automatic stabilization; JSTOR lists only 11 articles on automatic stabilizers in the last 20 years, most of them from the earlier part of the period. Several issues concerning automatic stabilizers need to be examined.

Table 2.1
Response of GDP to a Tax Shock

Country	Sample	Quarters Elapsed					Max.	Min.
		2	4	8	12	20		
USA	all	0.06	0.23	0.54*	0.44*	0.08	0.54*(8)	0.03 (1)
	S1	0.43*	0.88*	1.01*	0.84*	0.18	1.04*(9)	0.18 (20)
	S2	-0.18	-0.54*	-0.90*	-0.81*	-0.20	-0.10 (1)	-0.92*(9)
DEU	all	-0.34*	0.00	0.49*	0.02	-0.31*	0.56*(7)	-0.43*(1)
	S1	-0.40*	-0.08	-0.00	0.53*	-0.50*	0.53*(12)	-0.54*(1)
	S2	0.03	0.24*	-0.19	-0.52*	0.18	0.26*(3)	-0.52*(11)
GBR	all	-0.09*	-0.11*	-0.16*	-0.21*	-0.15*	-0.08*(1)	-0.21*(12)
	S1	-0.09*	0.15*	0.12*	-0.06	0.01	0.20*(4)	-0.18*(1)
	S2	-0.16*	-0.32*	-0.39*	-0.28*	0.04	0.04 (20)	-0.40*(7)
CAN	all	0.09*	0.43*	0.57*	0.37*	0.14	0.59*(7)	0.05 (2)
	S1	-0.05	0.00	-0.18*	-0.21*	-0.08	0.06 (1)	-0.23*(9)
	S2	0.08	0.49*	0.80*	0.67*	0.35*	0.87*(7)	0.08 (2)
AUS	all	-0.47*	-0.40*	-0.42*	-0.23*	-0.05	-0.05 (20)	-0.49*(5)
	S1	-0.53*	-0.24*	-0.28*	-0.21	-0.21*	-0.18 (10)	-0.67*(1)
	S2	-0.33*	-0.42*	-0.49*	-0.17*	-0.04	-0.04 (20)	-0.57*(7)

Note: Effects on GDP of a net tax shock equal to -1 percentage point of GDP, from benchmark model described in text. Sample indicated by "all" covers 1960 to 2000. "S1" covers the subperiod 1960 to 1980. "S2" covers the subperiod 1980 to 2000.
* Asterisk indicates significance.

First, there is a distinction between truly automatic stabilizers and those that are triggered. Truly automatic stabilizers require absolutely no intervention by anyone. So, for example, the income-tax or unemployment benefits will work without anyone making a decision. But there are automatic stabilizers that are triggered; they depend on some aggregate measure crossing some level. The extension of unemployment benefits in the United States would be an example: When the unemployment rate goes above some level, then the period for which benefits are paid becomes longer. This type of stabilizer is not quite as good; they respond to something that is measured with a lag. Unemployment benefits are triggered in response to published unemployment numbers, and there is room for manipulation; that is, if you want to trigger this benefit, you can probably play with the numbers.

Second, one wants automatic stabilizers to be appropriate for most shocks, and that is an issue that bears more investigation. For example, unemployment benefits, mentioned by Blinder as a good automatic stabilizer, may not be the greatest tool when the source of the increasing unemployment is an increase in the natural rate. In this case, unemployment benefits may not be an appropriate tool. To take another example, the investment tax credit may not be the best tool if the source of a recession is a consumption collapse.

The third point is well known and very important; it concerns "the bang for the buck." I agree with Blinder that, while intertemporal income shifts can have some effect, they are clearly much weaker than intertemporal price shifts; and the method one uses to get a lot of bang for the buck by changing intertemporal prices—whether through investment tax credits, VAT cuts, and so on—raises many issues. For example, using the investment tax credit creates accounting problems. And if one aims at increasing people's sensitivity to these policy levers, people will soon come to know the tax code quite well and will play with it.

Fourth, I think one wants a stabilizer that is self-eliminating—even if it is the case that recessions typically do not last much longer than the two or three quarters that Blinder mentions. One wants these policy levers to work in such a way that, at some point, the decision to use them becomes a decision by the fiscal authority to do the right thing. Therefore, automatic stabilizers should not be in effect forever; they should be phased out.

Is there a perfect automatic stabilizer? Unfortunately, I believe the answer is no. I cannot think of an automatic stabilizer that works through intertemporal price shifts and is truly automatic. So, I think that the policy intervention must be triggered, and must depend on some aggregate that is measured.

In the end, one comes up with a list that has been explored before, but I think we should return to it. The investment tax credit clearly looks like something we should revisit. Another option is value-added-tax (VAT) decreases. Changing sales taxes in the United States would require a deal between the federal government and the states. Also, if one opts for a general VAT decrease, it is rather inefficient. With a general VAT decrease, one is including goods for which there is little possibility of intertemporal substitution. Such a measure should probably be targeted towards durable goods, and this can be done. The question is, for how long? If it is open ended, under rational expectations it would actually work quite well. So long as unemployment is above some level, the VAT on cars is decreased by 5 percent. At the beginning, there would probably be bunching. When people know that it is going to cross the threshold, they wait; and when it crosses the threshold, they buy cars. After that, nothing much would happen until the end, when people believe that the unemployment rate is about to go below the critical level. Then, bunching will occur again. These are issues that we should be thinking about much more, instead of just taking what we inherited from history and leaving it at that.

References

Blanchard, Olivier, and Roberto Perotti. 2002. An empirical characterization of the dynamic effects of changes in government spending and taxes on output. *Quarterly Journal of Economics* 117(4) November: 1329–1368.

Perotti, Roberto. 2002. Estimating the effects of fiscal policy in OECD countries. Working Paper at IGIER – Università Bocconi. September.

Comments on Blinder's "The Case Against the Case Against Discretionary Fiscal Policy"

Christopher A. Sims

Alan Blinder's outline of the history of ideas about countercyclical fiscal policy documents how events, academic fashion trends, and—possibly—the improved understanding of the economy have changed those ideas over time. I found his report useful, a reminder for most of us that, at any given time, the number of people who share the current consensus view on what is good macroeconomic policy is not a reliable indicator of the probability that that view is correct.

1. Evidence of Imperfect Optimization or Imperfect Markets

Blinder's paper goes on to survey evidence, some of it recent, that individual spending behavior departs significantly from the predictions of theories that assume complete markets and perfect dynamic optimization. That there are such departures is clear. Less clear are the reasons for the departures and the quantitative reliability of predictions based on them.

The Hsieh results [Hsieh (2003)] on the Alaskan Permanent Fund payments are particularly interesting. Here, in contrast to most of the other episodes that have been studied, the timing of the actual payments did not seem to matter much. The timing and size of these payments were more uniform across people and better publicized than in most of the other incidents studied. It is likely that when a payment or rebate is modest in size, many people don't expend the effort to determine in advance the size and timing of their own payment and adapt their spending patterns accordingly, even though they could do so fairly easily. But when the size and timing are uniform, it is hard to escape that knowledge. Also, one can imagine personal loan companies developing a product—borrow now against your rebate, with repayment due the day after the rebate. Eligibility for the rebate would be far easier to check than the usual calculation of ability to pay. These considerations suggest to me that Hsieh's unusual results imply a need for caution in predicting the effects of formula-based, systematic, countercyclical fiscal policy. It could be that the more systematic and prompt such policy is, the smaller its effect on the timing of expenditures.

2. The Intertemporal Government Budget Constraint

In his paper, Blinder deals too casually with both private and public intertemporal budget constraints, perhaps relying on the arcane terminology of "transversality" to get the reader's assent to sweep these issues under the rug. Transversality is a fancy name for a simple idea: If you acquire wealth, you will, at some point, recognize that you are richer and will want to spend more. The same applies in reverse if you lose wealth or borrow money. The effects of wealth on spending are not necessarily immediate, but they can be quick; and they are not connected to maturity of the instruments in the spender's portfolio.

For exactly the same reason, public expectations of future deficits or surpluses can have effects *now.*

• If it seems clear that debt is going to be rolled over or even expanded indefinitely, the fact that it carries a 10-year term will not prevent it from generating a real shift in tax burden from current to later generations. This will have consequences for real savings and investment—*now,* not in the distant future.

• If it becomes a political axiom that taxes cannot be increased in response to growing government debt, that will generate inflationary pressure that the Fed cannot resist—*now,* not in the distant future.

• If, in the face of persistent deflation, monetary and fiscal policy are seen to be "committed" to maintaining in the future the growing real value of government liabilities, deflation becomes dangerous—*now,* not in the distant future.

3. Is the Business Cycle Bad?

Missing from among the paper's list of reasons why countercyclical fiscal policy is out of fashion is one of the most important: increasing acceptance of the idea that "all that cycles is not market failure." The extreme real business-cycle view that most fluctuation that we observe at business-cycle frequencies is efficient and that policy should not try to interfere with it remains a minority view. But, in contrast to both monetarists and Keynesians in the 1960s and 1970s, most macroeconomists now probably do accept the idea that enough of observed cyclical fluctuation is associated with necessary resource reallocations that it does not make sense to use costly policies simply to counteract every deviation of growth from trend. For example, the end of the dotcom boom reduced the value of portfolios and required people to search for jobs outside that sector. Should we have tried to prevent completely, via changes in fiscal and monetary policy, the GDP and unemployment rate changes that were associated with these real reallocations?

4. "Discretionary" versus "Countercyclical"

Blinder's title refers to *discretionary* fiscal policy. But, in most of the text, this seems to be taken to be equivalent to *countercyclical* fiscal policy, and these are not the same thing. One can believe that fiscal policy needs to react to developments in the economy, and that the appropriate reactions are not best reduced to rigid rules. And one can do so without believing that the business-cycle phase or the growth rate of GDP is the only relevant economic index, or that the effects of fiscal policy on "aggregate demand" are the only relevant considerations in fiscal-policy changes at business-cycle frequencies.

5. The Case for Thoughtful and Vigilant Fiscal Policy

Despite my disagreement with some of the paper's implicit and explicit assumptions, I do agree that fiscal policy is important and should not simply be put on some kind of autopilot. However, my list of the important types of contingencies to which fiscal policy should respond differs from Blinder's.

"Countercyclical" fiscal policy ought to be targeted at those aspects of fluctuations that seem likely to reflect incompleteness or distortions in markets. A good example is one that Blinder cites—recession-induced extensions of unemployment insurance (UI) benefits. UI offsets one kind of market failure, while inducing an incentive distortion of its own. When many have been thrown out of work by economy-wide developments, the balance of these factors shifts, so that extending benefits clearly makes sense. To the extent that this mitigates the decline in output, this is probably also efficient. Making such extensions automatic probably would make sense.

Investment tax credits (ITCs) are a different kind of example. We expect wide fluctuations in investment as opportunities arise and are exhausted, even without any market failure. Distorting these fluctuations with taxes surely would result in some inefficiencies. If we thought most fluctuations represented inefficiencies, or that we were constantly on the edge of a new great depression, the case for systematic cyclical ITCs might be strong, but otherwise the case is weak.

When a liquidity panic or a severe overinvestment cycle makes government paper attractive relative to private assets, the monetary and fiscal authorities need to keep this from developing into an accelerating contraction in real activity. The required policies are not complicated, but historically they have not always been understood. Because these conditions go with near-zero interest rates, the required actions always have at least a partially fiscal character, even if they are undertaken by the central bank. Deficit-financed public spending or transfer payments can be helpful, if the resulting increased debt is not seen as implying a corresponding future tax burden. The central bank can shore up the banking system or other institutions by freely discounting illiquid private assets like bank loans. Doing so has a fiscal dimension, however, as it generates a central bank balance sheet that could be subject to capital losses and negative net worth. A central bank with negative net worth that needs to combat inflationary pressures will need support, in the form of recapitalization, from the treasury.

If the government borrows now and makes it clear that taxes to finance the new debt will occur far in the future (or claims to believe they will never be necessary), "transversality" will make savings fall now. This immediate effect is the mechanism by which the tax burden is shifted to later generations. Calculations of how much shifting is going on, and how much would be fair, need constant updating, because they depend on long-run projections that will inevitably be updated regularly. Discussion of these issues and adjustment of policy in light of the discussion ought to be—but, of course, is not in fact—a central, "discretionary" component of fiscal policy.

6. Conclusion

Out of this list of caveats and quibbles, I end up agreeing in substance, though sometimes for different reasons, with most of Blinder's direct policy recommendations.

- Countercyclical fiscal policy is not "normally" very useful.
- In sustained deflationary contractions, the fiscal policy vehicle must come out of the garage.
- Institutional innovation to replace or reform the European Stability and Growth Pact would be a good idea.

My main disagreement with the paper on direct policy issues concerns what I see as an omission. I would have put more emphasis on the need to guard continually against intergenerationally unfair crowding out.

References

Hsieh, Chang-Tai. 2003. Do consumers react to anticipated income changes? Evidence from the Alaska Permanent Fund. *American Economic Review* 93(1) March: 397–405.

3

American Fiscal Policy in the Post-War Era: An Interpretive History

American Fiscal Policy in the Post-War Era: An Interpretive History

Alan J. Auerbach

From a macroeconomist's perspective, the central issue surrounding fiscal policy has traditionally been its efficacy as a tool for stabilization. This focus on aggregate activity typically has led to a parallel concentration on fiscal aggregates: revenues, spending, and deficits. But a focus on aggregates masks significant changes that have occurred over the post-war years in U.S. fiscal policy. Some of these changes, in turn, have consequences for the practice of stabilization and budget policy. Given the continuing evolution in the composition of revenues and spending, a look below the surface will provide some insight into the future challenges to the practice of fiscal policy.

This paper begins, in the next section, with an overview of U.S. fiscal policy during the post-war period. Section 2 considers the determinants of fiscal-policy actions over this period, asking, in particular, how business-cycle and budget conditions have affected tax and spending behavior. Section 3 provides a discussion of how the changing composition of spending, from discretionary spending to old-age entitlements, is likely to affect short-run spending behavior, and also how this shift affects budget sustainability and the way in which we judge this sustainability.

1. A Brief Overview

Spending

Since 1962,[1] federal spending (excluding interest) has been relatively stable as a fraction of GDP. As seen in Figure 3.1, this share has ranged between just over 16 percent and just under 20 percent throughout the period. But the relative stability of the overall share masks considerable

Percent of GDP

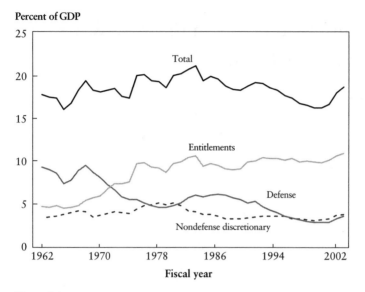

Figure 3.1
Federal noninterest spending as a share of GDP. *Source:* Congressional Budget Office, Budget and Economic Outlook: Fiscal Years 2005 to 2014, Appendix F.

changes in spending components. Defense spending has been trending steadily downward from a peak of nearly 10 percent at the height of the Vietnam War, with interruptions in this trend during the first half of the Reagan administration and since September 11, 2001. Nondefense discretionary spending rose during the mid-1960s and again in the mid-1970s and fell sharply at the beginning of the Reagan administration, but it has maintained a roughly constant share of spending since 1986— between 3.3 and 3.8 percent of GDP.

The main spending growth over the post-war period has occurred in entitlement programs, which grew sharply in the 1960s and 1970s and continued to grow, albeit more slowly, for the remainder of the period. Entitlement spending has more than doubled as a share of GDP since the early 1960s, absorbing the "peace dividends" provided by the ending of both the Vietnam and Cold Wars. Figure 3.2 shows spending on the three main entitlement programs—Social Security, Medicare, and Medicaid—over the same period. While spending as a share of GDP on these fast-growing programs stabilized for a time in the 1990s, in part because

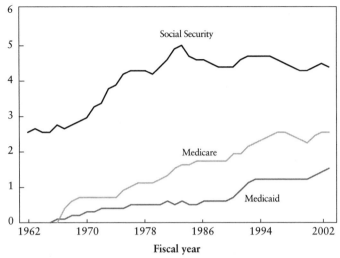

Figure 3.2
Trends in entitlement spending. *Source:* Congressional Budget Office, Budget and Economic Outlook: Fiscal Years 2005 to 2014, Appendix F.

of the economy's rapid growth during this period, growth relative to GDP has resumed; and, as long-range projections make quite clear, these programs as currently structured will continue to grow quite rapidly relative to GDP for the foreseeable future. Within these three programs, the share going to medical care has been increasing steadily, to the point that combined federal spending on Medicare and Medicaid is now nearly as high as that on Social Security.

Over the last four decades, then, federal spending has been relatively stable as a share of GDP, with this stability produced by offsetting trends in defense spending (down) and entitlement spending (up), while other discretionary spending has remained relatively constant. Over shorter periods, the trends have varied. During most of the Reagan years, cuts in nondefense spending balanced a temporary defense buildup. Throughout the George H.W. Bush and Clinton administrations, sharply falling defense spending more than offset entitlement growth, and aggregate spending fell as a share of GDP. During the George W. Bush administration, spending in all three areas has grown as a share of GDP for the first time since the Johnson administration's simultaneous pursuit of the Great Society and the Vietnam War.

Revenues

As with spending, federal revenues have been more stable in the aggregate, as a share of GDP, than have the important revenue components (see Figure 3.3). Prior to the late 1990s, revenues ranged between 17 and 20 percent of GDP, with the stability provided by offsetting trends in payroll taxes, which rose with the growth of the Medicare and Social Security systems to which they are dedicated, and in corporate income and other taxes, which fell. There were several important structural changes in the individual income tax that reduced marginal tax rates, notably in 1964 and 1986. Nevertheless, the individual income tax shows little trend, although it has risen over short periods, as during the late 1970s, when bracket creep and high inflation drove average tax rates upward, and even more throughout the mid-to-late 1990s, as income at the top of the taxable-income distribution

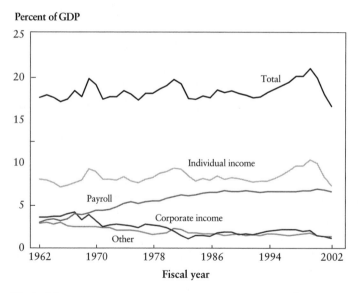

Figure 3.3
Trends in tax revenues. *Source:* Congressional Budget Office, Budget and Economic Outlook: Fiscal Years 2005 to 2014, Appendix F.

exploded with the economy and the stock market. Neither of these spurts in individual income-tax revenues was sustained; the first was reversed by the massive cut in individual income-tax rates included in the Economic Recovery Tax Act of 1981, the second by a series of tax cuts starting in 2001 and by the stock market "correction" that began in 2000.

Indeed, the years since 2000 have experienced a remarkably sharp drop in individual income taxes (as a share of GDP)—from 10.3 percent in fiscal year 2000 to 7.3 percent in fiscal year 2003. Further, this enormous drop in individual income taxes since 2000 has been accompanied by sustained declines as a share of GDP in each of the other revenue categories. In all, revenues fell from 20.9 percent of GDP in fiscal year 2000 to 16.5 percent in 2003, the highest and lowest shares of GDP, respectively, during the entire period since 1962.

The downward trend in "other" taxes reflects the declining use of indirect taxes as a source of revenue, a continuation of a trend of much longer duration. The modest level of corporate-tax collections has received renewed attention of late, but the biggest decline as a share of GDP occurred between the late 1960s, when corporate taxes reached 4 percent of GDP, and the early 1980s.[2] Since 1983, corporate-tax collections have ranged between 1.1 and 2.2 percent of GDP. During the last two decades, corporate taxes rose slightly after the Tax Reform Act of 1986, which shifted the tax burden from individuals to corporations, and again in the late 1990s with the economy's strong growth. The recent weakness in corporate-tax collections is clearly due in part to overall economic performance. Innovations in tax-avoidance techniques, including the use of offshore transactions, have also been implicated, although there is no precise estimate of their importance.

Deficits

Figure 3.4 brings together the post-war trends in spending and revenues to show the evolution of the federal government's budget deficit as a share of GDP. The strong growth in spending and the sharp decline in revenues over the past few years, as just discussed, have contributed to a remarkable drop in the federal budget surplus, from a high of nearly 2.5 percent in fiscal year 2000 to a deficit of 3.5 percent just three years

Percent of GDP

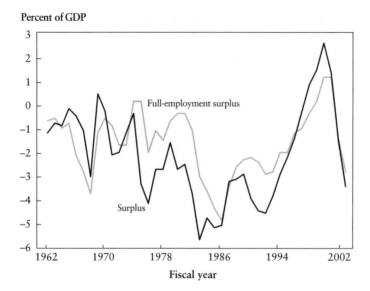

Figure 3.4
Federal budget surplus relative to GDP. *Source:* Congressional Budget Office, Budget and Economic Outlook: Fiscal Years 2005 to 2014, Appendix F.

later—a swing of almost 6 percent of GDP. This deterioration follows an equally remarkable eight-year rise that began in 1992.

Also represented in the figure is the full-employment surplus [as esti-mated by the Congressional Budget Office (CBO)], which is less volatile. As the comparison of these two series indicates, the strong surpluses of the late 1990s were attributable, in part, to strong economic performance; although the full-employment surplus in fiscal year 2000, at just over 1 percent of GDP, is still the highest value achieved over the entire period. Only a small part of the deterioration since then is directly attributed by the CBO to the business cycle. As a share of GDP, the current budget deficit, even when adjusted, is still smaller than in the mid-1980s. That is, taken in historical context, the 2003 budget deficit does not stand out, even though most of it remains after cyclical factors are removed.

2.   What Has Caused Policy to Change?

Over the longer term, the trends in various revenue sources and spending programs often have clear explanations, rooted in policy objectives and changing economic and demographic factors. For example, we have been turning away from indirect taxes as a revenue source for many decades, as our ability to collect direct taxes has improved; an aging population and steadily increasing per-capita medical spending have contributed to prolonged and rapid growth in Medicare spending. Over the shorter term, though, other political and economic objectives may influence changes in policy, and it is interesting to consider the strength of these different influences. A fundamental challenge to doing so, however, is the difficulty of identifying the magnitude and timing of policy changes, both of which are important in considering the macroeconomic effects of policy.

Automatic Stabilizers

Since the seminal paper by Brown (1956), it has been understood that measuring the magnitude of policy changes requires that one control for changes that are not policy driven. Increases in spending and, especially, declines in revenues that come about as a direct consequence of recession represent the automatic stabilizers implicit in fiscal policy. These automatic stabilizers, of course, may influence the magnitude of economic fluctuations, but they are not, in any sense, changes in the course of policy. Indeed, for those skeptical of the government's ability to time fiscal changes and practice discretionary fiscal policy effectively, automatic stabilizers provide at least some scope for countercyclical fiscal actions.

On the tax side, a key measure is the change in taxes with respect to a unit change in aggregate income. This may be roughly proxied by the tax share of GDP, but the two coincide only if the tax system is a proportional one, which ours is not. Changes in the structure of taxation and in the distribution of income can affect the strength of automatic stabilizers independently of the tax share of GDP. Given the changes that have occurred over the past several decades in the relative importance of different taxes, the progressivity of the individual income tax, and the income distribution, the relative stability of aggregate revenues as a share of GDP (as shown in Figure 3.3) does not necessarily imply a similar stability in the strength of tax-based automatic stabilizers.

Figure 3.5 presents estimates, for the period 1960–1997, of the response of individual income and payroll taxes, the two most important revenue categories, to a unit change in income. [The figure updates one in Auerbach and Feenberg (2000), and is based on the methodology

Change in taxes per dollar change in income

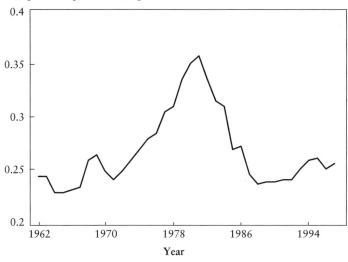

Figure 3.5
Automatic stabilizers: Individual income and payroll taxes. *Source:* NBER TAXSIM
model.

developed there.] There are several factors at work influencing this measure. Some, such as the widening dispersion of the income distribution,
should have increased the sensitivity of taxes to income, given the progressive individual income-tax rate structure. Other changes, such as the
various rounds of marginal tax-rate cuts that began in 1964 and continued in 1981 and 1986, should have decreased the sensitivity of taxes
to income (as should the inflation-indexing provision of the 1981 Act,
which took effect in 1985), to the extent that one assumes (as this calculation does) that inflation is sensitive to cyclical income changes.

   All in all, though, the measure in the late 1990s stands roughly where it
did in the early 1960s. The tax cut of 1964 had a relatively small impact,
given the very high incomes at which previous top marginal rates had
applied. The 1981 and 1986 Acts had more noticeable impacts, but these
simply undid the very large rise in sensitivity that had occurred during the
1970s as a result of bracket creep. The 1993 tax increase had a small effect,
and, if the figure were extended to the present, it would probably show that
this increase was more than undone by the tax cuts of 2001 and 2003.[3]

Further Adjustments

It is common to use changes in the full-employment deficit to measure changes in discretionary fiscal policy, given that these changes have been purged of the effects of automatic stabilizers. But there are considerable problems with this interpretation, as the following case study from the period leading up to September 11, 2001, illustrates.

As we now know, the economy had gone into recession several months prior to September 11, and the weakening economy contributed to the declining budget surplus. As Figure 3.6 shows, the full-employment surplus was relatively stable through the second quarter of 2001, while the unadjusted surplus was declining. However, the sharp drop in the surplus during the third quarter of 2001 is only slightly weakened by the full-employment adjustment, suggesting that a major expansionary policy change occurred during this quarter, either just before or just after September 11.

But what was this "policy" change? There were few changes in spending programs during the period; however, there were two factors, other than the economic slowdown, that contributed to a decline in revenues.

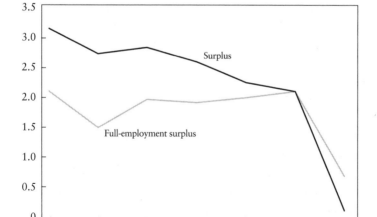

Figure 3.6
The budget surplus and September 11th. *Source:* Congressional Budget Office.

One was the phase-in of the Economic Growth and Tax Relief Reconciliation Act (EGTRRA), enacted in the spring of 2001. The other was the sharp decline in revenues attributable neither to legislation nor to the economic slowdown, and hence categorized by the CBO as "technical" changes. Due to such causes as the decline in the stock market and the resulting drop in tax revenues from capital gains and compensation options, the CBO (2002) revised its annual revenue forecasts downward by about $50 billion from those reported during the summer of 2001.

Thus, the large apparent change in discretionary policy that occurred during the third quarter of 2001 derives mainly from two sources; one was a policy change adopted earlier in the year, the other was not a policy change at all. Clearly, the second source should not be counted as a change in policy; as to the first, some of the policy effects may have been delayed until taxes actually were reduced, but this is not relevant if we are seeking to understand the determinants of policy *decisions*.

An Alternative Measure of Policy Changes

To avoid counting previously announced policy changes and changes in the budget that are not attributable to policy at all, I rely on a measure developed in Auerbach (2002, 2003), based on explicit policy changes. As described more fully in those papers, the changes in revenue and expenditure policy come from successive CBO forecasts that attribute changes from the previous forecasts of revenue and expenditures to legislative action, changes in macroeconomic projections, and changes in other economic factors not captured by macroeconomic projections. Thus, they measure changes in the government's explicit policy trajectory that occurred during the period.

The available information provides a continuous, roughly semiannual series (summer to winter, and winter to summer) of policy changes in revenues and expenditures, beginning with changes between the winter and summer of 1984. As each update includes policy changes for the current fiscal year and several subsequent years, I construct a summary measure equal to the discounted sum of the current fiscal year's change and that for the next four fiscal years, using a discount rate of 0.5.[4]

This measure of policy changes has its own problems, of course. Perhaps most notable is that even policies specified by legislation need not be credible. Indeed, in recent years, the credibility of legislative changes to the tax code has been undercut by the use of "sunset" provisions. These provisions repeal tax cuts after a specified number of years; in many cases, those crafting the legislation have made quite explicit their intent that the provisions be permanent.[5]

Such a legislative maneuver may be understood as a response to the multiyear budget window used to evaluate and constrain tax legislation; changes that are intended to be permanent may be enacted at a lower measured revenue cost if they are scheduled to expire during the budget window.[6] But, if the changes are intended to be permanent, and if these intentions are credible, then it is not clear how the policy change in years beyond the sunset should be treated. Presumably, at least some weight should be given to an extension of the policy. Fortunately, the relatively short policy period (five years) considered, along with the heavy discounting of the policy changes for future fiscal years, makes this issue relatively unimportant here.

Empirical Results

The first column of Table 3.1 presents a regression, with this summary measure of policy changes in revenue as the dependent variable and with the previous quarter's GDP gap and the previous fiscal year's surplus as explanatory variables. (All variables are scaled by the contemporaneous CBO estimate of potential GDP.) The second column of the table presents the same regression, except that the dependent variable is policy changes to noninterest expenditures. In both equations, the coefficients indicate that policy has responded in a countercyclical manner and has been responsive to budget conditions, as well. The responsiveness in the two equations is of roughly the same order of magnitude. The coefficients suggest that about 12 percent of an increase in the budget surplus is immediately eroded by tax cuts and spending increases.

One of the advantages of this data source is that it provides projections of the budget surplus under existing policy, which may be a more accurate measure of fiscal conditions than the lagged budget surplus. Using a weighted average of the lagged surplus and the projections of surpluses for the current and next three fiscal years,[7] I construct an alternative measure of fiscal conditions. Using this alternative measure, the results

Table 3.1
Determinants of Policy Changes, Fiscal Years 1984–2004
Dependent Variable: Semiannual Policy Change in Revenues or Expenditures (excluding interest) Relative to Full-Employment GDP (standard errors in parentheses)

Independent Variable	Sample Period and Dependent Variable:							
	1984:2–2004:1		1984:2–2004:1		1984:2–1993:1, 2001:2–2004:1		1993:2–2001:1	
	Revenues	Expenditures	Revenues	Expenditures	Revenues	Expenditures	Revenues	Expenditures
Constant	−.001 (.0003)	.002 (.0005)	−.001 (.0004)	.002 (.004)	−.002 (.001)	.002 (.001)	−.0003 (.0005)	.001 (.0003)
Budget Surplus (−1)	−.061 (.015)	.078 (.018)	—	—	—	—	—	—
GDP Gap (−1)	−.052 (.021)	.076 (.026)	−.059 (.023)	.095 (.027)	−.046 (.029)	.096 (.039)	−.034 (.049)	.071 (.030)
Projected Surplus	—	—	−.066 (.016)	.094 (.019)	−.084 (.021)	.098 (.028)	−.042 (.036)	.085 (.022)
$\bar{R}^2$	.285	.291	.278	.366	.386	.331	.070	.656
Number of Observations	40	40	40	40	24	24	16	16

Data Source: Congressional Budget Office.

for revenues and expenditures are shown in the third and fourth columns of Table 3.1. The results for revenues are similar to those based on the lagged surplus, while the fit for expenditures is better, and the estimated coefficients are larger.

Using these estimates, it is interesting to consider when policy has followed—and when it has deviated from—these simple feedback rules. Figure 3.7 presents residuals for the equations in the third and fourth columns of Table 3.1. On the spending side, there are notable negative shocks during the Gramm–Rudman–Hollings period in the late 1980s. The fall 1990 budget agreement between President George H.W. Bush and Congress produced a positive revenue shock and a negative spending shock, with both contributing to smaller subsequent deficits. The 1993 Clinton tax increase produced a positive revenue shock, but there were few other surprises during the Clinton period. Policy volatility returned during the current Bush administration, with the tax cuts of early 2001 and early 2003 producing large negative revenue shocks. The 2003 shock is larger than the 2001 shock, even though the 2001 tax cut was bigger, because of the different budget situations in the two years. When the

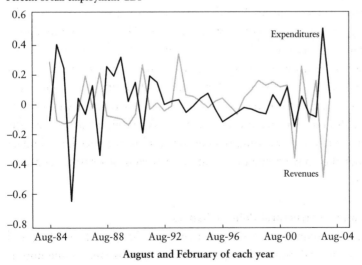

Figure 3.7
Policy residuals. *Source:* Author's calculations.

2001 tax cut occurred, there was a large budget surplus, and President Bush argued that it was the taxpayers' money and should be returned to them. When the 2003 tax cut occurred, the surplus was gone, replaced by a deficit, but tax cutting continued.

Also notable about the first part of 2003 is the large contemporaneous positive shock to spending. Note that this spending shock is due primarily to large increases in defense and nondefense discretionary spending. It does not include the introduction in the fall of 2003 of the Medicare drug benefit, which does not register as a large change because its major budget impact will not be felt in the next few years.

Do recent fiscal actions indicate a change in behavior? With so short a sample period of observation, it is difficult to tell. As the last four columns of Table 3.1 show, if one breaks down the entire sample period by presidential party (that is, Reagan, Bush, and Bush *versus* Clinton), the estimated behavioral responses are relatively similar across parties. The estimates suggest stronger responsiveness by Republicans to both the GDP gap and the projected surplus, for both revenues and expenditures. These differences, though, are not significant. The differences in intercepts indicate that, for a zero budget surplus and a zero GDP gap, Republicans would increase spending more than Democrats, and cut taxes more. It follows that, for conditions like those in the spring of 2001, when the budget was in surplus and there was a positive GDP gap, the predicted Republican response involves larger tax cuts and higher spending than the predicted Democratic response. Thus, some of the recent behavior may simply reflect a return to a Republican policy rule, but, again, it is hard to be certain, given the short sample period of observation. The real test will come during the next few years, as we observe how the government's tax and spending policies respond to the very large budget deficits that they have helped to create in a period of relative economic prosperity.

Determinants of Structural Policy Changes

Although it is common to focus on aggregate changes in spending and revenues, structural policy changes are important, as well. Some important tax reforms, such as the Tax Reform Act of 1986, were designed to be revenue-neutral, while attempting to change incentives to work, to allocate and finance capital, and to engage in tax-avoidance transactions. While one may apply a similar methodology to that used above to study changes in particular incentives,[8] the tax changes are generally difficult to summarize using concise measures suitable for econometric analysis. This leaves the case study as an alternative approach to understanding the timing and shape of structural tax changes.

Much writing has been devoted to understanding the economic and political factors that precipitated the major tax changes of the 1980s— both occurring under President Ronald Reagan: the Economic Recovery Tax Act of 1981 and the Tax Reform Act of 1986.[9] Equally challenging to summarize and explain is the reform process since then, as marginal tax rates crept upward until 2001, and gaps in the taxation of different forms of income (notably the favorable treatment of capital gains) reappeared.

3.   Implications of the Evolving Public Sector

Figures 3.1 and 3.2 showed that entitlement spending, particularly spending on Social Security, Medicare, and Medicaid, have been growing rapidly over the past few decades, accounting for a larger and larger share of total federal spending. There is little to suggest that this process will abate any time soon. Figure 3.8 provides the most recent intermediate projections by the Social Security and Medicare Trustees of benefits for their respective programs as shares of GDP, through 2080. According to the projections, these two programs alone, if not altered, would account for more of GDP in 2080 than has all federal spending combined in any year shown in Figure 3.1. Recent long-term projections for Medicaid (CBO 2003) paint a picture of growth for that program through 2050 similar to that for Medicare.

In the context of this paper, there are at least three important issues raised by this strong and persistent trend in entitlement spending. First, what are the implications for the feasibility of fiscal policy? Second, how will short-run policy responses be influenced by the changing composition of spending? Third, how does this shift in spending affect the meaning of standard measures of fiscal balance and fiscal policy, such as the budget surplus?

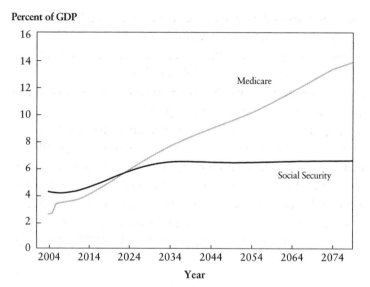

Figure 3.8
Social Security and Medicare projections. *Source:* Social Security: 2004 OASDI Trustees Report, Table VI.F5; Medicare: 2004 Medicare Trustees Report, Table II.A2 (interpolated 2013–2080).

Policy Feasibility

The answer to the first of these questions is simple. Given the Trustees' projections for Social Security and Medicare as well as the CBO's projections for Medicaid, current U.S. fiscal policy is clearly unsustainable. Table 3.2 presents a variety of measures of how far policy is from being sustainable, all from recent calculations provided by Auerbach, Gale, and Orszag (2004).

The first two columns of Table 3.2 are based on the assumption that the current CBO baseline for taxes and spending as a share of GDP prevails through 2014, with taxes and all noninterest spending components, other than Social Security, Medicare, and Medicaid, growing with GDP thereafter. The last two columns adjust this baseline to incorporate more realistic assumptions for the next decade about discretionary spending growth (for example, that discretionary spending grows with prices and population), and about taxes (that sunset provisions do not take effect and that the alternative minimum tax is not allowed to affect a growing share of taxpayers).

Table 3.2
Fiscal Gaps

	Official Baseline		Adjusted Baseline	
	2004–2080	Permanent	2004–2080	Permanent
As a Percent of GDP	4.60	7.73	7.20	10.47
In Trillions of Present-Value Dollars	23.1	63.1	36.3	85.5

Source: Auerbach, Gale, and Orszag (2004).

The first row of Table 3.2 presents estimates of the permanent increase in the primary surplus needed to make policy feasible under these two baselines. Columns 1 and 3 measure this necessary increase over the period 2004–2080, where feasibility is associated with achieving the same debt-to-GDP ratio in 2080 as in 2004. Columns 2 and 4 measure the necessary increase over the infinite horizon, identifying the permanent increase in the primary surplus-to-GDP ratio needed for the present value of revenues to equal the present value of spending plus the initial stock of publicly held national debt.

Under the official baseline assumptions, the fiscal gap through 2080 is 4.6 percent of GDP. This implies that an immediate increase in taxes or cut in spending of 4.6 percent of GDP—or almost $500 billion per year in current terms—would be needed to maintain fiscal balance through 2080. The fiscal gap is larger under the adjusted baseline, because it assumes a lower level of revenue and a higher level of discretionary spending than the official baseline. Under the adjusted baseline, the fiscal gap through 2080 amounts to 7.2 percent of GDP. The fiscal gap is even larger if the time horizon is extended, since the budget is projected to be running substantial deficits in years approaching and after 2080. If the horizon is extended indefinitely, the fiscal gap rises to 7.7 percent of GDP under the official baseline and to 10.5 percent of GDP under the adjusted baseline. The required adjustments represent substantial shares of current spending or revenue aggregates. A fiscal adjustment of 7.7 percent of GDP, for example, translates into a reduction in spending of 29 percent or an increase in revenues of 40 percent.

One may also express these measures in absolute terms, rather than as a share of GDP, by calculating the present value of the required increases in the primary surplus. This alternative method of presentation has recently been suggested by Gokhale and Smetters (2003) as a way of emphasizing how large the total imbalance is relative to the explicit national debt. These numbers are presented in the second row of Table 3.2, for the same assumptions as those in the first row of the respective columns.

Changing Short-Run Fiscal Behavior

In attempting to deal with this large fiscal gap, one problem that must be faced is that entitlement programs are more difficult to change than are other types of spending. Particularly when old-age programs, such as Social Security and Medicare, are concerned, long-range planning is involved on the part of beneficiaries, and this translates into the need for long-range planning for changes on the part of government. This suggests that short-run fiscal adjustments on the spending side should be smaller now than in the past, and should be smaller still in the future.

In illustration of this point, Table 3.3 presents regressions to explain annual changes in spending on discretionary items and on Social Security, Medicare, and Medicaid as a share of full-employment GDP. The independent variables, as before, are the lagged values of the budget surplus as a share of GDP and the full-employment gap.[10] As shown in the first three columns of Table 3.3, over the full available sample period, 1963–2003, total discretionary spending was responsive to both explanatory variables, although neither coefficient is statistically significant. The exclusion of defense spending, which clearly has other important determinants as well, substantially reduces standard errors, making the budget surplus coefficient statistically significant. Note, though, that spending on the three major entitlement programs bears essentially no relationship to these same determinants; indeed, the coefficients, while insignificant, are actually negative.

Given that Medicare didn't even exist in 1963, and that budget rules governing discretionary spending have varied greatly over the full period, a look over a shorter, more recent period may be advisable. The last three columns of Table 3.3 present results since 1993. The coefficients for both discretionary spending aggregates are much larger and more significant

Table 3.3
Determinants of Spending Changes, Fiscal Years 1963–2003
Dependent Variable: Annual Change in Spending Component Relative to Full-Employment GDP
(standard errors in parentheses)

	Sample Period and Dependent Variable					
	1963–2003			1993–2003		
Independent Variable	All Discretionary	Nondefense Discretionary	Social Security/ Medicare/ Medicaid	All Discretionary	Nondefense Discretionary	Social Security/ Medicare/ Medicaid
Constant	−.0001	.001	.001	.002	.001	.001
	(.001)	(.001)	(.0004)	(.001)	(.0004)	(.0005)
Budget Surplus (−1)	.057	.051	−.022	.381	.124	.026
	(.049)	(.022)	(.015)	(.070)	(.039)	(.053)
GDP Gap (−1)	.024	.024	−.017	.441	.158	.077
	(.038)	(.017)	(.012)	(.096)	(.054)	(.073)
$\bar{R}^2$	−.016	.071	.013	.754	.451	.146
Number of Observations	41	41	41	11	11	11

Data Source: Congressional Budget Office.

over this period, indicating considerable responsiveness. Even the major entitlements now show some responsiveness to the budget and the business cycle, but these effects are still insignificant and are much smaller in magnitude, relative to the corresponding average level of spending over the sample period.

The Meaning of Traditional Fiscal Measures

In the fall of 2003, Congress enacted a major expansion of the Medicare program, the new Part D, which will provide partial payment for prescription drugs for Medicare beneficiaries. Although there was considerable controversy regarding its cost over the official 10-year budget window, the short-run cost pales in comparison with the long-run cost, because (1) the program is not fully effective immediately; and (2), as with the rest of Medicare, the annual cost is projected to grow more rapidly than GDP for the foreseeable future.

The jump in projected Medicare spending visible over the next few years in Figure 3.8 represents the phasing in of this new program, which is projected to account for roughly one-fourth of all Medicare spending and 1 percent of GDP by 2015.[11] In present-value terms, the program has added an estimated $6.2 trillion of implicit liability, net of premium payments by beneficiaries and projected contributions from states. This increment alone is larger in magnitude than the current explicit national debt.[12]

This episode highlights the problem of evaluating changes in the entitlement programs, like Medicare, that are occupying a growing share of federal spending. Like essentially all other components of spending, Medicare is accounted for on a cash basis, with trust fund accumulations duly recorded, but increments to future liabilities ignored.

There is no ideal way to account for these liabilities. Treating them as equivalent to explicit debt suggests that they carry the same commitment, which they don't in a legal sense. But ignoring them suggests that they carry no commitment at all, which historically has certainly not been the case. Also, finding that the present value of a stream of future spending is very large does not imply that the spending is unwise or unsustainable; after all, the stream of future tax revenues is large in present-value terms, as well. But a *change* in policy that increases future spending commitments and provides no offset in the form of spending cuts or tax increases does worsen the government's fiscal position.

How one accounts for these large liabilities doesn't affect their magnitude, but it could affect policy decisions. Consider the illustrative calculations in Table 3.4, which update the estimates in Auerbach (2002, 2003) and are explained in more detail there. For the debt of the Social Security system (OASDI, or Old Age, Survivors, and Disability Insurance), the table presents annual estimates of the "closed-group" liability, equal to the present value of benefits less contributions for those 15 years of age and older in the year of the calculation.[13] This is one possible measure of the system's net liability, although there are others, as well.

In the second column is the deficit, equal to the change in the debt from the beginning of the current year to the beginning of the next year. The change in the closed-group liability from one year to the next equals the sum of two terms: increases in obligations to those remaining in the system plus the difference between liabilities to those entering the system and those leaving the system.

The next two columns provide a breakdown of the deficit into two exhaustive categories. The first of these categories, labeled "Base Year,"

Table 3.4
Implicit Debt and Deficits of the OASDI System
(billions of dollars)

Year	Debt	Deficit	Portion of Deficit Due to Change in	
			Base Year	Projections
1997	7,724	426	523	−97
1998	8,151	173	581	−408
1999	8,324	765	604	161
2000	9,089	878	677	201
2001	9,967	704	731	−27
2002	10,671	403	731	−328
2003	11,074	797	747	50
2004	11,871			

Source: Author's calculations.

measures what the deficit would have been had no economic or demographic projections changed during that year; this measures the change in the debt, holding projections fixed. The second residual category, "Projections," measures the remaining portion of the deficit, the part due to changes in projections. This portion of the deficit is sometimes negative and sometimes positive, averaging –$64 billion over the seven-year period. But the component due to the changing base year is always positive, and it averages $656 billion per year. This measure is positive and large, reflecting the fact that the retirement of the baby boom cohort is approaching.

Deficit estimates, such as these for the Medicare system, likely would be considerably larger, given the relative magnitudes of the closed-group liabilities for the two systems. For the past year, this would be especially so, as the deficit would include the $6.2 trillion unfunded liability of the new Medicare drug benefit.

Would there have been a substantial tax cut in 2001 if a budget deficit of several percent of GDP had been reported, rather than a budget surplus? Would Congress have added a prescription drug benefit to Medicare in 2003, with no offsetting spending reductions or tax increases, had the full cost of the change been featured in the debate?

4. Conclusion

During the past several decades, fiscal policy has responded to changing circumstances. Spending on defense has risen and fallen with national security needs, and old-age entitlement programs have grown along with the aging and elderly populations. In the short run, spending and taxes have responded to cyclical and budget forces. But aging and increasing healthcare expenditures present unprecedented challenges to the fiscal system's ability to respond, for they generate a large sustainability gap that is not well characterized by the traditional budget measures to which policy has responded in the past. The major fiscal changes required over the coming years may require changes in fiscal accounting, as well.

■ *I am grateful to James Duesenberry and Douglas Elmendorf, my discussants at the Federal Reserve Bank of Boston's conference on "The*

Macroeconomics of Fiscal Policy," June 14–16, 2004, as well as other conference participants, for comments on an earlier draft.

Notes

1. The historical data in Figures 3.1 through 3.4 are from the CBO (2004), which provides historical fiscal data since 1962.

2. For an analysis of the causes of this decline, see Auerbach and Poterba (1987).

3. Auerbach (2002) constructs an alternative time series for the strength of automatic stabilizers, based on the CBO's full-employment deficit series. That series has different year-to-year patterns, but has the same general shape over time, with the value in 2001 slightly below the value in 1960.

4. This high discount rate is chosen based on goodness-of-fit criteria. Because policy revisions between the winter and summer take effect starting midway through the current fiscal year, I reduce the weight on the current fiscal year by one-half and increase weights on subsequent years correspondingly, for winter-to-summer revisions.

5. See Gale and Orszag (2003).

6. See Auerbach (2005), forthcoming, for further discussion.

7. The weighting scheme is the same as that used for the dependent variables.

8. For example, Auerbach (2003) relates changes in the user cost of capital for U.S. business fixed investment to lags in the output gap and the budget surplus, as well as to lagged investment. The results suggest that, as with aggregate revenues, investment incentives are responsive to cyclical and budget conditions.

9. See, for example, Steuerle (1992).

10. The use of actual spending data is necessary, because there is not a consistent breakdown by category in the CBO policy data used in Table 3.1. There is a potential problem that actual spending data will include changes that might be the automatic result of cyclical factors. This should not be a major concern, though, given that most automatic responses at the federal level are on the tax side or in entitlement programs other than those considered in Table 3.3.

11. See the 2004 Medicare Trustees' Annual Report [Boards of Trustees, Federal Hospital Insurance and Federal Supplemental Insurance Trust Funds (2004)], Table II.A2.

12. 2004 Medicare Trustees' Annual Report, Table II.C23.

13. I am grateful to Kristy Piccinini for performing these calculations. The closed-group measures in Table 3.4 are somewhat lower for 2003 and 2004, respectively, than are those provided by the corresponding Trustees' Annual Reports ($11.9 trillion and $12.7 trillion, respectively), presumably as the result of differences in assumed tax and benefit profiles. One cannot use the figures from the Trustees'

Annual Reports to perform these calculations, because they are not published for earlier years and do not offer a breakdown of the sources of change from one year to the next.

References

Auerbach, Alan J. 2002. Is there a role for discretionary fiscal policy? In *Rethinking stabilization policy: A symposium sponsored by the Federal Reserve Bank of Kansas City,* 109–150. Kansas City: Federal Reserve Bank of Kansas City.

Auerbach, Alan J. 2003. Fiscal policy, past and present. *Brookings Papers on Economic Activity* 1:75–122.

Auerbach, Alan J. 2005. Forthcoming. Budget windows, sunsets, and fiscal control. *Journal of Public Economics.*

Auerbach, Alan J., and Daniel Feenberg. 2000. The significance of federal taxes as automatic stabilizers. *Journal of Economic Perspectives* 14(3) Summer: 37–56.

Auerbach, Alan J., William G. Gale, and Peter R. Orszag. 2004. Sources of the fiscal gap. *Tax Notes* 103 (May 24): 1049–1059.

Auerbach, Alan J., and James M. Poterba. 1987. Why have corporate tax revenues declined? In *Tax policy and the economy* 1, ed. L. Summers, 1–28. Cambridge: MIT Press.

Board of Trustees, Federal Old-Age and Survivors Insurance and Disability Insurance Trust Funds. 2004. *2004 annual report.* March 23.

Boards of Trustees, Federal Hospital Insurance and Federal Supplementary Insurance Trust Funds. 2004. *2004 annual report.* March 23.

Brown, E. Cary. 1956. Fiscal policy in the 'thirties: A reappraisal. *American Economic Review* 46(5) December: 857–879.

Congressional Budget Office. 2002. *The budget and economic outlook: Fiscal years 2003–2012.* January.

Congressional Budget Office. 2003. *The long-term budget outlook.* December.

Congressional Budget Office. 2004. *The budget and economic outlook: Fiscal years 2005–2014.* January.

Gale, William G., and Peter R. Orszag. 2003. Sunsets in the tax code. *Tax Notes* 99 (June 9): 1553–1561.

Gokhale, Jagadeesh, and Kent Smetters. 2003. *Fiscal and generational imbalances: New budget measures for new budget priorities.* Washington, DC: The AEI Press.

Steuerle, C. Eugene. 1992. *The tax decade: How taxes came to dominate the public agenda.* Washington, DC: Urban Institute Press.

Comments on Auerbach's "American Fiscal Policy in the Post-War Era: An Interpretive History"

James S. Duesenberry

Making good fiscal policy requires good judgment. I was told some years ago by a man reputed to be wise that good judgment can be attained through experience. Experience, he said, comes from bad judgment. We have had plenty of bad fiscal policy judgment in the last 40 years; but to use the experience well, we need to know what really happened and why. When we study the effects of fiscal events, we need to separate endogenous elements from policy-driven elements in the data on revenues and expenditures, but it is difficult to do a thorough job of it. Professor Auerbach has taken that problem seriously and has developed a solution that will prove to be a substantial contribution to macroeconomic analysis. The first part of Auerbach's paper deals with the measurement and determination of budget surpluses and deficits over the last 20 years. The second part deals with the implications of projected cost increases for Social Security and Medicare.

Auerbach begins with a review of the major movements of federal spending and revenue and the resulting surpluses or deficits (mainly the latter) in the last quarter-century. He then examines the role of fiscal policy in determining surpluses and deficits.

It has long been recognized that actual revenues and expenditures reflect movements of GDP, which is influenced, but not determined, by fiscal policy. The full-employment surplus provides one measure of fiscal policy independent of actual GDP movements. However, Auerbach shows that other nonpolicy influences—for example, tax revenue from capital gains—can change the full-employment surplus without a policy change. His discussion of the problems of identifying and measuring policy actions is particularly valuable, because it deals with a very common problem, which—though not ignored—is seldom dealt with in a systematic way.

In seeking a better measure of budget changes due to fiscal policy, Auerbach has decided to outsource the problem. His alternative measure of fiscal policy is based on the breakdown of budget changes by the Congressional Budget Office (CBO) into those due to economic events, those due to so-called technical factors, and those due to policy. A very sensible decision.

The next step is to see how policy is related to stabilization problems. Auerbach uses the CBO data in regressions, with measures of policy-induced changes in revenues and expenditures as dependent variables. The lagged GDP gap and the lagged fiscal surplus serve as explanatory variables. The results of a number of specifications of the regressions are shown in his Table 3.1. In all the regressions, expenditures and revenues have the expected response coefficients; but, in most cases, the regressions explain only a fraction of the changes in expenditures and revenues.

These results suggest a modest degree of rational stabilization response in the making of fiscal policy. It must be remembered, however, that some fiscal actions were taken in order to undo the damage done by earlier ones. More important, fiscal policy choices are not always motivated by stabilization objectives. They also reflect concerns about income distribution, the size of government, and the desire to finance certain expenditure objectives; they have often been justified on supply-side grounds. Tax deductions would, it has been argued, raise the long-term growth rate by increasing incentives for saving and investment.

1. Fiscal History

In this section, I shall try to support those observations by a brief review of fiscal history. To do so, I shall have to widen the field of vision to cover a somewhat longer period and to take into account monetary policy.

In Figure 3.4, Auerbach shows the movement of actual fiscal surpluses and of full-employment surpluses from 1962 onward. The year 1962 makes a useful starting point for my history. I shall use Figure 3.4 to highlight an account of the main fiscal policy events over the last 40 years. The experience of the late 1950s and early 1960s showed that decision and implementation lags ruled out public works expenditures as remedies for short recessions. Longer-term programs required Congressional support. The Kennedy administration, seeking faster growth, but lacking Congressional approval for permanent expenditure programs, resorted to a permanent tax reduction. The tax change began to affect demand just as President Lyndon B. Johnson was simultaneously succeeding in selling Great Society programs and accelerating expenditures for the Vietnam War. After nearly three years of growing inflationary pressure, a temporary tax surcharge and expenditure cuts were adopted. Those actions plus rising interest rates were sufficient to cause a short recession, but were insufficient to check a wage-price cycle.

In Auerbach's Figure 3.4, the V-shaped path of the full-employment surplus line from 1965 to 1970 reflects the fiscal actions of the Johnson administration. That experience undermined the idea of using fiscal policy for stabilization purposes, making monetary policy the only game in town.

The inflation begun in the 1960s continued in the 1970s, driven by inflation history, supply shocks, strong unions, and managements willing to accept cost-of-living adjustments (COLAs) as a norm. The experience fostered the NAIRU (nonaccelerating inflation rate of unemployment) approach in academic analysis. In spite of disputes over how to play the game, the idea that control of money growth could bring down inflation at an affordable cost, in terms of lost income and employment, gained academic adherents. However, political support for testing that argument was lacking. Following the second oil shock, Paul Volcker bit the bullet. At considerable cost, he brought about a disinflation and launched the idea that a long-established, inflationary wage-price spiral could be halted by a firm commitment to disinflation, although at a high cost. Volcker's success reflected his perception that his policy would receive popular support. Whether that support would have been forthcoming five years earlier will remain a question. In view of that success, and the Fed's newfound prestige, the task of restarting the economy might have fallen to the Fed. As inflation receded, reductions in real, as well as in nominal, interest rates would have been appropriate. Some permanent tax reductions might also have been appropriate, given the way in which full-employment revenue tends to rise. Instead, the Reagan program was sold as a spur to long-term growth of supply, as well as a stimulus to short-term demand. It did serve as a demand stimulus—one that was far too strong. The demand was met by reduction in unemployment and excess capacity, as well as by a massive trade deficit and, in time, by expenditure restraint and higher taxes. If, as many believe, its objective was to limit the growth of government, it succeeded; but it was hardly an example of good stabilization policy.

In Figure 3.4, the decline in the full-employment surplus line from 1981 to 1986 reflects the Reagan tax cuts and expenditure increases. The recovery of the full-employment surplus line from 1986 to 1992 resulted from tax increases, expenditure restraint, and, of course, the gains from rising full-employment income. The continued rise of the full-employment surplus line reflects the expenditure restraint as well as the growing full-employment income during the Clinton administration. The most recent developments in fiscal policy resemble those of the early 1980s: a massive demand stimulus creating deficits that may last for years.

Whatever else may be said of the fiscal policies of the last 40 years, they were not examples of good stabilization policy. In the 1960s, the budget was driven by war and the launching of Great Society programs. The Reagan and George W. Bush administrations both appear to have seized the need for a short-run fiscal stimulus to enact tax reductions that would permanently slow the growth of government.

2. An Alternative Policy

We need a fiscal policy/monetary package for stabilization that avoids, as much as possible, a conflict between long-term objectives and the short-term changes needed to deal with recessions. It should avert politically motivated wrangles over the long-run effects of those programs and should avoid disputes over the use of stabilization programs with major income distribution effects. I envisage a monetary/fiscal policy package, including:

1) a budget balanced at full employment as a norm;

2) a stabilizing monetary policy based on gradual adjustment of the funds rate in response to signals of either excess demand or deficient growth; and

3) automatic fiscal stabilizers.

So-called automatic stabilizers have long played an important role in limiting fluctuations in demand. Maintaining the budget program while tax revenues decline in response to falling income is, in itself, an important stabilizer, reducing the multiplier effects of any cut in private investment expenditures. Payments for unemployment compensation strengthen that effect.

In the event that unusually strong private demand threatens inflation, we must usually rely on monetary restraint, even at the risk of creating serious problems in the financial sector. Those are times when good judgment is particularly important. If the threat is real, early action would minimize the cost of averting inflation; but early action could prove to be very costly if the danger has been exaggerated.

In such circumstances, fiscal restraint would be extremely valuable. It would reduce the pressure on the Fed to choose between the risk of inflation and the risk of costly damage to the financial system or to especially vulnerable sectors like housing. Various legislative rules limiting expenditure growth have been used in the interest of deficit reduction. Similar rules could be used in the interest of limiting inflation and high interest rates.

Conversely, there may be times when easy money and automatic stabilizers prove insufficient to produce a quick recovery from recession. There will then be demands for *ad-hoc* fiscal actions—tax cuts or expenditure increases, or both. Costly errors could be avoided by the use of "semiautomatic stabilizers," such as:

• temporary suspension of payroll taxes;

• compensation of states for losses of revenue due to the reduction of GDP;

• extension of unemployment compensation; and

• provision of investment tax credits or other measures to stimulate investment.

These measures should be preplanned but not activated until some trigger point is reached. Preplanning would require that the Congress reach agreement on all the details of these programs, including the length of the initial period of their operation and the procedure for extending them. Auerbach has emphasized the importance of avoiding large tax reductions in view of the problems of financing Social Security and Medicare. I wholeheartedly agree with him on that point. I turn now to discuss briefly the second part of his paper.

3. Long-Term Problems

The second part of Auerbach's paper deals with the problems of financing Social Security and Medicare and Medicaid. Once the baby boom generation retires, the costs of these programs are expected to rise faster than GDP for many years. Auerbach clearly demonstrates that very large increases in tax rates would be required to fund these programs. He concludes that "aging and increasing healthcare expenditures present unprecedented challenges to the fiscal system's ability to respond, for they generate a large sustainability gap that is not well characterized by the traditional budget measures to which policy has responded in the past."

One can hardly disagree with that statement. The emphasis should be on the need for a response to the challenge. The most costly developments will not materialize for more than a quarter-century. Costs will rise gradually and, in the case of Social Security, scheduled benefit payments will exceed Social Security tax revenues in a few years.

We should not sit around waiting for costs to rise. We should soon arrange gradual changes in programs to slow the increase in costs.

Comment on Auerbach's "American Fiscal Policy in the Post-War Era: An Interpretive History"

Douglas W. Elmendorf

Over the past several years, Alan Auerbach has written a set of papers that has given us important insights into the behavior of fiscal policy during the post-war period and into the macroeconomic consequences of that policy (Auerbach, 2000, 2002, 2003, 2004). My comments address three topics that arise in Auerbach's work: the determinants of fiscal policy actions, the evolving focus in economic analyses of fiscal policy, and the long-run fiscal challenges facing the country.

1. Determinants of Fiscal Policy Actions

Auerbach's papers have explored the way in which fiscal policy responds to economic and budgetary conditions. He has shown that policy tends to move countercyclically and to push the budget back toward balance when it has ended up out of balance. I agree with those conclusions, but would emphasize that fiscal policy over the past quarter-century has not been driven primarily by this sort of incremental response. Instead, fiscal policy has been dominated by two dramatic episodes in which policy actions swung the budget sharply from surplus to deficit—with a long period in between those episodes of incremental efforts to restore budget balance. Auerbach addresses this point briefly by examining the residuals from his regressions, but I think this perspective deserves more prominent treatment.

One way to appreciate the episodic nature of fiscal policy is to look at Figure 3.9, which plots the Congressional Budget Office's projected budget surplus five years hence (shown on an annual basis and scaled by

Percent of potential GDP

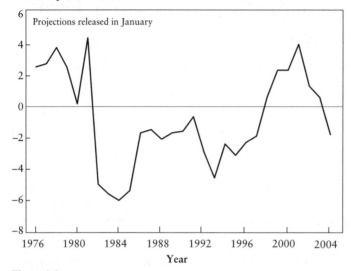

Figure 3.9
CBO projected budget balance for fiscal year five years ahead. *Source:* Congressional Budget Office, Budget and Economic Outlook, various years.

potential GDP).[1] Examining projections, rather than budget outcomes, minimizes the influence of economic conditions and highlights the role of policy actions in a given year.

The first sharp swing to budget deficit occurred in the early 1980s. In January 1981, the projected budget balance in 1985 was a *surplus* equal to 4 percent of potential GDP; one year later, in January 1982, the projected balance five years ahead was a *deficit* equal to 5 percent of potential GDP. This 9-percentage-point swing was caused largely by policy actions. For example, David Stockman (1994, p. 270) describes a "tax bidding war,...an auctioning off of a massive chunk of the revenue base,... and the consequent 7 percent of GDP 'hole in the budget' that became the defining condition of the 1980s."

Over the next two decades, a succession of presidents and Congresses took a series of steps to move the budget back toward balance, beginning in 1982 and running through the Gramm–Rudman–Hollings deficit limitation measures of the late 1980s, the 1990 budget agreement between President George H.W. Bush and the Congress, President Bill Clinton's budget plan in 1993, and the Balanced Budget Act of 1997. The history of fiscal policymaking is recounted for the 1980s by Jim Poterba (1994) and for the 1990s by Jeff Liebman, David Wilcox, and me (2002). The chart shows that the process of restoring budget balance was gradual—owing to the political difficulty of raising taxes and cutting spending—and faced significant setbacks—due to shifting tides in other forces affecting the budget. But the bottom line is that policy changes, combined with improving economic and technical factors, had returned the budget and the projected budget to a substantial surplus by the end of the 1990s.

The second sharp swing to budget deficit occurred in the past few years, with the projected budget balance five years ahead dropping by nearly 6 percent of potential GDP between January 2001 and January 2004. As in the early 1980s, policy actions played a central role—but not an exclusive one—in this worsening of the budget outlook. The experience of the preceding decades suggests that fiscal policy in the coming years is likely to be dominated by efforts to restore budget balance. We will need to await a future conference to judge whether history really does repeat itself—but the challenge is acute, as I will discuss further in a moment.[2]

The impression conveyed by this chart—of two marked swings to budget deficit separated by a long, halting move toward budget surplus—is confirmed by examining the sources of revisions to the CBO budget projections. Table 3.5 extends the calculations reported by Elmendorf, Liebman, and Wilcox (ELW) to include the 2001–2004 period. Policy actions generated ongoing improvement in the budget outlook between 1990 and 1998, but then undid some of those gains at the end of the decade, owing, in particular, to an increase in the unrealistically tight discretionary spending caps that had been set in 1997.[3] Yet, even this shift was dwarfed by the dramatic deterioration due to policy actions during the past few years.

A final perspective on the pattern of fiscal policy changes over the past decade is provided by Figure 3.10. This figure (also updated from ELW) decomposes the difference between actual budget outcomes and the CBO's January 1993 budget projection. Policy changes considerably improved the budget balance through 2000; however, the policy changes

Table 3.5
Sources of Change in the CBO's Budget Projections

Source of Revision	Revision to Projected 5-Year Surplus		Revision to Projected 10-Year Surplus			
	Jan. 1990 to Jan. 1993	Jan. 1993 to Jan. 1995	Jan. 1995 to Jan. 1998	Jan. 1998 to Jan. 2001	Jan. 2001 to Jan. 2004
Total	-$782 billion	$1,603 billion	$3,107 billion	$3,196 billion	-$8,487 billion
	(100%)	(100%)	(100%)	(100%)	(100%)
Policy	460	1,570	501	-1,606	-4,934
	(59%)	(98%)	(16%)	(50%)	(58%)
Economic and Technical	-1,242	33	2,606	4,802	-3,553
	(159%)	(2%)	(84%)	(150%)	(42%)

Notes. Revisions are from January to January of the years shown. Decomposition is by the CBO, cumulated by the author across projection updates; the economic and technical category includes revisions where the source was not reported by the CBO. Percentages apply to the total revision during the period indicated and are computed without regard to sign.

Billions of dollars

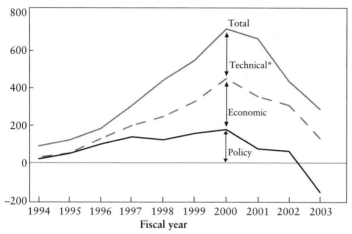

Figure 3.10
Revisions to CBO projected budget balance since January 1993. *Source:*
Congressional Budget Office, Budget and Economic Outlook, various years.
*Includes revisions where source was not reported by CBO.

enacted between 2001 and 2003 more than reversed the effect of the previous eight years' policy changes, with the net effect of reducing the 2003 budget balance by about $150 billion.

2. Evolving Focus in Economic Analyses of Fiscal Policy

The program for this part of the conference lists several objectives of fiscal policy: public-good provision, income redistribution, social insurance, and macroeconomic stabilization. Indeed, all these objectives have been key influences on policymaking and important considerations in economic analyses of policy. However, this list is missing the objective that has been most central to discussions of fiscal policy over the past decade or so, namely, the effect of that policy on national saving. Why have the consequences of fiscal policy for saving garnered increasing attention over time? In my view, for several reasons:

First, as discussed by Alan Blinder (2005), is a diminishing sense of the importance of discretionary fiscal policy for macroeconomic stabilization. I agree with Blinder that one should not dismiss the countercyclical possibilities of fiscal policy, as demonstrated anew by the apparent effects of the 2001 and 2003 tax cuts in boosting aggregate demand.[4] However, this consideration is undoubtedly less important today than it was several decades ago.

Second is an increasing emphasis among macroeconomists on economic growth rather than on stabilization as the key to people's well-being. This shift in emphasis is due both to changing economic circumstances (in part, a reduced volatility of economic activity) and to evolving research strategies and findings. Although this shift also may have been taken too far in some cases, I think that economists appropriately have an increased interest in the effect of fiscal policy on long-term growth, such as through its influence on saving.

A third factor is the striking demographic change underway in this country. With a substantial fraction of government outlays going to benefits for old people and sick people, and with the relative share of old people and the relative price of healthcare both rising over time, we can foresee a large increase in demands on the budget in coming decades. The increasing imminence of those demands has focused analysts' attention on what sort of preparations our country and our government should be making, perhaps in the form of greater saving.[5]

3.   Long-Run Fiscal Challenges Facing the Country

Auerbach's recent work has contributed to a burgeoning literature on the sustainability—or lack thereof—of the country's current tax and spending policies. Even in late 2000, when the budget was projected to run considerable surpluses during the subsequent decade and beyond, the CBO (2000, p. 1) reported that "under most assumptions,... an imbalance between spending and revenues will emerge." With the deterioration in the budget picture since that time, the long-term outlook is even bleaker today.[6] In Auerbach's parlance, the "fiscal gap" is quite large.

In that context, it is clear to me that we need a new framework for making fiscal-policy choices. During most of the post-war period, the underlying fiscal objective was generally perceived as balance in the total or unified budget, at least on average over the business cycle. Of course, this simple guideline was not strictly optimal, as many economists noted over the years. When inflation was high, for example, the measured deficit gave a distorted view of the real change in the government's financial position—and, even aside from measurement problems, a zero balance in the budget possessed no particular economic magic. Still, aiming to balance the unified budget was a reasonable goal on the merits, and that objective had a simplicity and a transparency that made it comprehensible to both policymakers and the public.

Unfortunately, this objective is much less appropriate now that we are confronting a substantial long-term uptrend in spending. As Auerbach observes in his paper, "...a large sustainability gap...is not well characterized by the traditional budget measures to which policy has responded in the past." As a result, policy formed by looking at the traditional measures is not likely to result in a very sensible intergenerational distribution of the fiscal burden. When we can predict, with some confidence, that fiscal conditions will be quite different in coming decades, balancing the current budget—or even the projected medium-term budget—is simply not forward-looking enough.

The difficult question is, what should our fiscal objective be instead? We need to find a new way to frame choices about fiscal policy, and that framework needs to satisfy two principal criteria: First, it should bring the relevant information to bear on fiscal-policy choices. It should give us a sense, over an extended time horizon, of what fiscal conditions are likely to be in the absence of policy changes, and of how alternative policies are likely to affect fiscal conditions. As Auerbach notes, "How one accounts for these large liabilities [from retirement programs]...could affect policy decisions." Second, the framework should be sufficiently simple and transparent that it can inform not only discussions among experts, but also debate in the public arena. We need a fiscal objective that enhances people's understanding of the government's finances and that fosters effective communication between people and their elected representatives.

The objective that I personally favor is one that David Wilcox and I have spent some time evaluating, which is to balance the budget excluding Social Security and Medicare (on average over the business cycle) and to achieve projected long-term solvency of those programs. By itself, this objective leaves open the question of how solvency should be achieved, and, in particular, whether the programs should be substantially pre-funded (and, if so, whether sufficient assets can be accumulated in the public sector).[7] Those decisions should be made within the context of the broader framework. I think this framework presents the necessary information about the budget outlook in a comprehensible manner and, thus, represents the best, feasible way to set long-term fiscal policy.

■ *I appreciate helpful comments from Peter Orszag, William Wascher, and David Wilcox. The views expressed are my own and not necessarily those of the Federal Reserve Board or other members of its staff.*

Notes

1. I am grateful to Thomas Laubach for providing this time series culled from the publications of the Congressional Budget Office (CBO).

2. Gale and Orszag (2004, p. 915) argue that the CBO's "baseline projections use mechanical assumptions that may not be the best representation of current policy," and that more realistic assumptions imply an even greater challenge in balancing the budget than is apparent from the official projections.

3. The relative lack of policy actions in the face of large and growing surpluses in the late 1990s could be viewed as an active contribution of policy compared with a previous tendency to balance the budget. The positive residuals that Auerbach reports for his revenue equations during that period are consistent with this view. Note also that the table reports nominal dollar amounts, thereby understating the relative importance of earlier changes when the baseline amounts of revenues and outlays were smaller.

4. Elmendorf and Reifschneider (2002) show that the direct expansionary effect of tax cuts or government spending increases can be attenuated considerably by the response of forward-looking financial markets to the associated increase in expected budget deficits. However, their analysis suggests that the net effect is usually expansionary.

5. Fiscal policy alters national saving both directly, by changing public saving, and indirectly, through its effect on private saving. In particular, private saving responds to the incentives created by tax policy, to the rules governing entitlement programs, and to the aggregate amounts of taxes and government outlays. [Elmendorf and Mankiw (1999) survey the extensive literature on this last topic.] Therefore, rising interest in the long-run implications of fiscal policy has affected the sorts of policy changes and the aspects of proposed changes that garner the most attention. For example, many of the present Bush administration's tax pro-

posals have aimed to reduce the tax burden on capital income, with the expressed hope of spurring additional saving and investment.

6. See Gale and Orszag (2004).

7. Many analysts have argued that the aging of the U.S. population provides a rationale for a large boost to national saving. However, the appropriate saving response to population aging is not clear-cut: While aging boosts the demands on future resources, it also changes the rate of return the U.S. economy can expect from saving; the net effect of aging on desired saving is ambiguous [Elmendorf and Sheiner (2000)]. In addition, some analysts who favor prefunding of retirement benefits believe that this goal can be achieved only through private accounts, because the political process will dissipate any attempted saving on the government's part. Whether or not this belief is true depends critically on the framework of fiscal-policy choices [Elmendorf and Liebman (2000)].

References

Auerbach, Alan J. 2000. Formation of fiscal policy: The experience of the past 25 years. *Federal Reserve Bank of New York Economic Policy Review* 6(1) April: 9–23.

Auerbach, Alan J. 2002. Is there a role for discretionary fiscal policy? In *Rethinking stabilization policy: A symposium sponsored by the Federal Reserve Bank of Kansas City*, 109–150. Kansas City: Federal Reserve Bank of Kansas City.

Auerbach, Alan J. 2003. Fiscal policy, past and present. *Brookings Papers on Economic Activity* 1:75–122.

Auerbach, Alan J. 2005. American fiscal policy in the post-war era: An interpretive history. Prepared for the Federal Reserve Bank of Boston conference, Macroeconomics of Fiscal Policy, June.

Blinder, Alan S. 2006. The case against the case against discretionary fiscal policy. In *The macroeconomics of fiscal policy*. Cambridge: MIT Press.

Congressional Budget Office. Various years. *Budget and economic outlook*.

Congressional Budget Office. Various years. *Budget and economic outlook: An update*.

Congressional Budget Office. Various years. *An analysis of the President's budgetary proposals*.

Congressional Budget Office. 2000. *The long-term budget outlook*. October.

Elmendorf, Douglas W., and Jeffrey B. Liebman. 2000. Social Security reform and national saving in an era of budget surpluses. *Brookings Papers on Economic Activity* 1:1–52.

Elmendorf, Douglas W., Jeffrey B. Liebman, and David W. Wilcox. 2002. Fiscal policy and Social Security policy during the 1990s. In *American economic policy in the 1990s*, eds. Jeffrey A. Frankel and Peter R. Orszag, 61–119.

Elmendorf, Douglas W., and N. Gregory Mankiw. 1999. Government debt. In *Handbook of macroeconomics,* vol. 1C, eds. John Taylor and Michael Woodford, 1615–1669.

Elmendorf, Douglas W., and David L. Reifschneider. 2002. Short-run effects of fiscal policy with forward-looking financial markets. *National Tax Journal* 55(3) September: 357–386.

Elmendorf, Douglas W., and Louise M. Sheiner. 2000. Should America save for its old age? Fiscal policy, population aging, and national saving. *Journal of Economic Perspectives* 14(3) Summer: 57–74.

Gale, William G., and Peter R. Orszag. 2004. The budget outlook: Updates and implications. *Tax Notes* 102 (February 16): 915–929.

Poterba, James M. 1994. Federal budget policy in the 1980s. In *American economic policy in the 1980s,* ed. Martin Feldstein, 235–270. Chicago: University of Chicago Press.

Stockman, David. 1994. Comment on federal budget policy in the 1980s. In *American economic policy in the 1980s,* ed. Martin Feldstein, 270–279. Chicago: University of Chicago Press.

4

Fiscal Policy in the Reagan Administration's First Term

Fiscal Policy from Kennedy to Reagan to G.W. Bush

C. Eugene Steuerle

To review contemporary fiscal policy requires first asking: Just what is it? Is it countercyclical budget policy? Pro-growth, "supply-side" incentive policy, primarily achieved through lower marginal income-tax rates? Budget policy, defined mainly by deficit reduction or control?

And what considerations have been given short shrift, and do they matter? If targeted on short-run economic growth, can the long run be ignored? If aimed to be countercyclical, can it be applied only on the half-cycle? (For that matter, are we always in a recession, just coming out of a recession, or going into a period of slowdown?) If focused on the deficit, when does federal cash flow matter, as opposed to changes in longer-term liabilities and promises? And, can debt, explicit or implicit, really be ignored?

Finally, in this milieu, just where does fiscal policy end and traditional tax and expenditure policy begin? Or is it merely of secondary importance that government programs be designed according to such principles as equal justice or horizontal equity, efficiency, simplicity, and progressively spending where needs are greatest and taxing most those with the greatest ability to pay? *Reductio ad absurdum*, can government tax and expenditure policy continually be subservient to demands that fiscal policy engage in the continual quest to "grow" the economy more? Does it matter whether the programs work?

Having just finished a comprehensive review of post-war tax policy (Steuerle 2004), with particular emphasis on the period since the ascendancy of Ronald Reagan to the presidency, I can state definitively that scholars and politicians, alike, share no consensus on the relative importance to attach to these questions, much less to their answers. Most economists, when they approach fiscal policy, seem to come from a single perspective, whether it be Keynesian, supply-side, income-tax or consumption-tax theory, tax-expenditure measurement, advocacy for capital formation, reduced capital gains and estate taxation, progressivity, or removal of tax expenditures. The fiscal policy they pursue often reflects that single-minded perspective.[1]

What is clear in the contemporary period is that:

1. Economics is never far separated from politics. In that vein, fiscal theory, at least that floating around Washington, has been turned more and more into a series of apologetics for whatever fiscal policy Congress or the administration is pursuing at the time. Economists find that their influence increases especially when their apologetics support the preexisting desire of politicians to make tax cuts or expenditure increases appear to be costless, or at least a great bargain. Let us call this the "bargain lunch" view.[2]

2. Economics is never far separated from accounting, or from the government's fundamental balance-sheet requirements over time. Let's call this the "green eye-shade" view.[3]

There is, of course, merit to both views. The search for efficient budgetary changes is not inconsistent with attempts to make sure that we pay for what we get. At least, bargain lunches still must be paid for. Attempts to balance fiscal policy across the economic cycle represent one perfectly rational effort to reconcile the two views—getting more out of underemployed resources, while maintaining long-term budget flexibility. Herb Stein was, in many ways, the best representative of that reconciliation for many years, and I must confess that I am a dutiful adherent of his type of prudent approach to fiscal policy. It has been difficult, however, for politicians—and, in truth, many economists—to give both approaches credence at the same time in the political arena.

If we try to impose some order to the fiscal debate in the United States since World War II, I suppose it represents primarily a going back and forth between the bargain lunch and the green eye-shade views. And, while all generalizations are dangerous, it is probably fair to say that the political parties largely switched roles around the time of President Reagan, with the Democrats now more likely to invoke the green eye-shade view (largely in opposition to Republican initiatives rather than in promotion of their own), rather than *vice versa*. This turnaround may reflect as much the role taken on by the opposition party as any change in underlying political philosophy of the parties.

The switch was anticipated by Jude Wanniski, the self-proclaimed "primary political theoretician" in the supply-side camp. In 1974, he began to argue on the *Wall Street Journal* editorial pages for a "two Santa Claus" policy. The notion was that Democrats got to vote for more spending, while Republicans were stuck in the role of opposing spending and occasionally accepting tax increases down the road to balance the budget—a losing political strategy, since Democrats got to be "Santa Claus." He argued that the Republicans should begin to push for tax cuts without paying for them, thus forcing Democrats to be the Scrooges who now had to deal with the deficit.

In many ways, the "two Santa Claus" policy has become the order of the day, but with an interesting and dangerous twist: *Both Santa Clauses are now showing up at the same time!* Wanniski and the *Wall Street Journal* editors also believed that their Santa Claus would, in the end, provide more generous gifts to the economy through enhanced growth.

Of course, even this history simplifies a great deal. Politicians have always had an incentive to vote for tax cuts and expenditure increases, rather than the reverse, and their campaigns always emphasize what they are going to "give" the voter. Many Keynesian and supply-side economists appealed to that tendency. Few politicians want to acknowledge that somebody will pay, much less who that somebody will be. And lobbyists almost all line up on the "gimme" rather than the "let me help pay" side of the ledger. One consequence is that, since the initiation of the federal income tax in the United States, there have been no *large* and obvious legislated income-tax increases other than in wartime or depression. (I say "obvious" because of automatic growth through bracket creep; also, the same constraint has applied less to Social Security taxes for several decades of that program's growth, partly because those taxes were largely imposed on future generations to pay for enhanced benefits to current ones.) When it comes to obvious legislated income-tax increases since the Korean conflict, they have been confined to the small increases of 1990 and 1993, which raised income-tax rates only on about the top one percent of taxpayers, and a small, two-year wartime surtax sold as part of a longer-term tax cut in 1969.

In the remainder of this paper, I will focus on a comparison of presidential fiscal policy over roughly the past half-century, with particular emphasis on the three major rounds of tax cuts: Kennedy–Johnson, Reagan, and G.W. Bush. The emphasis helps highlight four issues I wish to address:

(1) extent of each major stimulus;
(2) sustainability (long-term direction of the budget);
(3) micro-foundations of macro policy; and
(4) concern for traditional tax- and expenditure-policy principles.

A summary of my conclusions in each of these four areas is as follows. As we have progressed from the Kennedy to the Reagan to the G.W. Bush era:

• The changes in fiscal posture have been increasingly "stimulative"— not entirely due to the tax cuts *per se*—although with questionable effectiveness.

• The cuts have become progressively less sustainable, but less because of their size than because of other budget developments—in particular, the automatic growth of entitlements and related tax subsidies.

• Ignoring budget issues related to sustainability, the ability of these tax cuts to generate growth through microeconomic changes in the economy was most solid once the 1986 tax reforms were added to the 1981 tax cuts—less because of simplistic supply-side theory than because of the ways in which these changes moved capital toward more productive investment.

• Finally, none of these cuts gave much credence upfront to traditional policy principles, and this then caused other economic problems and inevitable reversals down the road.

1. Extent of Stimulus

Figures 4.1–4.6 show, by president or four-year presidential term, several measures of surplus or deficit, starting with the crude measure of nominal deficit. Figure 4.1 shows the nominal federal budget surplus or deficit. Adjusting for changes in the real value of interest payments due to inflation yields a measure of what I have labeled a "debt-adjusted surplus or deficit (Figure 4.2)." I provide some CBO or adjusted CBO numbers on the cyclically adjusted surplus or deficit, both nominal (Figure 4.3) and "debt-adjusted (Figure 4.4)," and then on the CBO "standardized surplus or deficit (Figure 4.5)." The CBO standardized deficit differs from the cyclically adjusted surplus mainly by taking out the inflationary component of interest payments, capital gains, and some lesser items such as timing adjustments and asset sales.[4] Also shown is the debt-to-GDP ratio (Figure 4.6).[5]

One of the most obvious points to note is that from the end of World War II to about the mid-1970s, the real deficits are often about zero. Real surpluses show up frequently. The debt-to-GDP ratio is falling, sometimes rapidly, a story to which we will return when discussing sustainability.

What is the amount of actual stimulus? Well, there are a variety of ways to measure it, but not enough space here to fully engage this subject. The stimulus obviously cannot be measured simply by the size of the nominal deficit itself, but among the alternatives are inflation-adjusted deficits, cyclically adjusted deficits, and standardized deficits relative to potential GDP. I prefer looking at changes over time, rather than levels. Note that in examining these periods as a whole, for the most part I am not attempting to measure the amount of discretionary stimulus promoted by tax legislation by itself, since automatic adjustments as well as delayed implementation of past legislation may also provide stimulus or restraint. Indeed, automatic factors such as declining taxes in a recession are usually dominant, and discretionary changes are of a smaller order of magnitude. Among other issues is the change in fiscal posture—whether to include capital gains that fall or rise with an economic cycle as part of the change in fiscal posture. The CBO either includes (in cyclically adjusted measures) or excludes them (in standardized surplus measures), simply because it doesn't feel capable of separating the discretionary from the automatic portions of the capital gains changes.

In spite of all these caveats, under almost any measure, the Kennedy round of tax cuts is relatively modest by comparison with the other two major tax-cutting periods. Looking purely at our adjusted real mea-

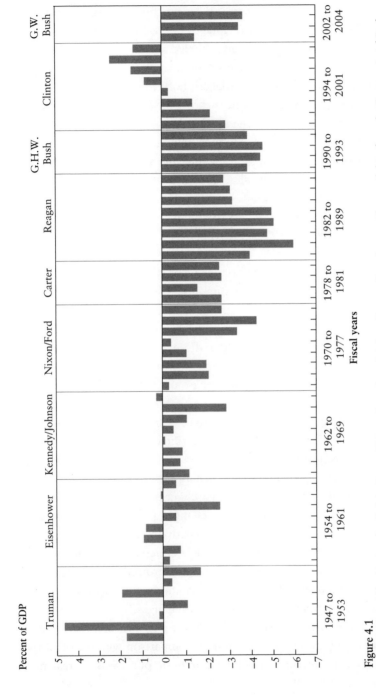

Figure 4.1
Nominal federal budget surplus/deficit. *Source:* Eugene Steuerle and Adam Carasso. Based on supplemental data from the Congressional Budget Office, Budget and Economic Outlook: Fiscal Years 2006–2015.
Note: The ongoing fiscal year in which a term begins is attributed to the president during the previous term.

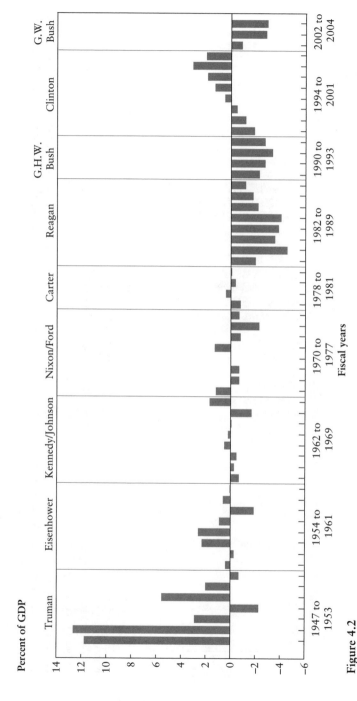

Figure 4.2

Debt-adjusted surplus/deficit. *Source:* Eugene Steuerle and Adam Carasso. Based on supplemental data from the Congressional Budget Office, Budget and Economic Outlook: Fiscal Years 2006–2015.

Note: The ongoing fiscal year in which a term begins is attributed to the president during the previous term. "Debt adjustment" removes the inflationary component of interest payments on publicly held debt.

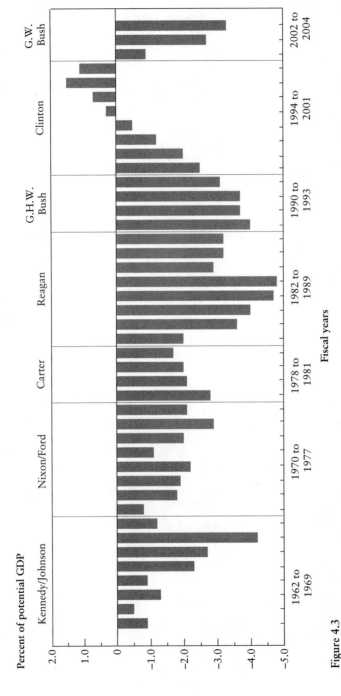

Figure 4.3

Cyclically adjusted surplus/deficit. *Source:* Eugene Steuerle and Adam Carasso. Based on supplemental data from the Congressional Budget Office, Budget and Economic Outlook: Fiscal Years 2006–2015.

Note: The ongoing fiscal year in which a term begins is attributed to the president during the previous term. The CBO defines the cyclically adjusted surplus as the normal budget surplus with adjustments to exclude the effects that cyclical fluctuations in output and unemployment have on outlays and revenues.

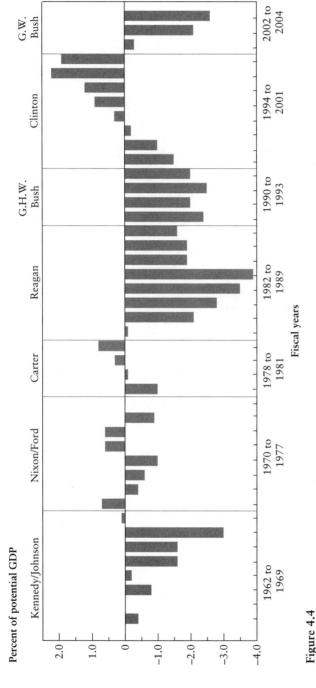

Figure 4.4
Debt-adjusted, cyclically adjusted surplus/deficit. *Source:* Eugene Steuerle and Adam Carasso. Based on supplemental data from the Congressional Budget Office, Budget and Economic Outlook: Fiscal Years 2006–2015.

Note: The ongoing fiscal year in which a term begins is attributed to the president during the previous term. "Debt adjustment" removes the inflationary component of interest payments on publicly held debt. The CBO defines the cyclically adjusted surplus as the normal budget surplus with adjustments to exclude the effects that cyclical fluctuations in output and unemployment have on outlays and revenues.

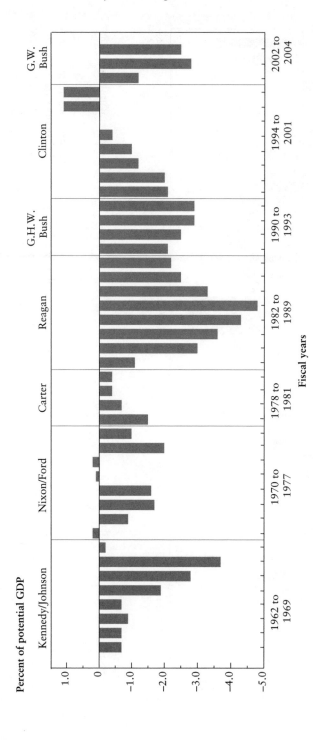

Figure 4.5
Standardized surplus/deficit. *Source:* Eugene Steuerle and Adam Carasso. Based on supplemental data from Congressional Budget Office, Budget and Economic Outlook: Fiscal Years 2006-2015.

Note: The ongoing fiscal year in which a term begins is attributed to the president during the previous term. The CBO defines standardized surplus as the normal budget surplus with adjustments to exclude the effects that cyclical fluctuations in output and unemployment have on outlays and revenues, as well as other minor adjustments.

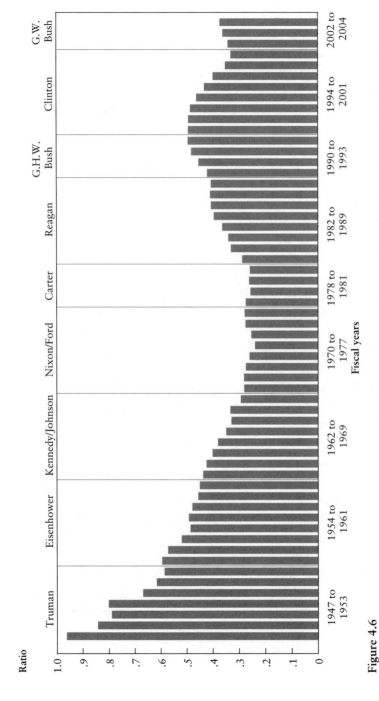

Figure 4.6
Debt-to-GDP ratio. *Source:* Eugene Steuerle and Adam Carasso. Based on supplemental data from the Congressional Budget Office, Budget and Economic Outlook: Fiscal Years 2006–2015.
Note: The ongoing fiscal year in which a term begins is attributed to the president during the previous term.

sure of the CBO's standardized budget surplus or deficit, Reagan's and G.W. Bush's are much larger. However, if we turn to figures on the *change* in either the real deficit or in the real standardized deficit, the Bush years stand out significantly, even relative to the Reagan period. The only four years in a row between 1948 and 2004 in which the real deficit as a percent of real GDP increased every year was from 2001 to 2004.

One crude way to try to gauge the early 21st-century stimulus can be found by comparing the CBO's projection of the budget deficit or surplus for 2004 in the 2000 fiscal budget with its projections in 2004. It turns out that the switch is on the order of around $800 billion, or close to two-fifths of government expenditures or revenues. (The actual switch from surplus to deficit from 2000 to 2004, as shown in the figures, is of a similar, but slightly lower, order of magnitude, since the surplus would have grown from 2000 to 2004 under the original projections.) Note that this comparison of projections for the same fiscal year combines everything that might be counted in fiscal policy—legislation, automatic adjustments, and the significant falloff in capital gains and other revenue due to the bursting of the bubble stock market.[6]

There are, of course, problems with this crude measure. Some would not count the falloff in capital gains revenue or in stock options in the stimulus pot. (I would not agree.) Some prefer looking at nominal rather than debt-adjusted measures, and so forth. But one comes to very similar conclusions whether one looks at the change in the cyclically adjusted surplus or the standardized surplus.

The size of this change must be compared with the level of decline in the economy. The 2001 decline was relatively modest and short lived. Combined, the turnaround in the government's fiscal position, under almost any measure, is greater than the entire decline or shortfall in the economy.[7] Thus, however one makes adjustments, the amount of stimulus was remarkable. The government essentially put more back into the economy than the economy lost. It didn't just prime the pump; it replaced the entire flow. The various measures suggest that, *in terms of fiscal stimulus, the recent episode is the greatest ever in the history of the United States, other than during a world war.*

2. Sustainability and Fiscal Slack

By "sustainability," I refer to whether the policy change by itself can be sustained without some further budget changes. I do not confine myself strictly to whether debt-to-GDP ratios would explode under "current law," since those extrapolations often involve rather implausible assumptions, such as allowing discretionary policy to collapse toward zero percent of GDP.[8] By "fiscal slack," I mean nothing more than budget flexibility and room for discretionary action.

Fiscal policy in the post-war era cannot be understood without noting the tremendous amount of fiscal slack in the budget throughout almost two centuries of the nation's existence, the gradual elimination of that fiscal slack, and, finally, the movement into an era (today) when the slack has become negative, and most (soon, more than all) future government revenues are committed even before the needs of the future are known. In the post-war period, this movement can be broken into three periods: the era of easy finance (essentially post-World War II to the mid-1970s); an era of tight finance (roughly, the mid-1970s to the beginning of the 21st century); and the early 21st-century era of required structural reform. These three periods successively define the fiscal conditions already prevalent when the Kennedy, Reagan, and G.W. Bush tax cuts were enacted. Of course, as with most history, it is not linear. Within these dominant cycles are some other important cycles, including the rise and fall of inflation, and the more recent late-1990s rise and fall (and renewal in the early 2000s?) of a bubble asset-valuation market.

Regardless of the size of the early-1960s stimulus, it was easily sustainable. The reason is simple. From the green eye-shade point of view, it didn't really matter whether or not the Keynesians of the day were right about its impact on economic growth. The increase in nominal debt was modest and was occurring even as debt-to-GDP was dropping. Most important, most of the budget was discretionary in nature; and even what might be called "mandatory" or "entitlement spending" was modest, partly because Medicare and Medicaid had not yet been enacted, and healthcare costs were a much smaller percentage of GDP, no matter what their growth rate.

With spending largely discretionary, any 5- or 10-year projections would have shown an increasing surplus *under current law*, almost regardless of what economic growth rate was assumed.

The early 1960s were still part of a post-war period that Elliot Brownlee and I have labeled the "era of easy finance" (Steuerle, 1996). Inflation was leading to substantial bracket creep in the income tax. Because inflation was gradually increasing, there was also a windfall gain to the government and a windfall loss to holders of government debt, or, alternatively, the effective *ex post* real interest rate on government bonds was often close to zero. Defense spending was in the middle of its fall from 14 percent of GDP at the end of the Korean conflict down to 3 to 4 percent of GDP by the end of the century. [9] And, to top it off, the higher level of debt with even a constant rate of inflation meant a higher differential between the nominal deficit and a debt-adjusted deficit, that is, a deficit adjusted for the impact of inflation on the measured interest payments. To see this, consider the difference between an economy with a debt-to-GDP ratio of 50 percent and one with no public debt. If the nominal deficit is 2 percent of GDP and the inflation rate is a constant 4 percent, then, in the former case, the real value of the public debt does not increase at all, while in the latter case it increases by 2 percent of GDP. [10]

By way of contrast, when Ronald Reagan became president, almost all of these elements of easy finance were in decline or about to go into decline. In his first term, the president continued the Carter-initiated increase in defense spending at the same time that his tax cuts were enacted. As inflation rates were dampened by Federal Reserve policy, there was a windfall loss to the government in terms of the value of its outstanding debt, or, alternatively, effective *ex-post* real interest rates rose significantly. Inflationary (but not real) bracket creep was ended after 1984 as part of the 1981 Tax Act. The stock of debt relative to GDP was also lower, making it harder to sustain real deficits and still have declining debt-to-GDP ratios.

Perhaps most important, entitlements were a much larger share of the budget and were growing at a faster rate than revenues under what, in budget parlance, is called "current law." Even faster economic growth was not much help, since retirement and health programs are generally designed to grow faster than the economy, whatever its growth rate. The

Reagan tax cuts and defense-spending increases were, for the most part, not sustainable, and deficit cuts in 1982, 1984, 1987, 1990, and 1993 were enacted, partly as a consequence.

By the time of the G.W. Bush tax cuts and spending increases, none of the easier sources of finance were available. The one modest and new exception would be bracket creep into the alternative minimum tax (AMT), which both political parties have pledged to stop (maybe, somehow). At even greater play by the beginning of the 21st century was the dominant position of the retirement and health entitlements.

Even without the tax cuts and spending increases enacted under President George W. Bush, Social Security, Medicare, Medicaid, defense, and interest on the debt were scheduled to absorb all revenues within a few decades (actually sooner, if deficits were to increase). However, after enactment of tax cuts, a drug bill, and defense increases, these elderly and defense programs (along with interest on the debt) will now absorb *all* revenues by 2014 if we merely keep current law on the tax and spending side. (The assumption here, which is not meant to reflect what Congress *will* actually do, reflects more the explicit and implicit promises that it has made: that the tax cuts of 2001 to 2003 are essentially retained and that our international posture will not go back into decline (for this calculation, defense and international affairs are assumed to fall modestly from their current level to about 4 percentage points of GDP). The basic point is that current commitments, if kept, would essentially wipe out hundreds of domestic programs, because no revenues would be left for other domestic spending.[11] Deficits might or might not delay the day of reckoning, depending upon how quickly they are allowed to compound; in the end, of course, they merely make the budget squeeze tighter still.

One issue at play is that the baby boom retirement begins in 2008, but most popular analyses focus only on the impact on benefits paid under elderly programs. In 2008 and beyond, if current retirement patterns merely continue (that is, if people still retire at the same age), labor-force growth slows considerably. The net impact on the economy from that potential decline is roughly equivalent to an increase in the unemployment rate of about three-tenths to four-tenths of one percent every year for almost three decades running—a macro event never before experienced by this country, and one potentially accompanied by a never-before-experienced decline in adult labor-force participation in other industrial countries. For instance, my calculations show that while Japan is scheduled to lose one-eighth of its population over the next three decades, it will lose one-fourth of its workforce if existing retirement patterns hold.

The macro implications are not yet fully known. Indeed, the U.S. economy has witnessed almost continual increases in adult labor-force participation in the post-World War II era, with some rare exceptions during recession years *and* the beginning of the 21st century. (The rapid rate of increase in number of retirement years of males was more than offset by increased female labor-force participation.)[12] Simple Cobb–Douglas types of models tend to show a moderate slowdown in the rate of economic growth and, importantly for budget calculations, in revenues; but these models, for the most part, assume away any multiplier effect (Keynesian or otherwise) from the decline in demand, and also assume that the rate of technological improvement maintains some constancy in its effect on the economic growth rate, even with fewer workers coming along.

Of course, the budget scenario of wiping out all other domestic policy to support existing retirement, health, and tax policies will not play out. Nor do I believe most projections on adult labor-force participation, since people roughly from ages 55 to 75 now displace women as the largest underutilized pool of human talent and capital. Adjustments will be made, one hopes, sooner rather than later. The simple point is that, over the post-war period, we have moved increasingly toward a more unsustainable path. Of course, once on an unsustainable path, it is also impossible to accept the supply-side argument that the economy has gained from businesses making plans on the basis of permanent changes in tax rates, since their permanency is highly in question. One provision of the tax cuts, for instance, wipes out the estate tax only for the year, 2010, presumably leading to increases in saving only for those who plan to die that year.

Let me repeat that it is the large growth in entitlement spending, along with the slowdown in revenue growth due to the practice of retiring people for the last third of their adult lives in the face of declining birth rates, that is the driving force here. Whatever its merits, the latest fiscal episode of cutting average tax rates by about two percentage points of GDP from an all-time high of about 20 percent of GDP certainly could have been sustainable under a traditional regime where most spending was discretionary in nature.

3. An Important Micro-Foundation of Macro Policy: More Productive Investment

Here, I am not attempting to engage in the larger economic debate over what behaviors might lead the public to respond to some change in fiscal policy (for example, why people would spend more with increased cash flow in the face of increased public debt, or why they might work harder because of lower tax rates, with their potential substitution and income effects). Instead, I refer to those aspects of tax policy that lead to faster or slower economic growth because of the shifting of investment toward more productive uses.

In that regard, one particular economic problem was uniquely prevalent in the early 1980s—the interaction of inflation and tax rates and its related impact on economic growth.[13] I have written elsewhere on how the bad accounting systems that accompany inflation often lead to bad investment decisions, once real returns are measured poorly (ranging from equipment to bank loans to tax shelters to second homes). Indeed, I believe that the confusion of nominal and real returns remains the best explanation of why inflation can still lead to real economic stagnation (stagflation). Although these accounting problems are prevalent even without a tax system, when the tax system comes into play and interacts with inflation, enormous opportunities for tax arbitrage are created. In simplest terms, these tax-arbitrage opportunities can, as they often did in the late 1970s and early 1980s, lead to an enormously poor channeling of scarce saving into inefficient and even unproductive investment.

In its simplest form, the problem is related to the tax rate (t) times the inflation rate (i). For instance, when interest deductions are taken, "t times i" equals the subsidy rate per dollar of borrowing. Borrowing to purchase even unproductive investments (not just business equipment, but unused second homes or commodities) can be offset only by very high nominal interest rates. However, the level of interest rate necessary to prevent unproductive investment at high inflation rates is impossible to sustain, partly because it, in turn, creates enormous financial arbitrage opportunities (for example, selling stock short to buy bonds). In simpler terms, for an investment purchased entirely with borrowed dollars, the real return on the asset can be negative if the after-tax interest payment is negative—which it often was in the late 1970s and early 1980s. Negative after-tax interest rates are especially pernicious in inducing unproductive investment and the movement of saving toward less risky assets. However, as the marginal tax rate and the interest rate are reduced, these problems are dissipated.

Unfortunately, most macroeconomic debates center either on short-run views of demand (often Keynesian and emphasized in econometric models) or long-run views of supply (usually supply-side and emphasized in general equilibrium models). But there are times when the change in microeconomic incentives can have a fairly strong effect that I might call "intermediate," at least in the sense that it does not fit easily into the traditional short-term demand-side and long-term supply-side categories. I suggest that the cut in tax rates in 1981 and 1986, combined with the Federal Reserve attack on inflation, had this kick to macro policy (although, see the discussion below of how the 1986 tax reforms were also necessary to remove some of the perverse effects of the 1981 cost-recovery provisions in favoring tax sheltering). By reducing substantially the subsidy for debt borrowing (t times i), the returns to debt and equity fall more into line with each other and limit tax-arbitrage and tax-shelter activity.[14] Net saving does not necessarily increase, but investment becomes much better directed.

Can a similar statement be made about the macroeconomic policies of the early 1960s and early 2000s? I don't think so. The attempt at corporate integration in the latter period likely will lead to some more efficient equity investment, but the change was modest enough, and done badly enough (many of the subsidies go to investments that were not double taxed), that it is hard to believe that the gains themselves are more than moderate in the intermediate term. And this indirect form of corporate integration was only a modest component of the overall tax cuts. In fact, one fear for the early 2000s is that after-tax interest rates again became negative for some taxpayers, leading once again to problems like excess demand for commodities, but this is more a function of monetary than fiscal policy, and the Federal Reserve apparently meant that policy to be temporary.

Perhaps the simple lesson to be learned here is that micro-foundations of macro-policy, just like the demand- and supply-side effects, vary widely from period to period and are hard to generalize.[15] What, at first glance, may appear to be a fiscal policy similar to one implemented in the past, for example, a cutting of tax rates by some percentage of GDP at a similar stage of a slowdown or recession, may be very different in the way it works in the economy of the time.

4. Traditional Policy Concerns

By traditional policy concerns, I refer to issues of horizontal equity or equal justice, efficiency (mainly inter-asset or intra-temporal), and simplicity, not to broader macro demand- or supply-side considerations. Here, none of the major tax-cutting eras comes out looking very good. In a sense, the "free lunch" group pretty much crowds out those with traditional policy concerns.

Presidents John F. Kennedy and Lyndon B. Johnson were perhaps the first to push deficit-increasing tax cuts as good for the economy and were also the first to suggest that the macroeconomic aspects of tax policy were even more important than the microeconomic aspects. Indeed, Kennedy was given a choice between his modest traditional reforms (which, I found, upon historical review, to be very few) and his cuts to spur the economy. He chose the latter, quickly abandoning the politically more difficult choices.

Since that time, the very definition of "tax policy" has been in a state of flux, no longer meaning primarily the application of principles to the raising of revenues to pay for government programs. There are many, myself included, who, though sympathetic at some level to both demand- and supply-side considerations, believe that the abandonment of core principles has been detrimental to the functioning of government.

In the 1960s, the investment credit, as it was designed then, favored shorter-lived over longer-lived properties. It discriminated in favor of already profitable and established businesses, as most new and less-profitable businesses lacked the income to be able to make full use of the credits. In fact, by size, elimination of the investment credit was the largest base-broadening provision of the Tax Reform Act of 1986.

The 1981 tax cuts exaggerated the problems of the investment credit by creating a cost recovery system that was quite accelerated, even while interest deductions were fully allowed (thus discounting any argument that it was consumption-tax treatment that was sought). In an era of inflation, these combined investment incentives in the presence of full interest deductions increased even more the channeling of saving into the tax shelter market (see the discussion of tax arbitrage above). Like the 1960s' investment incentives, the 1981 tax cuts also created distortions among assets by not relating incentives more neutrally to the lives of the assets. Thus, the 1981 tax cuts, too, became one of the major sources for base broadening in the Tax Reform Act of 1986.

Returning in some ways to old times, the 2002 and 2003 tax cuts created a system of first-year writeoffs of 30 percent, and 50 percent, respectively, of equipment costs. The incentives were heavily stacked in favor of profitable, existing firms and against loss-making firms and startup firms. Also, these incentives did not even go into effect until well after the recession was over. While many economists criticize discretionary fiscal policy because of its inability to go into effect early enough, the timing—or mistiming—issue is just as important when the incentives are removed—an area long ignored in most analyses. Thus, with temporary investment incentives, the classic argument against discretionary fiscal policy comes in spades: Congress is unlikely to get the timing right on either end.

Still another macroeconomic consideration relates to economists' strange notion that they are intellectually cleverer than noneconomists and know how to impose windfall taxes on old capital, for example, by granting the tax breaks only to new capital. But shouldn't planned "surprises" come to be expected? And, if so, doesn't this mean that businesses will change their expectations? Then, when the next downturn starts, might those expectations not add to that downturn by delaying any new investment? After all, Congress has now built up an expectation that it may get around to enacting yet another set of "temporary" incentives.

To be fair to all three cycles of tax cuts in the post-war era, they did, for the most part, emphasize tax rates. For any given level of revenues, economists generally believe that lower rates are preferable to higher rates and a narrower base. Opponents of the tax cuts often offer fewer and smaller rate cuts and more new programs hidden in the tax code as an alternative, suggesting along the way that they get better distributional results and a smaller increase in the deficit. Whether or not these alternatives are better as a deficit-policy matter, as a matter of tax policy they are still likely to be inferior to rate cuts of a similar size and distribution.

5. Conclusion

It is no longer possible—if it ever was—to view fiscal policy as the change in a single measure, such as net government cash flow to taxpayers or effective marginal tax rates. Fiscal policy has short-run, intermediate-run, and long-run implications. The size of the stimulus is largely affected by factors other than just the enactment of legislation, factors including all the automatic features of the tax and expenditure system that change revenues and spending over time. The sustainability of the stimulus affects its success and also the extent to which offsetting policies then become required at inopportune times down the road. Intermediate-run, as well as long-run, effects derive from micro-foundations related to the efficient allocation of saving to the most productive capital, not just from aggregate changes in real levels of work or saving. Fundamental tax- and expenditure-policy considerations affect whether the policy is effective over the long run in promoting growth. Taxing or spending poorly does have fiscal ramifications.

■ *I would like to thank Van Doorn Ooms, Rudolph Penner, and Frank Russek for extremely valuable comments. I am especially indebted to Adam Carasso for both advice and help with the data and figures.*

Notes

1. Other principles and perspectives are sometimes acknowledged when they produce a consistent result. For instance, capital formation advocates will sometimes invoke consumption-tax theory, supply-side economics, and even Keynesian theory when pushing for expensing of capital assets, although they have historically abandoned any or all of them when it also meant recognizing that

interest deductions would not be allowed in a consumption tax that included such expensing of assets.

2. I use the term "bargain lunch" to recognize that there are more efficient policies that may, indeed, be a bargain for the public, especially when there are underutilized resources. At the same time, there were economists who promoted both the Kennedy and Reagan tax cuts with the notion that the bargain was so good that it would be "free," even to the government. That is, some promoted the view that revenues would rise by more than the cost of the tax cut, even when recessions were mild or tax rates were not very high. Thus, there is inevitably tension when economic advice is sought for finding efficient policy changes, but is often accepted by politicians only when advisors suggest that opportunity costs can be almost entirely ignored.

3. As in the case of "bargain lunch," I use a term that implies a mixed message. Policy must be made with balance sheets in mind; but, of course, government doesn't exist to balance those sheets, and it doesn't exist to reduce its deficit. Presumably, all government action, at some level, should be leading to a better society, or else it should not be undertaken.

4. For many purposes, I have attributed the ongoing fiscal year in which the term begins to the president during the previous term (for example, fiscal 2001 is attributed to President Bill Clinton). Usually, this makes little difference, although there are some exceptions. For instance, the 2001 tax cut under President G.W. Bush contained features allocating up-front benefits to taxpayers during that same, 2001, fiscal year.

5. If one assumes a relatively constant supply of financial saving or demand for interest-bearing instruments as a percent of income, then a declining government debt-to-GDP ratio implies more loanable funds available for private investment and private consumer loans.

6. A part of the debate over what to count also relates to what the CBO calls "technical" adjustments. See Note 8, below.

7. A valid objection to this simple measure is that one would not want to count all technical errors of the forecast. The complication here is that the CBO has classified changes in capital gains and stock option realizations as technical errors, when, in fact, there was a dramatic falloff in their realization that accompanied the stock market plunge. Many reviewers, such as myself, view those changes as more "economic" than "technical." It is not economic in the sense that real GDP changed work or real saving, but it is economic in the sense that reduced capital gains and stock options mean lower levels of taxes paid to government, regardless of the size of the economy. The falloff in realized incomes did drastically reduce revenues relative to what would have happened with an economy that remained in the 1999–2000 bubble stage. One can argue that the tax saving went to higher-income households, and, therefore, had less demand stimulus associated with it, but, again, only occasionally do we measure stimulus by weighting who gets each dollar. Having said all this, one comes to a similar conclusion about the extraor-

dinary size of the stimulus at the beginning of the 21ˢᵗ century, whether looking at the changes in standardized deficits or in cyclically adjusted deficits.

8. The standard definition of sustainability merely asks whether the growth rate of the economy (g) exceeds the rate of interest on the debt (r), or, when it does not, whether the primary deficit (the deficit less interest payments) is of such a size as to create a continually growing debt-to-GDP ratio. Strong assumptions are often made about what percent of GDP is discretionary.

9. The Social Security tax was also easily increased to pay for past promises. From 1950 to 1990, almost every decade witnessed a three-percentage-point increase in the employer-employee tax rate alone.

10. Note, for instance, that the debt-to-GDP ratio falls significantly over the post-war period to the mid-1970s. By the mid-1970s, when economic growth declines, the government's nominal deficits are eating up a greater fraction of real financial saving in the economy, even if their nominal amounts represent the same percentage of GDP. It is this type of consideration that leads me to favor what I call "debt-adjusted measures of the deficit" to the nominal deficit. It is also related closely to earlier, separate work by Benjamin Friedman and myself that tried to assess the importance to macroeconomic policy of the total-debt-to-GDP ratio.

11. See Steuerle (2003b).

12. It remains to be seen whether the early 20ᵗʰ-century observation will be only recession related; with the baby boomers starting to retire, the post-2001 recession period and the early baby boom retirement period will also come close to merging.

13. An entire book on this subject can be found in Steuerle (1984).

14. To this day, many people view the falloff in the real estate market in the 1980s as due to the direct anti-shelter provisions of the 1986 tax reform, when, in fact, it was probably due more to the drop in interest rates and tax rates, which made the real, after-tax interest rate positive again.

15. When it comes to demand- and supply-side effects, note that in the early 1960s, the potential fiscal drag of the unindexed tax system was greater than when the system became indexed, and the top individual rate was quite high; either a straightforward Keynesian or a supply-side argument might suggest that there was more bang per buck out of that stimulus.

References

Auerbach, Alan J. 2003. Fiscal policy, past and present. *Brookings Papers on Economic Activity* 1:75–122.

Brown, E. Cary. 1956. Fiscal policy in the 'thirties: A reappraisal. *American Economic Review* 46(5) December: 857–879.

Brownlee, W. Elliot, and C. Eugene Steuerle. 2003. Taxation. In *The Reagan presidency*, eds. W. Elliot Brownlee and Hugh Davis Graham, 155–181. Lawrence: University Press of Kansas.

Eisner, Robert. 1986. *How real is the federal deficit?* New York: The Free Press.

Eisner, Robert, and Paul J. Pieper. 1984. A new view of the federal debt and budget deficits. *American Economic Review* 74(1) March: 11–29.

Friedman, Benjamin M. 1992. Learning from the Reagan deficits. *American Economic Review* 82(2) May: 299–304.

Russek, Frank S., and Stephen M. Miller. 1999. The relationship between large fiscal adjustments and short-term output growth under alternative fiscal policy regimes. University of Connecticut, Department of Economics Working Paper 1999–2004.

Steuerle, C. Eugene. 1985. *Taxes, loans, and inflation.* Washington, D.C.: The Brookings Institution.

Steuerle, C. Eugene. 1996. Financing the American State at the turn of the century. In *Funding the modern American State, 1941–1995: The rise and fall of the era of easy finance*, ed. W. Elliot Brownlee. Washington, D.C.: Woodrow Wilson Center Press and Cambridge University Press.

Steuerle, C. Eugene. 2003a. Do we really need more stimulus? *Tax Notes* 98 (January 27): 597–598.

Steuerle, C. Eugene. 2003b. The incredible shrinking budget for working families and children. National Budget Issues Brief No. 1. Washington, D.C.: The Urban Institute.

Steuerle, C. Eugene. 2004. *Contemporary U.S. tax policy.* Washington, D.C.: The Urban Institute.

Sutherland, Alan. 1997. Fiscal crises and aggregate demand: Can high public debt reverse the effects of fiscal policy? *Journal of Public Economics* 65(2): 147–162.

Vickrey, William. 1992. Meaningfully defining deficits and debt. *American Economic Review* 82(2) May: 305–310.

Economic Policy in the First Reagan Administration: The Conflict Between Tax Reform and Countercyclical Management

W. Elliot Brownlee

Ronald Reagan won election to the presidency in 1980 under unusual economic circumstances. He had waged his long campaign for the office during a wrenching episode that some economic historians now label "the Great Inflation."[1] In doing so, they imply that the episode ought to join "the Great Depression" as one of the two most serious economic disruptions of American life during the twentieth century. Whether or not this is accurate, the Great Inflation was the most severe bout of inflation during peacetime in American history, and the inflation was accompanied by a prolonged stagnation in productivity. Like the Great Depression, the Great Inflation had significant political implications. What the Great Inflation did politically was to create conditions that enabled an anti-government movement that had been gathering force only slowly since the early 1960s to take control of the federal government in the election of 1980.

During his presidential campaign, Ronald Reagan, like Franklin D. Roosevelt in 1932, sought to build a new coalition of workers and consumers around a program of relief from economic hardship and a reform of the conditions that had produced the hardship. While Roosevelt's focus was unemployment, Reagan's was inflation. To address the problem of inflation, the most important elements of Reagan's economic program consisted of a reform of taxation and a reform of countercyclical policy. The reform of taxation included a set of permanent tax cuts that he claimed would not only relieve the pain of inflation, but also end economic stagnation. The reform of countercyclical policy involved a diminished role for management of the business cycle by the federal government and a replacement of neo-Keynesian countercyclical policy with monetary policy. As it has turned out, the tax cuts that followed during his first administration have had a significant long-run effect on both the substance and the politics of tax policy. It is less clear what the long-term influence of Reagan's efforts to reform countercyclical policy has been.[2]

The remainder of Reagan's anti-government program, notably the idea of significantly slowing the growth of government, was less important to his building a winning electoral coalition in 1980. In fact, opposition to shrinking, or even slowing the expansion of government, particularly in the realm of national defense, was a significant force within the general public, Congress, and even the administration. This opposition helped push the federal budget deficit to levels unprecedented in peacetime.

This essay surveys how the Reagan administration struggled, in the face of budget deficits and economic instability, to reconcile the two economic policies that the administration had the greatest success in implementing: tax cutting and reform of countercyclical policy. As was the case with Franklin Roosevelt's program for economic reform, important elements of Ronald Reagan's program conflicted and forced major adjustments. From the campaign of 1980 through the end of his first administration, Reagan significantly modified his tax cutting in order to sustain his reform of countercyclical policy. Thus, while he engineered major tax cuts, his cuts would have been even larger without his effort to reform countercyclical policy.

1. The Economic Recovery Tax Act (ERTA)

Reagan's tax program, which he announced in 1977, included both indexing income-tax rates for inflation and cutting income taxes deeply— across the board by 10 percent for each of three successive years. These tax reforms, he argued, would provide economic relief, especially from the burden of "bracket creep," and would stimulate economic productivity. In addition, he made the startling claim that the cuts would actually reduce budget deficits and thus relieve the upward pressure on prices, including interest rates. This deficit reduction would occur, Reagan argued, because of the huge expansion of the tax base produced by American investors and workers invigorated by big cuts in tax rates.

Reagan thus seemed to embrace what became the most controversial proposition of the "supply-side" argument for tax cuts: The tax cuts would not only stimulate productivity, but would also reduce deficits. Martin Anderson, a central economic advisor in Reagan's first term as president, later claimed that supply-siders were actually moderate in their views, arguing only that tax cutting "would *not lose as much revenue as one might expect.*" Anderson was correct about most supply-siders, especially those who were professional economists, but not all. And, Reagan himself, on occasion, tended to express true belief in the extreme view, which implied almost no loss in revenues, even in the initial years. In the radio address in which he endorsed Jack Kemp's program, Reagan declared that "economists like Paul McCracken...Milton Friedman... Arthur Laffer...Allan Meltzer...(and) Arthur Burns...have each made it clear that government can increase its tax revenues...by lowering the tax rates for business and individuals."[3] The Kemp cuts, he said, "would reduce the deficit which causes inflation [*sic*] because the tax base would be broadened by the increased prosperity."[4]

In 1979, Reagan's campaign advisors fleshed out the tax program that Reagan had outlined two years earlier. In a policy memorandum that the campaign embraced, Martin Anderson set the proposed tax cuts within the context of what he called "Reagan's comprehensive economic program." The memorandum identified inflation as "the main domestic problem facing the United States today," and found that "the main cause of inflation" was "the massive, continuing budget deficit of the federal government." The memorandum did not explain the connections between deficits and inflation, nor their relationship with monetary policy. But Anderson argued that simultaneously "reducing the rate of growth of federal expenditures" and stimulating the economy through tax cuts and deregulation would eliminate the deficit. The memorandum did not provide a specific timetable, but declared: "The budget deficit must be reduced and eventually eliminated."[5]

During the summer of 1980, corporate lobbyists, with the support of economists who wished to lower the effective rate of taxation on capital income, succeeded in significantly modifying Reagan's tax proposals. They persuaded the Republican platform committee to propose a dramatic increase in the allowances to corporations and individuals for depreciation of tangible assets (the "10-5-3" proposal). In amending the platform, however, the Reagan campaign revealed that it had not accepted an extreme supply-side position. Reagan's economic advisors were sensitive to the reality that the tax cuts under consideration would increase deficits, at least in the short run, and the committee worried about the economic and political damage from the larger deficits. Thus, even in 1980, the Reagan forces adjusted tax proposals to take account of fiscal conditions. To pay for "10-5-3," Reagan's platform committee dropped entirely the proposal to index the individual income tax, even though it was of much greater benefit to labor income and middle-class income and was apt to produce more votes in November.[6]

With Reagan's nomination in July and the intensification of debate with President Jimmy Carter over the economy, Reagan's economic advisors continued to wrestle with the fiscal implications of major tax cuts. But they were not always able to persuade the president to agree to the changes they proposed. As would often be the case during the Reagan presidency, Reagan's personal views had a profound effect on the direction of policy. Less than three weeks after Reagan's acceptance speech, his economic advisors met with him, and most, including Alan Greenspan, advised Reagan that he ought to go slower and take five, rather than three, years to implement the 10-10-10 tax cuts. They had two goals in mind. First, they wanted to reduce the deficits. Second, they wanted to protect the proposed cuts in the tax on capital. They remained more interested in reductions in the taxation of capital than in the very large share of across-the-board cuts that would go to middle- and upper-middle-income workers. The supply-side economists among them also believed that the primary economic stimuli from the individual reductions would come from cutting the top rates, and that the large reduction in the bottom and middle rates would have little economic stimulus effect. All the advisors believed they might be able to have their cake and eat it, too: a tax cut on capital income *and* a lower deficit effect, because the tax cut on capital would be cheaper in terms of tax revenues than the across-the-board cut.

When Reagan's economic advisors had made their case and warned him about the deficits, he replied, "I don't care." Walker remembers that they all "nearly fell out of their chairs." Reagan had turned out to be the most extreme populist in the room. The president wanted to cut everyone's taxes, regardless of whether or not any particular economic theory supported him, and regardless of whether or not the cuts worsened the deficit. The president got his way, and the campaign stayed with 10-10-10. In general, the president, more than many of his advisors, wanted deep cuts in income taxes, and he did not want the cut focused on businesses and the highest-income individuals. His goal was to exploit broad popular support for a tax cut, pave the way for other policy initiatives, and produce a more profound realignment of voters.[7]

Most of Reagan's economic advisors believed the revenue benefits from economic stimulation would be slow in coming. Consequently, maintaining the deep cuts of the 10-10-10 proposal made it difficult for them to promise swift reductions of the deficits. In fact, during the summer of 1980, they concluded that the Reagan economic and defense programs would actually increase the deficits beyond what the Congressional Budget Office (CBO) was forecasting. When the CBO projected the emergence of a substantial budget surplus in fiscal year 1983, the Reagan advisors reached agreement among themselves that the Reagan programs would postpone a surplus budget for two years and, meanwhile, increase the deficit to levels over $50 billion in 1981 and 1982. Martin Anderson later wrote that this schedule "made good economic sense and good defense sense, but politically it was a problem, a real problem." Indeed, in September, the day before Reagan was scheduled to deliver a major economic speech that would, for the first time, detail his program, James Baker, then Reagan's campaign manager, told Anderson that he and Reagan's other political advisors, including Edwin Meese and William Casey, had concluded: "We just can't go with these $50 billion deficits. There must be something you can do." What Anderson did was discover that the Senate Budget Committee, in response to an apparent recovery from the brief recession of 1979–1980, had revised the CBO estimates to forecast larger revenues and smaller expenditures. Less than an hour before a press briefing, Anderson, backed up by Alan Greenspan, revised the deficit estimates downward. In Anderson's new estimates, the deficits were larger than what the Senate Budget Committee had estimated for 1981 and 1982, but they were only half as large as what the campaign had projected just 24 hours earlier, and the deficits would disappear altogether in 1983.[8]

With Reagan's election, the advisors who had come together during the campaign moved quickly to advance the program of tax cuts into legislation. They did so with the same sense of economic and fiscal optimism that they had had in September. On February 5, 1981, when the president addressed the nation on the state of the economy and formally called for his tax program, he once again forecast the disappearance of the deficit by 1983. When this happened, he said, "We can have further reductions in the tax rates." The next day, Secretary of the Treasury Donald Regan testified before the House Budget Committee and presented what became known as "Rosy Scenario." At the time, he predicted high real rates of income growth, including over 5 percent for 1982. On the inflation front, however, Regan was less optimistic. He forecast an inflation rate of 11 percent in 1981—a slight decline from a 12-percent rate in 1980. A decline would follow, Regan forecast, but the rate would still be 4 percent in 1986. But this was a crucial assumption for the tax program. With high inflation (and without the indexing for inflation that the Reagan campaign had abandoned in 1980), the administration could fund a major portion of 10-10-10 and 10-5-3 through bracket creep. Thus, for the new administration, the economic numbers still supported vigorous tax cutting accompanied by elimination of the deficit. That program still did not seem to require large supply-side boosts of revenue.

The night before, when Reagan had given his economic speech, he had included only one sentence on monetary policy: "In all of this," he said, "we will, of course, work closely with the Federal Reserve system toward the objective of a stable monetary policy."[9] Such a policy was, in fact, Reagan's ideal. During the 1970s, under the tutelage of Milton Friedman and others, Reagan had come to believe in the necessity of a steady, predictable rate of money supply expansion.[10] And this may well have been the objective of the Federal Reserve. But in his speech, Reagan papered over the reality that, since November of 1980, the approach of the Federal Reserve, under the leadership of Paul Volcker, had been one of aggressive tightening of the money supply, not of stable expansion, and that the administration supported Volcker's policy. The president had met with Volcker in January on the supposedly neutral ground of the Treasury and agreed on the need for a policy of "monetary restraint."[11]

Throughout the spring and summer of 1981, while the Economic Recovery Tax Act (ERTA) was under consideration, the Federal Reserve held to a policy of very tight restraint, as measured by both the Federal funds rate (held above 15 percent between November 1980 and October 1981) and monetary aggregates.[12] The Reagan administration continued to support this restraint. The Treasury regarded monetary policy, in the words of Beryl Sprinkel, the undersecretary of the Treasury for monetary affairs, as "an integral part of the economic program." It was "vital," Sprinkel wrote to the Cabinet Council on Economic Affairs, for the administration "to keep a close watch on the conduct of monetary policy, conveying to the Federal Reserve both support for their goal of long-run monetary control and suggestions for further improvement of their control procedures." Sprinkel went on to emphasize that the Federal Reserve could "stick to its monetary targets" even in the face of growing budget deficits. "Quite simply," he wrote, "there is no necessary linkage between budget deficits and the rate of monetary expansion." He explained: "Money is under the control of the Federal Reserve, and federal borrowing leads to accelerated money growth only when the monetary authorities attempt to counter short-term interest pressure." Sprinkel wanted the Federal Reserve to stay with its restrictive policy even in the face of increasing deficits. In July, the president reinforced his support of Paul Volcker, telling him that "I, and all members of my administration, appreciate the cooperation we have received from the Federal Reserve in working to reduce inflation," and that "we will stand firm in our fight against inflation." The president explained: "We recognize that high interest rates are a consequence of inflation, and will fall only as we bring inflation under control through continuing reductions in the growth of both spending and the money supply."[13]

The Federal Reserve eased its restraint slightly in October, but maintained its basic policy of tightness for almost another year, until July and August of 1982. In February of 1981, or even in August of that year, no one in the administration could foresee how prolonged, and how effective, monetary restraint would become. Almost certainly because of that tightening, inflation would fall far more rapidly than Secretary Regan had forecast, declining to the 4-percent level in 1982, rather than in 1986. And the tightening was the probable impetus for the severe recession of 1981–1982, which began during the third quarter of 1981 and continued until November 1982. (Over the course of the recession, GNP would fall by more than 3 percent, and unemployment would increase to more than 10 percent.) At the same time, as measured by either a supply-side or a demand-side criterion, fiscal policy was highly expansive. Between fiscal year 1981 and fiscal year 1982, the deficit increased from $79 billion to $128 billion, or from 2.5 percent to 3.7 percent of potential GDP. In fiscal year 1983, the deficit grew to $208 billion, or 5.6 percent of potential GDP. It would seem that during this episode of severe recession, an expansive fiscal policy had failed to offset the influence of a monetary policy working in the opposite direction.[14]

The effectiveness of monetary policy would, in time, present a massive fiscal problem for the Reagan administration and Congress as they faced the implementation of the tax cuts they had enacted in 1981. Working together, the decline in national income and the decrease in inflation would reduce revenue flows and increase deficits significantly beyond what they forecast.

At the time of the passage of ERTA in 1981, however, the Reagan administration and the Congress were responsive to economic and fiscal conditions. Between February 1981, when the Reagan administration introduced its tax-cut proposals, and August of that year, when ERTA became law, no clear, consistent signs appeared to signal that the economy was moving into a deep recession and that the defeat of inflation was imminent. To be sure, in June, the Treasury and the White House staff, in part to protect the tax cuts, ignored the warnings of Lawrence Kudlow, then associate director for economics and planning in the Office of Management and Budget, that monetary policy was likely to make the February estimates of GNP overly optimistic. And, economic activity did, in fact, decline slightly during the second quarter of the year. But forecasts could change quickly. The next month, Murray Weidenbaum told the president that the third quarter would probably also fall and "the current softness could continue through the rest of the year." But, "if we're lucky," he wrote, "the downturn won't be any sharper or longer." As it turned out, economic activity actually increased slightly during the third quarter, easing the administration's worries about deficits.[15]

Of course, in drafting ERTA, Democrats and Republicans engaged in a frenzied bidding war that may be one of the most egregious twentieth-century examples of special-interest politics. But even during the decoration of a "Christmas tree" bill, both the administration and Congress maintained some contact with fiscal reality. When Congressional leaders reinserted the very expensive indexing of tax brackets, they delayed its implementation until 1985. They anticipated that, until then, inflation would continue to move many people into higher tax brackets and thus reduce future deficits. Also, the Reagan administration supported transforming 10-10-10 into 5-10-10, thus providing for a 23-percent, rather than a 27-percent, net reduction in the tax rates for individuals.[16]

In addition, both the administration and Congress made pertinent political judgments. Veteran leaders in Congress believed that they would have opportunities to raise taxes in the future. Russell Long, chair of the Senate Finance Committee, recalled that, before the Reagan years, he "had voted for large tax cuts and for needed tax increases." He recalled, in particular: "We had twice repealed and subsequently reenacted the investment tax credit."[17] And the Reagan administration apparently believed that increases in the deficit would frighten Congress and prompt its leaders to cooperate in reducing the rate of increase in expenditures. Donald Regan told his Treasury staff: "My favorite part of the tax bill is the indexing provision—it takes the sand out of Congress's sandbox."[18] In February, President Reagan had said much the same thing. He invoked one of his homilies to justify going forward with a tax cut before trying to moderate or roll back spending: "Well," he said, "we can lecture our children about extravagance until we run out of voice and breath. OR, we can cure their extravagance simply by reducing their allowance."[19]

In fact, significant tax increases followed later on in Reagan's first administration. And discretionary spending for domestic purposes declined in fiscal 1982; it did not return to the level of 1981 until fiscal year 1985. Perhaps the political judgments that both Congress and the administration made in 1981 turned out to have some merit.[20]

2.   The Tax Equity and Fiscal Responsibility Act of 1982 (TEFRA)

Even before ERTA went into effect on October 1, 1981, the signs of recession and growing deficits became impossible for the administration to ignore. In early September, Murray Weidenbaum, the chairman of the Council of Economic Advisers, warned the president of the growing fiscal problem, and what he regarded as the worrisome economic consequences. There was "good news": "the progress in bringing down inflation." But prospects for a "strong upturn in the fourth quarter of early 1982" were now "clouded." Thus, there was "bad news": The "combination of slower growth and less inflation means less revenue and higher deficits than [in the forecast of] the July 15 midyear budget review." He reported that the administration's relatively optimistic "public forecasts" were part of "our credibility problem with financial markets." These markets were worried "that heavy deficit financing will absorb saving and keep interest rates high, thus interfering with private investment."[21]

In October, the president publicly acknowledged the onset of a recession. The administration had to scale back dramatically its revenue estimates. David Stockman recalled: "We now had to lower our forecast for 1982–1984 GNP by the staggering sum of *one-half trillion dollars.*" In response to this projection, and others like it, David Stockman called for a debate within the administration on a "mid-course correction" in fiscal policy. He noted: "Rosy Scenario is not yet the all-around beauty she was cracked up to be," largely because "the anti-inflationary monetary policy is working sooner, more thoroughly, and more successfully than might have been expected." He worried that "large fiscal deficits" in fiscal years 1982–1984 would "impose unacceptable pressure on financial and business balance sheets and unnecessarily large costs on the output and employment side of the economy" and "eventually jeopardize our capacity to maintain a steady reduction in the growth rate of money and credit, and sustain the dis-inflation process now under way." The debate ought to focus on "the combination—of revenue, entitlement, and discretionary spending changes—that will close the deficit gap."[22]

Stockman hoped to delay the second and third years of tax cutting, and he recruited James Baker, the president's chief of staff, and Richard Darman, Baker's deputy chief of staff and key advisor for economic matters, for an effort to win over the president. Meanwhile, Volcker confirmed Weidenbaum's characterization of financial markets and called publicly for a consideration of "new revenue sources." Robert Dole, chair of the Senate Finance Committee, told Frederick Schultz, vice chair of the Federal Reserve Board: "We are going to have to do something on the fiscal side."[23] Nonetheless, Stockman, Darman, and Baker failed to gain the support of Regan and Ed Meese, who served as counsellor to the president. The primary concern of both was to protect the long-term, supply-side benefits of the tax cuts. In addition, Regan may have been optimistic about recovery coming early in 1982.[24] And, he may have seen the situation in almost Keynesian terms and worried that tax increases would prolong the recession. "I was convinced," Regan recalled later, "that an increase in taxes, coupled to a monetary policy that was already starving business of capital, would make our economic troubles worse." He went on: "It was better to borrow money to finance the deficit while the economy recovered and people went back to work than to impose taxes that would cripple the recovery or prevent it altogether." He did not explain whether he thought the crippling effects would be via the demand or the supply side, but the former would be consistent with his description of Congress as "stomping on the accelerator of the economy" in 1982.[25]

Meese may also have used Keynesian terms to defend the tax cuts. On November 19, 1981, Richard Beal, director of the White House Office of Planning and Evaluation, urged Meese to "be cautious in discussing tax cuts as a Keynesian fine-tuning device to avoid or cure the recession."[26] On the same day, Jim Jenkins, another member of Meese's team, advised him that the restrictive monetary policy supported by the Reagan administration had caused inflationary expectations to wane and interest rates to fall. He urged Meese and the administration to stay with the "current noninflationary monetary policy" and warned against trying "to reverse the slowdown by the same old tried-and-failed methods of reacceleration of money growth, and massive, 'pump-priming' federal makework expenditures." Jenkins declared: "Keynes is dead, and so are his ideas. Hayek lives, and so do his ideas." Jenkins went on to explain: "An economy based on private property and which relies on market forces is inherently resilient and naturally gravitates towards full utilization of all its resources following any shock or depressive force such as droughts, wars, or destabilizing policies of government."[27]

The president stood firm behind the established schedule for the tax cuts. However, he allowed Regan to throw a sop to Baker and Stockman by recommending a small list of what became described to the public as "revisions in the tax code to curtail certain tax abuses and enhance tax revenues." The proposed revisions would reduce the deficits by the modest sum of $22 billion over three years.

During November and December, the president's economic advisors had great difficulty agreeing on specific forecasts. Nonetheless, they agreed that the deficit problem would amount to somewhere between $100 billion and $185 billion by 1984. (The actual number turned out to reach the high end of their range of estimates.) Stockman began to argue for increasing excise and consumption taxes, but the president, once again following the advice of his secretary of the Treasury and some political advisors in the White House, dug in his heels and resisted any significant tax increases.[28] On December 17, the president went on national television to announce that he would stand by his tax cuts. "You can balance the budget by robbing the people," but "you will find that you have torpedoed the economy." In January 1982, in his State of the Union address, Reagan said much the same thing: "I will seek no tax increases this year, and I have no intention of retreating from our basic program of tax relief."

Meanwhile, Stockman, Baker, Darman, and Weidenbaum turned their efforts to winning the president's approval for expanding the modest "revenue enhancements" obtained through loophole closing, and for allowing them to negotiate with Congress. By December of 1981, the administration was considering tax increases that would raise $45 billion in fiscal years 1983 and 1984. The administration worried about the impact on the 1982 elections of supporting tax increases, but, in January, the president approved a variety of tax-code revisions, including a new withholding tax on dividend and interest payments, which the Treasury believed would raise about $87 billion in new revenues over a three-year period.[29] Part of the reason for approving these tax increases was to protect the third year of tax cuts. As David Gergen explained, Congress would attempt to raise "that amount and a lot more" by "modifying the tax cuts and repealing the leasing, indexing, and oil provisions" rather than enacting "loophole closings, excise-tax increases, import fees, and the like" which "we consider best." He concluded: "We must, therefore, fight hard for our type of tax increases for the fiscal years 1983 and 1984, but make sure they do not undo our incentive tax cuts already in place."[30]

As Federal Reserve tightening continued into 1982, and as the recession deepened despite the 1981 tax cuts, some members of the Reagan administration became increasingly unhappy with Paul Volcker.[31] In his recollections, Donald Regan criticized Volcker for his "Delphic mysteriousness and a bureaucratic fascination with tinkering," which "created an atmosphere of fitful government activity and uncertainty in the market that, in my opinion, prolonged the slump well past the point of necessity.[32] Some suggested that it was the Federal Reserve's tight money policy, and not the deficits, that produced high interest rates and an economic slowdown. But Volcker also had defenders within the administration. In January, Lawrence Kudlow wrote a forceful memorandum to James Baker. He proposed that while the administration ought to engage the Federal Reserve privately over some technical issues, the Fed had improved its performance in 1981, and "the administration should be attempting to enhance the credibility of the monetary control program." Kudlow worried that the public would see through "scapegoating the Fed while we struggle with triple-digit deficits," and that Volcker might go public and "undermine the administration's attempts to present a credible fiscal program."[33]

In February, Alan Greenspan, in a memorandum for a Camp David retreat of senior advisors to plan the White House agenda for 1982, reinforced the importance of standing behind the Federal Reserve. It would be "a major mistake," Greenspan wrote, "to accuse the Federal Reserve of creating excessively high interest rates." He explained: "The major cause is, in fact, inflation and the budget deficits." He went further: "At root, our problem is that the markets believe that the federal deficit will continue to hemorrhage, inducing the Federal Reserve to create excessive money supply growth and hence inflation." Greenspan declared: "The president should be perceived as supporting of the Fed, although not acquiescing in all of its actions." He warned those who might want the president to be more aggressive in criticizing Volcker. "The press," Greenspan wrote, "will clearly support the Fed in any outward confrontation with the administration on this issue." In looking to the rest of the year, Greenspan was guardedly optimistic. He believed that interest rates were stabilizing, having fully discounted "budget deficits of $120–$140 billion in fiscal year 1984."[34]

In framing the agenda of the February retreat, Richard Darman had called out an "insufficiently prompt, strong, and sustainable economic recovery" as one of the major "substantive risks" to the administration's domestic agenda in 1982. He highlighted Greenspan's paper and seemed to accept his focus on interest rates. Darman worried that deficit projections of $120–$140 billion "or higher" were likely to become common, and that the administration's projections "will not be judged to be feasible—without movement on defense or taxes." But Darman appeared to see little likelihood of that happening, or of cutting entitlements. In apparent desperation, he recommended that the administration "distract attention from economic focus until the economy is clearly turning up."[35]

In March, the President's Economic Policy Advisory Board met and provided some support for the effort to close the deficit. The group was pleased by the progress in the fight against inflation, but, by the same token, saw little hope of immediate recovery. The "greatest barrier to a healthy and sustained recovery," the group concluded, "was high interest rates," and the administration had to concentrate on getting rates down. "Many members" regarded "large prospective budget deficits" as "the primary cause" of the high interest rates. "Financial markets" were "convinced that deficits and prospective deficits matter, regardless of the academic debate on the subject." Martin Anderson put "current deficit expectations in the $130–$150 billion range" and "observed that all other problems 'pale by comparison'." Herbert Stein urged immediate reduction of the deficit by $50 billion. The Board preferred reducing spending to increasing revenues, and urged keeping reductions in marginal rates; but some members supported stretching out the third year of the tax cuts, raising energy taxes and fees, raising excise taxes, and imposing new luxury taxes.[36]

At roughly the same time, the president became sufficiently worried about both fiscal conditions and his falling approval ratings to allow James Baker to launch negotiations with Congress to reduce deficits, and to offer up nearly $100 billion in "revenue enhancement." What followed was a prolonged and convoluted process in which the White House "triumvirate" of Baker, Meese, and Deputy Chief of Staff Michael Deaver tried to convince Congressional Republicans to agree on a deal that would reduce the deficit through conventional spending cuts as well as reductions in tax expenditures. The Treasury secretary reluctantly joined the negotiations. He remained concerned about tax increases deepening the recession, and he still worried about eroding the ERTA tax cuts. But he obtained assurances from Reagan that the president would stand behind the cuts, and Secretary Regan shifted his attention to relieving the tightness of monetary policy. He agreed to negotiate over deficit reduction after Paul Volcker, as Regan recalled, "assured me that he would try to be accommodating to the administration—he would ease money to bring interest rates down if he could see some movement by us on the deficits."[37]

The negotiating group grew in size until it was known as the "Gang of Seventeen." It had great difficulty estimating future deficits, but discussed numbers that approached $250 billion by 1985. The "Gang" seemed to reach agreement on a three-to-one ratio between spending cuts and new taxes, amounting to more than $400 billion in deficit reductions over three years. Secretary Regan urged the president to endorse the deal. He stressed that if "we show fiscal discipline," Paul Volcker would "help us with monetary policy." The secretary recalled saying to the president that if they pull off the $400 billion reduction, "it will startle Wall Street and the world, and we'll be on our way to a sound economy." Recovery would be the consequence, Regan told the president, of both greater investor confidence in the economy and a more expansive monetary policy.

In June 1982, the secretary of the Treasury recommended that the president adopt a tax package as administration policy, and Reagan subsequently did. One of the "basic principles" guiding its design was that "revenues must be increased by approximately $95 billion over the next three fiscal years, including at least $20.9 billion in fiscal 1983."[38] During the summer of 1982, when the loophole closing encountered resistance in Congress from conservative Republicans, the administration worked hard to pass the legislation. Behind the scenes, the administration lobbied the business community and won support for the bill as a whole from a wide variety of industries, even though many of them had reservations about particular provisions of the bill. In July, Elizabeth Dole reported to the "triumvirate" that this "marks the first time in anyone's memory that the business community has essentially supported a tax increase."[39] In public, Reagan began, for the first time, to adopt the language of a base-broadening tax reformer. In one of his longest speeches to the nation on economic affairs, the president emphasized that the legislation would promote "simple fairness" for "every American, especially those in lower-income brackets" by "closing off special-interest loopholes."[40]

The outcome of Reagan's leadership and the bipartisan cooperation was the Tax Equity and Fiscal Responsibility Act of 1982 (TEFRA). This act, which Congress passed in August 1982, imposed the first major tax increase during an election year in peacetime since 1932, and the first during a recession or depression, also since 1932. The process had been agonizing, but had resulted in some reductions in the projected deficits, both short term and long term. Just how much reduction actually followed became a substantive issue among the alumni of the Reagan administration.[41]

At roughly the same time that TEFRA became law, the Federal Reserve began to loosen monetary policy. From July through December 1982, the Federal Reserve eased monetary policy; and by November, economic recovery had finally begun. Whether the enactment of TEFRA contributed to the Federal Reserve's shift in policy remains a matter for conjecture. The shift may have done so, just as Donald Regan told the president it would. The process had not been pretty, and had probably taken too long, but the Federal Reserve, the Reagan administration, and Congress improved their coordination of fiscal and monetary policy.[42]

3. The Deficit Reduction Act of 1984 (DEFRA)

During the autumn of 1982 and the following winter, the search within the White House and Treasury for new revenues broadened in scope.

Making revenue forecasts remained a highly uncertain enterprise, and it was not yet clear when exactly economic recovery would take hold. In September, Martin Feldstein, who had just become chair of the Council of Economic Advisers (CEA) told the president and his Cabinet Council on Economic Affairs that "the recovery is likely to be relatively weak and slow" and that "the prognosis for capital investment in 1983 is poor." He advised: "A clear, early indication of a reduced deficit in future years could help to lower real long-term interest rates and accelerate the recovery." The administration had difficulty reaching agreement on an economic forecast for fiscal year 1983; but, by December, Feldstein had become more optimistic. He reported that the Treasury, OMB, and the CEA believed that the recovery would begin in the first quarter of 1983 and continue for the next six months. However, Feldstein noted, longer-term growth depended on reducing budget deficits to "less than $50 billion (one percent of GNP) in 1988."

The loss of conservative Republican seats in the 1982 Congressional elections, along with polls that pointed to loss of public confidence in the economic stewardship of the Reagan administration, focused minds on deficit reduction. Assistant Secretary for Tax Policy John (Buck) Chapoton worked especially closely with Congressional staff to develop deficit-reduction options. Within the White House, Richard Darman floated a variety of ideas, including delaying and reducing indexing and postponing the defense buildup. His goal was balancing the budget by fiscal year 1989, so that they would "leave future administrations (and future generations) a budget that is stably balanced."[43]

The most radical income-tax option that came under discussion in the White House during the last half of 1982 was the adoption of some form of a "flat tax." Over the Christmas holidays in 1982, during a round of golf, Secretary of State George Shultz pressed the idea upon the president who, according to David Stockman, saw classic supply-side possibilities.[44] "By the eighteenth hole," Stockman wrote, "the president was convinced this was a way to reduce the deficit without increasing taxes." In Stockman's account, the president pressed the idea on Treasury Secretary Regan and Edwin Meese as a way of both lowering taxes and immediately reducing the deficit. "Soon," Stockman recalled, "everyone around the White House was talking flat tax." Darman recalled that, by January

1983, a "faction . . . favored proposing radical tax reform, replacing the progressive income tax with either a flat tax or a consumed-income tax that would exempt net savings and investment from any tax at all."

Stockman, Darman, and Martin Feldstein, however, all had reservations about moving quickly toward a flat tax. They worried about versions that would increase deficits even further. They questioned the supply-side assumptions of a swift payoff in increased revenues that seemed to drive the president's interest in tax cutting. "They don't actually believe this mumbo-jumbo, do they?" Feldstein asked Stockman after a meeting in which the president pushed the flat tax as a revenue-raiser, working on the supply side.

Stockman and Darman developed an alternative plan, which Stockman later described as "perfectly disingenuous." They would accept the supply-side argument and assert that the flat tax, when adopted, would yield economic productivity gains of approximately $50 billion per year (about one percent of GNP). Then, they would argue for the adoption of a "placeholder" tax—a temporary increase in taxes—to raise this amount of revenue until the flat tax took hold, perhaps in 1986 or even later. "By hook or by crook, I was going to put $50 billion in new revenue into the budget," Stockman recalled.

In early January 1983, they made their case within the White House. Secretary Regan accepted the concept of the placeholder tax, but argued that its adoption should wait until 1986 when, presumably, the economy would be out of recession. Once again, Regan was worried about tax increases during recession. He argued, further, that the administration should wait to submit legislation for the placeholder tax until Congress had followed through on the commitment to three-for-one budget cuts. Meanwhile, Baker and Darman began to get cold feet as they contemplated the political fallout from radical reform along flat-tax lines—reform that would require, for example, repeal of the deduction of interest payments on home mortgages. In January, as Stockman recalled, "Shultz's original flat-tax idea was packed off to Siberia, in this case a 'deep study mode' at Treasury with a view to 'broadening, simplifying, and reforming the income tax'."

The idea of a placeholder tax, however, remained in the tax program, and took the form of a temporary tax that George Shultz had proposed:

an energy tax on domestic and imported oil. The chances of its enactment were, Stockman recalled, "about as likely as an invasion of Martians." But the president was not necessarily convinced of this and, in any case, he hated to even appear to be asking for tax increases. "Oh darn, oh darn," he complained, as he signed the 1983 budget submission for fiscal year 1984, which included the placeholder tax. "I had never seen him look so utterly dejected," Stockman later wrote.

On January 25, 1983, in his State of the Union address, President Reagan called for the provision of what he now called "stand-by" tax authority. Reagan declared that, "Because we must ensure reduction and eventual elimination of deficits over the next several years, I will propose a stand-by tax...." Reagan followed this declaration with the statement, stunning to some, that, "We who are in government must take the lead in restoring the economy." Darman has written that, with these two statements, the president "formally abandoned the supply-side principle" and revealed the truth that "the power of the Reagan Revolution's official fiscal policy was spent." In fact, however, the president had not yet given up on his conviction that cuts in taxes could generate larger revenues.[45]

As it turned out, the economy had begun to recover in November 1982. Expansion was strong throughout 1983, with real GDP increasing over 6 percent and unemployment falling 2.5 percentage points. Meanwhile, inflation remained under 4 percent. Both monetary and fiscal policy (at least on the demand side) encouraged the recovery. The Federal Reserve held the discount rate steady at 8.5 percent throughout the year. Between fiscal years 1982 and 1983, the deficit increased from $128 billion to $208 billion, and the deficit as a percentage of potential GDP increased from 3.7 percent to 5.6 percent. In fiscal year 1984, the deficit shrank slightly, to $185 billion, which amounted to 4.7 percent of potential GDP. Because of the strong expansion and the stable discount rate, complaints within the administration about the Federal Reserve Board subsided, although some of the president's political advisors may have remained uncomfortable with, or even resented, Paul Volcker's power and popularity. Regardless of their feelings, the president remained a supporter of Volcker. In June 1983, the president announced his decision to reappoint him as chair of the Board.[46]

As the economy expanded smartly throughout 1983, many Congressional leaders and members of the White House staff pondered how to help sustain the expansion. Reducing deficits still made sense to most of Reagan's economic advisors. Feldstein, for example, told the president that he was worried about "the continuation of vast deficits that add more than a half a trillion dollars to our national debt between now and 1987." But he advised against an increase in "tax rates this year or next." He urged, instead, the stand-by tax (which he described as the "delayed contingency tax"), and told the president that such authority would encourage confidence in the federal government, reduce real interest rates, and stimulate investment "with a delay of about one to two years" without dampening the current recovery. The stand-by tax appeared to be an attractive middle-of-the-road solution, and Bob Dole became enthusiastic about it. However, technical analysis by Treasury and Congressional staff raised daunting issues, and both Republicans and Democrats in Congress identified political problems with on-again, off-again taxes. For his part, the president remained convinced that Congress had failed to engage in serious reduction of the deficit through expenditure reduction, and he was unenthused about recommending any form of tax increase.[47]

In late 1983, as Reagan's advisors prepared for the State of the Union address and the February submission of a budget for the 1985 fiscal year, some of them resumed their campaign for a standby-tax. Feldstein not only promoted the tax, but also told the president that "the right kind of tax increase in future years—for example, a tax on consumption—could help the recovery by permitting interest rates to decline and providing more funds for investment." Darman also suggested both the appointment of a deficit commission and raising revenue from "a major tax simplification program."[48]

The president met the ideas for new taxes with his supply-side claims. In January, over a lunch, Reagan told Feldstein and Stockman: "There has not been one tax increase in history that actually raised revenue. And every tax cut, from the 1920s, to Kennedy's, to ours, has produced more." Feldstein immediately dashed off a brief history of tax revenues before and after tax increases and concluded: "*Every* increase in tax rates was followed by a rise in tax revenue." For good measure, Feldstein looked at the huge tax increases during World War II and concluded: "There is no evidence that the rising tax rates were incompatible with increased real GNP."[49]

The president, however, became persuaded that he needed to take the high ground of bipartisanship in preparation for the 1984 elections. While he refused to endorse any particular tax increases, he did agree that the high deficits were potentially a political liability, and that he ought to put as much responsibility as possible on Congress. In his 1984 State of the Union address, he called on Congress to enact spending and revenue measures on which bipartisan consensus existed. He offered up "measures to close certain tax loopholes." Such measures, the president said, could be a "downpayment" on further actions to restore a balanced budget.[50]

After the speech and submission of the budget, Feldstein pushed him to follow through. Feldstein argued: "It is certainly better to raise revenue by carefully chosen tax measures than to go on indefinitely with huge deficits that undermine the accumulation of capital." He told the president that he needed to persuade "financial investors and others that you are committed to move the economy toward a balanced budget."[51]

At the same time, the president received advice from Republican strategists that he ought to take the initiative in developing a deficit reduction program, and that the program could include "loophole closures."[52] In March, the president, once again, agreed hesitantly to a series of modest reductions in tax expenditures. Congress rejected most of these, but the president approved those that Congress substituted; in July, he signed the Deficit Reduction Act of 1984 (DEFRA, rhyming with TEFRA). Thus, Reagan took another step backward from his dramatic measure of 1981. Taken together, TEFRA and DEFRA raised revenues on the average of $100 billion per year at 1990 levels of income. Despite the president's hostility to taxes, tax increases this large had never been enacted except during major wars.[53]

4. Coda: The Tax Reform Act of 1986

After the passage of DEFRA, strong economic recovery, the continued success of the Federal Reserve Board in restraining inflation, and the successful reelection campaign of 1984, the Reagan administration lost interest in increasing tax revenues.[54] Instead, it returned to tax reform that reduced the highest marginal rates of income taxation. But the experience of the first term had been instructive. In promoting the Tax Reform Act of 1986, the Reagan administration accepted the discipline of revenue neutrality; the administration reduced corporate rates and the highest individual rates, but paid for them by slashed tax expenditures for the wealthiest individuals and corporations. Like ERTA in 1981, the Tax Reform Act of 1986 sought to promote economic productivity but, unlike ERTA, it followed the examples set by TEFRA and DEFRA in their sensitivity to fiscal reality. And, in shaping the 1986 Act, Reagan experimented with a different populist message—one based on tax fairness (in the form of horizontal equity) rather than on tax cutting. In his memoirs, Reagan gave ERTA and the 1986 Act equal billing. He declared: "With the tax cuts of 1981 and the Tax Reform Act of 1986, I'd accomplished a lot of what I'd come to Washington to do."[55] However, over the next two decades, it was ERTA, rather than the Tax Reform Act of 1986, that became more closely associated with the rhetoric and memory of a "Reagan revolution." If architects of taxation wish to use history to make taxation more responsive to fiscal and economic reality, they need to remember that 1981 marked only the beginning of the Reagan administration's reform of tax policy.

Notes

1. See Walton and Rockoff (2002), pp. 626–629.

2. On the long-run effect of the Reagan tax cuts and the other aspects of his tax program on the tax system, see Brownlee and Steuerle (2003), pp. 155–181, and Brownlee (2004), pp. 177–248. The precise nature of the impact of the Reagan tax reforms, as well as other shifts in U.S. tax policy, on the history of economic productivity remains very much a matter of conjecture. For discussion of this issue, see Brownlee (2002), pp. 71–93.

3. Some of these economists may have been surprised to learn that this was their view.

4. Reagan (2001a), p. 274 and p. 277. Reagan's commitment to the extreme version of supply-side economics appears to have come more than two or three years earlier than the briefing on the Laffer curve, delivered by Arthur Laffer just before Reagan's 1980 victory in the New Hampshire primary, that David Stock-

man and others believed marked Reagan's conversion. In 1976, in a newspaper column, Reagan suggested that the tax cuts of Presidents Harding and Kennedy had produced increased revenues. Sidney Blumenthal claims that at a dinner in 1977, Reagan told Arthur Laffer that he supported supply-side economics. In 1976 and 1977, Reagan may have been reading Jude Wanniski's *Wall Street Journal* editorials promoting Laffer's ideas. See Blumenthal (1986), pp. 166–167 and pp. 190–196, and Stockman (1986), p. 258. On the role of Wanniski's editorials, see Roberts (1984), pp. 27–30, and Anderson (1988), pp. 148–152.

5. Martin Anderson, Reagan's economic coordinator, organized a proposal for "a program—of at least three years' duration—of across-the-board tax cuts" and indexing "federal tax rate brackets, as well as the amount of exemptions, deductions, and credits." See Anderson (1988), pp. 113–121.

6. On the role of the lobbyists, including Charls Walker, see Birnbaum and Murray (1987), pp. 16–18, Conlan *et al.* (1990), p. 96, and Martin (1991), p. 47.

7. See Walker (1994), pp. 224–225.

8. For Martin Anderson's description of this episode, see Anderson (1988), pp. 122–138. The quotations are from p. 129.

9. See Reagan (2001), p. 492.

10. Reagan may have favored restoring the gold standard. William Greider suggests that he did, and that Reagan's advisors kept this from the public for fear "that it would sound 'kooky' and 'old-fashioned' to voters." In Reagan's first meeting with Volcker, according to Martin Anderson, Reagan told Volcker that people had suggested that "it is the Fed that causes much of our monetary problems and that we would be better off if we abolished it." Reagan proceeded to ask: "Why do we need the Federal Reserve?" See Greider (1987), pp. 379–381, and Anderson (1988), pp. 250–251.

11. In "Points on the Economic Package," probably drafted in February by Martin Anderson, the White House identified one of the four key elements of Reagan's comprehensive economic plan as "monetary restraint," and mentioned the meeting between Reagan and Volcker. (The other three components were "significant spending cuts," "tax cuts," and "regulatory relief.") See Economic Recovery Package (1981–1982). At this time, however, the administration's economic team worried both that Volcker might not stay the course with monetary restraint and that his policies might be too erratic, as they seemed to have been in 1980. On the criticism of Volcker from within the Reagan administration, see Greider (1987), pp. 363–364. For a description of the first meeting between Reagan and Volcker, which also included Edwin Meese, James Baker, Regan, Murray Weidenbaum, David Stockman, and Anderson, see Anderson (1988), pp. 250–251.

12. For the details of monetary policy, I rely heavily on Mussa (1994), pp. 81–145.

13. See Sprinkel (1981) and Anderson (1981).

14. See Congressional Budget Office, Table 11.

15. On the June estimates by Lawrence Kudlow, see Stockman (1986), pp. 330–332. On the July estimates, see Weidenbaum (1981a).

16. The president's Legislative Study had come to support the shift to 5-10-10 as a means "of deficit reduction and acceptance of selected other tax reduction proposals necessary to achieve a political majority." See Darman (1981). In May, the more extreme supply-siders within the administration "increasingly favored" the opposite approach—"front-loading" the tax cut through a 10-10, two-year program. See Gergen (1981).

17. See Long (1994), p. 221. For evidence of similar thinking on the part of other Congressional leaders, see Friedersdorf (1981).

18. For the quotation of Regan, see Hoover and Sheffrin (1992), p. 225.

19. See Reagan (2001), p. 490. For a further discussion of Reagan's intentions along these lines, see Brownlee and Steuerle (2003), p. 160.

20. For the trend of discretionary outlays, see Congressional Budget Office, Table 7.

21. Weidenbaum (1981).

22. There are three substantial accounts of the process that Stockman launched in September 1981, each by a central participant within the administration. The accounts are consistent with one another, but their emphases and their evaluations of the process differ widely. See Meese (1992), pp. 139–147; Regan (1988), especially pp. 171–184; and Stockman (1986), pp. 313–326 and pp. 353–354. See also Stockman (1981).

23. *Wall Street Journal* (1981). The Dole quotation is from Greider (1987), p. 424.

24. For the forecasts in November 1981 by Regan and his monetary advisor, Beryl Sprinkel, see Greider (1987), pp. 425–426.

25. Regan (1988), p. 174 and p. 172. Oddly, Regan described the proposal to increase taxes in 1982 as "the Keynesian solution." See p. 175.

26. Beal (1981).

27. Jenkins (1981).

28. Stockman (1986), pp. 340–342. Representative of the political advice was that given by Richard S. Williamson, assistant to the president for intergovernmental affairs and a former deputy to James Baker. On November 2, 1981, he wrote to Reagan's primary economic advisors urging them not to propose a major tax increase (in the range of $25–$50 billion per year). His objections were twofold. The first was political: The cut "would show that he did not know what he was doing with his Economic Recovery Program," and "the Administration would be Carterized." The second was structural: Without sustained cuts in taxes and spending, "America will go the way of most of Western Europe where 60 to 70 percent of income is taxed to support government programs that redistribute wealth, subsidize the middle class, and choke individual initiative." See Williamson (1981).

29. Presidential decision memorandum (1982). See also Regan (1988). p. 176.

30. Gergen (1981a). On the administration's concerns about the 1984 elections, see Beal (1982).

31. Michael Mussa has suggested that the Federal Reserve may have, in fact, "kept monetary policy too tight for too long during 1982." See Mussa (1994), pp. 113–114. For a similar view, see Greider (1987), pp. 446–448.

32. Regan (1988), p. 172.

33. Kudlow (1982).

34. Greenspan (1982).

35. See Darman (1982a) and (1982b).

36. President's Economic Policy Advisory Board (1982). The President's Economic Policy Advisory Board (PEPAB) consisted of outside economists, including Milton Friedman, William Simon, and others who had held economic policy positions in earlier administrations. On the role of the PEPAB, see Anderson (1988), pp. 265–271, Friedman and Friedman (1998), pp. 391–395, and Roberts (1984), p. 210. Edwin Meese described Friedman as "a particular favorite of the president." See Meese (1992), p. 127.

37. Regan (1988), p. 178. Volcker may have said the same thing to others in the White House. For William Greider's quotation of David Stockman, see Greider (1987), p. 478.

38. Regan (1988), p. 183; Regan (1982).

39. Dole (1982).

40. "Text of the Address by the President to the Nation" (1982). On the administration's efforts to highlight the base-broadening elements in TEFRA, see "Fact sheet: The Tax Equity and Fiscal Responsibility Act of 1982" (1982).

41. Reagan later concluded that he had been, in the words of David Stockman, "badly double-crossed" by the Democrats. They had not, Reagan believed, delivered on the three-for-one spending cuts that they had promised in 1982 for the TEFRA tax increases. For the rest of his administration, Reagan became even more rigidly opposed to significant tax increases. For Reagan's conclusion that the Democrats had "reneged on their (TEFRA) pledge," see Reagan (1990), pp. 314–315. While Edwin Meese supported TEFRA in 1982, he later described the compromise as "the greatest domestic error of the Reagan administration." See Meese (1992), p. 147. David Stockman, however, has described the notion that the Democrats failed to deliver on their side of the bargain as the "big lie" of the supply-siders. See Stockman (1994), pp. 277–278. Part of the reason for the president's possible misunderstanding was the technical impossibility of including the expenditure reductions in the same bill as the tax cuts. See Darman (1982c).

42. Michael Mussa concludes: "The Federal Reserve's concern over the effect of the deficit on interest rates was genuine." But he regards the evidence regarding the effect as "ambiguous." And, he finds "no clear evidence" of the influence of the passage of TEFRA on the Federal Reserve. See Mussa (1994), p. 115. On

the other hand, William Greider maintains that the Federal Reserve had decided to ease up a month earlier, even though it was skeptical of the willingness of Congress to act. Greider also discounts the role of Congressional threats to the autonomy of the Federal Reserve as "adolescent bravado" that Volcker did not take seriously. See Greider (1987), p. 478 and pp. 514–516.

43. For the forecasts for 1983, see Feldstein (1982), Poole *et al.* (1982), and Feldstein (1982a). On Darman's program, see Darman (1982).

44. The following discussion of deliberations within the White House in late 1982 and in 1983 draws upon the consistent recollections of David Stockman and Richard Darman. See Stockman (1986), pp. 355–365, and Darman (1996), pp. 118–199.

45. Reagan (1983).

46. On the substance of monetary policy during the first year of the recovery, see Mussa (1994), pp. 116–118. For the data on the deficit, see Congressional Budget Office, Table 11. On the administration's discussion of Volcker's reappointment, see Greider (1987), pp. 555–574.

47. On the Dole proposal and the reaction to it within the administration, see Regan (1983) and Fuerbringer (1983). For Feldstein's position, see Feldstein (1983), (1983a), and (1983b).

48. See Feldstein (1984), (1984e), and (1984f). For Feldstein's linkage of deficits and inflation, see Feldstein (1984b) and (1984d). For overviews of the preparations for the 1984 State of the Union address, see Stockman (1986), pp. 374–375 and Regan (1988), pp. 196–201. The president's budget for fiscal year 1985 included the revenue that a contingency tax might raise. In December 1983, Darman wrote: "There is no disagreement among key players here (including the President) that the budget must include the revenue represented by the contingency tax." If it did not, Darman explained, "there will be no plausible way to show deficits coming down satisfactorily; interest rates may rise some in the second half of next year; the economy would suffer some; and so on." See Darman (1983).

49. Feldstein (1984g). The recollection of Reagan's statement at lunch is Stockman's. See Stockman (1986), p. 374.

50. Reagan (1984).

51. Feldstein (1984a) and (1984c).

52. Kenneth Khachigian, for example, wrote in this way to the president. Khachigian said: "I'm told the revenue increases are strictly limited to those which do not inhibit the recovery, which protect the individual cuts and indexing at all costs, and which do not substantially affect the middle class or the poor." But he added: "The bottom line: this far and no further. America cannot tax itself to prosperity and balanced budgets." See Khachigian (1984) and Darman (1984).

53. For an overview of the tax increases, see Steuerle (1992), pp. 64–69. The Treasury, as well as David Stockman and the Office of Management and Budget, recommended that the president sign the legislation. See Stockman (1984).

54. Baker and Darman, however, considered developing an even larger tax increase—one that Darman described as a "big fix." They may have discussed an increase amounting to as much as two percent of GDP, and contemplated heavy taxation of consumption. For the comments of Richard Darman, see Walker (1994), p. 232. In his recollections of this episode, Darman implies that he continued to consider further deficit reduction after the passage of DEFRA. See Richard Darman (1996), p. 124. Donald Regan prepared for the possibility that the "[p]resident would be forced to yield" and accept a huge tax increase. The secretary asked his staff "to explore the possibilities of a value-added tax (VAT) and other forms of sales taxes." See Regan (1988), p. 205.

55. Reagan (1990), p. 335.

References

Anderson, Martin. 1981. "Talking Points" for meeting with Paul Volcker and cue cards for the president. Memorandum for the president, July 16. Office of the President: Presidential Briefing Papers, CFOA 739, casefile 043477. Ronald Reagan Library.

Anderson, Martin. 1988. *Revolution*. San Diego: Harcourt Brace Jovanovich.

Beal, Richard S. 1981. Possible unified position of administration on the economy. Memorandum to Edwin Meese, November 19. David Gergen Files: OA 10523, Economic Policy, February 1981 to December 1981. Ronald Reagan Library.

Beal, Richard S. 1982. Political impact of tax increase. Memorandum to Edwin Meese and Martin Anderson, January 19. Edwin S. Meese III Files: OA 9456, Polls/Information-R. Beal. Ronald Reagan Library.

Birnbaum, Jeffrey H., and Alan S. Murray. 1987. *Showdown at Gucci Gulch: Lawmakers, lobbyists, and the unlikely triumph of tax reform*. New York: Random House.

Blumenthal, Sidney. 1986. *The rise of the counter-establishment: From conservative ideology to political power*, 166–167 and 190–196. New York: Random House.

Brownlee, W. Elliot. 2002. Economic history and the analysis of 'soaking the rich' in 20th century America. In *Tax justice: The ongoing debate*, eds. Joseph J. Thorndike and Dennis J. Ventry Jr. Washington, D.C.: The Urban Institute Press.

Brownlee, W. Elliot. 2004. *Federal taxation in America: A short history*. 2nd ed. Cambridge: Cambridge University Press.

Brownlee, W. Elliot, and C. Eugene Steuerle. 2003. Taxation. In *The Reagan Presidency: Pragmatic conservatism and its legacies*, eds. W. Elliot Brownlee and Hugh Davis Graham. Lawrence: University Press of Kansas.

Congressional Budget Office. Historical Budget Data, Tables 7 and 11. Available at: http://www.cbo.gov/showdoc.cfm?index=1821&sequence=0.

Conlan, Timothy J., Margaret Tucker Wrightson, and David R. Beam. 1990. *Taxing choices: The politics of tax reform*, 96. Washington, D.C.: CQ Press.

Darman, Richard G. 1981. Meeting of Legislative Strategy Group, May 12. Craig L. Fuller Files: OA 10972, Economic/Budget Policy, May 1981. Ronald Reagan Library.

Darman, Richard G. 1982. Key (abstract) elements of program. Attachment to Legislative Study Group Agenda, December 13. Craig L. Fuller Files: OA 10972, Economic/Budget Policy. Ronald Reagan Library.

Darman, Richard G. 1982a. Legislative outlook, February 4, in "Briefing book for long-range planning meeting, Camp David, February 5." Richard G. Darman Files: CFOA 76. Ronald Reagan Library.

Darman, Richard G. 1982b. Objectives and priorities, February 4, in "Briefing book for long-range planning meeting, Camp David, February 5." Richard G. Darman Files: CFOA 76. Ronald Reagan Library.

Darman, Richard G. 1982c. Tax bill facts. Memorandum to the president, August 9. M.B. Oglesby Jr. Files: OA 8619, Tax Bill 1982. Ronald Reagan Library.

Darman, Richard G. 1983. Flat tax/Tax simplification. Memorandum for Richard B. Wirthlin, December 2. White House Office of Records Management File: FI 0101–02 [295346]. Ronald Reagan Library.

Darman, Richard G. 1984. To Mr. President, February 29. James A. Baker III Files: OA 10514, Dick Darman's File. Ronald Reagan Library.

Darman, Richard G. 1996. *Who's in control: Polar politics and the sensible center*. New York: Simon & Schuster.

Dole, Elizabeth H. 1982. Tax bill recap. Memorandum for Edwin Meese III, James A. Baker III, and Michael Deaver, July 22. Michael K. Deaver Files: OA 7621, Miscellaneous Memos/Correspondence, July 1982 to December 1982. Ronald Reagan Library.

Economic Recovery Package. folder 2 of 7. Martin Anderson Files 1981–1982, CFOA 0083. Ronald Reagan Library.

Fact sheet: The Tax Equity and Fiscal Responsibility Act of 1982. 1982. Frederick McClure Files: OA 14862, Tax Issues (3). Ronald Reagan Library.

Feldstein, Martin. 1982. Economic framework and outlook (September). White House Office of Records Management File: ID #101525, FG010–02 (101000-103999). Ronald Reagan Library.

Feldstein, Martin. 1982a. The new economic forecast. Memorandum for the president. White House Office of Records Management File: ID #111579, BE004 (111500-111999). Ronald Reagan Library.

Feldstein, Martin. 1983. Success at reducing taxes and spending. Memorandum for the president, October 13. Martin Feldstein Files: OA 9815. Ronald Reagan Library.

Feldstein, Martin. 1983a. Tax changes and recovery, November 2. Martin Feldstein Files: OA 9815. Ronald Reagan Library.

Feldstein, Martin. 1983b. Tax increases and economic recovery, October 18. James A. Baker III Files. OA 10514. Ronald Reagan Library.

Feldstein, Martin. 1984. Cut in tax rates since 1960s. Memorandum for the president, January 4. Martin Feldstein Files: OA 9815. Ronald Reagan Library.

Feldstein, Martin. 1984a. Deficit reduction package. Memorandum for the president, March 16. Martin Feldstein Files: OA 9815. Ronald Reagan Library.

Feldstein, Martin. 1984b. Deficits and inflation. Memorandum for the president, January 8. Martin Feldstein Files: OA 9815. Ronald Reagan Library.

Feldstein, Martin. 1984c. Memorandum to Jack Kemp and the president, March 28. Martin Feldstein Files: OA 9815. Ronald Reagan Library.

Feldstein, Martin. 1984d. State of the Union address. Memorandum for the president, January 20. Martin Feldstein Files: OA 9815. Ronald Reagan Library.

Feldstein, Martin. 1984e. Taking the offensive on the budget deficit. Memorandum for the president, January 2. Martin Feldstein Files: OA 9815. Ronald Reagan Library.

Feldstein, Martin. 1984f. Tax cuts since 1981. Memorandum for the president, January 3. Martin Feldstein Files: OA 9815. Ronald Reagan Library.

Feldstein, Martin. 1984g. Tax rates and tax revenue. Memorandum for the president, January 10. Martin Feldstein Files: OA 9815. Ronald Reagan Library.

Friedersdorf, Max L. 1981. Meetings with Representatives John J. Duncan, Bill Archer, and Bill Frenzel, March 27. Office of the President: Presidential Briefing Papers, CFOA 738, casefile 043366. Ronald Reagan Library.

Friedman, Milton, and Rose Friedman. 1998. *Two lucky people: Memoirs.* Chicago: The University of Chicago Press.

Fuerbringer, Jonathan. 1983. Reagan sees contingency tax plan. *New York Times.* December 13.

Gergen, David. 1981. The tax cut. Memorandum to Jim Baker, Mike Deaver, and Edwin Meese, May 18. Craig L. Fuller Files: OA 10972, Economic/Budget Policy, May 1981. Ronald Reagan Library.

Gergen, David. 1981a. Coming economic policy issues, December 4. David Gergen Files: OA 10523, Economic Policy, February 1981 to December 1981. Ronald Reagan Library.

Greenspan, Alan. 1982. Comments in "Briefing book for long-range planning meeting, Camp David, February 5." Richard G. Darman Files: CFOA 76. Ronald Reagan Library.

Greider, William. 1987. *Secrets of the temple: How the Federal Reserve runs the country.* New York: Simon and Schuster.

Hoover, Kevin D., and Steven M. Sheffrin. 1992. Causation, spending, and taxes: Sand in the sandbox or tax collector for the welfare state? *American Economic Review* 82(1) March: 225–248.

Jenkins, Jim. 1981. The true economic situation. Memorandum to Edwin Meese, November 19. Edwin S. Meese III files: OA 9944, Monthly Reports 1981 (Fuller/Jenkins/Beal). Ronald Reagan Library.

Khachigian, Kenneth. 1984. Memorandum for the president, February 27. James A. Baker III Files: OA 10514, Dick Darman's File. Ronald Reagan Library.

Kudlow, Lawrence A. 1982. Monetary discussion. Memorandum to James A. Baker III, January 30. Craig L. Fuller Files: OA 10972, Economic/Budget Policy, January 1982. Ronald Reagan Library.

Long, Russell. 1994. Tax policy. In *American economic policy in the 1980s*, ed. Martin Feldstein. Chicago: University of Chicago Press.

Martin, Cathie J. 1991. *Shifting the burden: The struggle over growth and corporate taxation.* Chicago: The University of Chicago Press.

Meese, Edwin III. 1992. *With Reagan: The inside story.* Washington, D.C.: Regnery Publishing.

Mussa, Michael. 1994. U.S. monetary policy in the 1980s. In *American economic policy in the 1980s*, ed. Martin Feldstein. Chicago: University of Chicago Press.

Poole, William, Lawrence Kudlow, Manuel Johnson, and Robert Dederick. 1982. Forecast. Memorandum for T-1, December 13. Craig L. Fuller Files: OA 10972, Economic/Budget Policy. Ronald Reagan Library.

Presidential decision memorandum: Selected tax code revisions, January 29, 1982. Craig L. Fuller Files: OA 10972, Economic/Budget Policy, January 1982. Ronald Reagan Library.

President's Economic Policy Advisory Board. 1982. Edwin S. Meese III Files: OA 9448, Economic Policy Advisory Board, March 18. Ronald Reagan Library.

Reagan, Ronald. 1983. Address before a joint session of the Congress on the State of the Union, January 25. Available at: http://www.reagan.utexas.edu/archives/speeches/1983/12583c.htm.

Reagan, Ronald. 1984. Address before a joint session of the Congress on the State of the Union, January 25. Available at: http://www.reagan.utexas.edu/archives/speeches/1984/12584c.htm.

Reagan, Ronald. 1990. *An American life: The autobiography.* New York: Simon & Schuster.

Reagan, Ronald. 2001. Economic speech—Address to the nation, February 5, 1981. In *Reagan, in his own hand*, eds. Kiron K. Skinner, Annelise Anderson, and Martin Anderson. New York: Free Press.

Reagan, Ronald. 2001a. Taxes, October 18, 1977. In *Reagan, in his own hand*, eds. Kiron K. Skinner, Annelise Anderson, and Martin Anderson. New York: Free Press.

Regan, Donald T. 1982. Proposed administration tax package. Memorandum for the president, June 22. White House Office of Records Management: FI 010-02, Income Tax, 094585PD. Ronald Reagan Library.

Regan, Donald T. 1983. Dole tax proposal. Memorandum for the Honorable James A. Baker Jr., October 17. James A. Baker III Files: OA 10514, Issues (1), Box 8. Ronald Reagan Library.

Regan, Donald T. 1988. *For the record: From Wall Street to Washington.* San Diego: Harcourt Brace Jovanovich.

Roberts, Paul Craig. 1984. *The supply-side revolution: An insider's account of policymaking in Washington.* Cambridge: Harvard University Press.

Sprinkel, Beryl. 1981. Domestic Monetary Policy. Memorandum to the Cabinet Council on Economic Affairs, March 20. Cabinet Council on Economic Affairs: Meeting Files, CCEA 23, OA 8637. Ronald Reagan Library.

Stockman, David. 1981. Stockman's comments. David Gergen Files: OA 10523, Economic Policy, February 1981–December 1981. Ronald Reagan Library.

Stockman, David. 1984. Enrolled Bill H.R. 4170. Memorandum for the president, July 11. Edwin S. Meese III Files: OA 11837, Deficit Reduction Act. Ronald Reagan Library.

Stockman, David. 1986. *The triumph of politics: How the Reagan revolution failed.* New York: Harper & Row.

Stockman, David. 1994. Budget policy. In *American economic policy in the 1980s,* ed. Martin Feldstein. Chicago: University of Chicago Press.

Steuerle, C. Eugene. 1992. *The tax decade.* Washington, D.C.: Urban Institute Press.

Text of the address by the president to the nation, August 16, 1982. Frederick McClure Files: OA 14862, Tax Issues (4). Ronald Reagan Library.

Walker, Charls. 1994. Summary of discussion: Tax policy. In *American economic policy in the 1980s,* ed. Martin Feldstein. Chicago: University of Chicago Press.

Wall Street Journal. 1981. Tax increases may be needed, Volcker warns. November 12.

Walton, Gary M., and Hugh Rockoff. 2002. *History of the American economy.* 9th ed. Stamford: Thomson Learning.

Weidenbaum, Murray L. 1981. Economic update. Memorandum for the president, September 8. Craig L. Fuller Files: OA 10972, Economic/Budget Policy, September 1981, folder 1. Ronald Reagan Library.

Weidenbaum, Murray L. 1981a. What's ahead for the economy. Memorandum for the president, July 31. Martin Anderson Files: CFOA 103, Staffing Memorandums, July 1981, folder 5. Ronald Reagan Library.

Williamson, Richard S. 1981. Tax increase issue. Memorandum to James A. Baker III, Michael K. Deaver, Edwin Meese III, Donald T. Regan, David Stockman, and Murray Weidenbaum, November 2. Craig L. Fuller Files: OA 10972, Economic/Budget Policy, November 1981. Ronald Reagan Library.

Reflections on Congressional Fiscal Policy in the 1980s

Van Doorn Ooms

"Congressional fiscal policy" may be an oxymoron, at least in the late Herb Stein's sense of "a policy that determines an appropriate size of the deficit or surplus, to which decisions about expenditures and revenues are then adapted."[1] Nevertheless, I'll use it to fit in with the landscape of this conference.

This paper reflects an attempt to organize my own thinking about several aspects of the Congress's budget efforts during recent years, but, particularly, those when I was on the staff of the Senate (1976–78) and House (1981–91) Budget Committees and the Office of Management and Budget (OMB) (1978–1981). The four topics treated are selective, and in no way are treated comprehensively, but they do touch on matters of some importance to the recent evolution of fiscal policy. I discuss:

1. the emergence of the budget as a public political battleground;
2. the Reagan program and the demise of fiscal stabilization policy;
3. the ensuing "piecemeal deficit reduction"[2] mode; and
4. the economic assumptions and baseline issues in deficit reduction.

1. The Budget as Public Political Battleground

The Congressional Budget Act of 1974, with its provision for Congressional budget resolutions and the Senate and House Budget Committees to design them, created a framework for political debate and conflict over broadly defined priorities. This framework opened the opportunity—and the potential pitfalls—of a debate on "guns and butter," as distinct from separate fights about the F-14 and the dairy support program. Budget issues, and especially taxation and military expenditures, have, no doubt, been at the heart of political controversy since time immemorial. Nor, of course, have such issues always been dealt with singularly; the Congress historically was not bashful about circumscribing presidential spending ambitions with the limitations of financing. However, the new environment did offer a framework for routinely and institutionally debating broad choices and tradeoffs, as compared with the prevailing issue-specific or bill-specific discussions.[3]

The problem, of course, is that legislation does not make choices about guns and butter, but about the F-14s and dairy support programs (and everything else in the budget), over which the budget committees had no authority. The budget resolutions could make "assumptions" about the details of tax and spending legislation, but these were given little weight by the committees of jurisdiction, unless, as was sometimes the case (especially in the House), they had been dictated by them. As a result, there developed a strong tendency for the budget committees and the House and Senate floors to become highly partisan debating forums on general economic policy during budget considerations.[4] During the 1981 markup of the House Budget Committee resolution, extended elaborations on supply-side work and saving incentives and the merits of the gold standard were provided by Representatives Phil Gramm and Jack Kemp, without evident import. Meanwhile, the substantive legislative work went forward in the relevant committees. The budget committee chairs became featured on the Sunday-morning talk shows; their tax and appropriation committee counterparts, in a quieter and less partisan manner, proceeded to divide and serve up the pie.

Notwithstanding the lack of immediate legislative impact, the budget debates tended not only to delineate and solidify party "mega-positions" on economic and fiscal policy, but also to complicate them. The long-standing Republican desire to cut taxes now had to be reconciled with the realities of Social Security and Medicare expenditure growth and the budget deficit.[5] Democrats, on the other hand, now faced the accusations of "tax and spend" more explicitly; if the programs of their constituents were to be preserved, it was harder to appeal to the tooth fairy for financing. This situation, while, on the one hand, delineating the fiscal positions of the two parties more sharply, also made the requirements for compromise at least more explicit, if no easier to meet. But budget resolutions to compromise such mega-positions often lacked enough political support to pass, so that negotiations involving the House and Senate leadership and the president were required in order to make major changes in fiscal policy, as in 1982, 1984, 1985, 1987, and 1990. Even when agreements on major changes were successfully negotiated, the slippage between "paper assumptions" and legislated policy changes was large enough to leave deficits well above the officially agreed-upon projections.[6]

In many years, this budget debate played out in a conventional scenario that greatly changed the role of the administration's budget in making fiscal policy. Prior to the Reagan era, the president's budget recommendations were used as the framework and "baseline" for the budget resolution markups. As "the budget" became the battleground for broad and deep partisan disagreement, however, the president's proposals took on more of the character of an "opening offer" in what was to be a prolonged debate. In the standard first act of this drama, the Congressional Democrats would characterize the president's budget as "dead on arrival," and the House and Senate would proceed to construct alternatives that used some variant of "current policy" as the framework for markup. The absence of a common framework, and the resulting confounding of policy differences with estimating differences, was the source of endless confusion for lawmakers. (Some of the estimating assumption issues are discussed below.)

Finally, the emergence of the budget as a central political battleground also made it the arena of choice for the display of raw political power and party discipline essential to establishing control of the policy process more generally. In 1981, the new, conservative Democratic chairman of the House Budget Committee, James Jones of Oklahoma, entered into the process with the hope of negotiating a compromise budget comprising a one-year tax cut, an accelerated defense buildup, and many of the president's proposed domestic spending cuts. It was quickly evident that this was not what the new administration had in mind. As OMB Director David Stockman later noted, the goal was a "decisive power play" that demanded "surrender" of the House Democrats.[7] The political "blitzkrieg" of spring and summer 1981, which enticed and/or frightened the southern "Boll Weevil" House Democrats into the president's camp, gave the administration effective political control of the Congress. A somewhat analogous situation arose with the new George W. Bush administration in 2001. With very narrow majorities in both houses, and lacking President Ronald Reagan's apparent electoral mandate, a new president again used a large tax cut as the instrument for displaying an impressive party discipline that enhanced his political control.[8]

2.   The Reagan Program and the Demise of Fiscal Stabilization Policy

Large and continuing structural budget deficits—and projections of such deficits for years ahead—emerged from the Reagan program in the early 1980s. This effectively led to the end of significant attempts by Congress to use the budget for countercyclical policy and into the new era of 15 years of "piecemeal deficit reduction," discussed below.

In the early years of Congressional budgeting during FY 1976–1978, the discussions and the budget resolutions themselves had a strong Keynesian flavor, even though the latter largely reflected the tax and expenditure plans of the legislating committees. Congress's recommended deficits in those years consistently exceeded those proposed by Presidents Gerald R. Ford and Jimmy Carter.[9] The macroeconomics practiced at the Congressional Budget Office (CBO) had a similar flavor, with considerable interest in a "closing the loop" macro model that emphasized the budgetary feedback effects of Keynesian multipliers. For most lawmakers, this foray onto the unfamiliar terrain of macroeconomic policy was novel and often puzzling, producing interesting variations in the pronunciation of the last name of John Maynard Keynes and his alleged doctrines. Certainly, the discussions were largely innocent of the profound developments in academic macroeconomics during the previous decade.

This mode of operation changed significantly as inflation accelerated during 1978–1980. Both the Carter administration and the Congress shifted into an anti-inflation stabilization stance, where the byword was "fiscal restraint." This was a period of deficit reduction *as* stabilization policy. That the historically high deficits and inflation during the 1970s were directly related was a simple article of faith, but one that was hardly unreasonable, given the significant monetary accommodation prior to late 1979. However, it was never explained how the relatively small fiscal changes proposed or enacted (or even feasible in the very short term) were to significantly reduce inflation. Thus, President Carter's FY 1981 budget, with a deficit of $16 billion (or 0.5 percent of GNP), was rejected by the Congress, which demanded budgetary balance.

The 1981 Reagan budget plan was certainly advertised as a critical component of anti-inflationary policy during the presidential campaign, even though monetary restraint was also a major part of the program. The radical supply-side enthusiasts claimed that large increases in productive capacity resulting from the tax cuts would bring down inflation, especially in the context of the rapid and sharp revision in inflation expectations that was to result from firm commitments to monetary restraint, domestic spending cuts, and a balanced budget by 1983. It was, as Herb Stein wrote, "the economics of joy"—low taxes, low inflation, rapid growth, high employment, and balanced budgets.[10] Just what was needed to relieve the economics of malaise.

The economic results proved disappointing to those with high supply-side expectations. There was little evidence, as the decade progressed, of the increases in labor supply, savings, investment, and growth that had been projected.[11] With respect to fiscal policy, as Stein pointed out, there *was* no fiscal policy, in the sense noted above.[12] The program reflected two very firm goals: a large tax reduction and an acceleration of the defense buildup begun in the Carter administration (with a strong push from the Congress). Domestic spending reduction was a softer and more flexible goal. Although the Congress did pass about 85 percent ($35 billion) of the administration's proposed domestic cuts for FY 1982,[13] and additional cuts were sought in succeeding budgets, the well quickly ran dry politically. David Stockman learned that attacking weak claims rather than weak clients was politically unrealistic, and the Senate stingingly rejected the administration's designs for cutting Social Security's actuarially generous early retirement benefits.[14] By FY 1985, domestic expenditures had been cut by about 1.5 percent of GNP (relative to a pre-Reagan baseline), but two-thirds of that had been consumed by rising interest costs.[15]

In the context of these goals, the budget deficit was essentially a residual, subject to the constraint that politically acceptable progress towards balance needed to be shown in the projections. (Budget balance was projected for 1983 during the campaign; for 1984 in the 1981 program; and then for later and later years, as the budget projections were overtaken by economic realities on the ground.) This constraint was satisfied by the famous "magic asterisk," which represented "additional savings to be proposed" of $160 billion during 1983–1986, and the equally famous "Rosy Scenario," which made the numbers add up by assuming three years of strong growth in output, employment, and incomes notwithstanding the Fed's severe economic restraint, strongly supported by the president.[16]

The problems of Rosy Scenario can hardly have been a surprise, except perhaps to a few ardent supply-siders in the Treasury, who soon left the administration. Certainly, both Republican and Democratic mainstream economists publicly noted the internal inconsistencies in the program before its public appearance in early 1981.[17] House Budget Committee Chairman James Jones warned of the program's "fiscal policy risks" and projected continually rising deficits that reached the then-unthinkable level of $130 billion by FY 1984.[18] But few private or public economists foresaw the magnitude of the sharp recession and disinflation that took place in late 1981 and 1982.

Table 4.1 summarizes the unhappy fate of Rosy Scenario when conventional economics caught up with radical supply-side and expectations theories:

• The Fed's monetary restraint reduced inflation more sharply and quickly than expected (or probably intended),[19] and the lower price level brought revenues far below the projections by reducing both nominal incomes and the bracket creep in the individual income tax prior to the advent of indexing in 1985. Thus, the size of the real tax cut grew, enhanced by the ornamentation added during the 1981 bidding war to secure its passage.[20]

• The disinflation simultaneously raised real spending levels for nonindexed programs and increased the real size of the defense buildup.

• Despite the sharp disinflation, fantasies about rapid revision of inflation expectations were disappointed; monetary restraint produced a sharp recession, reducing real output and incomes, notwithstanding the expansionary effects of the growing structural deficit.[21] This further

Table 4.1
1981 Projections and Subsequent Outcomes for 1984

	Projected	Actual	Percent Difference
Economics (calendar years)			
GNP ($ billions)	4,098	3,633	–11.3
Real GNP (1972$ billions)	1,711	1,639	–4.2
GNP Deflator (1972=100)	239.5	223.4	–6.7
Unemployment Rate (percent)	6.4	7.5	1.1 (points)
Interest Rate, 91-Day Treasury Bills (percent)	7.0	9.6	2.6 (points)
Budget (fiscal years, $ billions)			
Receipts	770.7	666.5	–13.5
Outlays	770.2	851.9	10.6
Deficit	0.5	–185.6	na
Debt Held by Public	868*	1,307	50.5

Note: "Projected" estimated from 1982 projected level and 1983, 1984 projected deficits in OMB (1981).
Source: OMB (1981) and Bureau of Economic Analysis, National Income and Product Accounts, March 1985.

reduced revenues and increased cyclically sensitive expenditures, such as unemployment compensation.

• Finally, the large deficits added to the stock of debt, raising expenditures for debt service as the deficit began to "feed on itself." As noted, the additional interest costs offset about two-thirds of the reductions in domestic expenditures by 1985.

Although these effects took several years to unfold completely, fears of large future deficits began to affect policy planning before the ink was dry on the tax cut enacted in August 1981. The markets (apparently also innocent of expectations theory) now reacted sharply after passage of the tax cut; long rates rose, and the stock market fell in September and October. In September, the administration was back on Capitol Hill with new proposals for spending cuts and a modest "revenue enhancement." While these were unsuccessful, they set the stage for the budget actions of 1982: the Tax Equity and Fiscal Responsibility Act of 1982 (TEFRA), which would claw back an estimated $100 billion of revenues for FY 1983–1985, and a much smaller set of expenditure reductions in a reconciliation bill. Both the administration and the Congress had now begun a 15-year journey of piecemeal deficit reduction.

The shift into deficit reduction mode was gradual, often ambivalent, and never strong enough to resolve the problem fully. It became, in effect, a policy of deficit management in fits and starts that resulted from changes in the deficit projections and the frustrations of the participants in the process. Many in the Congress would never enlist in the cause of major spending cuts or tax increases and remained largely outside the process. The administration also took time to adjust; from some officials, there was a litany of objections to deficit reduction that would resurface 20 years later:

• The fiscal program is working; economic growth will eliminate the deficit.

• Deficits don't matter (or at least don't raise interest rates).

• Deficits are desirable; they "starve the beast," ravenous for tax revenues to spend.

Nevertheless, a broad consensus was forming that large deficits should be eliminated; and this consensus hardened in 1983 when the deficit was moving towards 6 percent of GNP and the CBO projected large and rising deficits of 5.6 percent of GDP for FY 1984–1988.[22] Inflation was down sharply, but stabilization policy was no longer the name of the game.

3. Deficit Reduction Mode

The shift into deficit reduction mode was locked in place with the incorporation of income-tax indexing into the budget projections for the years after 1984.[23] In a nonindexed inflationary world, the effects of bracket creep had always produced future surpluses "on paper," leaving policymakers room for future tax cuts or spending. (In July 1981, the CBO projected that a FY 1981 $48 billion deficit would be transformed into a $209 billion surplus by 1986, a swing of 6 percentage points of GNP.) As Fullerton has noted, tax cuts were temporary prior to indexing; now, they would be permanent. In tax policy, the creation of tax expenditures would give way to a search for new revenues through base broadening.[24] Similarly, in fiscal policy, indexing meant that the easy option was gone, and the politics would turn from pleasure to pain.

The deficit became the preoccupation of Congress, almost to the point of obsession. Because it put a straitjacket not just on stabilization policy, but also on virtually all policy initiatives with budget consequences, it absorbed great time and energy and produced enormous frustration. It may also have produced some bad policy, when committees, to meet their almost-annual reconciliation bill requirements for more revenues or lower expenditures, sought to avoid major policy changes by tweaking the details of tax and pension law or by searching for new targets for user fees. And because the frustration was seldom able to surmount the political obstacles to comprehensive deficit reduction, it became manifest in the persistent quest for a "silver bullet" of budget process change, such as a balanced budget Constitutional amendment or the Gramm–Rudman–Hollings (GRH) law, that might force major deficit reduction policies on recalcitrant legislators.

Why the preoccupation with deficit reduction? While to economists it would come to signify a shift in policy focus from short-term economic stabilization to long-term resource allocation and growth, such abstractions carried little weight on the ground. For most legislators, the concern appeared to grow far more from a moral conviction that "deficits are bad" (and would have to be "paid off" by their grandchildren) than from any clear economic rationale. To the extent that economics was involved, there were multiple, and sometimes inchoate, views. The belief that deficits always cause inflation, which held sway at the beginning of the decade, weakened, as inflation fell sharply in the face of rising deficits. Some then decided, in light of the 1981–1982 experience, that deficits, working through high interest rates, cause recessions, but the ensuing strong recovery made this argument hard to sustain. (However, the proponents of GRH argued in 1985 that restrictive fiscal policy would increase economic activity, and they produced econometric model runs to "prove" it.) The emergence of the "twin deficits," with unexpectedly large dollar appreciation and negative impact on traded-goods sectors, brought some to see the deficit as a source of "deindustrialization," especially after the chairman of the Council of Economic Advisers, Martin Feldstein, emphasized the relationship among budget deficits, capital inflows, and exchange rates.[25] Finally, there were some who realized that deficits might reduce saving, capital formation, and growth, and perhaps even a few who saw this problem in the context of the baby boomers' retirement. However, at the time, this was 30 years off, an eternity in the Congressional political calculus.

In fashioning deficit-reducing budgets, the Congressional fiscal policy rule was simple. The budget resolution deficit must be no larger than that proposed by the president or, in the late 1980s when GRH was in effect, the deficit targets set in that legislation. There was to be no effective disagreement on fiscal policy writ large; all the battles were to be fought over "how to get there"—the deeply political issues of spending cuts versus tax increases and the composition of each. In some years, the regular legislative process would gridlock, and "summit negotiations" involving the Congressional leadership, and sometimes the president, would be required to agree on a new deficit target and the composition of a deficit reduction package. However, such negotiated settlements could also come to grief, as in 1985, when President Reagan "sold out" the Senate Republicans, who had produced a far-reaching budget resolution that included a freeze on Social Security cost-of-living adjustments. After first backing the Senate resolution, the president then agreed with Speaker Thomas P. O'Neill to give up the Social Security benefit reductions in exchange for a higher level of defense spending. The ensuing frustration among Senate Republicans may have fueled the drive to adopt GRH later that year.[26]

The apparent singular preoccupation with deficit reduction raises the question of whether fiscal policy was nevertheless countercyclical, as Alan Auerbach finds in his paper for this conference.[27] I find myself somewhat in the position of Moliere's Monsieur Jourdan, who belatedly discovered that he had been speaking prose.[28] Certainly, fiscal policy during the 1980s did not appear to be countercyclical from a staff perspective; neither the discussions nor decisions in designing the budget resolutions normally involved cyclical considerations.[29] However, this is not, in fact, inconsistent with Auerbach's findings. His multivariate regressions of Congressional legislative budget actions on a lagged GDP gap and a lagged (or prospective) budget surplus/deficit produce significant (but relatively small) coefficients, of the appropriate sign, on both the economic and budget variables. However, the countercyclical relationship, of course, is *conditional* upon the reaction of budget policy to the surplus/deficit. Univariate regressions show significant Congressional legislative policy changes in reaction to the budget variables, but the coefficients on the lagged GDP gap are insignificant (effectively zero) and, in fact, of the wrong sign. This suggests that Congress, in its sporadic way, consistently pursued deficit reduction, or deficit enhancement, once budget surpluses appeared in the late 1990s. However, the *intensity* of this pursuit was sensitive to the state of the economy. Budget decisions at the margin apparently "leaned against the cyclical wind," even though, in a global sense, they tended to be noncyclical or even procyclical.[30]

Deficit reduction mode effectively continued until the budget negotiations that produced the Balanced Budget and Taxpayer Relief Acts of 1997. Although this legislation produced only modest deficit reduction, by late 1997 strong economic growth that spawned unexpectedly large revenues, the 1993 tax increase, spending restraint resulting from the spending caps and pay-as-you-go rules of the 1990 Budget Enforcement Act, and political gridlock had produced projections of budget surpluses by 2002. When even stronger revenues poured in and the budget swung suddenly into near-balance or surplus in 1998–2000, the appetite for deficit reduction quickly disappeared. The Congress turned to disposing of the surplus, which it did expeditiously and effectively, first by evading its own budget rules and then by embracing another new president's large, campaign-driven tax cut in 2001.

4. Economic Assumptions and Baselines in Deficit Reduction

As noted above, the political competition within the Congress, and between the Congress and the administration, centered on the deficits projected in the president's budget and the budget resolutions. Differences in deficit projections, however, resulted both from policy differences and from differences in the economic and other assumptions on which the revenue and spending projections were constructed. The political competition on deficit reduction, therefore, spilled over from policy changes, which were politically painful, to estimating differences, which usually were not. Given the notorious unreliability of economic forecasts and the budget projections, the attraction of adopting estimates that are slightly more favorable is hardly surprising. What lawmaker would sacrifice $2.6 billion of military procurement, housing subsidies, or tax preferences in next year's budget when offered the alternative (for instance) of a 100-basis-point reduction in forecast interest rates?[31] (Such competition also spilled over into artifices such as end-of-year delays in public employee pay dates and bountiful asset sales, which are still another story.)

The practice regarding economic and budget assumptions changed, over time, in an effort to reduce the confusion caused by estimating differences and, to some degree, to reduce these competitive temptations. Originally, each budget committee had produced its own economic forecast; these had to be reconciled in the budget resolution conference, which resulted in the incongruous spectacle of lawmakers debating the intricacies of competing economic forecasts. After the bipartisan dissatisfaction with Rosy Scenario in 1981, the budget committees tried to adopt the CBO's forecast as a neutral standard. However, this was only partially successful, since differences remained between the CBO and the administration, and pressures to update or modify the CBO assumptions continued.[32] With the enactment of GRH in 1985, OMB became the arbiter of the automatic cuts provided under "sequestration." Congress then had little choice but to conform to the administration's economic forecast, which, for the first time, provided a common standard. When GRH was replaced by the 1990 Budget Enforcement Act, however, Congress moved to the CBO forecast as its standard (albeit with occasional modifications) and, with the exception of the House-passed FY 2003 resolution, this has remained standard practice. Differences between the administration and CBO forecasts remained, but such differences no longer had serious consequences for decision-making, once the era of deficit-reduction policy had passed after 1997.

Another continuing source of difficulties relates to the policy assumptions used in the CBO baseline projections. (In principle, this is not a serious issue for the president's budget, which incorporated his proposed policies. However, in practice, the expenditure estimates have often failed to reflect those policies fully, as in recent budgeting for the Iraq War.)

Although the CBO's baseline is often characterized as a "current policy" projection, in which the budget is on "automatic pilot," this characterization leaves unanswered many questions that have major political implications. Should projected annual appropriations (which cannot be on automatic pilot) be inflation adjusted? Should expiring tax provisions that have always been renewed be projected to expire? Should policies that seem virtually certain to be modified be projected to continue? In dealing with these questions, the CBO necessarily has adopted a set of rules to provide consistent treatment and avoid politically hazardous judgments. The two most important are that: (1) current law is generally used for projections of tax revenues and the expenditures authorized by "permanent" legislation, and (2) projected annual appropriations are adjusted for inflation to approximate a continuation of "real" program levels.

While these are reasonable rules, they by no means protect the baseline projections from becoming quite unrealistic representations of the fiscal future. Three problems in particular arise with respect to the budget outlook as of 2004:

1. *Discretionary Spending Requirements.* Projecting current appropriations adjusted for inflation may not provide a good indication of likely future program requirements. In particular, it appears likely that expenditures on defense and homeland security will rise faster than this, as reflected in the administration's defense program (although not fully in its budget). On the other hand, while nonsecurity-related domestic expenditures historically have increased faster than the projected baseline, the budget environment could become austere enough to slow this growth considerably.

2. *Unrealistic Baseline Policies.* As noted above, the assumption in 1981, that (nonindexed) effective individual tax rates would be allowed to rise sharply, produced very unrealistic projections of future revenues and deficits. Today's functional equivalent of this inflationary bracket creep is the individual alternative minimum tax (AMT), which is projected to ensnare one-third of individual taxpayers and raise $124 billion by 2010.[33] No one expects the AMT to survive without substantial modification, and short-term, temporary fixes have been adopted for several years. Yet, these phantom revenues have supported a tax-cutting agenda for the past four years, although the problem was well understood in 2001.

3. *Expiring Tax Provisions.* For many years, lawmakers have found it expedient to "sunset" certain tax credits and renew them later; this both inflated the revenue estimates and gave the proponents of such credits recurring opportunities to show their appreciation to legislators. However, what had been a relatively minor problem has recently become so large that it effectively undermines the projections. To evade budgetary constraints, the entire 2001 tax cut was designed to sunset at the end of 2010, and additional sunsets were incorporated in the 2002 and 2003 legislation, although the president and the Congressional leadership have supported making the tax cuts permanent. By 2013, these sunsets inflate revenues by about 2.5 percent of GDP relative to an extension of the tax cuts.[34]

These baseline policy problems are illustrated in Figure 4.7, which compares the current CBO 2004–2014 baseline (March 2004) with a modified baseline that attempts to capture the thrust of current budget policy, while using the same CBO estimating assumptions. In the modified baseline, the expiring tax cuts are extended, as proposed by the administration and the Congressional leadership; the temporary AMT relief enacted for 2004 is extended; defense expenditures and homeland security expenditures are modified to reflect the administration's defense and homeland security plans; and other domestic expenditures are assumed to keep pace with population and inflation. The difference is dramatic. Whereas the CBO baseline shows the budget close to balance by 2012–2014, the modified baseline projects deficits that rise continually (at full employment) after 2006 and reach 3.5 percent of GDP ($641 billion) by 2014.

5. Conclusion

The history of deficit reduction policy in the 1980s and 1990s naturally prompts the question of whether fiscal policy will move again in that direction. In 2001, as in 1981, a new president engineered a large tax cut that grew out of his campaign platform. In both instances, the large current and projected deficits that resulted were initially attributed to economic recession, but appeared on realistic examination to be structural, and only in part related to rising national security requirements.

However, to date, the similarities appear to end there, and the differences between the two episodes are striking. In 1980–1981, high infla-

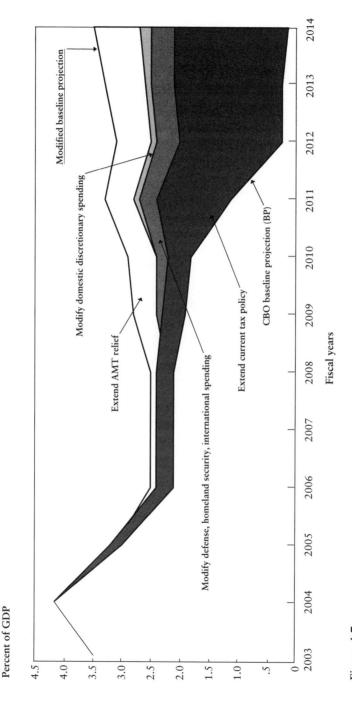

Figure 4.7
Projected federal deficit according to CBO and modified baselines as of March 2004. *Source:* Center on Budget and Policy Priorities *et al.* (2004).

tion had produced a sense of economic crisis that both motivated the new economic program and conditioned responses to it. In particular, both the markets and the administration reacted quickly in late 1981 to the "discovery" of structural deficits, and policy soon shifted to deficit reduction. In the current episode, there has been neither market nor policy reaction. The markets, perhaps captivated by extraordinarily low inflation, have appeared surprisingly indifferent to the deterioration of the fiscal outlook, especially in view of the massive financing problems known to lie ahead during the 2010–2030 demographic transition.[35] This environment has allowed the administration to appear equally indifferent to the budget outlook, firmly committed to further tax reduction, and unwilling to restrain expenditures significantly.[36]

It is uncertain whether this situation is sustainable, however. As the economy strengthens further and interest rates rise, market participants again voice concerns about future inflation. As in the mid-1980s, Congress is becoming somewhat restive in the face of projections of growing deficits, and the administration has signaled plans to restrain domestic spending in the FY 2006 budget. Only small straws in the wind at this juncture, perhaps, but a prolonged continuation of current policies seems unlikely in our present uncertain and dangerous world.

Notes

1. Stein (1994), p. 290.

2. The term is James Poterba's. See Poterba (1994), p. 250.

3. The novelty and unfamiliarity of this new framework comes through strongly in the reactions of members of the early budget committees in the mid-1970s. See Havemann (1978), especially Chapter 7.

4. The outstanding example is provided by the annual "Humphrey–Hawkins" debates during House budget resolution consideration that derived from the 1978 Humphrey–Hawkins Act. These were usually the House's most extensive and wide-ranging discussions of economic issues, but they had little apparent effect on policy.

5. It is sometimes remarked that the political parties have recently "switched positions" on budget policy. This may be true of the Republican position on budget deficits, but it is hardly the case regarding tax cuts. On the two occasions that Republicans controlled Congress prior to 1995, in 1947–48 and 1953–54, they had pushed through tax cuts against the opposition of President Truman and the "reluctance of President Eisenhower." See Stein (1994), p. 237.

6. The key consideration here was usually whether the adopted budget resolution contained significant "reconciliation instructions" that required tax and spending committees to report legislation implementing unspecified spending reductions and revenue increases outlined in the resolution.

7. See Stockman (1987), Chapter 6.

8. I say "apparent" mandate because political developments after 1981 suggest that the electorate never bought into the expenditure reductions required to make the "Reagan program" fiscally viable. But the "mandate for change"—whatever the policy—was certainly larger than suggested by Reagan's 51-percent popular vote majority, given the discomfort with the inflation of the late 1970s and his personal popularity. That no such "mandate for change" existed in 2001 makes President Bush's political success impressive.

9. See Havemann (1978), Appendix B. A detailed account of these years is provided in Schick (1980).

10. Stein (1994), Chapter 7.

11. Friedman (1992). For a somewhat more sympathetic earlier view, see Boskin (1987).

12. Stein (1994), p. 290.

13. Poterba (1994), p. 246.

14. See Stockman (1994), Chapter 7.

15. Mills (1984).

16. Office of Management and Budget (1981), Table 6.

17. See Penner (1981) and Stein (1981).

18. See House Budget Committee (1981), Section III and Jones (1981), pp. 5–12.

19. See Volcker (1994).

20. See Stockman (1987), pp. 107–108.

21. These effects were substantially mitigated by the unexpectedly large appreciation of the dollar, which reduced domestic demand for exports and import substitutes. Conventional expectations were for a larger rise in interest rates, with smaller capital inflows, and a stronger impact on construction, consumer durables, and other interest-sensitive sectors. See Frankel (1994).

22. Congressional Budget Office (1983), Summary Table 2.

23. Indexing was not part of the administration's proposal, but was added (along with a large number of other provisions) in the "bidding war" during the House and Senate tax bill debate.

24. See Fullerton (1994), especially pp. 185, 204–206.

25. See Council of Economic Advisers (1983), Chapter 3.

26. Penner (1988), p. 69.

27. Auerbach (2004), Table 3.1 (of this volume).

28. "Good Heavens! For more than forty years I have been speaking prose without knowing it." From *Le Bourgeois Gentilhomme*.

29. However, an escape clause was inserted into GRH to cancel its application during recession, and there were discussions during consideration of the Budget Enforcement Act of 1990, as the economy was entering a recession, as to whether the proposed deficit targets were too *procyclical*.

30. For those 23 observations for which the lagged GDP gap exceeded one percent of GDP, Congress took procyclical actions exceeding 0.1 percent of GDP eight times, countercyclical actions exceeding 0.1 percent of GDP five times, and "neutral" actions of less than 0.1 percent of GDP 10 times.

31. This is the 2004 tradeoff. See Congressional Budget Office (2004a), p. 105. In earlier years of lower debt levels, the effect on net interest expenditures, of course, would have been smaller.

32. The source of the economic assumptions used in budget resolutions during FY 1976–2004 is given in Congressional Research Service (2004), Appendix G.

33. Burman, Gale, and Rohaly (2003), Table 1.

34. Gale and Orzag (2003) and Center on Budget and Policy Priorities, Committee for Economic Development, Committee for a Responsible Federal Budget, and Concord Coalition (2004), backup materials.

35. See Penner (2004).

36. From FY 2001 to FY 2004 (estimated), discretionary expenditures have grown at an 11.3-percent annual rate and nondefense discretionary expenditures, excluding homeland security, at a 7.1-percent annual rate. Congressional Budget Office (2004b), Table 1-4 and Center on Budget and Policy Priorities, Committee for Economic Development, Committee for a Responsible Federal Budget, and Concord Coalition background calculations.

References

Auerbach, Alan J. 2004. American fiscal policy in the post-war era: An interpretive history. Prepared for the Federal Reserve Bank of Boston conference, The Macroeconomics of Fiscal Policy, June.

Boskin, Michael J. 1987. *Reagan and the economy: The successes, failures, and unfinished agenda*. San Francisco: ICS Press.

Bureau of Economic Analysis, National Income and Product Accounts, March 1985.

Burman, Leonard E., William G. Gale, and Jeffrey Rohaly. 2003. The AMT: Projections and problems. *Tax Notes* 100(1) July 7: 105–117.

Center on Budget and Policy Priorities, Committee for Economic Development, Committee for a Responsible Federal Budget, and Concord Coalition. 2004. The current course: Deficits "as far as the eye can see." April 20.

Congressional Budget Office. 1983. Baseline budget projections for fiscal years 1984–1988. February.

Congressional Budget Office. 2004a. The budget and economic outlook: Fiscal years 2005–2014. January.

Congressional Budget Office. 2004b. An analysis of the president's budgetary proposals for fiscal year 2005. March.

Congressional Research Service. 2004. Congressional budget resolutions: Selected statistics and information guide. February 9.

Council of Economic Advisers. 1983. The United States in the world economy: Strains on the system. In *Economic Report of the President 1983*. Washington, D.C.

Frankel, Jeffrey A. 1994. Exchange rate policy. In *American economic policy in the 1980s*, ed. Martin Feldstein. Chicago: University of Chicago Press.

Friedman, Benjamin M. 1992. Learning from the Reagan deficits. *American Economic Review* 82(2) May: 299–304.

Fullerton, Don. 1994. Tax policy. In *American economic policy in the 1980s*, ed. Martin Feldstein. Chicago: University of Chicago Press.

Gale, William G., and Peter R. Orzag. 2003. Sunsets in the tax code. *Tax Notes* 99(10) June 9: 1553–1561.

Havemann, Joel. 1978. *Congress and the budget*. Bloomington: Indiana University Press.

House Budget Committee. 1981. Report of the Committee on the Budget, U.S. House of Representatives, First Concurrent Resolution on the Budget, Fiscal Year 1982. April 16.

Jones, James R. 1981. Additional views of Hon. James R. Jones. In Report on the Second Concurrent Resolution on the Budget for Fiscal Year 1982, Committee on the Budget, U.S. House of Representatives. November 18.

Mills, Gregory B. 1984. The budget: A failure of discipline. In *The Reagan record*, eds. John L. Palmer and Isabel V. Sawhill. Washington D.C.: The Urban Institute.

Office of Management and Budget. 1981. Budget revisions for fiscal year 1982.

Penner, Rudolph G. 1981. Ronald Reagan's radical economics. *New York Times*. February 22.

Penner, Rudolph G. 1988. *Broken purse strings: Congressional budgeting, 1974 to 1988*. Washington, D.C.: Urban Institute.

Penner, Rudolph G. 2004. The financial consequences of fiscal paralysis. Urban Institute National Budget Issues 2. June.

Poterba, James M. 1994. Budget policy. In *American economic policy in the 1980s*, ed. Martin Feldstein, 235–270. Chicago: University of Chicago Press.

Schick, Allen. 1980. *Congress and money: Budgeting, spending, and taxing.* Washington, D.C.: Urban Institute Press.

Stein, Herbert. 1981. Another new economics. *AEI Economist.* April.

Stein, Herbert. 1994. *Presidential economics.* 3rd ed. Washington, D.C.: AEI Press.

Stockman, David A. 1987. *The triumph of politics.* New York: Avon Books.

Volcker, Paul A. 1994. Comment on monetary policy. In *American economic policy in the 1980s,* ed. Martin Feldstein. Chicago: University of Chicago Press.

Fiscal Policy During President Reagan's First Term

Rudolph G. Penner

Watching President Ronald Reagan operate from my perch at the Congressional Budget Office, I reached the conclusion that perhaps we need a constitutional amendment allowing only actors to run for president. He was truly remarkable. Time and time again, after his initial tax cuts were enacted, he opposed Congressional initiatives to raise taxes and trim his proposed defense increases. Time and time again, he compromised, and the Congress did raise taxes and limit his defense buildup. Time and time again, he enthusiastically declared victory regardless of what happened, and most of the public believed him.

The first budget documents of the new administration were not logically consistent. They promised huge tax cuts, a massive defense buildup, and a balanced budget in 1984, with revenues and expenditures equal to 19 percent of GDP. They also promised extremely rapid economic growth. But even that was not sufficient to bring together revenues and outlays. They had to rely on yet-unspecified spending cuts—the famous magic asterisk.

It is, of course, not that unusual to find implausible economic and fiscal assumptions in budget documents. The most unusual feature of the first Reagan budget was that it opined on monetary policy, as well. Under the influence of the monetarist Beryl Sprinkel, then undersecretary of the Treasury, the budget enunciated a target for the growth rate of the money supply. It would have taken an unprecedented surge in the velocity of money to make the assumption regarding GNP growth consistent with the monetary target.

It was easy for outside observers to argue that the Reagan goal of a balanced budget would never materialize, and soon outsiders were predicting deficits in excess of $100 billion for the first time in the nation's history. Although Reagan was much criticized for his "Rosy Scenario," outsiders have largely escaped rebuke—and I was among them—for being far too optimistic, as well. By 1983, the deficit had exceeded $200 billion.

It is hard to remember, but, early in 1981, it was far from certain that Reagan's initiatives would be passed. Rosy Scenario was much debated, and she would not have won a beauty contest. I remember believing that the proposed tax cut would be pared considerably, and that there would be a heated debate between those advocating across-the-board income-tax cuts and those favoring targeted cuts for investment and saving, such as the accelerated depreciation proposed by the president and a number of saving incentives favored by members of the Congress.

The most important event in the tax debate turned out to be the assassination attempt on President Reagan. He handled almost being killed with grace and humor, saying, "I hope that you doctors are Republicans." His popularity soared. Soon after leaving the hospital, he gave a dramatic speech to the Congress, promoting his fiscal initiatives. After that, there was no rejecting his fiscal proposals. The question was no longer how much Reagan's tax cuts would be reduced, but how much they would be expanded. The Congress did not choose between targeted and across-the-board cuts, but passed them all, paying for only a portion of the expanded package by cutting back and delaying the first-year, across-the-board cut in rates. Most dramatically, they indexed the personal rate and exemption structure for inflation, beginning in 1985. Who could have predicted that Jodie Foster would have such an important influence on tax policy?

The collapse of the economy into a 1982 trough, deeper than any since the Great Depression, combined with the legislated tax cuts to bring about an 11-percent fall in the real value of revenues between 1981 and 1983. The real economic decline in GDP was in reaction to the Federal Reserve's aggressive anti-inflation initiatives, although few predicted, at the time, that the economic cost of the Fed effort would be so significant. Reagan deserves much praise for not hassling the Fed while it put the economy through a wringer.

As the economy declined, inflation responded much more quickly than anyone had anticipated. In 1981, I contributed an article to a volume ironically called, *Shock Therapy or Gradualism? A Comparative Approach to Anti-Inflation Policies* (Penner 1981). I think it fair to say that we tried gradualism and got shock therapy by accident.

The fall in inflation had profound effects on the economy and on the budget. As people again became more confident of the real value of money, it became more attractive to hold. Therefore, the velocity of money fell, instead of rising at the rapid rate implied by the budget assumptions.

A significant part of the personal income-tax cut had been planned to counter the effects of inflation's pushing people into higher tax brackets; that is to say, to counter the real tax increase expected under constant law. When inflation fell surprisingly, the tax cut became very real. At the time, I estimated that, were it not for subsequent tax increases, revenues would have fallen to about 17 percent of GNP in 1984, as opposed to the 19 percent promised in the original budget documents.[1]

Traditional Keynesian theory would imply that the positive demand impact of the massive tax cuts should have made the recession shallower and the recovery more rapid than it would have been otherwise. Interestingly, many of the economists in the new administration were aggressively anti-Keynesian. Many were supply-siders, others were monetarists, and some were both. The supply-siders did not admit that tax cuts would have much impact on aggregate demand. They emphasized the increased economic efficiency and, thus, the economic growth resulting from cutting marginal tax rates. The supply-siders blamed the delay in enacting the tax cuts and their phased-in nature for the fact that the cuts did not make the recession shallower and the recovery more robust.

There was another theory floating around, but it did not garner much attention outside the economics profession. Mundell (1963) and Fleming (1962) had argued that, in an open economy with flexible exchange rates, a fiscal expansion would raise interest rates, attract foreign capital, appreciate the dollar, and create a trade deficit whose contractionary impact on aggregate demand would counter the expansionary thrust of fiscal policy.

In the early 1980s, the dollar did soar, and a large current account deficit emerged that moved almost in lockstep with the budget deficit. Much was written, at the time, about the twin deficits. More cautious observers argued that the deficits were not twins, but siblings, and international econometric models implied that a one-dollar increase in the budget deficit would cause an increase in the current account deficit of 50 cents or less (Helliwell 1991). As budget deficits turned to surpluses in the late 1990s and the current account deficit soared, the two deficits certainly did not appear to be twins or siblings. Indeed, they did not even appear to be distant relatives.

Of course, the two deficits are simply two important components of an identity. The most important disturbance to the economy can come from one component, say, the federal budget deficit, in one period, and from another, say, business investment, in some other period. I do not rule out the federal deficit as the main cause of the current account deficit in the early 1980s, even though the two appear unrelated later. But that is an unconfirmed conjecture. I do not think that we, as yet, fully understand how much DNA the current account and budget deficit shared in the early 1980s, but it is a vitally important question in understanding the economics of the period and the potency of fiscal policy.

It is interesting that David Stockman, a noneconomist ally of the supply-siders early in the administration, ultimately rationalized the tax cuts politically rather than economically. He was of the "starve the beast" school, arguing that the tax cuts' main effect would be to starve government of resources, thus reining in spending and government power.

The deficits of the early 1980s and those of recent years are similar in size, once corrected for inflation, and they are also similar in that we were caught by surprise in both cases. The consensus forecast of the future budget balance was far too optimistic in both 1981 and 2001.

The crucial difference between the two deficit episodes lies in the reaction of the Congress. In the early 1980s, the Congress immediately reacted to the negative surprise by undoing some of Reagan's tax cut. We had the Tax Equity and Fiscal Responsibility Act (TEFRA) in 1982; Social Security reform in 1983; and the Deficit Reduction Act (DEFRA), largely a business tax increase, in 1984. Currently, the Congress is still more interested in tax cutting than in tax raising; and the only evidence of some concern about the deficit is that discretionary appropriations, outside defense and homeland security, were quite subdued this year and are likely to be very stringent for fiscal year 2005. The other huge contrast with today is that the deficit-reducing measures in the early 1980s had to be bipartisan, because the Senate was Republican, and the House, Democratic. Strong leadership in the effort came from Senators Howard Baker, Robert Dole, and Pete Domenici in the Senate, and from Representatives Dan Rostenkowski and James Jones in the House, all of whom, except for Senator Domenici, have since departed the scene. Conservative Democrats, called "Boll Weevils," and moderate Republicans, called "Gypsy Moths," played a significant role in the process. There are not many conservative Democrats or moderate Republicans left, either.

The Congress became frustrated as we moved from 1984 to 1985. They had endured much political pain in raising taxes and in restraining nondefense spending, and, yet, the 1984 deficit still neared $200 billion and represented 4.8 percent of GDP. Their response was to pass the Gramm–Rudman–Hollings Act (GRH) in 1985. It established a declining set of targets for the deficit, and the targets were to be enforced by automatic cuts in spending, based on a complex formula.

I was very puzzled by the administration's support for GRH. It seemed evident that, if it worked, it would force Reagan to give up either a large portion of his tax cuts, his defense build-up, or both. That was evident to the Democrats, as well, and they strongly supported GRH. I first attributed administration support to the close personal friendship between Jim Miller, then Reagan's budget director, and Phil Gramm, the main designer and proponent of the bill. The real reason may have emerged as GRH neared passage. Iran Contra broke, and, I suspect, not much attention was being paid to fiscal policy at the highest levels of the administration.

In any case, the odds against GRH's working were pretty formidable. The basic problem is that, in any one year, the economy and technical factors typically have a much bigger impact on the budget balance than do legislated policy changes. Even worse, economists are not very good at predicting the effects of the economy on the budget balance. Consequently, the Congress might think that it was complying with a target, but be surprised if the deficit turned out worse than expected. When that happened, the required automatic cuts in spending or other possible deficit-reduction measures were likely to be far more painful than the political system could tolerate.

That is exactly what happened. The deficit targets had to be revised upward once in 1987 and then were abandoned altogether in 1990. President George H.W. Bush in 1990, and President Bill Clinton in 1993, negotiated major deficit reduction packages that were effectively enforced by the Budget Enforcement Act of 1990. But I shall not go into all that, since it was far beyond Reagan's first term.

To me, the most interesting aspect of the budget restraint that began in 1982 and lasted through 1997 was that the Congress essentially gave up on using countercyclical fiscal policy. The 1982 tax increase was passed long before we knew that the recession of 1982 was ending. No one much discussed the contractionary effects of Social Security reform in 1983 or DEFRA in 1984, even though the unemployment rate remained well above 7 percent. The strongly procyclical effect of GRH, if it had worked, was barely debated. The 1990 budget deal was enacted in the face of economic weakness, although it was not yet clear that we were in an actual recession; and the 1993 deal was enacted before we were completely sure that we were in a sustainable recovery.

Watching this process up close, it has become my strong view that it is not practical to pursue an active countercyclical policy and fiscal discipline at the same time. Certainly, it is theoretically possible, but it is simply too easy for a majority of legislators to argue that we are in a recession, that a recession is imminent, or that a recovery is not fast enough. Unfortunately, economic forecasts are not credible enough to knock down phony claims of economic weakness.

In the many reviews of Reagan's economic policies since his death, he is often accused of "tripling the national debt." That is clearly unfair criticism. It would have been madness to try to balance the budget in 1981 and in the years immediately following the trough of 1982. But how much excess debt can we accuse Reagan of creating?

That depends, for one thing, on whether monetary policy could have been looser if fiscal policy had been tighter. I suspect that traditional

Keynesians, monetarists, and rational expectations theorists would give different answers to that question.

My own concern, at the time, was more serious than whether stabilization policy was appropriate or whether the government was draining off too much national saving. I thought that there was some risk that things would get completely out of hand. Between 1981 and 1988, the debt rose from 25.8 percent to 40.9 percent of GDP. The interest bill rose from 2.2 percent to 3.0 percent of GDP, despite falling interest rates. One could envision the growth in the debt becoming explosive, with no other resort but to monetize. The risk of this happening may have been very, very low, but even the smallest risk of such an outcome was worrisome because of its horrendous implications.

The probability that the debt will explode is lowered greatly if the deficit can be held below the interest bill on the public debt.[2] In the mid-1980s, it was not clear whether we would achieve this goal. It was, in fact, not attained until 1989, and the deficit edged above the interest bill again in the early 1990s. It did not go below the interest bill again until 1995.

Again, it is possible to estimate the "excess" debt created by Reagan only if one is willing to define an optimum fiscal policy for the period. Robert Barro (1989) wrote during the 1980s that deficits were not far from his definition of "the optimum," in part, because inflation was reducing the real value of the debt so rapidly. If one applies a more stringent, but arbitrary, standard, and says that the cyclically adjusted deficit should have been brought below the interest bill by 1985, and the cyclically adjusted budget should have been balanced by Reagan's last complete fiscal year in 1988, about $500 billion less debt would have been created. But, then, one must ask how much blame is due Reagan for the dismal fiscal situation that he bequeathed to President George H.W. Bush and for the fiscal situation ultimately passed on to President Clinton.

In assessing the Reagan record in macroeconomics, it is important to examine some of his microeconomic actions, as well. Certainly, the firing of the air traffic controllers had a sufficient impact on Reagan's credibility and on the power of unions to have beneficial macroeconomic implications. His deregulatory efforts, though less dramatic, may have had a similar beneficial impact.

There is one area in which my view of Reagan's policy has changed with the passage of time. In the early 1980s, I felt that his defense buildup was terribly wasteful. Now, many argue that it played some role in hastening the collapse of the Soviet Union; and, even if it played only a small role, it was well worth it to eliminate the risks posed by the Cold War sooner rather than later.

Mikhail Gorbachev has argued that our buildup played a minor role, because the Soviet Union was near collapse anyway (Kaiser 2004). However, it seems reasonable to believe that the collapse was hastened, as we pushed the Soviets into spending more on defense than they would have otherwise.

But, although there are many references, in recent reviews of Reagan's record, to his desire to win the Cold War outright, I do not remember this being a large part of the argument at the time. The defense buildup was not justified because it would push a weak opponent over the edge. It was largely justified by the notion that our foe was formidable and dangerous.

If the defense buildup did contribute to the end of the Cold War, it was clearly an investment that enhanced our safety and that of our children. Was there, therefore, a rationale for financing it with debt rather than taxes? In retrospect, one might make that argument, but I think that it would have been very difficult to make at the time. In 1981, few people foresaw the quite remarkable events that would unfold at the end of the decade.

Notes

1. There have been many important revisions to economic data since I made my calculation, and it may be difficult to replicate this finding with today's version of past history.

2. This is easy to see intuitively. Suppose the average interest rate on the debt is 6 percent and the growth of the economy is 6 percent. If the deficit exactly equals the interest bill, the debt will grow by 6 percent, the same rate of growth as the economy. That is to say, the ratio of the debt to income will be stable. If the interest rate on the debt exceeds the growth rate of the economy, it is necessary

to keep the deficit below the interest bill to achieve stability in the debt-to-GDP ratio; however, over time, interest rates and economic growth rates tend to be relatively close together.

References

Barro, Robert J. 1989. The Ricardian approach to budget deficits. *Journal of Economic Perspectives* 3(2) Spring: 37–54.

Fleming, J. M. 1962. Domestic financial policies under fixed and under floating exchange rates. *IMF Staff Papers* 9 (November): 369–379.

Helliwell, John F. 1991. The fiscal deficit and the external deficit. In *The great fiscal experiment*, ed. Rudolph G. Penner. Washington, D.C.: Urban Institute.

Kaiser, Robert G. 2004. Gorbachev: We all lost the Cold War. *Washington Post.* June 11.

Mundell, Robert A. 1963. Capital mobility and stabilization under fixed and flexible exchange rates. *Canadian Journal of Economics and Political Science* 29 (November): 475–485.

Penner, Rudolph G. 1981. The impact of alternative strategies on the public sector in the United States. In *Shock therapy or gradualism? A comparative approach to anti-inflation policies*, ed. William John Fellner, 73–87. New York: Group of Thirty.

5

Government Finance in the Short and Long Run

Deficits and Debt in the Short and Long Run

Benjamin M. Friedman

The return of large-scale fiscal irresponsibility to U.S. economic policy-making has brought back to center stage a set of questions that dominated the public discussion a decade and a half ago, but then mostly faded from view during the course of the 1990s: To what extent do government budget deficits, maintained even when the economy's resources are fully employed, raise real interest rates and impair the economy's ability to undertake productive investment? To what extent do they force either the government or the private sector, or both, to borrow from abroad? What implications follow over longer periods of time, as persistent deficits accumulate into an ever-larger stock of government debt outstanding, and persistent borrowing from abroad accumulates into ever-greater net foreign indebtedness for the nation as a whole? In the meanwhile, do deficits stimulate greater real economic activity if resources are not fully employed?

Marx observed that history repeats itself, first as tragedy and then as farce. In the 1980s, President Ronald Reagan's fiscal program, combining tax cuts, increased military spending, and unwillingness to cut large-dollar federal programs in the nonmilitary sphere, led to post-war record deficits and a doubling of government indebtedness relative to the national income. The consequences included record-high real interest rates, diminished net investment in new factories and machinery, and the transformation of America internationally from a net creditor country to a net debtor. Since 2001, President George W. Bush's fiscal program, combining tax cuts, increased military spending, and increases in nonmilitary programs like farm subsidies and prescription drug benefits for the retired elderly, has already led to sizable (though not record-size) budget deficits. Whether the economic phenomena that accompanied the deficits of the Reagan era will ensue this time, as well, is the central question under debate.

At the same time, what policies might—or potentially will—narrow or even eliminate this new round of deficits is also very much a part of the national debate on this issue, although that is not the focus of this paper. The route from the Reagan deficits to the surpluses of the late 1990s involved three major changes in budget policy, first under President George H.W. Bush, then under President Bill Clinton, and then after the new Republican majority assumed control of the Congress. The process required six years, not counting the additional time for the new policies, once enacted, to have their effect. (Importantly, the process also involved active participation, albeit in different ways, by elected members of both political parties.) But this time around, six years from the present day will take the United States to the year in which the oldest members of the post-war baby boom generation become eligible for full retirement benefits under Social Security, as well as for Medicare coverage. Hence, even a repeat of what happened in the policy arena last time—if such were possible now—would be unlikely to lead to parallel consequences for the budget and the economy.

This paper begins by examining, in a longer retrospective, how persistent movements in the U.S. Government's budget posture tend to be, and whether the degree of persistence depends on what gives origin to budget deficits in the first place (tax cuts? military spending? nonmilitary programs? attempts at economic stabilization?). The paper then asks what we know, both theoretically and empirically, about the economic effects both of higher debt levels and of the deficits that produce them. The concluding section offers some thoughts on the intellectual tensions created by simultaneously knowing that a situation will not persist indefinitely and seeking to take action to end it.

1. Debt and Deficits in the Post-War Period

When the government spends more than the revenues it takes in, it must cover the overage by borrowing.[1] Each year's deficit, therefore, adds to the government's existing stock of outstanding debt. Conversely, when revenues exceed spending, the surplus allows the government to pay off rather than roll over its maturing debt, or even to buy back some of its obligations, so that the stock of outstanding debt decreases. For purposes of most economic questions, however, what matters is not the absolute dollar size of the deficit or the debt, but rather its relationship to economic quantities like national income or, in the case of a deficit, the flow of private saving. Hence, taking into account the expansion of economic activity over time must also be an important element of any analysis of the effect of government deficits and debt over time. In compact form, the essential relations are:

(1) $DEFICIT(t) = EXPENDITURES(t) - REVENUES(t)$

(2) $DEBT(t) = DEBT(t - 1) + DEFICIT(t)$

(3) $DEBT(t)/GDP(t) = [1/(1 + g)]DEBT(t - 1)/GDP(t - 1)$
$\quad + DEFICIT(t)/GDP(t)$

where g is the growth rate of the (nominal) national income.

The United States emerged from World War II with nearly $1.10 of federal debt outstanding for every dollar of the year's national income.[2] Borrowing had been extraordinary, just as the war effort had been. [By 1944, the U.S. Government had commandeered 45 percent of the entire gross domestic product (GDP), even with the services of more than 11 million uniformed military personnel, priced at Army–Navy pay scales, and those of many senior government officials, recorded at $1 per year.] But rapid income expansion in the immediate post-war years, together with a quick return to approximate budget balance, soon reduced the government's relative indebtedness. By 1956, the end-of-war debt load had been cut by half.

As Figure 5.1 shows, the post-war experience falls into three fairly distinct periods. First, until the end of the 1970s, the government continued to reduce its debt relative to the national income, not by running surpluses and buying back its bonds, but simply by keeping its annual deficits small enough so that the continuing growth of national income (as time passed, increasingly including a significant inflation component) outpaced the more modest growth in the outstanding stock of government obligations. In 1959, for example, President Dwight D. Eisenhower

Percent of GDP

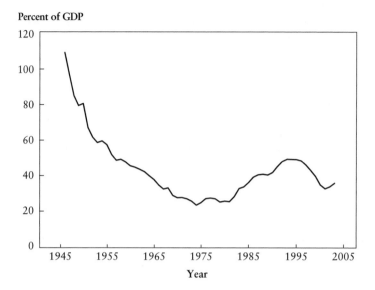

Year

Figure 5.1
Outstanding debt held by the public as a percent of GDP, 1946–2003. *Source:*
Council of Economic Advisers.

reacted to the sudden emergence of the largest-yet post-war deficit (2.6
percent of the year's GDP) with a budget retrenchment that delivered a
small surplus the following year.

In many respects, the pattern followed during these three and a half
decades was parallel to what the experience had been before World War
II, dating back to the founding of the Republic: Government borrowing
during each of the nation's wars had increased the debt-to-income ratio,
and, with minor exceptions due mostly to temporary economic downturns, the debt ratio had then declined until the next war occurred. (The
one exception that was not so minor was the depression of the 1930s.)
On the eve of the OPEC cartel's quadrupling of oil prices in 1973, the
outstanding debt was down to 24 cents' worth for every dollar of the
national income. Despite three recessions in the next eight years, at the
end of fiscal 1981 it was still below 26 cents.

The 1980s and early 1990s were different. Now, the government was
borrowing in sufficient amounts that, even in years when the economy
was strong and the nation was not at war, the debt ratio rose almost con-

tinuously. By 1993, the outstanding debt had reached 49 cents for every dollar of national income, nearly double what it had been 12 years earlier (though still not even one-third of the way back to the high point reached at the end of World War II).

Since 1993, the debt ratio has fluctuated more irregularly, declining during the years of shrinking deficits, and then actual surpluses—along with rapid, but mostly noninflationary, economic growth—in the mid and late 1990s, and, most recently, since 2001, beginning to increase once again. At the end of the government's 2003 fiscal year, the debt ratio stood at 0.36, up from the recent low of 0.33 two years before. The latest "baseline" projections by the Congressional Budget Office (CBO) indicate a debt ratio of 0.38 for the end of fiscal 2004, rising to 0.41 by the end of the decade.[3]

Figure 5.2 shows the record of annual deficits, and occasional surpluses, behind this half-century of fluctuation in the government's debt ratio—measured, once again, relative to the national income. The preponderance of deficits throughout, in contrast to the absence of any long-term upward

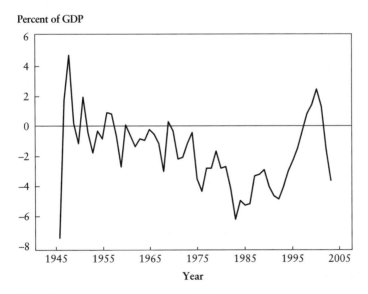

Figure 5.2
Unified federal surplus/deficit as a percent of GDP, 1946–2003. *Source:* U.S. Department of the Treasury, Office of Management and Budget, U.S. Bureau of Economic Analysis.

trend in the outstanding debt ratio, immediately reconfirms the importance, for this purpose, of the economy's growth, as indicated in equation
(3). The year-by-year pattern also reveals, more or less, the same three
distinct periods that stand out in Figure 5.1. For three decades, deficits,
though clearly outnumbering surpluses, were mostly small compared
with the national income. Moreover, when larger deficits did emerge—in
1959, or 1968, or 1971–72—they did not persist. The latter half of the
1970s marked a transition, however; and by the early 1980s, deficits had
become both persistent and far larger on average, even in relative terms.
Beginning in 1993, the deficit shrank, then gave way to a surplus, and
then returned in size (albeit not yet so large as in the 1980s and early
1990s). The largest deficit of the post-war period to date has been 6.0
percent of national income, in 1983.

Although the deficits or surpluses that the government runs clearly
reflect underlying policy decisions—most basically, the level at which to
set tax rates and how much to spend on which government activities—
part of the fluctuation shown in Figure 5.2 is merely passive. Economic
downturns depress incomes and profits, thereby reducing tax revenues.
To a lesser, but also significant, extent, recessions also boost spending,
as more workers receive unemployment compensation and some elderly
workers decide to start drawing Social Security benefits early.

As Figure 5.3 shows, however (now only for the four decades for
which the CBO calculates "standardized-budget" concepts), allowing for
the budgetary effects of stronger or weaker economic activity does not
change the overall historical experience in a major way.[4] The most sizable
changes are to the Vietnam War period in the 1960s, where the deficit
now looks larger (because the economy was over fully employed), and to
the post-OPEC years of the late 1970s and early 1980s, where the deficit
now looks smaller (because the economy was underemployed). On this
metric, the largest deficit of the post-war period has been 4.8 percent of
the national income, in 1986. The 3.4-percent deficit recorded in fiscal
2003 translates into a 2.8-percent deficit on a standardized-budget basis.
But the basic pattern—mostly small deficits or even surpluses in the early
years, then large and persistent deficits in the 1980s and early 1990s,
giving way to surpluses in the late 1990s, and then deficits again most
recently—describes the standardized-budget experience as well.

Percent of GDP

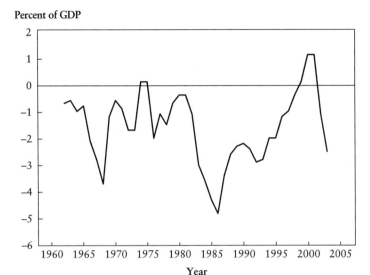

Figure 5.3
Standardized-budget surplus/deficit as a percent of potential GDP, 1962–2003. *Source:* Congressional Budget Office.

2. The Persistence of Deficits and Debt

Whether a government deficit is transitory or persistent is crucial for assessing its economic implications, and the same is true for fluctuations in debt. Especially when the economy's resources are underemployed, either tax cuts or increases in government spending plausibly stimulate overall economic activity.[5] Such was presumably the case in 2001 and 2002, just as it was during 1982 and 1983. Even at full employment, fiscal stimulus can, for a while, lead to production at levels above the economy's potential output. In time, however, active stimulus enables an economy that started out underemployed to reach full employment (under most macroeconomic theories it would do so anyway, only more slowly), and any above-potential production is presumably temporary, as well. Much of the concern frequently expressed about large deficits and rising debt levels focuses on what happens next.

Central to that concern are typically the implications of deficits and debt for capital formation and, in an open economy, for net foreign borrowing. But both of these are inherently dynamic processes. Especially in a mature industrialized economy like that of the United States, a diminished investment rate for a year or two normally has only a minimal impact on the trajectory of capital accumulation, and, hence, implies little discernible cost in terms of lower levels of productivity and diminished living standards in the long or even the medium run. Similarly, enlarged foreign borrowing, maintained for just a brief period of time, has little ultimate impact on a country's net creditor or debtor position.

Figure 5.4(a) displays the average persistence properties of U.S. Government deficits or surpluses (measured as a percentage of national income), estimated as a univariate autoregressive process, using quarterly data spanning 1959–2003.[6] The (arbitrary) value plotted for the initial quarter is the standard deviation of the estimated shock to the deficit ratio process over this sample, 0.63 percent of GDP. The outer lines indicate the two-standard-error confidence band around the estimated deficit trajectory. As inspection of Figure 5.4(a) suggests, the deficit process exhibits considerable, but clearly finite, persistence. After an initial further increase, the deficit begins to decrease a year or so later. By quarter 12, the decay back to the series mean is half complete.

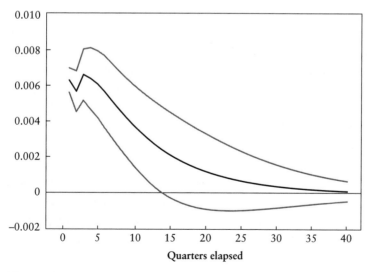

Figure 5.4(a)
Deficit persistence (univariate representation). *Source:* Author's calculations.

Also, as is apparent from the data exhibited in Figure 5.2, since the Reagan era, movements in the federal government's budget position have become not only larger in scale, but also more persistent. Figure 5.4(b) displays the results of estimating the same univariate autoregressive process, using only the post-1980 portion of the sample. Here, the standard deviation of the shock is smaller—0.54 percent of GDP—but the tendency for the deficit to build after the initial shock is both greater and longer lasting than in the full sample. The time required for the decay back to the series mean to be half complete is 17 quarters.

The process by which the deficit goes away presumably includes some combination of policy responses (raising taxes in response to a deficit, as in 1990 and 1993; reducing spending, as in 1993 and 1995; or cutting taxes in response to a surplus, as in 2001) and induced economic responses (higher national income—and, therefore, increased revenues—following from fiscal stimulus, as in the late 1960s and the early and mid-1980s). A simple univariate representation of this highly complex set of political/economic interactions not only misses the specifics of what is happening but also risks incorrectly estimating even the summary dynamics of the process. Figure 5.5, therefore, shows the analogous

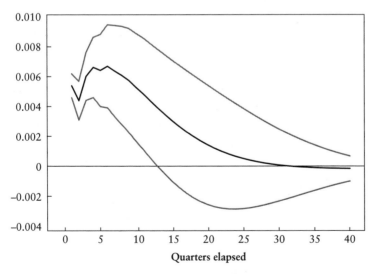

Figure 5.4(b)
Deficit persistence, post-1980. *Source:* Author's calculations.

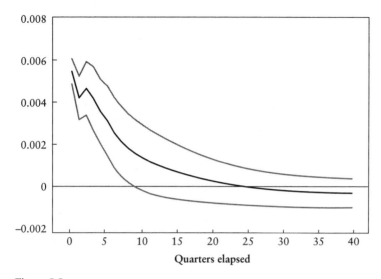

Figure 5.5
Deficit persistence (VAR representation). *Source:* Author's calculations.

representation estimated from a three-variable vector autoregression (VAR), including the growth of real output, price inflation, and the deficit ratio (ordered in that way). The more specific question being asked, therefore, is how the deficit ratio responds over time to an initial one-time "deficit shock," meaning a movement in the deficit ratio not attributable to prior movements of either output growth or inflation. Narrowing the inquiry to purely policy-originating deficit movements and explicitly allowing for the additional output growth and inflation that the deficit shock induces along the way leads to reduced estimated persistence for the deficit itself. Here, the half-life of the decay is only 7 quarters. In the post-1980 data (not plotted), it is 13 quarters.

What about debt levels? Because changes in the deficit are persistent, and deficits add to the outstanding debt, it is natural to expect debt levels (even compared with the national income) to exhibit an even greater tendency for any initial shock to build up, and, for whatever decay back to the baseline takes place, to be stretched out over a longer period of time. As Figure 5.6 shows, the univariate autoregressive representation of the debt-to-GDP ratio process exhibits just these properties. The post-shock buildup takes the debt ratio to a level more than twice as great as the

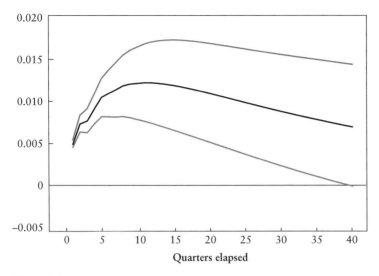

Figure 5.6
Debt-ratio persistence. *Source:* Author's calculations.

size of the initial quarter's shock, and the series returns to the level of the initial shock only after 55 quarters. The half-life of the entire response is 85 quarters. Estimating a four-variable VAR, including output growth, inflation, the deficit, and the debt ratio (in that order) leads to similar, but even more pronounced, results, shown in Figure 5.7.[7] In response to an initial "deficit shock," the debt level builds for nearly five years and returns to baseline only over a very long time period.

Even within the category of policy-originating movements, deficits (and changes in the debt ratio) arise for any number of specific reasons, and some of these initiating events may well lead to different degrees of persistence in the deficit than others. For example, a buildup in military spending, perhaps due to a war, may end after just a few years, while a new entitlement program, or some other occasion for increased government spending, may continue indefinitely. Similarly, taxes, once cut, may be politically difficult to raise.[8] Examining the univariate autoregressive representations of standardized-budget spending and revenues confirms that different elements of the federal budget exhibit different degrees of persistence. The half-life with which movements in spending disappear is 22 quarters, while the corresponding half-life for revenues is only 7

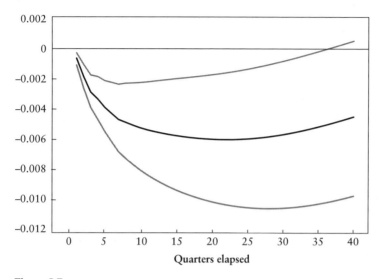

Figure 5.7
Debt-ratio response to deficit shock. *Source:* Author's calculations.

quarters. The results shown in Figures 5.2, 5.4, and 5.5 suggest that even deficits attributable to the introduction of new entitlements do not persist indefinitely, however. (The entitlement may go on forever, but, in time, increased taxes and/or cuts in other spending programs can finance it.) The relevant question is to what extent the degree of persistence in the deficit differs according to the kind of policy action from which it arises.

Table 5.1 reports the results of investigating this question through a series of four-variable VARs, including, in each case, real output growth, inflation, a specific component of the government's budget, and the deficit (in that order, and with both the budget component and the deficit measured as a ratio to GDP). The budget components included, in this one-at-a-time way, are defense spending, nondefense spending, total spending, standardized-budget spending, total revenues, and standardized-budget revenues. The question being asked, in each case, is how the deficit responds to a one-time increase in the included budget component.

As Table 5.1 shows, there are distinct (and somewhat surprising) differences in the persistence of the induced deficit across these six elements of the federal budget. The respective half-lives with which the deficit ratio returns to its baseline after a one-time shock from each of the sources

Table 5.1
Persistence of Deficits in Response to Movements in Specific Budget
Components

Budget Component	Half-Life in Quarters
Total Expenditures	9
Defense Expenditures	16
Nondefense Expenditures	3
Standardized-Budget Expenditures	9
Total Revenues	7
Standardized-Budget Revenues	7

ranges from only 3 quarters, for nondefense spending, to 16 quarters, for defense spending. The persistence of deficits resulting from changes to total spending falls in between, as does that of deficits resulting from revenue changes. (In neither case does using the CBO's standardized-budget measure make a noticeable difference for this purpose.) Hence, sustained runs of enlarged deficits, like those of the 1980s and early 1990s, presumably result not from single events, but from sustained series of policy measures, repeated or renewed over time.

Finally, what about the debt level? Consistent with the results already reported above, adding the debt ratio as a fifth variable to any of these four-variable VARs delivers a pattern not unlike that shown in Figure 5.7. When the government increases military spending, or cuts taxes, the result is—for a while—to increase the *deficit* ratio compared with what it otherwise would have been. Until the enlarged deficit has decayed back to its original baseline level, the further result is to raise the *debt* ratio, compared with what it otherwise would have been, as well. In time, the induced boost to the deficit ratio disappears. The induced higher debt ratio does so, also, but only over very long periods of time.

3. Debt Levels, Interest Rates, and Capital Formation

What matters for most considerations of public policy is not the government's debt or deficit *per se*, but the consequences that ensue for key aspects of economic activity. Throughout the post-war era, but especially during the period of sustained larger-than-average deficits and a climbing debt ratio in the 1980s and early 1990s, the central issue in this discussion has been implications for investment and, therefore, the economy's accumulation of productive capital.

The version of the link between capital formation and the government's fiscal posture that fits most naturally into standard economic theory focuses on the level of outstanding debt. Standard dynamic models of optimal wealth-holding typically imply a fixed equilibrium ratio of wealth to income. The key question, for these purposes, is whether—and, if so, to what extent—government debt is a part of that wealth. Insofar as people anticipate higher tax liabilities in the future, in order to service higher levels of government debt, those anticipated liabilities offset whatever government obligations they hold, leaving their net asset–liability position unaffected.[9] If people do not take such future tax liabilities into account, however—because their consumption-saving behavior is income constrained to begin with, or because they believe the government will be able to engineer a once-for-all increase in its debt level (that is, they perceive the debt level to be nonstationary), or simply because of limited foresight—then, in equilibrium, higher government debt levels relative to income imply a lower capital-income ratio. Presumably, the question of whether the public perceives the government's debt as a net asset need not have a zero/one answer. In fact, attempts to address the question empirically have delivered answers that virtually span the spectrum between zero and one (and, embarrassingly, sometimes lie outside that interval).[10]

If the public does perceive part or all of the government's debt as an element of its overall wealth, so that higher debt means a lower capital stock (in both cases, relative to income), then implied changes in interest rates, and asset returns more generally, are an important part of the story. It follows immediately, from the diminishing-marginal-returns property of most standard models of the role of capital in the production process, that the lower equilibrium capital-output ratio implies a higher marginal rate of return. In addition, a higher interest rate on government debt, and, therefore, a higher rate of return that investors require to hold capital, are normally central to the process whereby the economy moves from the initial capital-income ratio to the new, lower equilibrium value. In the short run, before the capital-output ratio has adjusted, the marginal product of capital is also unchanged, and so the higher required rate of return must result from a fall in the price of capital assets. With a lower price of existing capital and a higher required rate of return, investors undertake less new capital formation. In equilibrium, after the capital-output ratio has fallen (via depreciation in a steady-state economy, or merely via reduced accumulation when income is growing over time), the price of capital assets returns to the reproduction level, and the higher required rate of return corresponds to the higher marginal product.[11]

A long history of efforts to establish an empirical relationship between observed deficits and observed interest rates—the first link in this causal chain—has generated widely varying estimates.[12] One difficulty is the need to separate out the effect of the business cycle, including the response of monetary policy. (A weak economy temporarily makes both the deficit and the debt larger, and it also often leads the central bank to lower interest rates.) Another is distinguishing real versus nominal interest rates. Yet another is that, apart from short-term interest rates (which are controlled by the central bank, anyway), rates of return set in speculative asset markets are inherently forward looking, and so what matters is not the debt or deficit at the moment, but what investors expect the government's fiscal posture to be at some relevant future time.

More recently, however, research that seeks to sidestep some of these problems by relating anticipated future real interest rates to anticipated future debt levels has achieved a fairly high degree of consensus. Laubach (2003) uses the observed yield curve on U.S. Treasury obligations, together with a set of survey-based measures of inflation expectations, to infer the real 10-year interest rate implied for five years in the future, and projections made by either the CBO or the Office of Management and Budget (OMB) to measure the level of government debt outstanding (relative to national income) expected to exist five years later. A battery of regression results delivers an effect of anticipated future debt levels on expected future interest rates in the range of 2.9 to 5.3 basis points for every one percentage point on the debt ratio. Engen and Hubbard (2004) carry out a similar analysis, also using the Treasury yield curve and the CBO projections of future debt levels, and controlling for a more expansive set of further influences. Engen and Hubbard's estimated impact on implied future interest rates varies from 3.4 to 5.8 basis points for every one percentage point on the debt ratio. Moreover, as both Laubach and Engen and Hubbard argue, estimates in these (nearly identical) ranges are plausibly consistent with the standard underlying model of optimal capital accumulation, with conventional values for key parameters like the capital-income ratio and the capital coefficient in the production function.[13]

These estimated effects are large, at least in the context of the observed fluctuations in interest rates and in the government's debt ratio since World War II.[14] From 1962 (when the data on the 10-year rate begin) to the present, the nominal yield on 10-year U.S. Treasury bonds has exceeded inflation (as measured by the GDP deflator) by an average 3.3 percent. This difference, over more than four decades, is probably a reasonable approximation to the average level of real interest rates expected by investors during this period.[15] Carrying out the analogous calculation for each decade individually implies average real interest rate levels ranging from 0.7 percent in the 1970s to 5.5 percent in the 1980s. Over a period as short as a single decade, of course, actual inflation may repeatedly differ from what was expected; and so these decade-averages may not be a reliable guide to the levels of real interest rates that investors actually anticipated. In all likelihood, investors underestimated what inflation would be in the 1970s, and overestimated inflation in the 1980s, so that the respective average differences between nominal interest rates and actual inflation during these decades far overstates the range within which anticipated real interest rates vary. In any case, the point is that the range is not very wide.[16]

Compared with that range, the impact due to, for example, the increase in government debt during the Reagan–Bush I period is sizable. The outstanding debt rose from less than 26 percent of national income at the end of fiscal 1981 to more than 49 percent in 1993. At, say, four basis points per percentage point of movement in the debt ratio—in about the middle of the range estimated both by Laubach and by Engen and Hubbard—the consequence was an increase of 94 basis points in the prevailing real interest rate. The corresponding decline in real interest rates, implied by the subsequent fall in the debt ratio to the recent low of just over 33 percent at the end of fiscal 2001, was 65 basis points. (As of the end of fiscal 2003, the latest rise in the debt ratio, to just over 36 percent, implies only a 12-basis-point increase in real interest rates.)

Establishing evidence for the second link in the chain—the effect of higher interest rates in reducing capital accumulation—has remained more problematic. With reference again to the Reagan–Bush I period, measured rates of investment did decline as the debt ratio rose in the latter half of the 1980s and on into the 1990s, and they revived as the debt ratio declined in the latter half of the 1990s (more on this below). But to what extent these movements were a direct consequence of the rising and then falling debt levels, as opposed to effects associated with deficit financing, remains unclear. Further, unraveling the consequences of fiscal policy from conceptually separate influences, such as business-cycle movements, trends in foreign competition, the introduction of computers and other new technologies, changing oil prices, and so on, is a task that apparently lies beyond the scope of what the economics profession has been able to agree upon to date. Efforts to pin down empirically such parameters as the interest-elasticity of investment (or, equivalently, for this purpose, the dependence of investment on the relationship between the market price and the reproduction cost of capital) have also led to little consensus. The one point on which most research does agree, however, is that the diminishing-marginal-returns effect associated with the role of capital in the production process is sufficiently gradual—in other words, the production function has sufficiently small curvature—that equilibrium changes in returns on the scale that either Laubach or Engen and Hubbard would attach to the Reagan–Bush I debt buildup imply large changes in the economy's equilibrium capital-output ratio.

4. Is There Something Special about Deficits?

A further source of frustration, for anyone attempting to apply the lessons of economic theory to analyze how actual fiscal-policy decisions affect economic activity, is that, while the theory refers primarily to *debt levels*, the public discussion of fiscal policy mostly focuses on *deficits*. The two are related, of course, as equation (3) shows, in that whether the debt-to-income ratio rises or falls depends on the size of the deficit in relation to the existing debt level and the growth of nominal income. But, especially for a country like the United States, where the outstanding debt is already large, even a sizable deficit makes only a small difference for the debt ratio if it is sustained for only a small number of years.

One resolution of this tension is simply to assume that deficits matter only if they are large enough, and sustained long enough, to matter via changes in the debt ratio—as happened, for example, during the debt buildup of the 1980s and early 1990s. By contrast, if the implied change in the debt ratio is small, then the sequence of portfolio adjustments outlined above is minor as well, with few, if any, consequences for interest rates, asset returns, or, especially, real economic activity.

The puzzle that remains, however, is what makes this stock-oriented portfolio balance conception consistent with the requirement that patterns of economic activity also satisfy, at each point in time, the saving-investment constraint,

(4) $SAVING(t) - DEFICIT(t) = INVESTMENT(t)$.

Again, especially for an economy like that of the United States, where private saving is normally only a small share of the national income, even a short-lived deficit that is also modest compared with national income may, nonetheless, bulk large compared with saving and, therefore, require large adjustments in other key economic flows. To the extent that private saving does not adjust in step with the government deficit along the lines suggested by Barro (1974), the implication is that even deficits not associated with a significant change in the government's outstanding debt ratio imply what may be large changes in the economy's investment flows. To be sure, there is no shortage of theoretically understood market mechanisms that would bring such changes about: The most familiar are rising (real) interest rates that depress the domestic component of investment; and appreciating (real) exchange rates that increase imports relative to exports and, hence, depress net foreign investment. The question is what causes interest rates to rise, and exchange rates to appreciate, if deficits matter only by changing the stock of debt outstanding, and that change is small because the deficit is only temporary.

The experience of the U.S. economy's saving-investment balance (measured net of depreciation on each side), summarized in Table 5.2, makes

Table 5.2
Elements of the U.S. Saving-Investment Balance

Years	Federal Budget Deficit	Net Private Domestic Investment	Net Plant & Equipment Investment	Net Private Saving	Net Foreign Investment
1961–80	0.9	8.2	4.2	9.9	0.4
1981–85	3.8	7.1	4.3	10.2	−1.1
1986–90	3.1	6.5	3.2	7.9	−2.3
1991–95	3.6	4.9	2.3	7.0	−0.8
1996–2000	−0.2	7.2	3.8	5.2	−2.4

Note: Figures are percentages of gross domestic product.
Source: National Income and Product Accounts.

the question clear.[17] In the early 1980s, the federal deficit quadrupled, on average, from the level of the prior two decades. The deficit then ebbed some in the latter half of the decade, as the economy returned to full employment, but rose again in the early 1990s. In the late 1990s, the budget was in surplus, on average. Until the latter half of the 1990s, there was no indication that private saving was moving to offset changes in the federal government's fiscal posture. Instead, the private saving rate declined sharply in the late 1980s, and it declined further in the early 1990s.[18] In the late 1990s, the decline in the saving rate continued, now in the presence of a turnaround in the federal budget. (Whether to think of this latest movement as a Ricardian response, or simply a continuation of the downward trend that began well over a decade earlier, is a question outside the scope of this paper.)

In the face of deficits that were large compared with the flow of private saving—and the more so because private saving not only did not increase as the deficit widened, but also moved in the other direction—both the domestic and the net foreign components of U.S. investment declined in the latter half of the 1980s and on into the early 1990s. By the early 1990s, net private domestic investment as a share of national income had fallen by more than one-third compared with the average of the 1960s and 1970s. The decline in the plant and equipment component of domestic investment was nearly one-half. In the latter half of the decade, as deficits gave way to surpluses, the investment rate recovered almost back to the average level of the 1960s–1970s, both for private domestic investment overall and for plant and equipment. In the meanwhile, net U.S. investment abroad turned from positive in the 1960s and 1970s (as it had been ever since World War I), to negative in the 1980s and beyond. Moreover, the negative foreign investment flows were, and have remained, large, compared with domestic investment.

One answer, but only a partial answer, is that U.S. real interest rates rose and dollar exchange rates appreciated in the 1980s, because investors understood that the deficits of the time were the product, not of temporary economic weakness, as in the past, but of a new set of fiscal policies that implied large deficits for some years to come and, therefore, in time, a significantly higher debt ratio. The reason this answer is only partially satisfactory is that, if the opposite had been true—that is, if the deficit had been large but had not persisted beyond a few years, so that the increase in the debt ratio had been minimal—during those years, some other component(s) of the economy's saving-investment balance would have had to adjust anyway. In the absence of higher real interest rates and dollar exchange rates, it is not clear what market mechanism would have induced those adjustments.

An alternative conception is that, because of investors' ability to rebalance their portfolios immediately and at no cost, deficit flows matter in ways apart from the changes they create in the stock of outstanding debt. There has long been evidence that financial flows more generally have an impact, often sizable, albeit temporary, on interest rates and asset returns.[19] There is also evidence that personal income matters for consumer spending, and business cash flows matter for physical investment. In each case, it is possible to conjecture that what appears to be an effect of flow variables *per se* is merely the effect of anticipated future changes in asset or wealth stocks, and that current flows only appear to matter because they are the basis on which investors and other decision-makers form their expectations. But, in the presence of costly adjustments, or borrowing constraints, this need not be the entire explanation.

A more detailed examination of the U.S. experience with fluctuating deficits (and sometimes surpluses) further adds to the impression that deficit flows matter. Figures 5.8(a) and 5.8(b) show the year-by-year

Percent of GDP

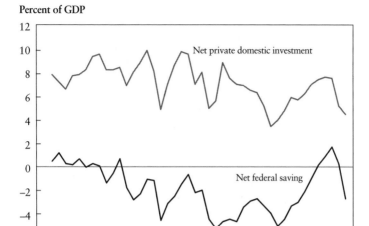

Figure 5.8(a)
Net private domestic investment and net federal saving, 1959–2002. *Source:* U.S. Bureau of Economic Analysis, National Income and Product Accounts.

Percent of GDP

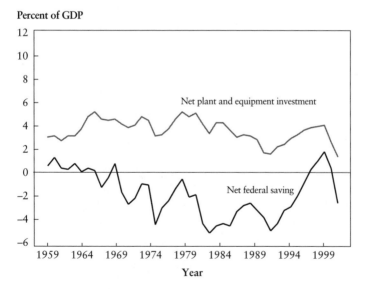

Figure 5.8(b)
Net plant and equipment investment and net federal saving, 1959–2002. *Source:* U.S. Bureau of Economic Analysis, National Income and Product Accounts.

comovements of the deficit (actually, net federal saving from the National Income and Product Accounts) with the economy's net private domestic investment and the plant and equipment component of net investment, over the last half-century, with all three flow variables measured as percentages of GDP. Net private domestic investment exhibits a substantial amount of covariation with the deficit (the simple correlation is 0.51). The covariation is smaller, but still readily visible, for net plant and equipment investment (correlation 0.31). Figure 5.9 shows the corresponding comovement of the deficit with U.S. net foreign investment. Here, the two series exhibited a substantial covariation until the late 1990s, but then moved sharply in opposite directions. (The correlation for the entire sample is just 0.15.)

In order to isolate the effect of fiscal actions on investment, holding aside the effect of economic weakness in simultaneously widening the deficit and depressing investment, Figure 5.10(a) shows the response of *gross* private domestic investment to a "deficit shock," as estimated from a four-variable VAR, including output growth, inflation, the deficit, and investment,

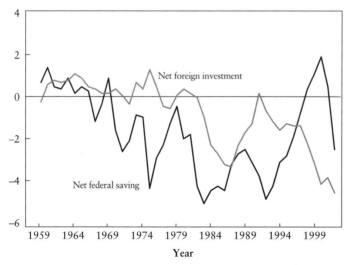

Figure 5.9
Net foreign investment and net federal saving, 1959–2002. *Source:* U.S. Bureau of Economic Analysis, National Income and Product Accounts.

Percent of GDP

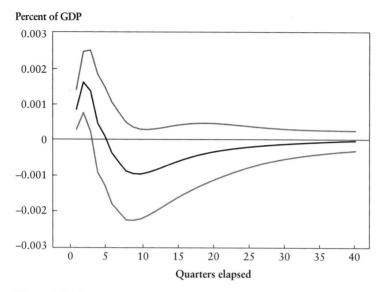

Figure 5.10(a)
Response of gross private domestic investment to deficit shock. *Source:* Author's calculations.

in that order.[20] The initial one-quarter deficit shock (actually an increase in the surplus) leads to an immediate increase in the investment rate that is statistically significant and that lasts for five quarters.[21] Interestingly, the estimated trajectory then indicates a decline, although it is not statistically significant. Figure 5.10(b) shows analogous results for a VAR with gross investment in plant and equipment. Here, the increase in investment spurred by a one-quarter deficit shock (again, actually an increase in the surplus) lasts for two years. Once again, the estimated trajectory indicates a decline thereafter, although it is not statistically significant.

In sum, the evidence appears to show that, on average, deficits do "crowd out" investment, including investment in plant and equipment, in particular. It is always possible, of course, that what appear to be consequences of deficit flows are really just consequences of changing debt stocks in disguise: Over the post-war period, deficits have been persistent—more so since the 1980s—and investors, perceiving this persistence, have reacted by moving real interest rates (and exchange rates) by enough to generate the observed response in investment flows.

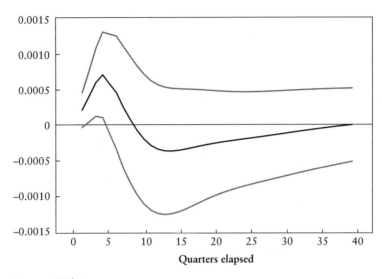

Figure 5.10(b)
Response of gross plant and equipment investment to deficit shock. *Source:*
Author's calculations.

Perhaps, if investors had not seen deficits as persistent, interest rates
would have responded in a more muted way, and investment flows would
have remained virtually unaffected. But, in that case, some other element
of the saving-investment balance—by elimination, private saving—would
have had to respond in a way quite different from the historical experience. Alternatively, to the extent that investors either cannot or simply do
not accomplish changes in their portfolio allocations without cost, financial flows also matter independently of the changes that they effect in the
corresponding asset stocks; and, in particular, the government's deficit
matters, apart from just the associated change in its debt outstanding.
The observed experience is certainly consistent with this interpretation,
as well.

5.   Concluding Remarks: The Perverse Corollary of Stein's Law

Government deficits, sustained year after year, even when the economy
is operating at full employment, reduce net capital formation and induce

foreign borrowing. Both effects accumulate over time. Both are harmful. As Table 5.2 shows, from the 1960s through the first half of the 1980s, the United States, on average, devoted 4.2 percent of its national income to net investment in plant and equipment. Since then, the average net investment rate has been just 3.0 percent.[22] Even without allowing for the induced higher output along the way, maintaining a 4.2-percent net investment rate since 1985 would have given the country approximately 16 percent more private capital today. With a capital coefficient in the production process of 1/3, that higher capital intensity would have meant a national income some 5 percent greater—roughly $500 billion per year in a $10 trillion annual economy. One can speculate endlessly about what the country would or could do with an additional $500 billion per year.

In the meanwhile, given the deficits that the government ran during much of this period, the only way the U.S. economy managed to achieve even a 3.0-percent average investment rate was by borrowing heavily from abroad—on average, an amount equal to 2.1 percent of the national income. The result has been a massive accumulation of net foreign indebtedness that is ever greater, not only in absolute dollars, but in relation to the size of the U.S. economy. The United States was a net creditor country until either 1986 or 1989, depending on whether assets and liabilities are measured at book or market values. As of year-end 2002, the country was a net debtor in the amount of either $2.4 trillion or $2.6 trillion. No one knows whether, or, if so, when, this large and growing net foreign debt position will create the conditions required for turmoil in the dollar exchange market, or, even more important, lead to an erosion of American influence in world affairs parallel to what has happened historically to prior creditor countries that have turned into net debtors.

For a while, in the latter half of the 1990s, changed fiscal policies—affecting both taxes and government spending—not only eliminated the government's deficit, but generated a surplus. That experience proved short lived. New policies, instituted beginning in 2001, rapidly returned the budget to deficit. Moreover, that deficit is already large compared with what the private sector of the U.S. economy saves—in all likelihood, the deficit will exceed 4 percent of the national income in this fiscal year—and it leads directly into the long-anticipated period when the federal government will come under even more intense fiscal pressures stemming from the changing demographic composition of the country's population. The resulting prospect is even less investment in productive capital, or yet further net accumulation of foreign debt, or both.

Oddly, the lesson many Americans seem to have drawn from the experience of the past two decades is that nothing need be done. One version of this argument is that since the country survived the Reagan–Bush I deficits with no ill effect, deficits are, therefore, harmless. This view is simply false. While the magnitudes are subject to debate—and they always will be—the reduced capital formation and buildup of net foreign debt that followed the enlarged deficits of the Reagan–Bush I period are now part of the U.S. economic-historical record.

A different version of the argument that nothing need be done, one that is impossible to address on the economic grounds alone, is what might be called "the Perverse Corollary of Stein's Law."[23] This argument acknowledges the long-run damage done by a policy of large and continuing deficits, but concludes, in effect, that nothing need be done because something will be done: In time, the Reagan–Bush I deficits "took care of themselves," and the same will happen this time. This argument has the virtue of not directly ignoring the relevant economic experience. It also appears to reflect a practical, real-politik approach to the making of economic policy. It is clearly of great appeal to opponents of tax increases, or cuts in spending, or any other changes that, if enacted, would reduce the government's budget imbalance.

This argument is (in a phrase once used by Jonathan Edwards) "almost inconceivably pernicious."[24] The Reagan–Bush I deficits did not take care of themselves, but shrank and ultimately gave way to surpluses only as a consequence of a series of visible policy actions, most prominently in 1990, 1993, and 1995. To ignore those key policy changes is to misrepresent the relevant experience no less than to ignore the reduced capital formation and increased foreign borrowing that occurred along the way. To suppose that some parallel set of policy changes will simply ensue on its own this time around is either to ignore how economic policy is made or (perversely, from the perspective of this argument) to posit some imminent crisis that will compel action by *force majeur*. Either is an invitation to continued fiscal irresponsibility.

■ *I am grateful to Susanto Basu, William Gale, and participants in the Federal Reserve Bank of Boston conference on "The Macroeconomics of Fiscal Policy," Chatham, Mass., June 14–16, 2004, for helpful comments on an earlier draft; to Richard Mansfield and Seamus Smyth for research assistance; and to the Harvard Program for Financial Research for research support.*

Notes

1. The government may also draw down any cash balances it maintains, or sell assets. In the context of the discussion here, the ability of most governments (including the U.S. Government) to avoid borrowing by drawing down cash balances is highly limited. Some governments abroad have sold assets in amounts large enough to be significant compared with ongoing budget operations, but their ability to do so is clearly limited as well. The U.S. Government has not done so in modern times.

2. The concept of debt outstanding used here (as in most discussions of this topic), "debt held by the public," treats the government as a unified entity apart from the central bank. In other words, Treasury obligations held in government accounts like the Social Security Trust Fund and the Highway Trust Fund are excluded, but obligations held by the Federal Reserve System are included.

3. Congressional Budget Office, The Budget and Economic Outlook: Fiscal Years 2005 to 2014 (January 2004).

4. The CBO's "standardized-budget" calculation takes account of not only the business cycle, but also "other adjustments," including deposit insurance, receipts from auctions of licenses to use the electromagnetic spectrum, and contributions from allied nations for Operation Desert Storm. See, for example, The Budget and Economic Outlook: Fiscal Years 2005 to 2014, Table F-13.

5. See, for example, Elmendorf and Reifschneider (2002) for an empirical investigation of these short- and medium-run effects, including, in particular, the bearing of forward-looking financial market responses (a key part of the story below in this paper). In recent years, a much larger literature has investigated the more aggregative short- and medium-run effects of fiscal policy, albeit without the explicit focus on forward-looking financial markets; see, for example, Fatás and Mihov (2001), Blanchard and Perotti (2002), Gali *et al.* (2003), Perotti (2004), and the many other papers that these authors cite.

6. The underlying autoregression includes four lags. The analogous AR(1) process looks similar, though, of course, without the "hump."

7. Because the "deficit" variable is actually the surplus, the debt ratio declines in response to a "deficit shock."

8. An interesting question that the analysis in this paper does not take up is whether tax cuts are more irreversible (in this sense of leading to greater deficit

persistence) than tax increases. Properly allowing for such asymmetries would probably require a longer data sample, including more instances of major tax increases and reductions, than what the post-war U.S. experience offers.

9. This is the position advocated by Barro, beginning in Barro (1974) and in numerous papers thereafter. There remains the possibility that augmenting people's portfolio by a combination of assets consisting of government bonds and liabilities for tax payments against future earnings leaves net wealth unchanged, but has effects on asset demand behavior, and, hence, on market-clearing interest rates and asset returns, nonetheless. See, for example, Fama and Schwert (1977).

10. For a recent survey of such results, see Elmendorf and Mankiw (1999). See also Bernheim (1987) and Seater (1993) for prior surveys.

11. This rendering of the process follows the classic account by Tobin, in a series of papers beginning with Tobin (1963), where the key variable is the required rate of return, and Tobin (1969), where the key variable is the price ratio.

12. See, for example, the estimates surveyed in Tables 1 and 2 of Gale and Orszag (2002).

13. Laubach (2003) and Engen and Hubbard (2004) also provide useful references to prior papers in this line of research.

14. They are large also in the context of familiar estimates of the rate of return on capital. Poterba (1998), for example, estimated that the pre-tax marginal product of capital employed in U.S. nonfinancial corporate business was 8.5 percent. Elmendorf and Mankiw (1999) suggest a 6-percent rate of return on aggregate capital.

15. For taxable borrowers, the average real interest rate would have been significantly smaller on an after-tax basis, and so the effects due to anticipated changes in debt levels, as estimated by Laubach (2003) and by Engen and Hubbard (2004), are even larger by comparison. With a 35-percent marginal tax rate (the current tax on corporate income for most corporations), the average nominal interest rate of 7.3 percent and inflation rate of 4.0 percent over 1962–2003 imply average real interest rates of 3.3 percent pre-tax, but only 0.7 percent post-tax.

16. As would be expected, the range of variation of real interest rates implied by survey-based expectations of inflation is much narrower. See, for example, the values for the United States plotted by Engen and Hubbard (2004) in their Figure 15.

17. The data in Table 5.2 are from the National Income and Product Accounts, and so the deficit measure does not exactly match that shown in Figure 5.2, above.

18. A substantial literature, at the time, questioned whether these movements might be consistent with the Ricardian idea, nonetheless, either because of technical mismeasurements (most prominently, the treatment of pension contributions) or because the relevant measure of saving from the Ricardian perspective includes

changes in wealth due to capital gains, which the NIPA excludes. A rough summary of that literature is that allowing for such additions would eliminate the decline in the private saving rate during this period, but would not produce an increase, as the Ricardian proposition would imply in the presence of historically outsized deficits. For purposes of this discussion, however, the point is that, even if the private sector perceives greater wealth because of capital gains, in the absence of an increased flow of saving, the flow of investment must decline.

19. See, for example, Friedman (1992).

20. Quarterly data in the National Income and Product Accounts are available for gross investment, but not for net investment.

21. It is somewhat surprising that the effect of deficits in reducing investment occurs immediately. Especially when the economy is operating below full employment, a deficit might be expected initially to "crowd in" investment, either through the traditional "accelerator" effect (including effects that operate by stimulating business cash flows) or by the kind of portfolio effects suggested in Friedman (1978), including effects operating via either interest rates or asset prices. But there is no evidence here of any such short-run "crowding in."

22. The calculation here goes through 2002. Net investment data are not yet available for 2003.

23. The late Herb Stein famously remarked that if something can't go on indefinitely, it won't.

24. Jonathan Edwards to John Erskine, 3 August 1757, in *The Works of Jonathan Edwards*, vol. 16, ed. George S. Claghorn (New Haven: Yale University Press, 1998), pp. 719–720.

References

Barro, Robert J. 1974. Are government bonds net wealth? *Journal of Political Economy* 82(6) November–December: 1095–1117.

Blanchard, Olivier, and Roberto Perotti. 2002. An empirical characterization of the dynamic effects of changes in government spending and taxes on output. *Quarterly Journal of Economics* 117(4) November: 1329–1368.

Bernheim, B. Douglas. 1987. Ricardian equivalence: An evaluation of theory and evidence. In *NBER Macroeconomics Annual*. Cambridge: MIT Press.

Congressional Budget Office. The Budget and Economic Outlook: Fiscal Years 2005 to 2014. January 2004.

Elmendorf, Douglas W., and N. Gregory Mankiw. 1999. Government debt. In *Handbook of macroeconomics*, eds. J.B. Taylor and M. Woodford, vol. 1C. Amsterdam: Elsevier Science.

Elmendorf, Douglas W., and David L. Reifschneider. 2002. Short-run effects of fiscal policy with forward-looking financial markets. *National Tax Journal* 55(3) September: 357–386.

Engen, Eric, and R. Glenn Hubbard. 2004. Federal government debt and interest rates. National Bureau of Economic Research Working Paper 10681. August.

Fama, Eugene F., and G. William Schwert. 1977. Human capital and capital market equilibrium. *Journal of Financial Economics* 4(1) January: 95–125.

Fatás, Antonio, and Ilian Mihov. 2001. The effects of fiscal policy on consumption and employment: Theory and evidence. CEPR Discussion Paper 2760.

Friedman, Benjamin M. 1978. Crowding out or crowding in? The economic consequences of financing government deficits. *Brookings Papers on Economic Activity* 3:593–641.

Friedman, Benjamin M. 1992. Debt management policy, interest rates, and economic activity. In *Does debt management matter?*, eds. Agell *et al.* Oxford: Oxford University Press.

Gale, William G., and Peter R. Orszag. 2002. The economic effects of long-term fiscal discipline. Brookings Institution Working Paper. December.

Gali, Jordi, J. David Lopez-Salido, and Javier Valles. 2003. Understanding the effects of government spending on consumption. Universitat Pompeu Fabra Working Paper.

Laubach, Thomas. 2003. New evidence on the interest rate effects of budget deficits and debt. Board of Governors of the Federal Reserve System Finance and Economics Discussion Series 2003–12.

Poterba, James M. 1998. The rate of return to corporate capital and factor shares: New estimates using revised national income accounts and capital stock data. *Carnegie–Rochester Conference Series* 48 (June): 211–246.

Perotti, Roberto. 2004. Estimating the effects of fiscal policy in OECD countries. IGIER Working Paper.

Seater, John J. 1993. Ricardian equivalence. *Journal of Economic Literature* 31(1) March: 142–190.

Tobin, James. 1963. An essay on the principles of debt management. In *Fiscal and Debt Management Policies*. Englewood Cliffs: Prentice–Hall for Commission on Money and Credit.

Tobin, James. 1969. A general equilibrium approach to monetary theory. *Journal of Money, Credit, and Banking* 1(1) February: 15–29.

Comments on Friedman's "Deficits and Debt in the Short and Long Run"

Susanto Basu

I am delighted to have a chance to discuss this very interesting paper by Ben Friedman. Actually, I shall step back a bit from the details of the paper to examine a premise that is implicit in this paper—indeed, in this whole conference. That is the assumption that deficits are bad, that no responsible fiscal policy would allow continual deficits of any size, and that sensible "mainstream" economists may soberly discuss the exact magnitude of these welfare costs, but that no one can seriously question the sign.

Let me begin by accepting the premise that expansionary fiscal policy lowers national saving, especially when the economy is near full employment. Consequently, we bequeath future generations either a smaller capital stock or a larger international debt. In either case, we reduce the consumption possibilities available in the future. The assumption I wish to examine is the general acceptance that this outcome is obviously bad. How do we know if we are leaving too little for future generations—or too much? There is nothing magical about a balanced budget; even having a zero deficit may mean that we are leaving too little for the future. Without a yardstick, we simply do not know.

Crucially, although the yardstick in question will affect economic choices, it is not, itself, a matter of economics. Generally, economics evaluates market transactions, where one thing of value is exchanged for another. But, as Joan Robinson famously asked, "What has posterity ever done for me?" We do not pass on resources to future generations as part of a market exchange, because the future never pays us back. We do so either because it gives us pleasure—in which case, we are free to reduce our gift whenever we want, if our preferences change—or because we are morally compelled to do so. To put it another way, economics evaluates policies and outcomes as more or less efficient. But—unless the U.S. economy is oversaving, which few suppose—to choose the size of the deficit is to choose among allocations that are all efficient. In order to make someone better off (future generations, if we reduce the deficit), we must make someone worse off (the current generation, which must save more and consume less). Friedman quite clearly agrees that the issue is not an economic one *per se*. For example, the paper talks not about inefficiency, but about "fiscal *irresponsibility*" (my emphasis). Friedman is even clearer on the moral dimension of this choice in his earlier book, *Day of Reckoning: The Consequences of American Economic Policy under Reagan and After* (1988, p. 3): "Americans have traditionally confronted such questions in the context of certain values, values that arise from the obligation that one generation owes to the next."

Thus, the problem that we confront in evaluating the deficit is one of intertemporal distributive justice. It is really a problem of political philosophy, not one of economics. Nevertheless, many distinguished economists have made important contributions to the field, because many of its problems can be analyzed by adapting some of the traditional tools of economics.[1] An appealing starting point is the idea of the "veil of ignorance," due to Harsanyi (1953) and Rawls (1971). As applied to intergenerational transfers, the idea is to think of an imaginary assembly of all people who have ever lived, or who will ever live, in a given society. These people agree to put aside the knowledge of their particular circumstances—their income, their own tastes, and even the time in which they live. They meet to design the rules of a just society, with the understanding that they will be bound by the constitution they devise, even after they step out from behind the veil of ignorance. Economists find this construct appealing, because it corresponds to the notion of an *ex ante* contract. Indeed, it is much like an insurance contract, which must be signed before the actual path of events is revealed.

What properties would such a contract have? Rawls argues persuasively that the social contract signed behind the veil of ignorance will have some of the properties of an insurance contract. In particular, people would agree that if they draw "a good hand" for their lives—high abilities or high inherited wealth, for example—they would consent to have some of the benefits of that good luck distributed to others who have been less fortunate. Rawls is less convincing in arguing for the "maxi-min" principle—that policies must be judged solely by the extent to which they help the *most* disadvantaged. As Arrow and others have argued, the maxi-min version appears to require that people behind the veil of ignorance have infinite risk aversion. But the basic principle stands: A just social contract is likely to require redistribution from the rich to the poor.

This principle permits a unified treatment of issues related to both intra- and intergenerational redistribution. Applied to fiscal policy at a point in time, it requires that we have net taxes on the rich and net transfers to the poor [subject to the caveats about incentives and civil liberties discussed at length in Rawls (1971)]. But there is no reason to limit the taxes to the rich alive today. After all, since economies become richer over time, the future rich will be even wealthier, on average, and we should also tax them to redistribute to the poor today. The only way to tax the future rich is to run deficits, financed by issuing bonds that will ultimately be paid off with taxes on the wealthy in the future. Thus, applied to intergenerational issues, the principle of an *ex ante* insurance contract suggests that we should, indeed, run deficits as a matter of course, so long as average income in the future is higher than average income today. (If, for some reason, people are expected to become poorer in the future, then the same reasoning dictates that we should run surpluses.) The exact magnitude of the deficits we should run will be determined by the growth rate of the economy (how much more wealth people in future generations are likely to have relative to those alive today), and by the degree of risk aversion of those behind the veil of ignorance. For example, the maxi-min principle says that we should run deficits until per-capita consumption is equalized between the current and future generations.[2]

From this perspective, the positions of both the right and the left in current U.S. politics appear inconsistent. The right implicitly favors intergenerational redistribution—by running larger deficits—but has worsened intragenerational equity by reducing net taxes on the very wealthy. The left favors intragenerational redistribution, but its anti-deficit stance makes it an opponent of intergenerational equity.[3] Sometimes, these positions can be understood in political terms. For example, the left's current emphasis on fiscal rectitude is at least partly rooted in its view that this is a way of opposing further tax cuts indirectly. However sensible this may be politically, we need not accept it on either ethical or economic grounds. There is no necessary connection between the method of raising taxes and the way in which those tax revenues are spent. We can—and the reasoning above says we should—run deficits in order to make transfers not to the rich, but to the poor.

Note that the Harsanyi–Rawls principle also suggests how fiscal policy should react to economic events. For example, an increase in the growth rate of income per capita should, *ceteris paribus*, increase the size of deficits that we run. The reason is that a higher growth rate means that the people who will live in the future are now expected to have a higher standard of living, relative to those alive today, and, thus, should be taxed more. This analysis implies that the George W. Bush deficits may be easier to justify than the Ronald Reagan deficits of a generation ago. The Bush deficits take place during a time of high productivity growth (although it is impossible to predict whether these growth rates will be sustained); while, under Reagan, the United States began running large deficits just when the productivity slowdown had become apparent.

While these remarks make a case that may be provocative, my intent is not to stress that we should run deficits of some particular size. Rather, what is important is a procedural conclusion: We need to apply the same rigorous thinking to a normative assessment of deficits that we apply when predicting their positive effects. For example, uncertainty is of great importance in the intergenerational context, since the future is never known with certainty. What does this uncertainty imply for a just national saving policy? For example, are we required to guarantee that future generations will be able to enjoy a particular agreed-upon level of consumption in every possible state of the world in the future? Or, is it enough to guarantee only an expected level of future consumption? These and similar questions still await thorough examination.

Notes

1. Kenneth Arrow, Partha Dasgupta, John Harsanyi, Edmund Phelps, and Amartya Sen are just a few of the names that come to mind.

2. "Consumption," here, needs to be understood in a broad sense. It encompasses public goods such as environmental quality and public safety, as well as private goods such as education and healthcare.

3. Like most such generalizations, this one needs qualification. Many on the left strongly favor continued large Social Security and Medicare deficits, while the Bush administration is trying to reduce the Social Security deficit even as it tries to make various deficit-enhancing tax cuts permanent.

References

Arrow, Kenneth J. 1973. Some ordinalist-utilitarian notes on Rawls's *Theory of Justice. Journal of Philosophy* 70(9): 245–263.

Friedman, Benjamin M. 1988. *Day of reckoning: The consequences of American economic policy under Reagan and after.* New York: Random House.

Harsanyi, John C. 1953. Cardinal utility in welfare economics and in the theory of risk-taking. *Journal of Political Economy* 61(5) October: 434–435.

Rawls, John. 1971. *A theory of justice.* Cambridge: Harvard University Press.

Comments on Friedman's "Deficits and Debt in the Short and Long Run"

Barry P. Bosworth

As usual, Ben Friedman has written an eminently sensible paper with which it is difficult to quarrel. The paper has three primary themes: (1) the persistence of budget deficits, (2) the economic costs of deficits, and (3) the focus on the deficit versus the debt as the appropriate measure of those costs. I would like to make a few points about each of these issues in the context of the current discussion of budget policy.

1. Deficit Persistence

I completely agree that persistence is an important issue, because many opponents of an active stabilization role for fiscal policy doubt that fiscal stimulus, such as that of 2001–2003, can be reversed in a timely fashion when circumstances change. Thus, a policy designed to counter a short-term recession may have a long-run effect of squeezing out private investment. Friedman measures this with several alternative autoregressive processes, and concludes that there has been a substantial increase in persistence after 1980: an increase in the half-life of the adjustment process from 7 months to 13 months.

We can also observe a significant shift in the politics of the budget around 1980 that is consistent with Friedman's hypothesis. Prior to 1980, the Democrats were the unvarying advocates of new programs, and the Republicans played the institutional role of stingy naysayers, arguing for fiscal prudence and a concern for budget deficits. This all changed in 1980, as the Republicans under Ronald Reagan became the cheerful gift givers, arguing that Americans deserved tax cuts. Democrats were forced onto the defensive ground of arguing that the country could not afford them. In that context, the budget deficit has come to be viewed as a political weapon that can be used to prevent the introduction of new programs and to force a scaling back of the old.

However, the outlook for persistent deficits shifted again in the years after 1995, when the projections of "large and growing deficits as far as the eye could see" changed within just a few years to promises of growing surpluses as far as the eye could see.[1] What happened? Did the politicians suddenly change and undertake policy actions to close the budgetary gap? I am afraid that the correct answer is that it was largely an accident, unanticipated by the budget projections, and not the result of policy change. Beginning in 1995, the Congressional Budget Office (CBO) began to make baseline budget projections over a 10-year horizon, based on current policy. Thus, we can actually track the CBO projection of the 2005 budget over a 10-year period. The annual revisions in the outlook are shown in Table 5.3. In addition, the CBO allocates the revisions among those that were due to legislative actions, those due to changes in the economic outlook, and those due to technical revisions in the estimates.

The cumulative effects of those revised estimates for the FY 2005 budget are shown at the bottom of Table 5.3. The most notable feature is the trivial role played by legislative changes between 1995 and 2000. Of a total change in the projected budget balance of $838 billion (from a $405 billion deficit to a $433 billion surplus), only $43 billion is recorded as the result of legislative actions. More was done in 1996–1997, when discretionary actions reduced the projected deficit by about $130 billion, but some of the restraint was offset in the runup to the 2000 election. In addition, the standard for measuring expenditure changes may be too restrictive in the eyes of some, since the Congress set a baseline of zero real growth in discretionary spending. Still, most of the improvements came from an unexpected surge in productivity growth, and a benign inflation outlook that allowed the achievement of an extraordinarily low unemployment rate. In addition, the importance of the unexpected runup of equity prices, options, and bonuses is largely captured in the technical revisions. In effect, the budget benefited from an extraordinary run of good luck, not policy change.

After 2000, the situation is much different. There has been a reversal of the prior contribution of the economic and technical revisions.

Table 5.3
Budget Projections and Changes for Fiscal Year 2005
billions of dollars

Projection Year	Initial Balance	Revisions			Revised Balance
		Legislative	Economic	Technical	
1995					−405
1996	−405	28	39	84	−254
1997	−255	95	151	85	75
1998	75	−3	65	120	256
1999	256	−11	86	47	376
2000	379	−66	55	65	433
2001	433	−197	−81	−51	103
2002	103	−64	2	−114	−73
2003	−73	−219	35	−104	−362
2004	−362	0	0	−2	−363
Changes:					
1995–2000		43	396	401	838
2000–2004		−480	−44	−271	−796

Source: Congressional Budget Office, Budget and Economic Outlook, various issues.

By 2004, the projection for FY 2005 had returned to almost exactly its value in 1995, but nearly two-thirds of the change was due to legislative actions. On the other hand, given the severity of the investment collapse in 2001 and the exhaustion of monetary measures, the tax cuts (admittedly adopted for other reasons) represent one of the best-timed fiscal stabilization actions in history. If we are to criticize them from an economic perspective, it must arise from a concern that they will not be reversed in a timely fashion in the future (persistence).

2. Economic Effects, and Deficits versus Debt

The recent empirical research, reviewed in Friedman's paper, marks a substantial methodological improvement, and I agree that a consensus on the links between deficits and interest rates has started to emerge. In recent studies, the increase in the public debt between 1981 and 1993 is estimated to have added about one percentage point to the long-term real interest rate. Actually, given the international openness of today's economy and financial markets, I am surprised that the empirical studies find economic effects as large as they do.

However, there is still a difference between those who focus on the deficit and those who link the interest rates to the stock of debt. I am more sympathetic to those arguments in Friedman's paper that emphasize the deficit over the debt as the appropriate issue of concern. The evaluation of the current debt must depend on the factors that gave rise to it. A large portion can be traced back to World War II. Other portions of the debt are a direct result of countercyclical policies at times of underutilization of resources. If there is an economic cost to such debt, it must be measured by future interest payments, not the stock. An emphasis on the stock of debt makes sense under two extremes: a small, open economy in which a portfolio model provides a reasonable framework, or an intertemporal general equilibrium model in which the interest rate is tied to the marginal product of capital (the capital-output ratio). In both cases, we have assumed away the problem of business cycles or any rationale for countercyclical fiscal policy.

However, the 2001–2003 tax cuts were, in part, a response to an inability to generate a recovery in investment and production at any positive rate of interest. In that case, it is hard to see that those years' increment to the public debt has reduced the capital stock, either now or in the future. The economic cost can only be judged in the context of the economy in which it occurs. When we integrate these past flows into a stock, we lose that context. A focus on the link between debt and interest rates must also involve political and institutional questions of the credibility of a government's commitment to repay its debt without default or monetization.

I found Friedman's Figures 5.10(a) and 5.10(b) to be eminently reasonable estimates of the *ceteris-paribus* investment costs of public-sector deficits—positive in the short term, negative over the intermediate horizon, and fading to zero in the very long run. One problem is that, as he states, the focus on cost to investment ignores the implication for the net foreign investment position. It need not make much difference whether the cost is in foregone domestic capital or greater net international debt: Net wealth is still reduced. These are the long-term costs of deficits, and they may not be well represented by a focus on the impact on interest rates.

Note

1. The CBO highlighted this reversal of fortunes with a graph on the cover of its July 2000 budget update, showing the change in the baseline projections between 1997 and 2000.

6

Is the United States Prone to "Overconsumption"?

Is the United States Prone to "Overconsumption"?

Jean-Philippe Cotis, Jonathan Coppel, and Luiz de Mello

"I can get no remedy against this consumption of the purse: borrowing only lingers and lingers it out, but the disease is incurable."
— William Shakespeare
King Henry the Fourth, Part II

1. Introduction

In 2003, U.S. national saving amounted only to 13½ percent of gross domestic product (GDP). This was the lowest rate in U.S. history since the Great Depression and also one of the weakest among OECD countries. Following a relatively brief upward trend over the mid-1990s, the saving rate started to decline during the penultimate years of the investment boom, and the decline continued during the subsequent investment slump. The weakening of national saving has been associated with a parallel shift of the external current account, with the deficit reaching 5 percent of GDP, a level widely seen as unsustainable.

In this context, commentators and policymakers outside the U.S. have become increasingly worried about a "structural" lack of saving in America, with potentially adverse consequences for capital accumulation worldwide. A major source of concern in the short run is a steep backup of long-term interest rates crowding out private investment at a premature stage of the recovery. From a longer-term perspective, too, the substantial fall of U.S. national saving is not seen as an optimal response to the acceleration in total factor productivity and potential output that the American economy has enjoyed since the mid-1990s. It is often felt that the U.S. investment boom has led to a costly diversion of foreign saving with detrimental consequences on potential growth elsewhere.

What would have been needed, instead, is a stronger contribution from U.S. domestic saving to the financing of the investment surge.

Whether these concerns are legitimate is an open question, as reflected in this session's title: "Is the United States Prone to 'Overconsumption'?" The issues, indeed, deserve a thorough examination, with a clear distinction between the past behavior of the U.S. economy and future prospects. In a nutshell, this paper will argue that *"prone to overconsumption"* is an excessively severe description of the past, but may well prove a real issue in the future.

Looking at past behavior in a purely descriptive way, it seems obvious that the United States has been consuming over and above what historical and cross-country standards would suggest. The American situation is not unique, however; and it bears many similarities to developments in the United Kingdom and other English-speaking countries, such as Canada and Australia, where either national saving or household saving has fallen to very low levels. It should also be added that these countries have in common a very robust macroeconomic performance in recent years. Their output growth has been strong, and their resilience during the past slowdown was impressive.

This common pattern of performance and behavior could be taken to suggest that falling saving rates are the desirable response in a variety of circumstances. For instance, during the past economic slowdown, falling public or private saving in English-speaking countries may have been key to stabilizing the world economy. Conversely, an overhang of precautionary savings may have proved detrimental to growth, as suggested by the lackluster performance of continental Europe.

In a world where capital has become very mobile, falling saving may also be appropriate for countries experiencing above-average growth and profitability. As foreign investors seek to share in these gains, home-country asset prices are driven up, generating substantial wealth effects and lower appetite for U.S. assets from domestic savers. In principle, this decline in domestic saving is welfare enhancing. It allows profitable portfolio diversification for foreign investors, and consumption smoothing for domestic households, without necessarily harming world capital accumulation.

With a bit of creativity, one can, therefore, find good reasons why apparent "overconsumption" was, in fact, desirable. Given the very steep fall of U.S. national saving, it may, nonetheless, be worth assessing the extent to which such a decline could be due to suboptimal public policies and "abnormal" behavior on the part of private agents, as well as what this may imply for the sustainability of output and consumption growth both in the United States and worldwide.

The objective of this chapter is to survey recent empirical work at the OECD and elsewhere that can shed some light, in a tentative and crude way, on a possible U.S. "overconsumption" problem. The chapter is organized as follows. The next section briefly reviews recent and longer-term developments in U.S. saving and considers how these compare internationally. It also addresses a number of important measurement issues. Section 3 discusses the concept of "prone to overconsumption" adopted in this paper and how it relates to the theoretical notion of optimum consumption. In Section 4, we try to identify periods of unusually high consumption, using econometric methods for *ex-post* analysis, and then assess judgmentally whether these situations represent cases of overconsumption in a normative sense. A fifth section considers the likely consequences for U.S. national saving and long-term growth of a lasting shift towards high structural public deficits. Section 6 summarizes our main conclusions.

2.   Past Saving Trends

Measurement of Saving[1]

Saving can be conceptualized as output produced in a period that is not consumed in the same period; instead, it is available for future consumption. In principle, a straightforward operational definition of saving is "income less consumption." But, in practice, saving statistics are fraught with measurement problems (see Box 6.1). These relate to the measurement of income, the classification of expenditures between consumption and investment, and the allocation of saving among households, businesses, and government sectors.

Not only do the effects of these measurement problems show up at the aggregate level, where the effects can be significant,[2] but also, sometimes more importantly, they influence the sector composition of saving. The household saving rate, for instance, is biased by revaluation effects due to inflation, by the partial treatment of capital gains in personal income, and by the treatment of unincorporated companies. Focusing on the level of saving in one or another sector is, thus, likely to be misleading.

Statistical uncertainties surrounding the measurement of saving may be less pervasive, however, when it comes to assessing long-term trends. Such a possibility is suggested, for instance, by Gale and Sabelhaus (1999) in the U.S. case. The authors adjust saving statistics for the classification of consumer durables in investment, the inflation tax, and the treatment of saving in government retirement plans and other federal social insurance trust funds. They find that, except for the inflation tax, adjustments to total private saving remain broadly constant over time, thus adding to the level, but not changing the profile of saving.[3] The adjustment for the inflation tax has fallen markedly, however, over the past few decades, moving from –2 percent of GDP during the 1970s, to –0.3 percent of GDP only in the late 1990s.

In sum, on the basis of U.S. experience, it appears that focusing on the level of private saving is potentially misleading, but the broad trends in private saving rates, as measured in the SNA, are probably more reliable.[4] Indeed, in the United States, the fall of the national accounts saving measure over the period reflected, to a large extent, a fall of the "true saving rate" alongside an easily identifiable decrease in the inflation tax,[5] while other adjustment factors played a relatively minor part.

Trends in Saving

Bearing in mind measurement caveats, historical trends in U.S. saving by sector relative to GDP are shown in Figure 6.1. The key features to observe, abstracting from cyclical variations, include the following:

• The household saving rate was broadly steady through the 1960s and 1970s. However, since the early 1980s, it has exhibited a downward trend, falling by the equivalent of some 7 percentage points of GDP to reach 3 percent of GDP, an historical low.

• In contrast, corporate saving, which is closely related to profit developments, has remained essentially constant relative to GDP over the past four decades, averaging about 11 percent.

• Trends in private saving, therefore, have mirrored those of households. Moreover, the private-sector saving rate is more stable than its household and corporate components. This seems to suggest that households pierce the "corporate veil," although empirical work usually indicates offsets are incomplete.[6]

Percent of GDP

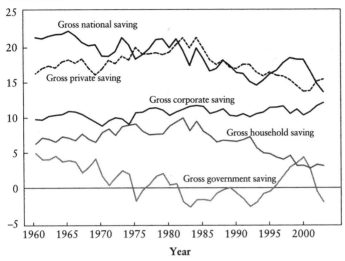

Figure 6.1
Historical trends in U.S. saving rates. *Source:* U.S. Bureau of Economic Analysis.

• Movements in the public saving rate have frequently coincided with opposite changes in the private saving rate. Thus, the national saving rate has tended to be more stable than either of its components, although it has declined somewhat over the past three decades.

• Measures of gross saving have fallen by less than net measures (not shown in Figure 6.1), in line with the shift in the composition of capital towards information, communications, and technology (ICT) equipment, which has a higher depreciation rate.[7]

Certain features of trends in U.S. saving are equally evident in other countries. For instance, changes in fiscal stance have often taken place concomitantly with opposite comovements in private saving, thus smoothing fluctuations in national saving (Figure 6.2), as discussed further in Section 5, below.[8] A decline in domestic saving has also been evident in Japan, France, and Italy over the past three decades, although the initial rate of saving in these countries was higher. And household saving rates have dropped considerably in most G-7 countries. There are also important differences among OECD countries. The German and Canadian national saving rates have been remarkably stable, while developments in

Percent

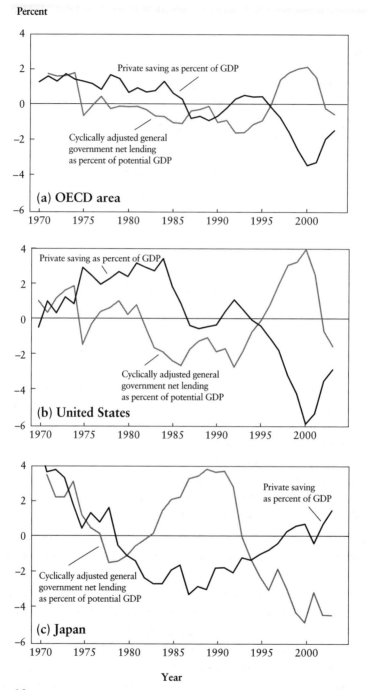

Figure 6.2
Private and public saving: Deviations from averages. *Source:* OECD Economic Outlook No. 76, December 2004.

Percent

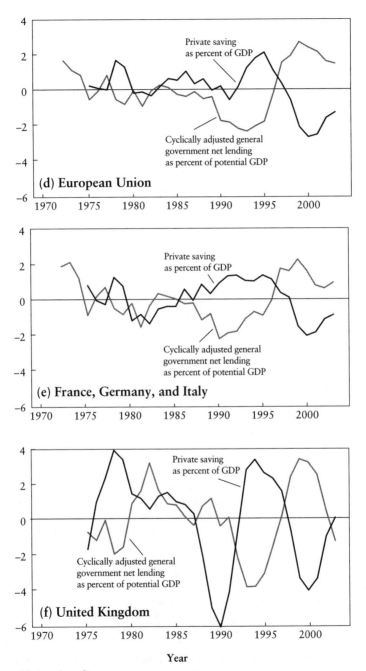

Figure 6.2 (continued)
Private and public saving: Deviations from averages. *Source:* OECD Economic
Outlook No. 76, December 2004.

Box 6.1
Some issues in measuring saving in the national accounts

The economic definition of saving differs from the one followed in the System of National Accounts (SNA). The SNA treats as income only those revenues that are generated from the current production flow, ignoring revaluation effects on the stock of wealth. Thus, for instance, when capital gains are realized, they are not included in personal income, even though taxes paid on them are fully deducted from income. This implies a shift of income, and, therefore, saving, from the household to the public sector.

A period of sustained capital gains can also lead to an artificial shift of saving from the household to the corporate sector, because of the treatment of saving through defined-benefit pension plans. Under such schemes, capital gains may enable employers to reduce their direct contributions to employee pension funds, while keeping the system fully funded. In this case, since employers' contributions are counted as "other" labor income, measured wages and salaries decline, even though the benefits to beneficiaries, and, hence, consumption plans, remain unchanged. Likewise, revaluation effects due to inflation cause a downward bias in the measure of household saving, since nominal interest payments are included fully as a component of current income, but the erosion of the real value of monetary assets and gains on debt are not.

The measurement of saving also depends on how certain expenditure items are classified. By convention, spending on education and on R&D funded by the public sector are treated as consumption, although, from an economic point of view, they could be considered as investment, given the fact that they contribute to raising future levels of potential output. It could also be argued that the purchase of a durable good by households should be treated as investment, as is currently the practice when the buyer is a firm.

The methodological difficulties in measuring saving are most evident at the sectoral level. Apart from the measurement problems already mentioned, this is due to the inconsistent treatment of like transactions across sectors and, more generally, to the arbitrary boundary between household and corporate saving. For example, although dividends and corporate repurchases both involve shifting funds from the corporate to the household sector, they have different effects on the sectoral composition of private saving. The trend in corporate finance away from dividend payments towards capital gains exerts downward pressure on the measured household saving rate. Similarly, incorporations of unincorporated companies result in shifting saving from the household to the corporate sector. Another example is the treatment of saving in pension plans. Transactions between households and government social security systems are considered as current, while those with private schemes are treated as capital transactions. The rationale for this difference reflects the view that households generally regard contributions to private pension schemes as financial investment, but consider social security contributions as being of the same nature as income taxes.

corporate saving rates have been diverse, rising in some countries and falling in others. Overall, however, the U.S. domestic saving rate is lower than that of all the other G-7 countries except the United Kingdom.

3. Conceptual Clarifications and Approach Adopted in the Chapter

"Overconsumption" is obviously a normative issue, whereas most empirical evidence is based on positive analysis. To bridge that gap, this section aims to clarify what could be meant by "prone to overconsumption" and how to use existing empirical studies to glean normative insights on this issue.

"Prone to Overconsumption": Some Conceptual Clarifications

"Overconsumption"
A highly normative notion such as overconsumption is intuitive, yet hard to pin down in practice. It refers to a situation where consumption is too high to be consistent with the maximization of consumers' welfare over the long term, leading to unduly low consumption in the future. Beyond this general definition, the challenge is to clarify, at least in broad terms, what lies behind the words "optimal consumption" or "optimal saving."

Maximizing the expected utility of consumption over time confers two major roles on saving: providing appropriate capital accumulation to prepare for future consumption and allocating consumption in a welfare-improving way over the life cycle. As a result, the optimal path of consumption should be as high and as smooth as possible. In the steady state, this would imply that consumption, as well as output and capital, would grow at the natural rate, defined as the sum of technical progress and the growth rate of the labor force.

The path for optimal consumption will, of course, deviate from the steady state when the economy is disturbed by shocks to technical progress and demographic growth, shifts in time preferences, or cyclical fluctuations. These disturbances will affect optimal consumption in sometimes conflicting ways. For instance, a positive shock to technical progress, which is obviously highly topical in the U.S. case, will call for an increase in optimal saving so as to stabilize the capital-to-efficient-labor ratio, but also for an offsetting reallocation of consumption towards the present to avoid "excessive" consumption in the future.

It is also important to determine what categories of agents should be involved in the optimization process. There are "natural" moral reasons to ensure maximum welfare for future generations. In the end, future consumption involves future consumers, not yet born, whose incomes will depend on the inherited capital stock. Nonetheless, taking a view about optimal consumption is impossible without deciding on the desirable degree of intergenerational altruism, with strong implications for fiscal policy, should the benevolent social planner discount the welfare of future generations differently than current generations do. In this respect, what would be very objectionable for an altruistic social planner[9] is a situation combining persistently large public deficits and continually deteriorating public net wealth—including unfunded liabilities—with limited intergenerational altruism on the household side.

In a context of high international mobility of capital, optimal consumption and saving also need to be cast in a worldwide framework. Although capital mobility does not really matter if all regions of the world share identical experiences, it matters much more with idiosyncratic developments in one region. A negative idiosyncrasy could materialize in the United States under the guise of persistently large public deficits, with possible adverse consequences for long-term world capital accumulation. Positive idiosyncrasies are also possible. The best recent example of such an idiosyncrasy is the rapid productivity growth and the steep fall in the relative price of ICT capital that the United States experienced over the past decade. Passing judgment on how well the U.S. economy reacted to this positive shock is obviously very important for this discussion.

Moving from a closed-economy to an open-economy framework makes the task much easier. Indeed, viewed in the context of a closed-economy framework, the way the U.S. economy departed from a well-behaved Solovian steady state seems rather paradoxical. What is puzzling in a closed-economy context is that both capital accumulation and the expansion of consumption have outpaced the natural Solovian output growth by such a wide margin (Figure 6.3).[10] Looking at consumption in isolation, it is tempting to prognosticate a blatant case of "overconsumption." But, then, how can we explain such an exuberant capital path?[11]

Explanations for this, in a closed-economy context, all seem unlikely. One could assume, for instance, that the steep fall in the relative price of capital observed in the United States could have induced both capital deepening and consumption growth above the natural rate, provided some special conditions were met. It would have been the case, for instance, if the fall in the price of capital elicited a modest increase in the volume of investment, thus freeing purchasing power for additional consumption.[12] However, would such a modest investment response have been enough to engineer the sort of exuberant capital deepening that the

Index 1995 = 1

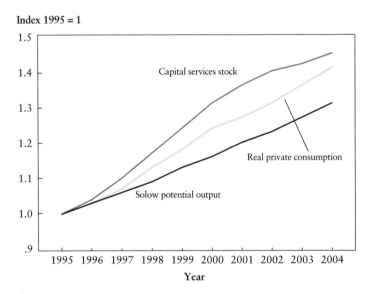

Figure 6.3
Solow potential output for the United States. *Source:* Organisation for Economic Co–operation and Development.
Note: Capital services data are extended after 2002 with the growth rates for overall business capital stock.

U.S. economy experienced? Alternatively, one could invoke wealth effects arising from higher technical progress to justify a declining saving ratio. But which domestic agents would have financed private-sector physical capital accumulation in the meantime?

If this scenario of very strong consumption growth and capital over-accumulation is an unlikely outcome in a closed economy, it is easily conceivable in an open-economy context. If, indeed, technical progress in one region is strong relative to the rest of the world, foreign savings should spontaneously tend to displace domestic savings and to increase the capital stock until the marginal product of capital is equalized world-wide. In the process, the price of capital relative to its price in the rest of the world should increase in the high-growth region, generating positive wealth effects and a higher optimal consumption path. Since it increases incomes in both regions, the new equilibrium should be welfare enhancing, providing it is not founded on mistakenly optimistic relative-return expectations.

Looking, therefore, at stylized facts, the case for overconsumption in the United States during the late 1990s is not at all straightforward, and it could just as well be said that other regions, such as Europe, suffered from excess savings. A more formal and thorough analysis may, therefore, be needed to deal more decisively with this issue.

"Prone" to Overconsumption

Being prone to overconsumption is understood here as a situation in which the economy, although not overconsuming when on its steady-state path, tends to play an amplifying role or a less-than-adequate smoothing role in the face of certain types of shocks, either cyclical or longer lasting. To illustrate this general statement, one could think of two arbitrary, but topical issues:

• From a cyclical perspective, "prone to overconsumption" may be seen as a tendency for household consumption to play a procyclical role during upswings.

• From a longer-run angle and looking at national savings, it may take the form of a difficulty in offsetting a lasting shift into larger public deficits through a significant increase in private saving.

The Approach Adopted: Empirical Analysis with Rough Notions of Optimal Consumption

What would be needed, ideally, to address overconsumption issues is an ambitious optimization exercise, using calibrated general equilibrium models to confront calculated paths of optimal consumption with reality. This exercise would obviously involve all areas of public policies to optimize consumption and output jointly. It might then be possible to pinpoint spells of overconsumption[13] and explain their putative existence by various types of imperfections: suboptimal regulatory, tax, and fiscal policies; market imperfections; or forecasting errors.

Despite its obvious attractiveness, this demiurgic program unfortunately goes well beyond the capacities of simple OECD mortals, and this paper has more modest ambitions. Rather, in this paper, we will confine ourselves to saving behavior. We first adopt a U.S. historical perspective, trying to identify, *ex post*, periods of unusually high consumption, using econometric analysis, and trying to assess judgmentally whether these situations represent cases of overconsumption in a normative sense. This approach is based on the notion that a long-run stable behavioral relationship, reasonably similar to what is observed abroad, is presumed to be optimal, and that departures from it may be suboptimal. We then switch to an *ex-ante*, forward-looking approach, trying to assess whether the projected path of persistently high U.S. budget deficits would be acceptable for an altruistic social planner. To this end, using a variety of econometric panel data models, we try to assess the propensity of households to generate private saving in response to public dis-saving, or *vice versa*. Although such offsetting movements in private and public saving can only be suggestive of households' altruism, their absence should make the social planner (policymaker) all the more cautious about the possible consequences of persistent public deficits.

4. Has U.S. Household Consumption Overshot Since the Late 1990s?

It was previously mentioned that saving had a role to play, both in providing for appropriate capital accumulation and in allocating consumption over time.[14] In this section, we focus on the efficiency of saving as a mechanism to allocate consumption in a welfare-improving way over the life cycle, knowing that the U.S. economy has not yet shown obvious signs of suffering from inadequate capital accumulation.

In this respect, there is *prima-facie* evidence, notwithstanding measurement issues, that the decline in the U.S. household saving rate over the past two decades is broadly in line with what one would predict, given the developments in household wealth (Figure 6.4). However, over the final years of the 1990s and the first few years of this decade, household net worth relative to disposable income declined, mostly because of a fall in the value of equity holdings, yet the household saving rate remained broadly steady. Some observers argued that this episode was a characteristic case of a consumption overhang that could unwind later with detrimental consequences for the U.S. economy. These worries are corroborated by simple historical benchmarks, such as the ratio of trend consumption to GDP estimated with a Hodrick–Prescott filter: This suggests that the ratio of U.S. household consumption to GDP

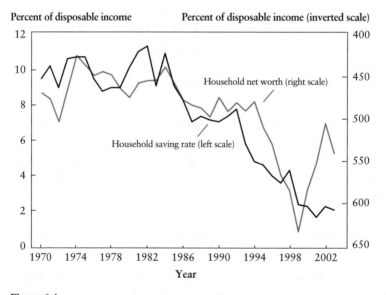

Figure 6.4
Personal saving rate and household net worth. *Source:* Board of Governors of the Federal Reserve System and U.S. Bureau of Economic Analysis.

was consistently above its long-term average (Figure 6.5). What could be at play is a kind of "ratchet effect" *à la* Duesenberry, involving not only household incomes, but also asset prices. In this context, the potential for a fall in consumption would be all the greater, given that: (a) household consumption overreacted markedly to wealth increases in the late 1990s, and (b) the overvaluation of equities at their peak was particularly large.

A careful econometric analysis of consumption (see Box 6.2 for the precise specification) shows that the ratchet hypothesis does not hold. At the peak of the asset price cycle in 2000, household consumption may have been a modest 2 percent above what could be predicted knowing wealth levels[15] (Figure 6.6). By 2003, this gap was down to 1 percent, suggesting that the resilience of consumption may have reflected favorable developments in short-term interest rates, house prices, and income: This may have counteracted the negative incidence of falling equity prices.

Index, 1995 = 100

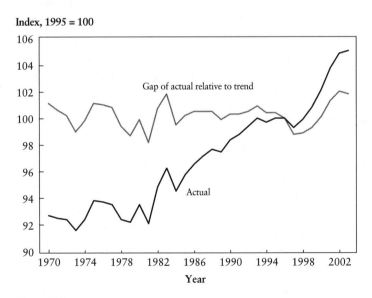

Figure 6.5
Ratio of consumption to GDP: Actual and actual relative to trend. *Source:* Organisation for Economic Co–operation and Development.

Box 6.2
Estimating private household consumption

A good basis to assess whether the level of consumption has deviated from its long-run equilibrium is to estimate a consumption model. This provides a foundation to compare actual consumption with the level predicted by the fundamental determinants of household spending. For this exercise, a model of U.S. consumption, within the framework of the life-cycle hypothesis, was estimated.[a] The approach relates, in the long run, trends in consumption to movements in income and wealth.[b] Consumption is able to deviate from the long-run equilibrium using an error-correction mechanism, where the short-run dynamic terms include lagged values of income and wealth, as well as interest rates, unemployment, and inflation.

The estimated short-run relationship is as follows:

$$\Delta(c) = \tau ect(-1) + \sum_{i=1}^{n} \gamma_i \Delta(c)(-i) + \sum_{i=1}^{n} \upsilon_i \Delta(y)(-i) + \sum_{i=0}^{n} \lambda_i \Delta(nfwr)(-i) + \sum_{i=0}^{n} \lambda_i \Delta(nhwr)(-i)$$

$$+ \sum_{i=0}^{n} \kappa_i \Delta(unr)(-i) + \sum_{i=0}^{n} \rho_i \Delta(irsr)(-i) + \sum_{i=0}^{n} \nu_i \Delta(inf)(-i)$$

where c is real consumption, y is real labor income excluding property income,[c] $nfwr$ represents real net financial wealth defined as financial assets minus financial liabilities other than mortgages, $nhwr$ is real net housing wealth defined as housing assets minus household mortgages, unr is the unemployment rate, $irsr$ is the real short-term interest rate, inf is the inflation rate, $ect(-1)$ is the error-correction term from the cointegrating vector, and Δ represents first-order differences.

The equation was estimated over the period from 1970 to 2002 by ordinary least squares (OLS), using the Stock and Watson procedure.[d] Consumption equations for other major OECD countries were also estimated, but the estimation period typically differed because of data limitations. The results showed significant wealth effects in most countries, broadly in line with previous research findings. For the United States, the estimated long-run marginal propensities to consume out of housing and financial wealth were 0.05 and 0.03, respectively. For housing wealth, the estimate is a little lower than that for the Netherlands and other OECD Anglophone countries, but larger than in Italy and Japan.

[a]See Catte *et al.* (2004) for a detailed specification of the model and its properties.
[b]The specification incorporates disaggregated wealth components, as different categories of wealth may affect consumption with different magnitudes. This is in line with results in Case, Quigley, and Shiller (2003). Boone, Girouard, and Wanner (2001), however, find different-sized wealth effects, depending on the class of asset, only in a minority of G-7 economies. The sensitivity of consumption to wealth also varies, depending on how wealth is measured.
[c]Property income is removed from disposable income to avoid the risk of double counting returns earned on financial assets.
[d]Stock and Watson (1993) suggest including leads and lags to address the endogeneity bias in OLS estimates of cointegrating relationships.

Billions of dollars

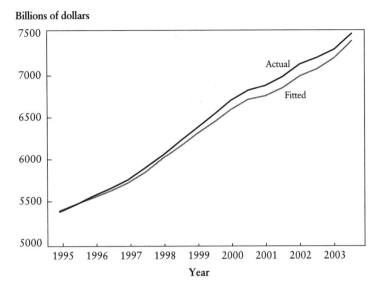

Figure 6.6
Fitted and actual levels of U.S. consumption. *Source:* Organisation for Economic Co–operation and Development.

Hence, on this basis, households do not seem to have erred in allocating consumption over time, given wealth developments.[16] It may be the case, however, that equity could still be overvalued. This is conceivable, for instance, according to the Gordon valuation formula, which relates the dividend-to-price yield to the real rate of interest, a risk premium, and the level of potential growth. Making reasonable assumptions for the normal risk premium and long-run real interest rate, the actual dividend-to-price yield implies a potential growth rate that was implausibly above most estimates of the late 1990s, and, at 4 percent in 2003, also probably above the current true potential growth in GDP (Table 6.1). However, and perhaps contrary to received wisdom, a similar exercise suggests that market valuations may have been much more out of line with "fundamentals" in the euro area, given the fact that the implied level of potential growth is considerably above all direct estimates. In comparison with the putative European overvaluation, the U.S. case may, therefore, look relatively benign, and its contribution to residual overconsumption may be modest, bearing in mind that such calculations are very sensitive to the specific assumptions made.

Table 6.1
Potential growth implied from the Gordon stock valuation method

	United States		Euro Area	
	Dividend-price ratio[a]	Implied potential growth[b]	Dividend-price ratio[a]	Implied potential growth[b]
1995	3.42	3.28	3.19	4.01
1996	3.15	3.55	3.08	4.12
1997	3.07	3.63	2.57	4.63
1998	2.21	4.49	2.23	4.97
1999	2.20	4.50	2.10	5.10
2000	2.05	4.65	1.88	5.32
2001	2.26	4.40	2.47	4.73
2002	2.55	4.15	3.07	4.13
2003	2.69	4.01	3.40	3.80

[a]Adjusted for share repurchases.
[b]Implied potential growth is defined as the real rate of interest plus the risk premium less the dividend-price yield. The risk premium for each market is defined as the average value of the difference between the earnings-price ratio and the real rate of interest from 1985 to 1995. The values are 3.2 for the United States and 3.7 for the euro area. The real rate was assumed to be 3.5 percent for each economy.
Sources: OECD and Datastream.

Looking at this issue of intertemporal allocative efficiency, Lettau and Ludvigson (2003) provide a radically positive assessment: Households generally do not incorporate transitory movements of wealth in their consumption decisions; and, thus, they immunized themselves from possible overconsumption in the late 1990s.

5.   Hysteresis in Public Deficits and Durably Low National Saving

The Need for an Increase in National Saving
Since 2000, real business investment as a share of GDP has fallen by 2.5 percentage points, and it is currently at the level that prevailed in 1997. It is not obvious that, at present investment rates, capital accumulation

will be sufficient to match a high potential GDP growth rate.[17] Should the rate of private investment increase, it is uncertain whether foreign savings could easily be made available to finance this expansion, knowing that the current account deficit is already around 5 percent of GDP and that the United States has a negative net asset position that is currently around 30 percent of GDP and steadily deteriorating. Hence, in the next few years, the U.S. economy may need to increase its investment rate, while reducing its recourse to foreign savings. This, in turn, may call for a strong increase in national savings, which have collapsed by more than 4 percentage points of GDP since 2000, because of a steep increase in structural public deficits.

With U.S. structural public deficits forecast by the OECD to remain very high for an extended number of years, the recovery in private saving may need to be strong. It is hard to visualize which public policies—other than fiscal retrenchment—could trigger such a surge in saving. A move towards a higher rate of saving could still occur spontaneously, however, if households were offsetting declining public net wealth by increasing their private net wealth positions.[18]

Uncertainties Surrounding the Rise of National Saving
Whether U.S. households are in a position to display such behavior remains an open question. One may argue that, during the 1990s, public and private saving tended to exhibit inverse movements. Such an inverse correlation has, however, been less strong since 2000. Hence, the post-2000 experience may cast doubt on whether the fall in private saving experienced in the 1990s reflected the marked improvement of public saving. Falling private saving could have, indeed, been primarily a consequence of rising private wealth.

This suspicion is heightened by the fact that the OECD-estimated consumption equations incorporating wealth, but not public saving (see above), as explanatory variables display relatively small residuals. It is also telling that a different type of private saving equation featuring public saving, but only indirectly accounting for private wealth through its fundamental determinants (for example, productivity growth), does an excellent job at out-of-sample forecasting from 1995 to 2000 (when the correlation between private wealth and public saving is strong), and a relatively poorer job in the period 2000–2003, when the correlation weakens (Figure 6.7). To try to clarify this issue, it may be worth examining the performance of private saving equations, including in the specification both public saving and indicators of housing and financial wealth, as well as short-run real interest rates, GDP growth, and other control variables.

Such work has been undertaken recently at the OECD using a panel data approach (see Box 6.3). It suggests that there is a relatively good case for a strong negative private saving offset to public saving in European countries and in Canada, but a much weaker case in the United States.

Testing for a Private Saving Offset in the United States

Looking ahead into an uncertain future, our benevolent social planner—or policymaker—may not be in a position to fine-tune precisely an optimal path for national consumption and the associated fiscal policy.

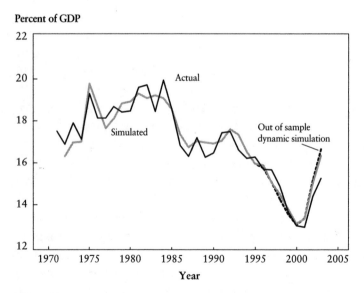

Figure 6.7
Gross private saving rates: Actual and simulated. *Source:* Organisation for Economic Co–operation and Development.

She or he does not necessarily have precise views about what the optimal private saving response should be to, say, a tax cut-induced public deficit.[19] In such a context, he or she may engage in limited optimization and try to avoid, for instance, worst-case scenarios. One such scenario would involve delaying fiscal adjustment for too long, only to discover that private savers were not offsetting changes in public saving. Our prudent social planner would certainly want to verify that private offsets have been reliably identified by the experts.

This section will try to carry out this preliminary check by using panel data analysis to test the existence of private saving offsets in the United States in response to movements in public saving. At this stage, we do not try to disentangle the various sources of offset (that is, Ricardian equivalence, substitutability between current public and private spending, etc.), but rather to verify whether, under one form or another, private saving offsets show up in the data.

We estimate the magnitude of private saving offsets to cyclically adjusted public deficits for a sample of 16 OECD countries in the period 1970–2002. Based on pooled cross-country and time-series data, this empirical exercise aims to compare OECD-wide and U.S. saving.[20]

Estimation of the baseline regressions yields the parsimonious models reported in Table 6.2.[21] The private saving offset to changes in cyclically adjusted public net lending is estimated in the sample of OECD countries at about one-half in the short term, and two-thirds in the long term.[22] As regards wealth variables, the equity market index negatively affects private saving in the long term, and housing wealth is negatively associated with private saving in both the short and long terms.

Estimates of the private saving offset (not reported) do not change significantly in magnitude when other measures of public saving are used. This is so, even though measuring public saving by the budget balance uncorrected for the business cycle is likely to create endogeneity biases arising from the size of automatic stabilizers, to the extent that causality may run from private to public saving, and not conversely. Nor does the offset coefficient vary significantly in magnitude when the fiscal stance is measured by the primary budget balance (adjusted for the cycle)—arguably a more accurate measure of discretionary fiscal impulses.

Box 6.3
Estimating private saving

There are several options for estimating the relationship between private and public saving. Our preference is for a reduced-form, error-correction setup, in which private saving is regressed on public saving, and short- and long-term dynamics are modeled explicitly.[a] Unit root tests for the individual time series and the panel as a whole, as well as residuals-based cointegration tests for the pooled data, suggest that this is a valid approach to estimating the dynamic relationship between private and public saving.[b] In particular, the saving equation to be estimated can be written as:

$$(1)\ \Delta S_{it}^{priv} = (\beta_0 - \beta_2\alpha_0) + \beta_1\Delta S_{i,t-1}^{priv} + \beta_2\Delta S_{i,t-1}^{priv} + \beta_3\Delta S_{it}^{pub} - \beta_2\alpha_1 S_{i,t-1}^{pub}$$
$$+\beta_4\Delta X_{it} - \beta_2\alpha_2 X_{i,t-1} + e_{it}$$

where ΔS_{it}^{priv} and S_{it}^{pub} denote, respectively, the private and the public saving ratios in country i at time t, X_{it} is a vector of control variables, e is a disturbance term, and Δ is the first-difference operator.

The set of control variables is standard in empirical literature and includes the old-age dependency ratio, the real interest rate, consumer price inflation, changes in the terms of trade, the ratio of broad money (M2) to GDP, and the growth rate of per-capita GDP. Proxies for wealth effects (equity market and housing price indices) are also included in the estimating equation, because, as noted above, the extent to which movements in private saving offset those in the cyclically adjusted budget balance is also affected by fluctuations in household wealth, which may, themselves, be correlated with budget action.[c]

[a] A more conventional approach is to estimate the reduced-form saving equation in a partial equilibrium setup, in which the lagged dependent variable is included in the set of regressors primarily in order to deal with inertia in saving behavior. However, we prefer the error-correction specification because the partial-equilibrium setup allows for only very simple dynamics, making the estimation of long-term private saving offsets often unrealistically high. The approach adopted here also differs from that followed in De Serres and Pelgrin (2002). They focus on gross public saving, defined as the general government financial balance plus gross public-sector investment. Here, public saving is defined as cyclically adjusted net lending of the general government.

[b] A variety of unit root tests were carried out for the individual time series, and the IPS test was carried out for the panel as a whole, suggesting that the variables of interest are nonstationary. The Pedroni–Kao cointegration test was also carried out, suggesting that there is a stable long-term relationship between private and public saving.

[c] The decline in equity wealth since 2000 has taken place concomitantly, with an expansionary fiscal stance and an increase in private saving rates after 2001. Whether coincident with budgetary changes, or in part related to them, it is difficult to disentangle the effects of wealth-induced shifts in saving from those deriving from public-sector indebtedness *per se*, and exclusion of these proxies would arguably overstate the private saving offset.

Table 6.2
Sensitivity of private saving to fiscal stance: Panel analysis

Dependent variable: Private saving
(in percent of GDP, National Accounts definition):[a]

	Baseline	1	2
Private saving			
Lagged first difference	0.11**	0.09**	0.18***
	(0.047)	(0.047)	(0.060)
Lagged level	−0.27***	−0.29***	−0.34***
	(0.034)	(0.034)	(0.047)
Public saving (net lending[b])			
First difference	−0.51***	−0.51***	−0.43***
	(0.048)	(0.048)	(0.062)
Lagged level	−0.19***	−0.22***	−0.11**
	(0.034)	(0.036)	(0.054)
Net lending* U.S. (lagged level)		0.44***	0.36
		(0.133)	(0.225)
Controls			
Broad money (first difference)	−0.1***	−0.11***	−0.12***
	(0.271)	(0.027)	(0.036)
Change in terms of trade (first difference)	0.04***	0.04***	0.01
	(0.012)	(0.012)	(0.013)
Old-age dependency ratio (lagged level)	−0.28***	−0.29***	−0.03
	(0.057)	(0.057)	(0.112)
Per-capita GDP growth (first difference)	0.32	0.04	0.06**
	(0.027)	(0.027)	(0.031)
Housing price index (first difference)	−0.02***	−0.02***	−0.03***
	(0.008)	(0.008)	(0.009)
Housing price index (lagged level)	−0.02***	−0.02***	−0.02***
	(0.004)	(0.004)	(0.006)
Equity market index (lagged level)	−0.01***	−0.01***	−0.01
	(0.001)	(0.001)	(0.006)
Time period	All	All	Pre-1995
Number of observations	275	275	165
Number of cross-sectional units	16	16	16
Sargan test (overidentification, p-value)	0.99	0.99	0.99
First-order autocorrelation (p-value)	0.00	0.00	0.00
Second-order autocorrelation (p-value)	0.40	0.41	0.66

[a]All models are estimated using the Arellano–Bond difference-GMM estimator and include a common intercept (not reported). Standard errors are reported in parentheses. Statistical significance at the 1-, 5-, and 10-percent levels is denoted by, respectively, (***), (**), and (*).
[b]Net lending is cyclically adjusted.
Source: OECD Economic Outlook database.

How Different Is the U.S. Case?

To assess whether the estimated private saving offset differs in the United States from the OECD average, the cyclically adjusted budget balance (measuring public saving) was interacted with a dummy variable, taking value "1" for the United States, and "0" for all other countries in the panel.[23] Based on this methodology, the private saving offset appears to be positive, rather than negative in the United States over the longer term. Furthermore, we experimented with an interaction dummy for other selected G-7 countries (that is, the United Kingdom, Germany, France, Italy, and Canada), but the results reported in Table 6.3 do not suggest a lack of robustness of the negative private saving offset in those countries. For countries like the United Kingdom and Canada, which are characterized by strong wealth effects, the coexistence of negative offsets and wealth effects does not seem problematic.

This finding seems to suggest that very little consumption smoothing may be taking place in the face of long-term shifts in public deficits in the United States. Taken at face value, these results may also be seen to imply that U.S. households behave in a non-Ricardian way. Such a conclusion, although plausible, may be nonetheless premature. It must first be remembered that, in this exercise, the sources of changes in public deficit arise not only from the tax side, but also from changes in expenditures. Indeed, it is hard to conceive how tax-rate changes, alone, could ever generate a private savings offset that is neither negative nor null. For a positive offset to materialize, public expenditures need to be incorporated into the analysis, with a clear distinction made between temporary and permanent spending shocks. Permanent changes in public spending will not fit the bill, for instance, since they tend to generate negative offsets rather than the positive ones sought. A permanent increase in public spending will generate, for example, an increase in private saving through the workings of the intertemporal budget constraint. A temporary shock in public spending can, however, generate the required positive offset, provided that households see public and private consumption as complements.[24] As a matter of illustration, should complementarity prevail, a temporary increase in current public expenditure leading to a deterioration of net public lending would also deteriorate personal savings by stimulating personal consumption. In such a case, a positive offset would, indeed, be observed.[25]

It is also interesting to note, in the same vein, that expected future cuts in public spending are susceptible to reducing present savings via the workings of the intertemporal budget constraint as well as by a stronger preference for present private consumption, which would benefit from relatively stronger complementary public spending.

Incorporating expected public spending to the analysis is potentially of great interest to explain how truly Ricardian taxpayers may behave in an apparently non-Ricardian manner. Such would be the case, for instance, if, following a period of tax cuts and deficits, consolidation were expected to take place in the form of substantial cuts in public expenditures. In this scenario, the tax cut would generate an increase in private saving, while the expected reduction in public expenditures would push down savings, leading finally to a zero offset. All in all, U.S. households would not have the opportunity to exercise intergenerational altruism, since the benevolent planner would take prompt and credible action.

The hypothesis that the wealth effects associated with the housing and equity price cycles affect private saving behavior more strongly in the United States than in the remaining countries in the panel was investigated further. To this end, the housing and equity price indices were interacted with the U.S. dummy. The results suggest that a rise in equity prices may depress private saving by a higher amount in the U.S. than in the remaining countries in the panel, but the estimated coefficient is not significant at normal levels. Rather than dismissing this possibility, we believe that a failure to find a statistically significant link may be due to data inadequacies, given that housing and equity price indices are proxies for, rather than the actual measurement of, household wealth.

Altogether, this exercise suggests that the case for negative private saving offsets in the United States is probably less compelling than in many other OECD countries. An optimistic interpretation of this finding is that it may reflect a greater confidence of the U.S. public that deficits in their country are less persistent than elsewhere. Even more optimistically, one could deny the robustness of the econometric work or blame a set of exceptional circumstances for masking the forward-looking dimension of U.S. household behavior. A less optimistic interpretation would put greater emphasis on the likely risks that U.S. households do not behave in a Ricardian way. Whatever the case, the risk of overconsumption seems

Table 6.3
Sensitivity of private saving to fiscal stance: Panel analysis

Dependent variable: Private saving (in percent of GDP, National Accounts definition):[a]

	U.S.	U.K.	Germany	France	Italy	Canada
Private saving						
Lagged first difference	0.09**	0.10**	0.11**	0.11**	0.11**	0.10**
	(0.047)	(0.046)	(0.047)	(0.047)	(0.047)	(0.047)
Lagged level	−0.29***	−0.27***	−0.27***	−0.27***	−0.27***	−0.27***
	(0.034)	(0.033)	(0.034)	(0.034)	(0.034)	(0.034)
Public saving (net lending)[b]						
First difference	−0.51***	−0.51***	−0.51***	−0.51***	−0.51***	−0.51***
	(0.048)	(0.048)	(0.048)	(0.048)	(0.050)	(0.049)
Lagged level	−0.22***	−0.18***	−0.19***	−0.19***	−0.19***	−0.21***
	(0.036)	(0.034)	(0.034)	(0.036)	(0.036)	(0.038)
Net lending* country dummy (lagged level)	0.44***	−0.17	0.00	0.07	0.04	0.10
	(0.133)	(0.126)	(0.141)	(0.167)	(0.147)	(0.075)
Controls						
Broad money (first difference)	−0.11***	−0.10**	−0.10***	−0.10***	−0.10***	−0.10***
	(0.027)	(0.027)	(0.027)	(0.027)	(0.027)	(0.027)
Change in terms of trade (first difference)	0.04***	0.04***	0.04***	0.04***	0.04***	0.04***
	(0.012)	(0.012)	(0.012)	(0.012)	(0.012)	(0.012)
Old-age dependency ratio (lagged level)	−0.29***	−0.28***	−0.28***	−0.28***	−0.28***	−0.29***
	(0.057)	(0.056)	(0.058)	(0.057)	(0.058)	(0.058)
Per-capita GDP growth (first difference)	0.04	0.04	0.03	0.03	0.03	0.03
	(0.027)	(0.027)	(0.027)	(0.027)	(0.027)	(0.027)

Housing price index (first difference)	-0.02***	-0.02***	-0.02***	-0.03***	-0.02***	-0.02***
	(0.008)	(0.008)	(0.008)	(0.008)	(0.008)	(0.008)
Housing price index (lagged level)	-0.02***	-0.01***	-0.02***	-0.02***	-0.02***	-0.02***
	(0.004)	(0.004)	(0.004)	(0.004)	(0.004)	(0.004)
Equity market index (lagged level)	-0.01***	-0.01***	-0.01***	-0.01***	-0.01***	-0.01***
	(0.001)	(0.001)	(0.001)	(0.001)	(0.001)	(0.001)
Number of observations	275	275	275	275	275	275
Number of cross-sectional units	16	16	16	16	16	16
Sargan test (overidentification, *p*-value)	0.99	0.99	0.99	0.99	0.99	0.99
First-order autocorrelation (*p*-value)	0.00	0.00	0.00	0.00	0.00	0.00
Second-order autocorrelation (*p*-value)	0.41	0.36	0.40	0.40	0.40	0.37

[a]All models are estimated using the Arellano–Bond difference-GMM estimator and include a common intercept (not reported). Standard errors are reported in parentheses. Statistical significance at the 1-, 5-, and 10-percent levels is denoted by, respectively, (***), (**), and (*).
[b]Net lending is cyclically adjusted.
Source: OECD Economic Outlook database.

Table 6.4
Projected effects of aging on public spending, 2000–2050[a]

	Old-age pension and "early retirement" programs		Healthcare and long-term care	
	Level 2000	Change 2000–50	Level 2000	Change 2000–50
Australia	3.9	1.7	6.8	6.2
Austria	9.5	2.2	5.1	3.1
Belgium	9.9	3.4	6.2	3.0
Canada	5.1	5.8	6.3	4.2
Czech Republic	9.6	6.2	7.5	2.0
Denmark	10.1	2.8	6.6	2.7
Finland	11.3	4.7	8.1	3.8
France[b]	12.1	3.8	6.9	2.5
Germany	11.8	5.0	5.7	3.1
Hungary	7.1	1.6	—	—
Italy	14.2	–0.3	5.5	2.1
Japan	7.9	0.6	5.8	2.4
Korea	2.4	8.1	0.7	0.5
Netherlands[c]	6.4	5.2	7.2	4.8
New Zealand	4.8	5.7	6.7	4.0
Norway	7.2	9.7	5.2	3.2
Poland	12.2	–2.6	—	—
Spain	9.4	8.0	6.2	2.5
Sweden	11.1	1.2	8.1	3.2
United Kingdom	4.3	–0.7	5.6	1.7
United States	**4.7**	**2.1**	**2.6**	**4.4**
Average of countries above[d]	8.3	3.3	5.9	3.1

[a]The projections of public-spending implications of aging were undertaken in 2000–2001. For Austria, France, Germany, Italy, and Spain, projections concerning healthcare spending were not part of the original exercise, but have been elaborated subsequently, based on the same macroeconomic assumptions.
[b]For France, the latest available year is 2040.
[c]"Early retirement" programs only include spending on persons 55 years of age and older.
[d]OECD average excludes countries where information is not available.
Source: OECD (2001).

strong enough to warrant very substantial retrenchment in the next few years.

Fiscal Sustainability in the Longer Term

Fiscal retrenchment may also be needed to mitigate future public-spending pressures due to materialize towards the end of this decade when the baby boomers start to retire. These developments will place additional stresses on public finances and downward pressure on saving and capital formation. A recent OECD study [Dang, Antolin, and Oxley (2001)] projected the fiscal impact of age-related spending for OECD countries. The results, based on national models and using an agreed-upon set of assumptions about macroeconomic and demographic developments, suggest public spending on age-related pension and early retirement programs in the United States could rise by the equivalent of 2.1 percentage points of GDP over the next half-century (Table 6.4). Moreover, public spending on healthcare and long-term care was projected to rise by 4.4 percentage points of GDP.[26]

All in all, the large and persistent deficits projected over the coming years underscore the need to adjust revenue and spending levels so as to raise national saving and prepare for impending demographic pressures on budgetary positions. This would also help to lessen the external imbalance. Failing fiscal consolidation, budget deficits on the order of 5 percent of GDP would lead to a rising level of government debt, with adverse economic consequences. The latest OECD *Economic Survey of the United States* attempted to calculate the implications for national income. Based on a large number of assumptions,[27] it concluded that the beneficial effects of the tax reductions since 2001[28] on long-run labor supply were more than offset by the negative effects of the decline in national saving and capital formation.

6. Conclusion

This paper offers two main conclusions. First, it is difficult to talk about serious, "overconsumption" in the United States during the late 1990s. Lower U.S. saving did not hamper capital accumulation in a context where massive inflows of foreign saving led to an investment overhang.

There are no signs either that, given levels of wealth observed in the late 1990s, consumption had been incompatible with an efficient allocation of saving over time. There were, at least, no signs of an excessive propensity to consume out of wealth or income. There may have been, however, an element of "*ex-post* overconsumption" inasmuch as equity markets proved to be overvalued, and households may not have distinguished accurately between permanent and transitory wealth. It should also be noted that, based on standard equity valuation methods, current equity prices may still be somewhat overvalued. Moving into the future, it seems that the investment ratio will have to rise significantly from current levels in order to match U.S. natural growth, in a context where high public and external deficits are expected to persist over an extended number of years. What may then be needed is a large recovery in private saving.

Our second conclusion, however, is that the evidence of private saving offsets to public deficits in the United States is far less compelling than in many other OECD countries. One should not underestimate, in these circumstances, the risk stemming from a failure to lift national saving and its negative consequences on national income. Should the United States manage, however, to increase further its current account deficit in order to finance high public deficits and higher private investment, the consequences for the outside world may not be very positive: Foreign savers may still benefit from superior opportunities by investing in the United States, but saving available worldwide for private investment would be much lower. In this context, the risk of overconsumption seems strong enough to warrant very substantial retrenchment in the next few years in the United States, as well as in other large OECD countries.

■ *The authors thank the two discussants, Willem Buiter and Eric Engen, for their valuable comments on an earlier draft. Some of these comments have greatly helped to reshape the paper and its discussion of private saving offsets. The authors also thank Debbie Bloch for her expert statistical assistance and Alain De Serres, Jorgen Elmeskov, Michael Kennedy, Vincent Koen, and Thomas Laubach for useful comments and suggestions on earlier versions of this paper. The views expressed in this paper are those of the authors and do not necessarily reflect those of the OECD Secretariat or the Organisation's member countries.*

Notes

1. For a detailed discussion on the national accounts measurement of saving, see, for example, Gale and Sabelhaus (1999) and Price, de Mello, and Kongsrud (2004).

2. See Shafer, Elmeskov, and Tease (1992).

3. Between the 1970s and the late 1990s, these adjustment factors changed by less than 1 percent of GDP in aggregate. This overall stability reflects a certain inertia of the various adjustment factors as well as their tendency to offset one another's fluctuations over time.

4. Nonetheless, this tentatively reassuring statement needs to be qualified in various ways. The profile of saving may be altered, for instance, if it is expressed relative to numeraires other than GDP. For instance, with the declining trend in net factor income from abroad, the ratio of gross saving to national income is boosted over time. Conversely, net saving rates are likely to have trended lower with the rising proportion of ICT capital, which depreciates more swiftly than the economy-wide capital stock.

5. Compared with its average level in the 1970s, the national accounts saving measure of private saving was 4.6 percentage points of GDP lower in 1998, reflecting a 2.9-point fall in the inflation-adjusted saving rate and a 1.7-point fall in the inflation tax. The "true saving rate," which needs to be adjusted for factors other than the inflation tax, fell by 2.1 percentage points of GDP over the period.

6. See, for example, Thornton (1998).

7. Tevlin and Whelan (2000) estimate the average U.S. capital depreciation rate rose from around 4 percent in the late 1980s to nearly 9 percent in the late 1990s. Part of the increase reflects market, rather than physical depreciation.

8. The average correlation between changes in private saving and the cyclically adjusted budget balance between 1970 and 2003 is close to –0.5 for the OECD area as a whole.

9. As exemplified by the infinitely lived agent, *à la* Ramsey.

10. Figure 6.3 shows the path for potential growth from 1995, based on average total factor productivity growth over the period of 2.2 percent per annum and labor force growth of 1.3 percent per annum. There are several available measures of the capital stock for the United States. Each series, however, grew at a faster pace than the Solow potential over the period. Between 1995 and 2000, the U.S. capital stock had reached a level some 12 percent above the equivalent for potential output. And over the same period, private consumption had risen to a level almost 7 percent above the equivalent for Solow potential output. Similar profiles are evident when the same calculations are made over longer time periods.

11. Indeed, it was so strong that it was followed by an investment bust and lingering underutilization of production capacity.

12. This would happen in the case of a low elasticity of substitution between capital and labor.

13. However, depending on the choice of the model, the assumptions made about hardly observable variables (that is, rate of time preference, rate of decline of marginal utility over time, etc.), and the criteria chosen for the utility function, this approach could lead to many different, and, thus, speculative, optimal paths.

14. See Section 3.

15. As well as those of other explanatory variables.

16. Using a much more demanding and sophisticated approach, Scholz *et al.* (2004) found that a sample of people nearing retirement had accumulated an optimal stock of wealth in the late 1990s.

17. In fact, based on a simple version of the neoclassical growth model, and using conservative assumptions about the equilibrium capital-output ratio and depreciation rate, one finds the current investment rate to be below the sustainable or long-term equilibrium rate that is consistent with the 3.5-percent natural rate of GDP growth assumed earlier. The OECD's assessment is, indeed, that after growing by 4 percent per year on average during the late 1990s and early 2000s, the U.S. business capital stock grew by only 1.5 percent a year in 2002 and 2003.

18. A tightening of monetary policy, possibly associated with falling asset prices, could impact national savings. Should negative wealth effects and substitution effects outweigh income effects, an increase in interest rates may stimulate personal savings. At the same time, however, business and public-sector savings may decrease because of higher interest payments. The magnitude of changes in national savings in reaction to a monetary tightening, therefore, remains uncertain.

19. It is highly unlikely that a fully Ricardian reaction would be appropriate. Even in a world devoid of imperfections (liquidity constraints, etc.), a less-than-total offset from private saving may well be optimal. For instance, while, in principle, current generations of households cannot consume beyond their lifetime (human and financial) wealth, the government has the capacity to ease that constraint by shifting resources from future to current generations [Buiter (1988)]. In other words, the government can use its ability to tax resources of future generations to facilitate intergenerational consumption smoothing, provided that current generations do not have too strong altruistic motives *vis-à-vis* future generations. This is the case, for instance, in a world where population growth takes place not only within existing dynastic families, but also in future, unrelated families, such as immigrants, who will share the tax burden.

20. Country selection has been guided by data availability. The data set includes Australia, Belgium, Canada, Denmark, Finland, France, Germany, Italy, Japan, the Netherlands, Norway, New Zealand, Spain, Sweden, the United Kingdom, and the United States. The data set predates the latest U.S. re-benchmarking exercise, which resulted, *inter alia*, in a downward revision to the level of private saving in the United States.

21. Empirical literature based on reduced-form saving equations has also focused, on the one hand, on the association between public saving and private consump-

tion, as in Giavazzi and Pagano (1996), and national saving, on the other, as in Giavazzi *et al.* (2000). Previous empirical studies focusing on private, rather than national, saving as a left-hand-side variable in a reduced-form saving equation include Loayza *et al.* (2001), and De Serres and Pelgrin (2002). Exclusive focus on household, rather than private or national, saving, as in Callen and Thimann (1997), is relatively uncommon.

22. The estimated private saving offset is greater in magnitude in the short term than that reported by Loayza *et al.* (2001) for OECD countries (about 0.1), using a comparable generalized method of moments (GMM) estimator, but lower than those reported by Haque *et al.* (1999) and De Serres and Pelgrin (2002), using error-correction mean group estimators (about 0.9 and 0.7, respectively); by Masson *et al.* (1998), using a static, fixed-effects estimator (about 0.8), and by Edwards (1996), for both industrial and developing countries, using an instrumental variables estimator (about 0.6).

23. The option of running a separate regression for the United States, alone, could not be pursued because of data availability, with, at most, 30 observations per country in the panel.

24. There is complementarity when the marginal utility of private consumption is positively affected by public spending.

25. The joint intertemporal budget constraint of households and government suggests, of course, that, in the very long run, this fall in current private saving would be followed by a countervailing rise, with possible detrimental consequences for intergenerational equity. Future generations will not benefit from the temporary increase in current public consumption, but they may have to reduce their own private consumption as a result of the higher taxes that may be needed to repay a higher public debt and as a result of a weaker private capital stock. See Frenkel and Razin (1996) for a discussion of the intertemporal consequences of government spending.

26. These calculations exclude the recent extension of the U.S. old-age pharmaceutical benefit scheme (the 2003 Medicare Prescription Drug Improvement and Modernization Act), which may well reduce private saving previously committed to meeting future health-spending requirements.

27. For details, see Appendix 2.1 of the 2004 OECD *Economic Survey of the United States.*

28. The main tax-reducing acts were the Economic Growth and Tax Relief Reconciliation Act of 2001, the Job Creation and Worker Assistance Act of 2002, and the Jobs and Growth Tax Relief Reconciliation Act of 2003.

References

Auerbach, Alan. 1985. Saving in the U.S.: Some conceptual issues. In *The level and composition of household saving*, ed. H. Hendershott. Cambridge: Balinger.

Boone, Laurence, Nathalie Girouard, and Isabelle Wanner. 2001. Financial market liberalisation, wealth, and consumption. OECD Economics Department Working Papers 308.

Buiter, Willem 1988. Death, birth, productivity growth, and debt neutrality. *Economic Journal* 98(391) June: 279–293.

Callen, Tim, and Christian Thimann. 1997. Empirical determinants of household saving: Evidence from OECD countries. IMF Working Paper 97/181.

Carman, Katherine, Jagadeesh Gokhale, and Laurence Kotlikoff. 2003. The impact on consumption and saving of current and future fiscal policies. NBER Working Paper 10085.

Case, Karl, John Quigley, and Robert Shiller. 2003. Comparing wealth effects: The stock market versus the housing market. Berkeley University: Program on Housing and Urban Policy Working Paper W101–004.

Catte, Piero, Nathalie Girouard, Robert Price, and Christophe André. 2004. Housing markets, wealth and the business cycle. OECD Economics Department Working Papers 394.

Cerisola, Martin, and Paula De Masi. 1999. Determinants of the U.S. personal saving rate. In *United States: Selected Issues*. International Monetary Fund Staff Country Report 99/101.

Dang, Thai Than, Pablo Antolin, and Howard Oxley. 2001. Fiscal implications of aging: Projections of age-related spending. OECD Economics Department Working Papers 305.

De Serres, Alain, and Florian Pelgrin. 2002. The decline in private saving rates in the 1990s in OECD countries: How much can be explained by non-wealth determinants? OECD Economics Department Working Papers 344.

Frenkel, Jacob, and Assaf Razin. 1996. *Fiscal policies and growth in the world economy*. Cambridge: MIT Press.

Edwards, Sebastian. 1996. Why are Latin America's saving rates so low: An international comparative analysis. *Journal of Development Economics* 51(1): 5–44.

Gale, William, and Peter Orszag. 2002. The economic effects of long-term fiscal discipline. Urban-Brookings Tax Policy Center Discussion Paper 8.

Gale, William, and John Sabelhaus. 1999. Perspectives on the household saving rate. *Brookings Papers on Economic Activity* 1:181–224.

Giavazzi, Francesco, and Marco Pagano. 1996. Non-Keynesian effects of fiscal policy changes: International evidence and Swedish experience. *Swedish Economic Policy Review* 3(1): 67–103.

Giavazzi, Francesco, Tullio Jappelli, and Marco Pagano. 2000. Searching for non-linear effects of fiscal policy: Evidence from industrial and developing countries. *European Economic Review* 44(7): 1259–1289.

Haque, Nadeem, M. Hashem Pesaran, and Sunil Sharma. 1999. Neglected heterogeneity and dynamics in cross-country savings regressions. IMF Working Paper 02/208.

Lettau, Martin, and Sydney Ludvigson. 2003. Understanding trend and cycle in asset values: Re-evaluating the wealth effect on consumption. NBER Working Paper 9848.

Loayza, Norman, Klaus Schmidt-Hebbel, and Luis Serven. 2001. What drives private saving across the world? *Review of Economics and Statistics* 82(2): 165–181.

Lusardi, Annamaria, Jonathan Skinner, and Steven Venti. 2001. Saving puzzles and saving policies in the United States. NBER Working Paper 8237.

Maki, Dean, and Michael Palumbo. 2001. Disintegrating the wealth effect: A cohort analysis of household saving in the 1990s. Board of Governors of the Federal Reserve: Finance and Economics Discussion Series 2001–21.

Mankiw, N. Gregory. 2000. The savers-spenders theory of fiscal policy. *American Economic Review* 90(2): 120–125.

Masson, Paul, Tamim Bayoumi, and Hossein Samiei. 1998. International evidence on the determinants of private saving. *World Bank Economic Review* 12(3): 483–501.

Muhleisen, Martin, and Christopher Towe, eds. 2004. U.S. fiscal policies and priorities for long-run sustainability. IMF Occasional Paper 227.

Organisation for Economic Cooperation and Development. 2004. *OECD Economic Survey, United States*. Paris: OECD.

Parker, Jonathan 1999. The consumption function revisited. Princeton University Working Paper.

Pelgrin, Florian, Sebastian Schich, and Alain De Serres. 2002. Increases in business investment rates in OECD countries in the 1990s: How much can be explained by fundamentals? OECD Economics Department Working Papers 327.

Price, Robert, Luiz de Mello, and Per Mathis Kongsrud. 2004. Saving behavior and the effectiveness of fiscal policy. OECD Economics Department Working Paper 397.

Scholz, John, Ananth Seshadri, and Surachai Khitatrakun. 2004. Are Americans saving "optimally" for retirement? NBER Working Paper 10260.

Shafer, Jeffrey, Jorgen Elmeskov, and Warren Tease. 1992. Saving trends and measurement issues. *Scandinavian Journal of Economics* 94(2): 155–175.

Stock, James, and Mark Watson. 1993. A simple estimator of cointegrating vectors in higher order integrated systems. *Econometrica* 61(4): 783–820.

Tevlin, Stacey, and Karl Whelan. 2000. Explaining the investment boom of the 1990s. Board of Governors of the Federal Reserve: Finance and Economics Discussion Series 2000–11.

Thornton, John 1998. Corporate taxes and household saving: Panel evidence from five OECD countries. *Economia Internazionale* 51(2): 279–283.

Comments on Cotis et al.'s "Is the United States Prone to 'Overconsumption'?"

Willem H. Buiter

This paper contains a wealth of material and raises a host of issues. I won't even try to summarize the paper or respond to all the issues and questions it raises. Instead, I will make some points loosely motivated by the paper.

The question of whether the United States consumes too much can be rephrased as two questions. First, does the U.S. save too little? And, second, does the U.S. invest too little at home? In an economy with an open capital account, the two questions are not the same: The large and persistent U.S. external current account deficit means that, in the United States today, these two questions are not the same, although too many American economists continue to treat the issues of a savings shortfall and an investment shortfall as if they were equivalent.

If there is, indeed, too little saving in the United States today, the further question arises as to *who* saves too little? Is it the private sector? Within the private sector, is it the households or the enterprise sector? Is it the public sector? Does it matter? Today's discussions, thus far, all appear to be based on the tacit premise that we are in a Modigliani–Miller world. The corporate veil is well and truly pierced, although people aren't completely clear about the Ricardian veil. I'll come back to this.

I will focus mainly on the saving issue, which I think is the most pressing one. It is much less straightforward to make a *prima facie* case that the United States is investing too little than that it is saving too little. First, there is the persistent, large, and growing current account deficit, which has permitted a rate of U.S. domestic capital formation at levels 5 to 6 percent of gross domestic product (GDP) in excess of what domestic saving can finance. In addition, there is the often-spectacular decline in the relative price of many capital goods and the marked increase in their technical efficiency, both of which are probably underreported in the data. This means that *real* investment (using nonexistent constant hedonic prices) could be quite robust, despite a decline in the conventionally measured real investment rate.

1.   Measurement Issues

The paper also mentions measurement issues; I think too little has been made of measurement issues at this conference. I would like to reiterate some of the important ones, in addition to the failure to allow fully for the increasing quality of capital goods mentioned already. Household saving and investment in education and consumer durables should be reported both as saving and as capital formation. These two items must be taken seriously, as they are much more important quantitatively in affluent societies like the United States than in poorer societies. On the other side, resource depletion—natural resource rent extraction—is not accounted for properly in the national accounts; it should be counted in its entirety as depreciation. Because this is not done in practice, the true capital depreciation rate is underrecorded.

There is a wider problem: Much of what is recorded as public-sector consumption and value added, in line with conventional but misconceived national income accounting standards, is not, from an economic point of view, consumption and value added at all. Instead, it should be viewed as the production and use of intermediate public goods and services. Much of this expenditure is, no doubt, important or even essential, but it does not represent final output, value added in the form of consumption and investment. Intermediate public services encompass most of public administration, including law and order and defense spending. After all, only cannibals directly consume police officers and judges; the services provided by judges and police officers are not valued in their own right, but only because they enable or facilitate consumption that is valued intrinsically, or investment. This misclassification as public consumption of the production and using up of intermediate public services does not distort the measurement of the *amount* of saving; but, because it leads to the overstatement of public consumption and, thus, GDP, it does increase the denominator in the saving rate and, therefore, biases the measured saving rate downwards.[1]

Then, there is the point that saving behavior is just one of the two drivers of the variable of interest to economists: the change in real financial wealth. Over the past couple of decades in the United States, capital gains—changes in the value of existing financial claims—have been a much more important driver of the change in real financial wealth than have cumulative net savings. It is true that, since the distribution of financial wealth is much more unequal than the distribution of saving rates, it is important to look not just at aggregate financial wealth and the aggregate net saving rate, if one wishes to determine whether the representative American family is accumulating enough financial wealth to deal with retirement and other contingencies.

2. Is the U.S. Saving Rate Sustainable?

The short answer is: Probably not, but that, in itself, is not a cause for concern. The term "sustainability" has been used very loosely, and rather uninformatively, in the discussions here. What does it mean that something is "unsustainable"—just that it cannot go on forever? If something is unsustainable if it is not in a steady state, then not much is sustainable, and it need not matter very much that something is not sustainable. The current net national saving rate of the U.S. is 1.3 percent. Even allowing for all my measurement problems, this saving rate is probably not (indefinitely) sustainable. However, this does not mean that it cannot be part of a nonstationary, efficiently optimal plan for the national saving rate. This is very much the point made by Susanto Basu earlier in the discussion. You don't necessarily want to see a steady-state saving rate when the economy is, for good reasons, not in steady state.

If you don't have an operational benchmark of what optimal consumption is, or what optimal saving is, then you are inevitably reduced to time-series comparisons, cross-sectional (cross-country) comparisons, or, if you are lucky, to a panel data approach. Is the saving rate unusually low now in comparison with the past (or relative to some benchmark based on average past behavior)? Is the saving rate in the United States lower than in comparable countries? A problem is, of course, that there really are no countries comparable to the United States for the purpose of the study of saving behavior. I believe the United States to be much wealthier than even those countries that are recorded in the standard national accounts as richer than the U.S., because nontraded goods and services tend to be so much cheaper in the U.S. Even if, in a panel data approach, we can control for a number of determinants of saving behavior (that is, demographics, business cycle conditions, etc.), it is, I believe, extremely difficult to use other countries to determine a benchmark for what the United States ought to save.

3.   Is the U.S. Saving Rate Optimal?

There is an operational test for excessive, dynamically inefficient investment. It is whether the United States is on the wrong side of the golden rule. Has the marginal product of capital been depressed to the point that it is less than the natural growth rate? In a market economy, is the share of investment always larger than the share of profits? In a closed economy, excessive investment means excessive saving. So, we would have an empirically implementable test for excessive saving. I don't think there is much evidence to support the view that the United States suffers from excessive investment. There are historical examples of overinvestment: the Soviet Union towards the end of its life, Singapore in the 1980s and early 1990s, and, perhaps, China today.

There is no simple test for insufficient investment to complement the test for excessive investment. Even if there were one, the fact that the United States is financially open means that, in order to establish that the United States does not save enough, it is neither necessary nor sufficient to establish that there is insufficient U.S. investment.

What do we mean when we ask whether the United States saves enough? Are current and anticipated (using our best models and forecasts) future U.S. saving rates sufficient—given our best forecasts of future nonasset income (labor income), and given our best forecasts of the *modus operandi* of general government tax and transfer programs (including not just Social Security, Medicare, and Medicaid, but income taxes, other taxes, and transfer programs, as well)—to provide current and future generations with reasonable age-consumption profiles?

Restricting ourselves to current generations only, what factors make for inefficient saving and, specifically, for too low a saving rate? Myopia is one possible explanation, but that is a description rather than an explanation. Insufficient precautionary saving is another possibility, although I am uncomfortable putting my trust in anything that depends on the details of the third derivative of the utility function, but there could be a problem. Fiscal distortions leading to suboptimal savings are an obvious candidate: When the rate of return on saving is taxed, the private rate of return to private saving today is below the social rate of return to private saving. However, this will reduce saving only if the intertemporal substitution elasticity exceeds unity—something for which the empirical evidence (as distinct from the assumptions made by the calibrators) is mixed, at best. The state is unlikely to tell old people, who are destitute because they chose not to save an adequate amount while young, to get lost. Knowing this, people may rationally save less, knowing that they can always throw themselves on the mercy of the community when their working days are over. Some form of mandatory saving could mitigate this problem, provided it is impossible to undo the effect of the mandatory saving plan by dissaving more through other mechanisms (for example, by using the balance of the mandatory savings account as collateral for loans to finance additional consumption while young).

One empirically important form of myopia may well be the systematic overestimation, by generations currently of working age, of the future contribution of the government to their material well-being in old age, through Social Security, Medicare, and Medicaid. Alan Auerbach has estimated that meeting the budgetary demands of full implementation of current Social Security, Medicare, and Medicaid benefits/entitlements would require a permanent increase of government revenues of 10 percent of GDP.

While there are no insurmountable administrative barriers to raising 10 percent of GDP in additional revenues in the United States, and while this could be done without dramatic adverse incentive effects [say, by introducing a federal value-added tax (VAT) or final sales tax], the unique political economy of the United States means that such an increase, or anything like it, is extremely unlikely to materialize. Therefore, future Social Security, Medicare, and Medicaid benefits/entitlements are likely to be substantially less than implied by current laws, rules, and regulations. If this is not recognized by those of working age today, saving rates that seemed adequate *ex ante* may turn out to be inadequate *ex post*.

Is the U.S. saving rate sufficient, stepping away from an exclusive focus on the current generations, to address intergenerational equity concerns? Again, there may be a myopia/ignorance issue: Are the implications of demographic developments recognized? I would be surprised if they were. They are recognized here, at this conference, but this is hardly a representative sample of the wider U.S. public. The effect of demographic myopia would be too little saving. Against that, higher trend rates of productivity growth, of the kind that the United States appears to have been blessed with since the late 1990s, have obvious implications for intergenerational efficiency; and they make it less urgent to save now to take care of the future—both the future of generations currently alive and that of as-yet-unborn generations. Of course, higher investment in the U.S. economy than can be financed from U.S. savings, alone, may well be required to support the higher growth rate of trend productivity, if much of the higher total factor productivity is embodied in new vintages of capital goods. If the rest of the world does not enjoy similar investment opportunities, foreign saving could, efficiently, supplement scarce U.S. saving. This, indeed, is one interpretation of what drives the large and growing U.S. current account deficit.

I note, in passing, that conventionally defined investment (fixed investment in plant, machinery, and equipment; in structures; and in infrastructure) may well have negative, un(der)recorded, and improperly priced effects on the stocks of depletable and (partly) renewable natural resources, ecological and environmental capital—effects that often occur only with long, variable, and uncertain lags. Consumption may have similar externalities. Greater intergenerational concern may, therefore, call for lower conventionally measured investment rates, even if it calls for higher (or less negative) comprehensively measured investment rates.

From a global first-best perspective, the United States probably absorbs too much of the world's savings. The reason is that, in much of the world, private rates of return on investment are pitifully low, even though social rates of return (the returns that would be realized by a benevolent, competent, and well-informed central planner—not the returns that would be realized if the state were to control and direct the investment) are high. The reason is poor governance at all levels, from the state to the enterprise. Corrupt and predatory governments, absence of the rule of law and an independent judiciary, insecure property rights, weak or non-existent protection of the rights of creditors and minority shareholders, arbitrary taxation verging on selective and politically motivated confiscation and expropriation—all drive a massive wedge between the social and private rates of return on investment. In the United States, the wedge between social and private rates of return reflects mainly the taxation of capital income at the margin, but this is not of the same magnitude as the wedges seen in many emerging markets and developing countries.

The wedges that are depressing private rates of return below social rates of return in many emerging markets and developing countries are part of the reality that must be taken as given in any real-world counterfactual exercise. Yes, the fact that the most capital-rich country in the world, the United States, has a current account deficit is a reflection of institutional and policy failures, but the failures in question are overwhelmingly located outside the United States. Until the basics of good economic governance are rooted more firmly in the countries that continue to send their savings to the United States, it is difficult to argue that the United States should not absorb these savings.

4. The External Current Account and External Debt of the U.S.

There is something else that is unique about the U.S. It is not that the magnitude of its net external debt is unique: It stands at about 35 percent of GDP, using the current best guesstimate. There are lots of valuation problems on both sides of the balance sheet, but the figure does not seem unreasonable.

The key point is that U.S. gross external liabilities are of two kinds. Either they are real liabilities—equity and real estate—or they are financial liabilities denominated in U.S. dollars. This is a wonderful set of external liabilities for the United States to have. The "debt service" due on equity and real estate—dividends and royalties—does not consist of fixed contractual payments. One cannot default on equity. When times are tough, one stops paying dividends. The second type, U.S.-dollar-denominated bonds and other debt instruments, can be inflated away. So, the United States, as a debtor, is in a very strong position; and, if, at any time, the external debt were to become perceived as excessive by the holders, the resolution of this excessive debt problem would likely be more expensive for the creditors in the rest of the world than for the United States.

5. Ricardian Equivalence: Do Changes in Private Saving Offset Changes in Public Saving?

In 1979, I wrote a paper with Tobin [Buiter and Tobin (1979)], which had the same kind of regression of private saving on public saving that has been presented in Cotis's paper. Of course, it did not have the unit root and other stationarity tests, the error-correction specifications, and the tests for cointegration performed by Cotis. But, fundamentally, it involved the same regressions of private saving on current and/or lagged public saving, and it proposed the same "deep structural" interpretation of the estimated parameters: If the sum of private saving and public saving had a non-zero (preferably a positive) coefficient on public saving, this was taken to be evidence against debt neutrality or Ricardian equivalence.

Back in 1979, I got really hammered over the interpretation of these results, and I now know that those who wielded those hammers were right: The correlation between private saving and public saving, contemporaneous or lagged, is not at all informative about any deep structural relationships. There is no statute of limitations on mistakes. In a Ricardian economy (representative agent and lump-sum taxes and transfers), there exists a shock to public-sector saving that will be fully offset by a matching change in private-sector changes. The shock that produces the Ricardian association between private saving and public saving is an unexpected immediate cut in current lump-sum taxes, holding constant current and future public consumption. In that same Ricardian economy, there also exist shocks to public-sector saving that will be associated with a zero private-saving offset. The unexpected announcement of an immediate, one-period increase in public consumption will, with permanent-income consumption behavior, reduce current (and future) private consumption by a small fraction of the increase in private consumption. Assume that the government does not change its taxes in the current period. There is a reduction in public saving equal to the increase in public consumption, and an increase in private saving equal to a small fraction of the increase in public consumption. Finally, consider the case in which there is an unexpected announcement today of a permanent increase in future public consumption. There is no current change in public consumption or taxation, so public saving does not change. But, since their permanent income is down, private consumers consume less, and, with taxes unchanged in the current period, save more. This has private saving changing without any change in public saving.

In a pure (Old or New) Keynesian economy, I can have a partial offset, a negative offset, or a full offset of private saving and public saving, depending on the nature of the shocks. So, to answer the question: "Is the world Ricardian?," even in a world without real capital, there is no escape from jointly modeling private consumption, real endowments net of government consumption spending, and real interest rates, and testing restrictions across these processes. You cannot regress private saving or public saving, with or without lags, with or without error-correction mechanisms, and believe you are getting anything other than the summary of what happened in the sample.

■ *The views expressed are those of the author. They do not reflect the views of the European Bank for Reconstruction and Development.*

Notes

1. The same problem arises with many goods and services purchased by the household sector (including unincorporated businesses). Household financial services are not purchased because they are valued for their own sake (for the direct utility they yield), but because they are productive inputs into the production of the things that the household does value intrinsically. Since the bulk of household production of true consumption goods and services is not measured at all, the national income accountants adopted the shortcut of identifying all household purchases from nonhousehold agents as consumption.

References

Buiter, Willem H., and James Tobin. 1979. Debt neutrality: A brief review of doctrine and evidence. In *Social Security versus private saving*, ed. G. von Furstenberg. Cambridge: Ballinger.

7

The Twin Deficits – U.S. and International Perspectives

Budget and External Deficits: Not Twins but the Same Family

Edwin M. Truman

The United States has had a current account deficit for most of the past 30 years.[1] Since 1969, the deficit has averaged 1.5 percent of the gross domestic product (GDP)—2.9 percent over the past 10 years—and it reached 5.7 percent of GDP in 2004. As a result, the U.S. net international asset/liability position or net international investment position (NIIP) turned negative after the mid-1980s, and has been heading south ever since, reaching about minus 24 percent of GDP at the end of 2002 and 2003.[2] What is new is the reemergence of substantial U.S. fiscal deficits for the first time since the mid-1990s. Does this mark the return of the external deficit's twin?

In this paper, I first argue that the two deficits are linked through the saving-investment identity in the national income and product accounts (NIPA), but they are not analytical or behavioral twins. That is, when the supply of government saving declines (the fiscal deficit increases), the net inflow of foreign saving (the external or current account deficit) does not necessarily increase either dollar-for-dollar or with that sign. Both deficits are part of the same family in the sense that they are both U.S. problems, although they are also problems for the rest of the world.

Second, at their present rates, neither deficit is sustainable. However, this observation provides little insight into how long they can or will continue.

Third, with respect to economic implications, failure to correct the fiscal deficit would have adverse effects on growth and on the standard of living in the medium and longer term in the form of higher real interest rates, lower investment, and lower potential output.

Fourth, failure of the external deficit to narrow is likely to have milder negative effects over the same timeframe; the gap between GDP and the gross national product (GNP, that is, GDP plus net income receipts from abroad and minus net income payments abroad) will widen, but GNP would continue to expand. Because of the costs and uncertainties associated with shifting resources from the nontraded sector to the traded goods and services sector, correction of the external deficit via exogenous exchange-rate adjustment, in the absence of a change in fiscal or other policies, would likely involve negative effects on growth and the U.S. standard of living.[3] By assumption, net inflows of foreign saving to the United States would decline, real interest rates would be higher, and investment and potential output would be lower. As the gap between GDP and GNP reverses, the growth rates of both would probably slow.[4]

Fifth, prompt correction of the fiscal balance in the short run would entail somewhat slower growth, but it would be positive for growth and the U.S. standard of living over the longer run compared with delayed adjustment. Prompt correction of the external deficit via exchange-rate adjustment, even if it occurs smoothly, is likely to be associated with lower near-term growth and a lower standard of living than would otherwise prevail. A delayed correction of the external deficit may involve larger macroeconomic costs of transition to a sustainable position.

Finally, with respect to policy implications, a smooth, low-cost correction of the U.S. current account deficit would be facilitated by prompt correction of the fiscal deficit. An optimal strategy would be to seek delay in external adjustment until the fiscal adjustment is well in hand. However, while current account adjustment is inevitable, it is also endogenous, and we may not have the luxury of time to achieve optimal sequencing.

1.   Are the deficits related?

Dudley and McKelvey (2004) have articulated the twin-deficit view:

[T]he budget and trade deficits are intertwined. Chronic budget deficits create a shortfall of domestic saving. This leads to higher interest rates, a stronger dollar, and foreign capital inflows. In this way, the initial budget deficit becomes transformed into twin budget and trade deficits.

Figure 7.1 depicts net government saving and the net inflow (positive) of saving from abroad (the external or current account deficit), and Figure 7.2 depicts net investment and net private saving. The data are from NIPA.[5] Net government saving is federal saving plus state and local saving.[6] The net inflow of saving from abroad ("foreign saving," for short) is the NIPA translation of the current account balance with the sign reversed. Thus, the figures summarize the key components of the saving-investment identity.[7]

Visual inspection of Figure 7.1 reveals that net government saving and net saving from abroad do not generally move in opposite directions. In fact, their annual levels and changes as a percent of GDP are positively correlated (inconsistent with the twin-deficit story), at 0.04 and 0.24, respectively, although not significantly.[8]

Consider three episodes of large changes in net government saving over the past 25 years:[9]

• From 1979 to 1983, net government saving declined by 4.8 percent of GDP; from its low in 1980 to 1987, the net inflow of foreign saving rose

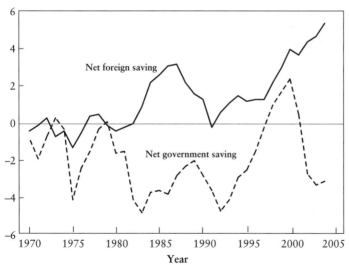

Figure 7.1
Net foreign and government saving. *Source:* U.S. Bureau of Economic Analysis, National Income and Product Accounts.

Percent of GDP

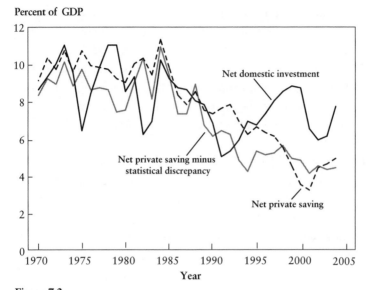

Figure 7.2
Net investment and net private saving. *Source:* U.S. Bureau of Economic Analysis, National Income and Product Accounts.

by 3.6 percent of GDP. This was the heyday of the twin-deficit story, but the story is somewhat undercut by the fact that, from 1983 to 1987, net government saving actually rose by 2.0 percent of GDP.

• From 1992 until 2000, net government saving increased by 7.1 percent of GDP, while the foreign saving inflow also increased by 4.6 percent of GDP, suggesting that something other than the twin-deficit phenomenon was occurring.

• From 2000 to 2003, government saving declined by 5.7 percent of GDP, while the foreign saving inflow increased by only 0.7 percent of GDP; this experience also is not fully consistent with the simple twin-deficit story.

During these three episodes, not only was fiscal policy changing in the United States, but also policies were changing in the rest of the world, and other developments were affecting the global economy. Consider a few examples to illustrate the basic point that there is no necessary systematic relationship between the behaviors of the two deficits. Table 7.1 presents a two-by-two matrix. On the side are increases or decreases in

Table 7.1
Analysis of Twin Deficits

	Inflow of Foreign Saving	
Net Government Saving	Increase	Decrease
Increase	Toward Fiscal Surplus and External Deficit	Toward Fiscal Surplus and External Surplus
Decrease	Toward Fiscal Deficit and External Deficit	Toward Fiscal Deficit and External Surplus

net government saving (toward fiscal surplus or deficit). Across the top are increases or decreases in the inflow of foreign saving (toward external, or current account, deficit or surplus).

The twin-deficit case involves an increase in discretionary U.S. government spending, with no monetary accommodation.[10] Net government saving decreases because of the expenditure expansion, and the inflow of foreign saving increases (current account deficit widens) because the boost to income sucks in more imports; see the lower-left-hand quadrant. In addition, interest rates rise, which tends to appreciate the dollar; net imports increase more; and some of the potential increase in the interest rate is ameliorated by an even larger inflow of foreign saving, in the form of a transfer to the rest of the world of claims on the United States. How all this works out in a general equilibrium context in the short, intermediate, and longer term depends on assumptions about various lags, sticky prices or wages, expectations formation, and balance-sheet constraints that may or may not be satisfied over particular time horizons.

Staying with the short term, consider impacts on the rest of the world. Treating the rest of the world as a single country with unchanged policies, it moves toward external surplus (a decrease in the use of foreign saving) and net government saving increases; see the upper-right-hand quadrant. Because the United States is a large country, the initial fiscal expansion tends to push up both U.S. and foreign interest rates, with adverse effects on investment and potential GDP in both countries.[11]

Consider a second case: a positive productivity shock in the United States. This stimulates investment, but also raises the real interest rate.

Net government saving increases (the fiscal deficit shrinks), and the inflow of foreign saving increases (the external deficit widens); see the upper-left-hand quadrant. In the rest of the world, the inflow of foreign saving is reduced (the rest of the world's external deficit narrows), but net government saving increases as well; see the upper-right-hand quadrant. Again, interest rates rise in both countries, but the rise is associated with an increase in investment and potential GDP in the United States, and the opposite in the rest of the world.[12]

Thus, the two deficits need not move systematically together. On the other hand, currently, the United States has both.

2.   Are the deficits sustainable?

Neither the U.S. budget deficit nor the U.S. current account deficit is likely to be sustainable at its current rate of roughly 6 percent of GDP. Herb Stein's famous remark is regularly quoted to reassure the U.S. that what is unsustainable will not continue indefinitely. What is more difficult to assess is how long either type of deficit can continue on a substantial scale, and whether there are differences with respect to their sustainability.

The External Deficit

On the external side, dating back to before I left the Federal Reserve in 1998, when the current account deficit was only 2.4 percent of GDP, it was already accepted that our external deficit could not continue indefinitely on its projected negative trajectory. Freund (2000) and Mann (1999) concluded from their studies of the experiences of other industrial countries that pressure for correction often arises when external deficits are in the range of 4 to 5 percent of GDP.

Greenspan (2003 and 2004a) has emphasized three points. First, one cannot predict with any precision how long external deficits and a growing negative NIIP can be sustained. Second, the adjustment process most likely will be triggered by the reluctance of foreign-country investors to continue to accumulate net claims on the United States. Third, the increased openness of the global financial system has contributed to a reduction in home bias.[13] This trend implies that deficits and surpluses could pile up for a longer period than in the past before a process of adjustment or correction begins. Greenspan (2004) also argues, "We may not be able to usefully determine at what point foreign accumulation of net claims on the United States will slow or even reverse, but it is evident that the greater the degree of international flexibility, the less the risk of crisis."

There is no consensus about the size of any U.S. external adjustment, once it gets under way. Truman (2005) describes a number of views as of early 2004, which range from moving the U.S. current account position into surplus and paying down some of the net external debt that has already accumulated to merely reducing the deficit to less than 4 percent of GDP.

Several considerations are relevant. One can ask what it would take to stabilize the ratio of the NIIP to GDP at the level of about minus 25 percent that prevailed at the end of 2002. If the normal or trend nominal growth rate of the U.S. economy is 6 percent, then the ratio could be stabilized at a current account deficit of 1.5 percent of GDP.[14] With net transfer payments of 0.5 percent of GDP and negligible net income payments or receipts, this would mean that the United States could still have an annual trade deficit of 1 percent of GDP and stabilize the NIIP ratio.

However, the U.S. NIIP consists disproportionately of interest-bearing, dollar-denominated liabilities. Those net liabilities were about $3.3 trillion at the end of 2003, compared with the overall NIIP of minus $2.6 trillion. The net liabilities are predominantly short term. At the abnormally low nominal dollar interest rates of recent years, the financial cost of those liabilities has been understated. At a more normal nominal short-term interest rate 300 basis points higher than it was in 2003, closer to 4 percent than 1 percent, the interest cost of the net interest-bearing, dollar-denominated liabilities would have been $100 billion higher, or about 0.9 percent of GDP.[15]

Even if the U.S. external adjustment process eventually stabilizes the NIIP ratio, the process will not be instantaneous. In the meantime, the ratio would rise along with the interest-bearing component. On the other hand, the adjustment process almost certainly would involve a substantial depreciation of the dollar well in excess of the 15 percent that was recorded from February 2002 through March 2005 on the Federal Reserve Board staff's broad index of the foreign-exchange value of the dollar, and the depreciation has tended to boost the dollar value of U.S. foreign assets relative to U.S. liabilities to foreigners.[16] If the NIIP ratio stabilized at minus 35 percent of GDP, a trend growth rate of U.S. nominal GDP of 6 percent implies a sustainable current account deficit of 2.1 percent of GDP. The associated trade deficit might be 0.5 percent of GDP, implying the need for reduction in the U.S. trade deficit of about 4¾ percentage points of GDP from the 5.2 percent in 2004.

The view that the eventual adjustment of the U.S. external position can and will be smaller rests on the proposition that the United States is, and will remain, an attractive place for residents of other countries (individuals, money managers, corporations) to invest. For example, the current account deficit may only have to narrow to 3 percent of GDP.[17] At a 6-percent nominal trend growth rate, a U.S. current account deficit of 3 percent implies that the NIIP ratio would stabilize at minus 50 percent of GDP. Moreover, it could be some years before that level was reached.[18]

Alternatively, Mann (2003) suggests normalizing the U.S. current account position on the margin to what would be consistent with the U.S. share of global GDP (about 33 percent) or with the U.S. share of non-U.S. global wealth, measured by market capitalization (about 55 percent). Mann's calculations, based on data as of mid-2002, imply U.S. current account deficits of 2.4 and 3.6 percent of GDP, respectively, in 2005.

Freund (2000) and Mann (1999), in their studies of industrial countries that have experienced substantial external adjustments, find that normally in these periods, external debt ratios stabilized but did not reverse. On the other hand, positing a partial adjustment of the U.S. current account in the next several years—say, to 3 percent of GDP—would not achieve stabilization. One might also think that if the U.S. NIIP ratio were headed for minus 50 percent of GDP, there might, at that point, be some correction or overshooting in the form of trade or current account surpluses to pay down some of the debt. In addition, if 50 percent were a *de-facto* market-induced limit, then there would be limited scope for deficits larger than 3 percent of GDP going forward. In effect, they would have to average around that figure; and the dollar's medium-term volatility, say, over the course of a year or two, might increase, even as the amplitude of its swings decreased.

It is difficult to prove anything in this area, but, based upon these considerations, my view is that, once the U.S. current account adjustment gets seriously under way, with the deficit narrowing to significantly less than 6 percent of GDP for a period of years, the low point will be closer to 1 percent than 4 percent. In other words, at a minimum, the correction will be 3 percentage points.

The Fiscal Deficit

Turning to the sustainability of the U.S. fiscal deficit, many of the same points arise. My sampling of the newer literature on the issue suggests substantial consensus that U.S. federal deficits of 5 percent of GDP should not, and will not, go on forever.[19] Perhaps, there is a greater consensus on this point than there is on the sustainability of the U.S. external deficit of the same size.

As Gramlich (2004) argues, fiscal deficits are less sensitive to market forces of self-correction than are external deficits. In the limit, of course, the U.S. government might be unable to float its debt, and the fiscal adjustments following such a crisis might be described as market driven. Long before that point is reached, we expect economic conditions to interact with political forces to bring about change. One potential economic channel is through slower growth associated with higher interest rates and lower investment, which tends to worsen the budget deficit and comes to be seen as the source of slow growth and malaise. It took more than a decade, from 1981 to 1992, for these forces to come fully into play politically. Arguably, political forces, this time, have advanced the process more rapidly.

Finally, with respect to the fiscal deficit, as in the case of the external deficit, views differ about how large an adjustment is desirable and over what time horizon. However, for the longer run, again, there may be a greater consensus than in the case of external deficits that the appropriate near-term (three to five years) objective for the unified federal budget deficit should be zero, or a small positive figure—more than enough to stabilize the debt-to-GDP ratio. That weak consensus rests on three considerations: maintaining room to maneuver fiscal policy either through discretionary action or the use of automatic stabilizers; increasing the overall rate of saving in the economy; and preparing for the demographic future. Different analysts emphasize different points, but they often reach similar conclusions.

Thus, it is generally agreed that neither the U.S. fiscal deficit nor the U.S. current account deficit is indefinitely sustainable at its current rate. However, the reasons and the associated logic differ somewhat. One explanation for this difference is that the economic and financial implications of the continuation of the two deficits are not entirely the same.

3.   Economic Implications of the Deficits?

The economic implications of U.S. fiscal and current account deficits for the U.S. and global economies are, in some respects, similar. Both deficits appear in the saving-investment identity. However, over the longer term, the U.S. fiscal deficit reduces U.S. and global saving, and the U.S. current account deficit merely redistributes saving from the rest of the world to the United States, and presumptively redistributes wealth in the other direction.

With respect to the fiscal deficit, in the short run such deficits normally stimulate economic activity; policy actions to reduce the deficit dampen economic activity. Over the medium and longer term, if fiscal deficits are not corrected, their stimulative effects wear off and turn negative. In a closed economy, the reduced level of national saving pushes up interest rates as the economy returns to full employment. This dampens investment, labor productivity, and potential output.

In an open economy, part of the impact on U.S. interest rates and investment may be muted, because saving can be sucked in from the rest of the world. However, foreign economies also share in the adverse effects of higher U.S. government debt; their interest rates are higher, investment is lower, labor productivity is lower, and potential output is lower.[20] They are partially compensated, of course, by higher returns on U.S. assets.

Most analytical and empirical studies agree with the basic thrust of these arguments, although there are differences in empirical magnitudes at each step of the analysis. Supply-side effects from tax reductions and, in principle, from more efficient government spending are a relevant qualification. However, my reading of the literature is that these effects may reduce the size of the negative longer-run effects, but they generally do not reverse their signs. Over the longer run, the enlarged stock of government debt dominates. In models with binding long-run balance-sheet conditions, this dominance of government debt has the additional implication that, unless the debt stock is restored to its original level—fiscal surpluses of equal size scaled by GDP follow deficits—the adverse effects on the U.S. and global economies persist, except to the extent that there is an offset from supply-side effects.

Analysis of the economic implications of current account deficits is complicated by the fact that those implications in size, and occasionally in sign, depend upon the causes of the deficits and conditions in the U.S. and global economies. The effects can be viewed as either positive or negative in both the short and longer runs.

For example, in the short run, a widening of the current deficit associated with slower growth abroad is associated with downward pressure on U.S. economic activity and employment, which may or may not be welcome, depending on the condition of the domestic economy. At full employment, the external deficit allows domestic demand to exceed supply, permitting an increase in domestic consumption and/or investment. To the extent that the dollar appreciates as part of the process, the positive terms-of-trade effect also boosts welfare in the form of the real value of consumption.

In the medium or longer run, the appropriate conditioning assumption is that the economy is at full employment. In this context, current account deficits again have both positive and negative effects, depending in part on the nature of the comparison. On the positive side, domestic demand exceeds supply; the country is permitted to live beyond its means. In addition, it is likely that the dollar is appreciated relative to where it would be without the deficit, which provides a positive terms-of-trade effect. On the negative side, the country is borrowing from abroad, which presumptively depresses the standard of living in the future. Even if the current account deficit permits a higher level of investment, the direct returns on that investment flow abroad. The level and growth rate of GNP are lower compared with a situation in which the same rate of domestic investment occurs without the current account deficit.

In popular and political discussions, correction of the U.S. external deficit is associated with a boost to U.S. employment and output. What this view ignores is that normally the economy should be operating at full employment.[21] Thus, a reduction in the external deficit, with production (GDP) unchanged, means gross domestic purchases (absorption or GDP less net exports) must be reduced. For example, if the U.S. trade and current account deficits have to be reduced by 3 percent of GDP, that implies a reduction of $1,350 per capita in gross domestic purchases at an unchanged level of GDP in 2004. During the 1987–1990 period of U.S. external adjustment, GDP per capita grew at an annual rate of 1.5 percent, compared with 2.7 percent during the previous four years. However, gross domestic purchases expanded only 0.9 percent per year, compared with 4.6 percent over the previous period. Consumption advanced at only 1.2 percent, less than a third of the average rate of the previous four years. "It was the economy, stupid," in 1992, but the source of the economic malaise was poorly understood; growth in standards of living had stagnated.

Because of these ambiguities, it is conventional to try to distinguish between current account deficits that are a larger or smaller source of concern; see, for example, Summers (2004). Is the economy with the current account deficit at full employment? Does it appear that the deficit is financing consumption or investment? Is the investment in the traded or nontraded sectors of goods and services? Is the deficit otherwise leading to distortions in the economy between those two sectors? Is the deficit financed by private or official capital inflows? If the flows are private, are they long term or short term? These are good questions, but rarely are they susceptible to definitive answers, even in a specific case, which limits their usefulness to guide policy.[22] Moreover, most of the questions implicitly relate not to the current account deficit *per se,* but to what happens when an unsustainable deficit begins to narrow.

A continuation of unsustainable U.S. current account deficits points to other potential global problems. One is the risk of a rise in protection, which imposes long-run costs on both the U.S. and the global economies. Geopolitical implications are also relevant; Summers (2004) refers to the "balance of financial terror" associated with large, concentrated official holdings of short-term dollar-denominated claims on the United States. More generally, countries that are large international debtors find it more of a challenge to exert leadership in political as well as economic

spheres. This challenge is complicated, on balance, though some say ameliorated, by the fact that the dollar is an international currency, in the
sense that it is widely used by countries as a unit of account, means of
payment, and store of value in circumstances in which U.S. residents are
not involved.[23]

Again, many of these concerns and considerations do not relate to the
U.S. current account deficit *per se*, but to the process of correction once it
is under way. Under these circumstances, the existence of an external and
a fiscal deficit in the same family, even if they are not twins, increases the
risks. Gramlich (2004) introduces the concept of a "credibility range,"
applying to each of the deficits a range in which neither type of deficit
has large effects on asset prices—interest rates or exchange rates. Extending his concept, when either deficit is large or has been expanding, the
credibility ranges narrow for both deficits. Confidence in U.S. financial
policy is undermined [Truman (2001)], and the risk of crisis rises. Rubin
et al. (2004) vividly describe a number of adverse scenarios, implicitly
disagreeing with Greenspan (2004), quoted above, who sees greater flexibility reducing the risk of crisis. Freund (2000), in her study of experiences of industrial countries with large current account adjustments,
brings out a key point: External financial crises are much more common
after the process of adjustment is under way than as a trigger to the
adjustment process.[24]

4. Implications for Economic Policies?

With two unsustainable U.S. deficits, policymakers should embrace policies to maximize the probability of a smooth adjustment. Policies should
aim at adjustment sooner rather than later, in effect reducing the probability of a crisis and preserving some room for maneuver, in order to
minimize the damage to the U.S. and global economies if things do not go
just right. U.S. policymakers might also hope for cooperative policies in
the rest of the world to boost growth, and for a large dose of good luck.
However, none of the effective strategies is risk-free or costless.

The core issue is the low U.S. saving rate. As stated by Summers (2004),
"I am reluctantly convinced that the most serious problem we have faced
in the last 50 years is that of low national saving, resulting dependence

on foreign capital, and fiscal sustainability, which has far-reaching implications for the U.S. and the global economy." Some economists think that the answer is to attract more and more saving from abroad, but that offers only a short-run fix. Some economists believe that changes in the tax code, normally reductions but also removal of the tax deductibility of mortgage interest payments, can lift the private saving rate. My impression is that there are fewer economists with these views than there once were. Most economists agree that the most reliable, but less than foolproof, method of increasing national saving is to reduce the fiscal deficit and raise government saving, whether by expenditure reductions or tax increases. The short-run impact on the economy may be to slow growth if monetary policy is unable to compensate fully, but the long-run impact will be to raise growth and living standards. Reducing the budget deficit should contribute to lower interest rates and may be associated with a weaker currency, which would tend to narrow the current account deficit and offset some of the short-term drag of fiscal policy.

Should the United States deliberately seek to weaken the dollar? No. We should have learned in the late 1970s that the United States could not devalue its way to prosperity even if we could successfully manipulate exchange rates, which we could not. It is a different question as to whether we should discourage other countries from manipulating or pegging their exchange rates, when doing so impedes the global adjustment process. The actions of the Chinese authorities in purchasing large quantities of dollars, and of the Japanese authorities doing the same thing, to the extent that the latter actions are effective, distort the global adjustment process. As Greenspan (2004a) observed with unusual candor, the Chinese authorities are delaying the adjustment process. The consequences of that delay may be a more disorderly adjustment process down the road.

If the distortions to the adjustment process that are associated with *de-facto* or *de-jure* dollar pegs were reduced or removed, presumably the yen would appreciate a bit further, the renminbi would be repegged at an appreciated rate, and the currencies of India and of other East Asian countries would adjust or be adjusted upward. It is possible that the dollar might be unchanged on average because the euro, Canadian dollar, and other currencies that have had large appreciations against the dollar over the past two-plus years would depreciate, and this would reallocate some of the U.S. external adjustment. A more likely result would be a smaller overall appreciation of those currencies over the longer run as the global adjustment process runs its course. If the U.S. external deficit has to contract by a minimum of 3 percentage points of GDP, about $350 billion as of 2004, and if we accept the rule of thumb that a real depreciation of 1 percent on the Federal Reserve Board staff's broad index of the foreign-exchange value of the dollar will be associated with $10 billion in current account adjustment, then the dollar's eventual adjustment will have to be at least 30 percent; we are at most halfway there.[25]

What about U.S. monetary policy? To the extent that the U.S. fiscal deficit is decisively narrowing, U.S. monetary policy can be easier. Let me be clear: Full employment and price stability would be associated with a lower federal funds rate in real and nominal terms than otherwise would be the case, absent a spontaneous surge in investment. At the same time, if the dollar were depreciating and the current account deficit were narrowing, monetary policy would have a role to play in restraining the growth of aggregate demand relative to aggregate supply, facilitating a faster expansion of output than of domestic demand. If the dollar were depreciating with little prospect of lower fiscal deficits, then monetary policy should be even tighter.

One question on which economists do not agree is whether exchange-rate adjustment can do it alone in narrowing a current account deficit or whether, in addition, growth should be deliberately slowed. Experience, reviewed by Freund (2000), suggests that growth does slow in most countries undergoing external adjustment and exchange-rate depreciation. However, these experiences reflect a range of policies interacting with a range of economic and financial conditions.[26] It is also another matter deliberately and permanently to lower the level of U.S. real GDP by 9 percent in order to reduce imports of goods and services by, say, 2 percent of GDP.[27]

On the other hand, adjustments in monetary and fiscal policies at home and abroad for countries undergoing an exchange-rate-induced external adjustment do play a significant role in determining how large the adjustment will be or how much exchange-rate change is needed to achieve an external adjustment of a given size.[28] More broadly, the IMF staff

(2004) has advocated a cooperative strategy to facilitate the orderly resolution of global imbalances: U.S. fiscal contraction, European structural adjustment, Japanese banking and structural adjustment, and increased exchange-rate flexibility and structural adjustment in Asia. To this package, I would add easier monetary policy in Europe to sustain European growth and to take some of the appreciation pressure off the euro. I would also add policies in Asia to stimulate consumption and discourage domestic saving. With increased saving in the United States, this would keep global saving and investment in balance and would reinforce the effects of exchange-rate changes on adjustment.

5. Summary

• The U.S. fiscal and external deficits are linked through the saving-investment identity, but they are not analytical or behavioral twins.

• Both deficits are unsustainable, although there is little consensus, especially for the external deficit, about what level would be sustainable.

• The economic implications for the U.S. economy of continuation or correction of each deficit are complex, and they differ somewhat. The adverse effects of continuation of the fiscal deficit are likely to be more pronounced than those associated with continuation of the external deficit. Correction of the external deficit could well be more problematic, precisely because its evolution is essentially endogenous.

• The fiscal deficit is more debilitating, and policy can do something about it. The exogenous external deficit is a source of risk and instability to the U.S. and global economies.

• It is difficult to imagine how the United States could achieve a substantial correction of the external deficit and still maintain a large fiscal deficit because of the size of the implied drop in the rate of domestic investment that would be involved.

• It is more critical to reduce the fiscal deficit, where policy has a greater role and the beneficial economic effects are more obvious.

■ *Thanks go to Frabrizio Iacobellis, Gunilla Pettersson, and Anna Wong for research assistance on this paper. I have also benefited from comments by Martin Baily, Ralph Bryant, Joseph Gagnon, Morris Goldstein, and Catherine Mann. Errors of fact and interpretation remain my own.*

Notes

1. The current account, as now computed, was in surplus in 1970. It returned to surplus in 1973–76, induced by the dollar's devaluation and a U.S. recession; and again in 1980–81, induced by the same two influences; and, most recently, in 1991, because of a large net inflow of Gulf War-related transfer receipts.

2. The estimated NIIP was 24.4 percent at the end of 2002 and declined slightly to 24.1 percent by the end of 2003, because $546 billion in net financial inflows—net new debt—were largely offset by $448 billion in positive valuation adjustments, primarily due to the dollar's depreciation. The resulting percentage increase in the NIIP was less than the percentage increase in nominal GDP.

3. At full employment, if the narrowing of the external deficit occurred as the result of acceleration in growth abroad, these effects might be somewhat ameliorated.

4. If the increase in the negative NIIP produces a large risk premium on U.S. liabilities on average, as well as on the margin, GNP growth will slow more than GDP growth.

5. Some might prefer to use stock concepts, for example, changes in wealth, but the accounting framework and statistical base for such analyses are not well developed for open economies.

6. Most of the action in net government saving comes from the federal sector.

7. Net private saving is presented alone and minus the statistical discrepancy; combining the statistical discrepancy with private saving does the least visual damage.

8. In dollar terms, the levels correlation is –0.22, and the changes correlation is 0.08. Neither is significant.

9. Of course, during each of these episodes, more than fiscal policy was affecting net government saving and net inflows of foreign saving. For example, business cycles affect government saving as well as the current account. According to the IMF's WEO database, the U.S. general government structural deficit widened by 3.8 percent of GDP from 1981 through 1986, tightening the twin-deficit pattern. However, the improvement from 1992 to 2000 was 5.3 percent of GDP, and the deterioration from 2000 to 2003 was 4.5 percent of GDP, providing little support for the twin-deficit hypothesis.

10. The liability side of the central bank's balance sheet is unchanged.

11. The situations would be reversed if the fiscal expenditure expansion were abroad.

12. Again, the situations would be reversed if the positive productivity shock were abroad. Moreover, if there were a negative productivity shock abroad, the rest of the world would move toward fiscal deficit and external surplus. In the United States, net government saving also would decrease and the inflow of foreign saving would increase, placing the United States in the twin-deficit quadrant in the lower-left-hand corner via another route.

13. Greenspan (2004a) reports a decline in the GDP-weighted correlation of saving and investment rates among OECD countries, from 0.97 in 1970, and 0.96 as recently as 1992, to 0.80 in 2002.

14. Analyses of debt sustainability are often couched in terms of real or nominal growth rates, interest rates, and primary surpluses or deficits, as well as debt levels. However, given the complexities of statistics on the U.S. NIIP, it is simpler to use the relationship that for the NIIP to stabilize, the annual addition to it (the current account deficit) must equal the nominal growth rate of the economy times the net stock of debt.

15. O'Neill and Hatzius (2004) estimate that if U.S. government bond yields rise to 6 percent, the average level of the 1990s, this would add 1.2 percentage points to the U.S. current account deficit relative to GDP.

16. The IMF (2004a) has estimated that a 25-percent depreciation of the dollar reduces the U.S. NIIP ratio by 7 percent of GDP.

17. O'Neill and Hatzius (2004) argue that deficits at this rate may well be sustainable "for a time."

18. If one thought that the U.S. current account deficit of 5 percent of GDP were sustainable, that would imply an eventual NIIP ratio of 83 percent.

19. The treatments in Gale and Orszag (2003); Gramlich (2004); IMF (2004 and 2004a); Laubach (2003); Mühleisen, Towe, and Cardarelli (2004); Rivlin and Sawhill (2004); Rubin, Orszag, and Sinai (2004); and Summers (2004), for example, tend to focus on the federal deficit rather than the general government deficit or surplus. However, most of the variability is at the federal level.

20. Simulations reported in IMF (2004a) suggest that by 2010, the current U.S. fiscal expansion will reduce the level of U.S. potential GDP by ¾ to 1¼ percent, and the level of potential GDP of the rest of the world as a whole by 1 to 2 percent.

21. Of course, deficits are likely to affect the distribution of employment and capacity utilization across sectors, with possible economic and obvious political implications, for example, calls for sectoral or country-specific protection.

22. The composition of the fiscal deficit also matters to some analysts. Are widening deficits associated with increases in investment or consumption? Should the focus be on the unified budget deficit or some other concept? What time horizon should be used in analyzing the issue? As is normally the case in such matters, answers to these questions often depend on the issue under examination and sometimes depend on who is doing the analysis. As a result, there is a lack of consensus.

23. This aspect of the dollar's role is much more relevant and complicating to the exercise of U.S. monetary policy than the dollar's limited reserve role because of the high degree of inertia in official reserve holdings; see Truman (2005).

24. Of the 25 episodes Freund reviews, 17 involved external financial crises, using a modified Frankel and Rose (1996) index approach, but only four occurred before the current account deficit reached its widest point.

25. These rules of thumb assume the dollar's adjustment is exogenous, an assumption that does not fully capture exchange-market developments since early 2002. Moreover, different models yield different results, and the results depend on assumptions about accompanying policies and objectives. Baily (2003) reports simulations of the effects of exogenous dollar depreciation in the Macroeconomic Advisers model; the results can be interpreted as implying a rule of thumb of about $20 billion per percentage point of dollar adjustment; U.S. real GDP also declines relative to baseline. On the other hand, in FRB/Global (Levin, Rogers, and Tryon 1997), an exogenous dollar depreciation produces about $6 billion per percentage point when monetary policies in the U.S. and abroad follow Taylor rules; here, U.S. real GDP rises relative to baseline. If U.S. and foreign real GDP were unchanged, the FRB/Global result would be closer to $10 billion per percentage point.

26. In the simulations reported by Baily (2003), an exogenous change in the dollar is associated with real GDP 4.8 percent lower after 10 years and a reduction of the current account deficit of 2.5 percent of GDP.

27. This calculation, which ignores price effects, is based upon U.S. 2004 nominal GDP of $11,725 billion, imports of goods and services of $1,750 billion, and an income elasticity of 1.7.

28. A permanent boost of 3 percent in the level of foreign GDP (U.S.-export-weighted) would raise exports of goods and services by $35 billion (0.3 percent of U.S. GDP) on a base of $1,150 billion and an income elasticity of 1.0, again ignoring price effects.

References

Baily, Martin. 2003. Persistent dollar swings and the U.S. economy. In *Dollar overvaluation and the world economy*, eds. C. Fred Bergsten and John Williamson. Washington, D.C.: Institute for International Economics.

Dudley, William C., and Edward F. McKelvey. 2004. The U.S. budget outlook: A surplus of deficits. Goldman Sachs: Global Economic Paper 106 (March 31).

Frankel, Jeffrey, and Andrew Rose. 1996. Currency crashes in emerging markets: An empirical treatment. *Journal of International Economics* 41(3–4) November: 351–366.

Freund, Caroline. 2000. Current account adjustment in industrialized countries. Board of Governors of the Federal Reserve System: International Finance Discussion Papers 692.

Gale, William G., and Peter R. Orszag. 2003. The economic effects of long-term fiscal discipline. Urban Institute: Urban-Brookings Tax Policy Center Discussion Paper 8.

Gramlich, Edward M. 2004. Budget and trade deficits: Linked, both worrisome in the long run, but not twins. Remarks at the Los Angeles Chapter of the National Association for Business Economics, March 31.

Greenspan, Alan. 2003. Current account. Remarks at the 21st Annual Monetary Conference, cosponsored by the Cato Institute and *The Economist,* November 20. Washington, D.C.

Greenspan, Alan. 2004. Globalization and innovation. Remarks at the Conference on Bank Structure and Competition, sponsored by the Federal Reserve Bank of Chicago, May 6.

Greenspan, Alan. 2004a. Current account. Remarks before the Economic Club of New York, March 2.

International Monetary Fund. 2004. Economic prospects and policy issues. In *World Economic Outlook.* Washington, D.C.: International Monetary Fund.

International Monetary Fund. 2004a. How will the U.S. budget deficit affect the rest of the world? In *World Economic Outlook.* Washington, D.C.: International Monetary Fund.

Laubach, Thomas. 2003. New evidence on the interest rate effects of budget deficits and debt. Board of Governors of the Federal Reserve System: Finance and Economics Discussion Series 2003–12.

Levin, Andrew T., John H. Rogers, and Ralph W. Tryon. 1997. A guide to FRB/ Global Board of Governors of the Federal Reserve System: International Finance Discussion Papers 588.

Mann, Catherine L. 1999. *Is the U.S. trade deficit sustainable?* Washington, D.C.: Institute for International Economics.

Mann, Catherine L. 2003. How long the strong dollar? In *Dollar overvaluation and the world economy,* eds. C. Fred Bergsten and John Williamson. Washington, D.C.: Institute for International Economics.

Mühleisen, Martin, Christopher Towe, and Roberto Cardarelli, eds. 2004. *U.S. fiscal policies and priorities for long-run sustainability.* Washington, D.C.: International Monetary Fund.

O'Neill, Jim, and Jan Hatzius. 2004. U.S. balance of payments, unsustainable, but…. Goldman Sachs: *Global Economics Paper* 104.

Rivlin, Alice M., and Isabel Sawhill. 2004. *Restoring fiscal sanity: How to balance the budget.* Washington, D.C.: Brookings Institution.

Rubin, Robert E., Peter R. Orszag, and Allen Sinai. 2004. Sustained budget deficits: Longer-run U.S. economic performance and the risk of financial and fiscal disarray. Presented at the AEA-NAEFA Joint Session, Allied Social Science Associations Annual Meetings, January 4.

Summers, Lawrence H. 2004. The United States and the global adjustment process. Remarks at the 3rd Annual Stavros S. Niarchos Lecture, Institute for International Economics, March 23. Washington, D.C.

Truman, Edwin M. 2001. The international implications of paying down the debt. Institute for International Economics: *International Economics Policy Briefs* PB01-7.

Truman, Edwin M. 2005. The euro and prospects for policy coordination. In *The euro at five*, ed. Adam Posen. Washington, D.C.: Institute for International Economics.

Twin Deficits and Twin Decades

Jeffrey A. Frankel

Fiscal policy of the current decade in many respects mirrors the fiscal policy of the 1980s. For example, growing budget deficits are reflected in growing current account deficits. The twin deficits are back!

Perhaps the most important contribution to open-economy macroeconomics in the 1960s was the Mundell–Fleming model, with its prediction that a fiscal expansion under conditions of high capital mobility would be largely reflected in a current account deficit. Previously, the closed-economy models of the time had, instead, emphasized crowding out of domestic investment. The new prediction, that fiscal expansion would crowd out net exports, was mitigated by two contributions of the late 1970s. First, an important theoretical point: Barro's debt-neutrality hypothesis suggested that an increase in the budget deficit might be offset by an increase in private saving. With no fall in aggregate national saving, there need be no crowding out, of either the trade balance or investment. Second, an important empirical point: Feldstein and Horioka suggested that capital mobility must not be as high as previously assumed, because most of a fall in national saving is observed to be reflected as a fall in national investment, after all, rather than as being financed by borrowing from abroad.[1]

1. The 1980s

Each of these propositions received its first major practical test in the early 1980s under "Reaganomics." Massive tax cuts and increases in spending produced the largest budget deficits of the post-war period. Figure 7.3 and Table 7.2 show the results.

Notwithstanding the fact that the tax cuts were supposed to be pro saving, the rate of private saving did not rise enough to offset the budget deficit, as one might have predicted from Barro's debt-neutrality proposition. In fact, the rate of private saving actually fell substantially during the latter part of the decade (as Table 7.2 and Figures 7.4 and 7.5 show). One does not want to reject a theory based on a single historical episode, regardless of the importance of the episode; but, by now, there are numerous empirical studies and theoretical explanations elaborating on the failure of debt neutrality.

Thus, the total rate of national saving fell sharply in the 1980s. The question then became: What sector would bear the brunt of the crowding out? Investment or the trade balance? Which prediction would prove correct: that of the Mundell–Fleming model under high capital mobility or the Feldstein–Horioka finding? Three key attributes made the 1980s the first real test of the Mundell–Fleming model. First, the dollar was

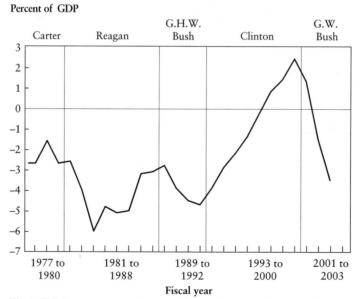

Figure 7.3
U.S. federal deficit, by presidential term. *Source:* Office of Management and Budget.

Table 7.2
Decomposition of National Saving and Investment

	Net Private Saving (% of GDP) (1)	Net Government Saving (% of GDP) (2)=(3)+(4)	Net State & Local Saving (% of GDP) (3)	Net Federal Saving (% of GDP) (4)	Net National Saving (% of GDP) (5)=(1)+(2)	Net Domestic Investment (% of GDP)	Current Account (% of GDP)
(average)							
1961–1964	9.9	1.4	0.9	0.5	11.2	10.4	0.8
1965–1968	10.6	0.7	0.9	-0.2	11.3	11.3	0.5
1969–1972	9.4	-0.4	0.8	-1.3	8.9	9.6	0.1
1973–1976	10.2	-1.6	0.6	-2.2	8.6	8.8	0.7
1977–1980	9.4	-0.9	0.6	-1.4	8.6	10.1	-0.1
1981–1984	10.3	-3.5	0.2	-3.7	6.8	8.2	-0.7
1985–1988	8.6	-3.1	0.4	-3.5	5.5	8.6	-2.8
1989–1992	7.5	-3.3	0.1	-3.4	4.2	6.2	-0.8
1993–1996	6.5	-2.7	0.2	-2.9	3.8	6.7	-1.3
1997–2000	4.9	1.2	0.5	0.7	6.1	8.5	-2.6
2001–2003	4.4	-1.8	0.0	-1.9	2.6	6.3	-4.3

Source: National Income and Product Accounts, Bureau of Economic Analysis, U.S. Department of Commerce.

Percent of GDP

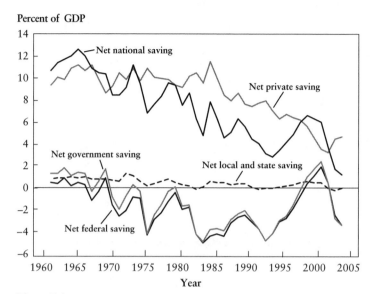

Figure 7.4
Budget balances, private saving, and national saving. *Source:* U.S. Bureau of Economic Analysis.

Percent of GDP

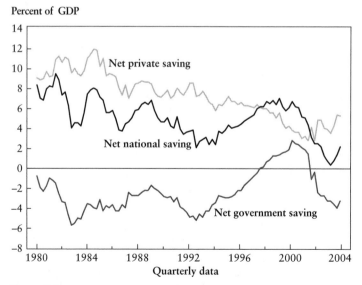

Figure 7.5
Private saving fails to rise to offset budget deficits; rather, national saving falls. *Source:* U.S. Bureau of Economic Analysis.

floating. Second, there were no controls on the capital account. These two structural aspects differentiated the experiment from the fiscal expansion of the 1960s (when President Lyndon B. Johnson increased military spending to fight the Vietnam War, while simultaneously expanding domestic spending under his Great Society and, at first, refusing to raise taxes to pay for it all). The third reason why the 1980s were the first clear test was that the Federal Reserve had adopted a tough anti-inflationary stance in 1980, and stuck with it thereafter (although the monetarist armor that had been adopted for this bold venture was wisely, but quietly, jettisoned after 1982). The predictions of the Mundell–Fleming model required that the fiscal expansion not be accommodated by expansion of the money supply, as it had been in the 1940s, 1960s, and 1970s. The stage was set as the 1980s began. Which sector would be crowded out by the fall in national saving?

Figure 7.6 and Table 7.2 tell the story. In the event, the Reagan deficits crowded out *both* the investment rate and the trade balance. Simple ratios for the U.S. data would imply that more than half the fall in national saving

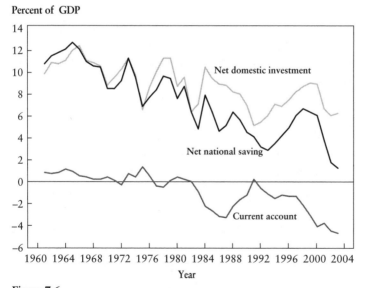

Figure 7.6
National saving, investment, and current account. *Source:* U.S. Bureau of Economic Analysis.

showed up in the trade balance, and less than half showed up in domestic crowding out. In this respect, the prediction of the Mundell–Fleming model was borne out, as was also the specific predicted mechanism of high real interest rates, net capital inflows, and real appreciation of the dollar. Updates of the Feldstein–Horioka regressions (either based on time-series or cross-section data) tended to suggest something different: that the Feldstein–Horioka coefficient was still a bit above half. Either way, the verdict seemed to be that international economists had jumped the gun in the mid-1970s by proclaiming perfect capital mobility, but that the system had been moving very gradually further in that direction subsequently. And, either way, the coefficient in the 1980s seemed to be not far from a half, comfortably in the middle of the range—close to neither zero nor one.

Quite possibly, the appropriate interpretation was that, although the United States and a few other major countries had removed their capital controls in 1973–1974, the United Kingdom and Japan did not begin liberalizing until 1979, and other countries still later. For deficits to be easily financed internationally, it is necessary that *both* the borrower and the lender be free of capital controls. Japan, in particular, became a major funder of U.S. deficits in the 1980s. It may also be relevant that the international debt crisis of 1982 marked a sudden reversal of what had been substantial capital flows to developing countries, thereby freeing up additional funds to pursue the high interest rates available in the United States.

The 1980s' combination of a large U.S. fiscal deficit and a large trade deficit became known as the "twin deficits." Martin Feldstein, as chairman of President Ronald Reagan's Council of Economic Advisers, was one of the first to popularize the phrase "twin deficits" and to forecast that the United States would soon lose its net creditor position as a result.[2] This was ironic, in light of the Feldstein–Horioka proposition.

The pattern was reversed in the 1990s. That the current account deficit briefly disappeared in 1990 was a coincidence, attributable to the U.S. recession and the contributions by Kuwait, Saudi Arabia, and other allies to cover the cost of the first war against Iraq. But paths of rising tax revenue and declining spending shares were established for the 1990s, with the result that they intersected by 1998, and record surpluses followed.[3] As a result, national saving rose. To be sure, the current account deficit continued to rise throughout the 1990s. But this was because investment was rising faster than saving. Whether one views the boom as having been propelled by a private-sector productivity boom led by information technology, by a perceived return of long-run fiscal virtue, or by a Fed that cooperated in bringing down interest rates, the resulting rise in investment and in the current account deficit is not surprising.

2. The Current Decade

The current decade is still too young to have received a convenient name ("00s"?). But the decade was only weeks old when it became clear that the United States was in for a new experiment with massive fiscal expansion.[4] Sure enough, the budget surplus vanished almost overnight, and record deficits soon returned.

There are many parallels between the current decade and the 1980s. In both cases, a major cause of the widening deficits was aggressive tax cuts, made against a background of (questionable) claims to long-run fiscal probity. In both cases, forecasts of growth rates and tax revenues that were predictably overly optimistic were part of the problem. (Figure 7.7 illustrates the repeated unidirectional errors in official budget forecasts that were made during the first three years of the George W. Bush presidency. Taking an unbiased look forward, Figure 7.8 illustrates the likely error that is built into the most recent official budget forecasts.) Further, in both cases, some in the administration, including the president, subscribed to the Laffer hypothesis that a reduction in U.S. tax rates would stimulate growth so much that tax receipts would go up, rather than down. In both cases, although the optimistic forecasts were soon shattered, the administration for a while continued to blame the deficits on recession and to repeat the claims that they would go away before long. In both cases, the failure of the budget outcomes to follow the scripts that had been prepared by White House speechwriters led to a switch to an alternative claim known as "starve the beast," that is, the proposition that deficits were a deliberate strategy to force the political process to cut spending. In both cases, this theory of political economy rang hollow in light of the proclivity of the Republican White House to continue to submit to Congress budgets with rapidly growing spending and to promise in speeches plans that were yet more extravagant than what was

Billions of dollars

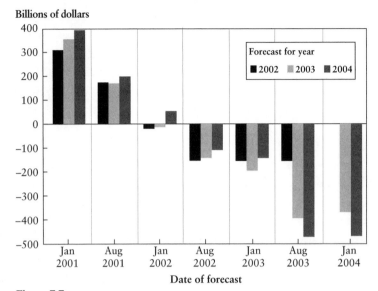

Figure 7.7
Three years of budget forecasts that soon proved too optimistic. *Source:*
Congressional Budget Office.

Percent of GDP

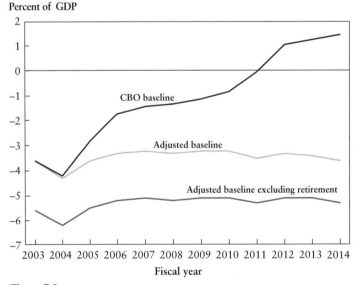

Figure 7.8
As of early 2004, the official budget forecasts were still too optimistic. *Sources:*
Congressional Budget Office, Budget and Economic Outlook: An Update, August
2003; and Rivlin and Sawhill (2004), Figure 1-4.

Percent of GDP

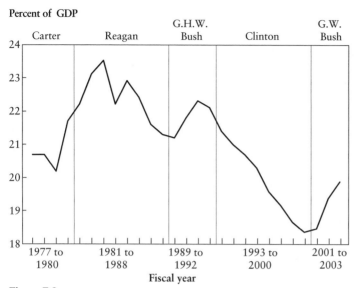

Figure 7.9
U.S. federal spending, by presidential term. *Source:* Office of Management and Budget.

built into the budget.[5] (Figure 7.9 shows the pattern. Spending as a share of GDP seems uncannily to rise whenever a Republican president takes office.) In both cases, economists debated the extent to which deficits affect interest rates. In both cases, private saving did not offset the new deficits—no Ricardian equivalence. In both cases, the fall in national saving was soon reflected as a fall in the current account. In other words, the twin deficits are back.

3. An Update of Feldstein–Horioka

It is important to acknowledge the role of cyclical factors. The recessions of 1981–1982, 1990–1991, and 2001 exacerbated the remarkable pattern, whereby new Republican presidents have presided over sharp deteriorations in the federal budget. (Return to Figure 7.3.) More generally, it is a regular pattern that national saving rates fall in recessions and rise in booms. Investment rates tend to vary cyclically, as well—even more so, with the result that current account balances tend to rise in recessions and fall in booms. Of the many critiques of Feldstein–Horioka, some attribute the saving-investment correlation to this endogenous cyclical pattern; and most of the rest attribute it to endogeneity of national saving with respect to some other particular factor, such as growth rates of productivity or population or changes in world interest rates. Many of the critics have failed to notice that Feldstein and Horioka (1980) and Feldstein (1983) were aware of the cyclicality and other endogeneity problems, and sought to address them by using decade averages, instrumental variables, and cross-sections instead of time series. The saving-investment correlation tends to emerge even with these corrections.[6]

The subject at hand is recent U.S. history, and full cross-section econometrics is probably overkill for the task. Instead, we ran a simple Feldstein–Horioka regression on an updated U.S. time series, covering the period 1964–2003. Table 7.3(a) reports a saving-retention coefficient of .60. When we allow for a time trend in the coefficient, it appears to be positive. As a check, we ran the regression in Table 7.3(b), with the current account on the left-hand side in place of the investment rate. In theory, the two regressions should be precisely equivalent, with the new coefficient equal to one minus the old (and the trend of opposite sign); but it is worth checking, because statistical errors and omissions, in fact, invalidate the national saving identity. In this case, we duly find a coefficient of .38: Fluctuations in national saving are 38 percent financed by borrowing from abroad, and 62 percent reflected as crowding out of national investment.

It is likely that cyclical fluctuations seriously raise the saving retention coefficient and perhaps its trend. In Table 7.3(c), we repeat the Feldstein–Horioka regression with cyclically adjusted rates of national saving and investment. Now, the coefficient for the overall sample falls to .49. The positive trend is no longer statistically significant. Table 7.3(d) repeats the regression with the current account as the dependent variable. The coefficient is essentially equivalent, at .50. There is now a significant and positive trend in the coefficient, implying, more plausibly, a gradual increase in the degree of capital mobility in the Feldstein–Horioka sense. Although these results are liable to charges of endogeneity and all the other critiques that have been launched against Feldstein–Horioka, they seem to confirm the findings of earlier studies, including those with instrumental variables: Fluctuations in national saving are

Table 7.3
Feldstein–Horioka Regressions for the United States, 1964–2003
(160 observations)

	Coefficient (Std. Error)	Coefficient (Std. Error)
(a). Dependent Variable: National Investment as Share of GDP, NOT Cyclically Adjusted		
National Savings as Share of GDP (NS)	.5969*** (.0246)	.6186 (.0253)
Trend in Coefficient on Saving (NS * t)		.0009 (.0003)
Constant	.0444*** (.0018)	.0387 (.0027)
R^2	.79	.80
(b). Dependent Variable: Current Account as Share of GDP, NOT Cyclically Adjusted		
National Savings as Share of GDP (NS)	.3798*** (.0335)	.3301*** (.0329)
Trend in Coefficient on Saving (NS * t)		−.0022*** (.0004)
Constant	−.0360*** (.0025)	−.0231*** (.0035)
R^2	.45	.52
(c). Dependent Variable: National Investment as Share of GDP, Cyclically Adjusted		
National Savings as Share of GDP, Cyclically Adjusted (CyclAdjNS2)	.4913*** (.0228)	.3967*** (.0551)
Trend in Coefficient on Saving (CyclAdjNS2 * T)		.0011* (.0006)
Constant		.0011 (.0008)
R^2	.75	.75
(d). Dependent Variable: Current Account as Share of GDP, Cyclically Adjusted		
National Savings as Share of GDP, Cyclically Adjusted (CyclAdjNS2)	.5027*** (.0332)	.3554*** (.0803)
Trend in Coefficient on Saving (CyclAdjNS2 * T)		.0018** (.0009)
Constant		.0018 (.0012)
R^2	.59	.60

***(1-percent significance); **(5-percent significance); *(10-percent significance)

Note: Cyclical adjustment of a series is accomplished by applying the residuals from a regression of the series against the logarithmic percentage difference between actual and potential output.

Data sources:

U.S. Bureau of Economic Analysis:
GDP Table 1.1.5, Line 1; Net Domestic Investment Table 5.1, Line 31; and Net National Savings Table 5.1, Line 2

OECD Economic Outlook:
GDPV, gross domestic product, volume, market prices; and GDPVTR, gross domestic product, volume, potential

reflected roughly half in the current account and half in investment, possibly with a gradual trend suggesting that the United States has found it easier, over time, to borrow in order to finance its deficits.

4.   Any Differences Between the Decades?

There are, to be sure, a number of important differences between the pattern of the 1980s and the current decade. Interest rates have been low (nominal and real) during 2001–2004, and the dollar began to depreciate in 2003—just the opposite of the Mundell–Fleming prediction and the experience of 1980–1984. But this is not surprising: The Federal Reserve lowered interest rates aggressively in 2001, just the opposite of what it did at the beginning of the earlier recession/presidency/decade (and in 1990, as well). The Mundell–Fleming prediction applies specifically to a fiscal expansion that is *not* accommodated by monetary policy, whereas the 2001–2004 expansion clearly *has* been accommodated, so far. In this sense, the Vietnam-era expansion of the late 1960s may be a better precedent for today's deficits than was Reaganomics in the 1980s. Not only were the two war-time fiscal expansions accommodated by monetary policy, but they also showed up in growing U.S. balance of payments deficits that largely put the dollar at the mercy of foreign central banks.

The real test for the current decade will come when the Fed responds to the recovery by raising interest rates; that is, assuming the central bank declines to play the role of enabler to the fiscal alcoholic, in the same way that Volcker declined to play the role of enabler to Reagan in the early 1980s (and the Bundesbank to the German government in the early 1990s). Furthermore, the tendency of central banks in Asia and other foreign countries to buy up U.S. Treasury securities, thereby keeping interest rates low and the dollar high, has been as important as the tendency of our own central bank to do so. But it is likely to come to an end, as well.

Another difference this time around is that our initial condition is a far higher national debt, and far fewer years to go until the baby boomers start to retire, than was the case in 1981. Admittedly, the current debt and prospects for likely future deficits have not yet shown up in long-term interest rates or stock market valuations. But it is *expectations* of

Table 7.4
Determinants of Long-Term Real Interest Rates: Six Countries

	US	Germany	France	Italy	Spain	UK
Constant	-0.001	-0.122***	-0.022	-0.081	-0.043*	-0.034
	(0.008)	(0.038)	(0.027)	(0.041)	(0.023)	(0.030)
Inflation	1.00	1.00	1.00	1.00	1.00	1.00
Debt Ratio	0.060**	0.182***	0.027	0.109	0.031	0.067
	(0.019)	(0.047)	(0.040)	(0.062)	(0.051)	(0.044)
Expected Change in Debt Ratio	0.144**	0.112***	0.177**	0.324**	0.289***	0.066
	(0.061)	(0.032)	(0.073)	(0.106)	(0.048)	(0.110)
Output Gap	0.388**	0.608**	0.252	0.297	0.218	-0.316
	(0.174)	(0.219)	(0.202)	(0.484)	(0.223)	(0.324)
Foreign Interest Rate	0.096	1.529***	0.923***	0.390	1.204***	0.815**
	(0.122)	(0.327)	(0.241)	(0.446)	(0.145)	(0.348)
N	15	15	15	15	15	15
Adjusted R2	0.32	0.51	0.82	0.77	0.82	0.55
D-W	2.24	2.50	2.47	1.70	2.47	1.44

Notes: OLS regression using annual data, in levels. Newey–West robust standard errors in parentheses. Percentage variables defined in decimal form. N is the number of observations.

*, **, *** denote significance at the 10-percent, 5-percent, and 1-percent levels, respectively.
Source: Chinn and Frankel (2003)

future deficits that matter most for long-term interest rates.[7] If respondents to political polls appear unaware of what are realistic forecasts for the budget deficits over the next 10 years, then perhaps it is not surprising that participants in the securities markets are also not yet fully aware of them. That Japan and Europe have debt and demographic problems at least as bad as ours is of some reassurance. But it only reinforces the prediction that the trend for world interest rates, from here on out, is likely to be upward.

■ *The author would like to thank Dora Douglass for efficient research assistance.*

Notes

1. Feldstein and Horioka (1980).

2. Council of Economic Advisers (1984); Feldstein (1986).

3. The author would give substantial credit to three deliberate policy decisions: (1) *The 1990 Budget Enforcement Act*. The first President Bush bravely revoked his "no new taxes" pledge, and spending caps and PAYGO provisions were established to prevent future budgetary giveaways unless they were paid for. (2) *The 1993 Clinton budget*. President Clinton gave up his middle-class tax cut and some other campaign priorities to put emphasis on the budget, renewing the caps and PAYGO provisions. (3) *The policy of "Save Social Security First" in the 1998 State of the Union Message*. This policy led to a bipartisan consensus to continue foregoing spending increases and tax cuts until Social Security was put on a firm footing. To be sure, a booming economy and stock market were a large part of the elimination of the deficit during the course of the decade. But some would claim that the boom was partly endogenous—mutually reinforcing, together with a credible path of fiscal discipline. Views of Robert Rubin, Martin Feldstein, and many others are represented in Frankel and Orszag (2002).

4. I am counting the decade as beginning on January 1, 2001. George W. Bush's inauguration took place on January 20.

5. In several respects, the record of the current administration is worse than that of the Reagan administration. In the first place, President Reagan allowed some exchange of views internally, for example, between the monetarists, who believed that exchange rates should float, and the supply-siders, who believed they should be pegged. In the second place, the Reagan administration began to adjust course after a year or two in office (like the first Bush administration after it), and to reverse some of the tax cuts, whereas the current administration has yet even to acknowledge fiscal reality. In the third place, we now have the example that was set by the 1990s as to how fiscal discipline can be restored: a

set of mechanisms (such as caps and PAYGO provisions) that constitute a system of shared sacrifice and the principle of budget neutrality for future changes. We know that the political economy of this approach can work to balance the budget ("I will forego my spending increase if you forego your tax cut"), unlike the political economy of "starve the beast" ("I will screw you on taxes, and you will forego your spending increase").

6. Frankel (1991) surveyed the critiques as of that date, and sought to address endogeneity by instrumental variables. Regression results using military spending as an instrument for government spending and the age-dependency ratio as an instrument for private saving showed little decline in the Feldstein–Horioka coefficient relative to OLS estimation. Imperfect integration across markets in securities and across markets in goods may be the culprit, despite high integration for short-term deposits and bills. However, the coefficient had, indeed, declined a bit between the 1970s and 1980s.

7. Table 7.4 reports some regression results for six countries. We see that expected future deficits have statistically significant effects on real interest rates, after remembering to control for a few other important determinants.

References

Chinn, Menzie, and Jeffrey Frankel. 2003. The euro area and world interest rates. Working paper presented at "Financial Globalization," Federal Reserve Bank of New York, December.

Council of Economic Advisers. 1984. The United States in the world economy: Challenges of recovery. In *Economic report of the president: 1984*. Washington, D.C.: U.S. Government Printing Office.

Feldstein, Martin. 1983. Domestic saving and international capital movements in the long run and the short run. *European Economic Review* 21(1–2) March–April: 129–151.

Feldstein, Martin. 1986. The budget deficit and the dollar. In *NBER Macroeconomics Annual 1986*, 355–392. Cambridge: National Bureau of Economic Research.

Feldstein, Martin, and Charles Horioka. 1980. Domestic saving and international capital flows. *Economic Journal* 90 (358) June: 314–29.

Frankel, Jeffrey. 1988. International capital flows and domestic economic policies. In *The United States in the world economy*, ed. Martin Feldstein, 559–627. Chicago: University of Chicago Press.

Frankel, Jeffrey. 1991. Quantifying international capital mobility in the 1980s. In *National saving and economic performance*, eds. D. Bernheim and J. Shoven, 227–260. Chicago: University of Chicago Press.

Frankel, Jeffrey, and Peter Orszag, eds. 2002. *American economic policy in the 1990s*. Cambridge: MIT Press.

The Current Account and the Budget Deficit: A Disaggregated Perspective

Catherine L. Mann

What's new to say about the relationship between the budget deficit and the current account deficit? The national accounts dictate that they add up, but the behavioral underpinnings of the components determine how they are related. Over the last 25 years, we have had all manner of relationships. In the 1980s, we had the "twin deficits." The widening fiscal deficit was associated with higher interest rates, an appreciated dollar, and a larger current account deficit. In the 1990s, the two were "estranged." Fiscal discipline narrowed the budget deficit, but unleashed economic forces that contributed to increased wealth, investment, consumption, and a larger current account deficit. Sometimes they are just "family," as Truman points out in this volume. In my comments, I emphasize, first, that disaggregating fiscal and trade balances into types of spending and buying reveals important insights into their economic relationship today. Second, I stress that trends in the two deficits create a negative feedback loop that will widen them both and fulfill the warning that they are unsustainable.

Figure 7.10 shows a decomposition of the national income and product accounts (NIPA). Net investment always exceeds net national saving. Fiscal balance was negative for most of the period, although it was briefly in surplus at the end of the 1990s. The trade deficit narrowed in the recession of 1991–1992 and then widened again, dramatically from about 1997 onward. The most notable feature of the NIPA is the 25-year declining trend in the household saving rate. This declining trend is the first element of the story that relates the fiscal deficit to the trade deficit of today. A low saving rate suggests strong consumption spending out of wage and salary income. But additional spending in the late

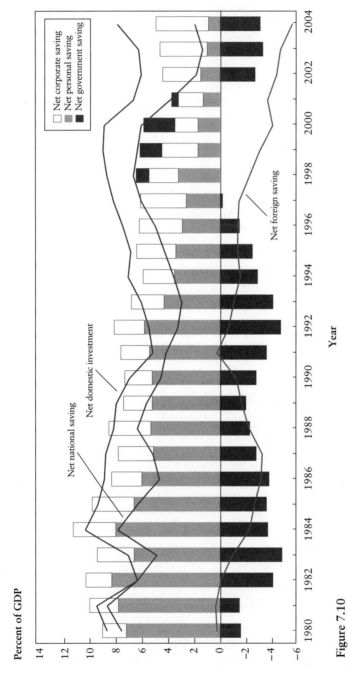

Figure 7.10
The NIPA in disaggregate: U.S. saving and investment, 1980–2004. *Source:* U.S. Bureau of Economic Analysis, National Income and Product Accounts and International Transactions Accounts; author's calculations.

1990s came as a consequence of high stock-market wealth, and, today, additional spending is coming from home-equity wealth. The tax cuts of recent years have further bolstered consumer demand.

Hence, a second element of the story relating the budget deficit with the trade deficit is the decomposition of the fiscal deficit into the sources of that deficit. Figure 7.11 shows the decline in the fiscal budget position since 2001 and projections for the budget over the next 10 years, under alternative assumptions regarding fiscal policy. According to the Congressional Research Service, 45 percent of the decline in the federal budget balance between FY 2000 and FY 2004 was accounted for by tax cuts [Esenwein *et al.* (2005)]. This translates into a great deal of potential consumption. In fact, in September 17, 2002, Macroeconomic Advisers (2002) calculated that the additional consumption associated with $30 billion in tax cuts in 2001 added about 1 percentage point to

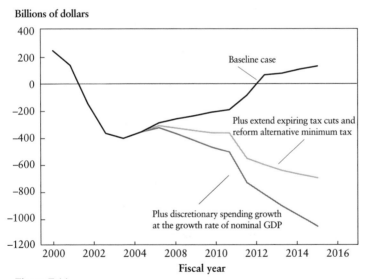

Billions of dollars

Figure 7.11
CBO's budget scenarios, January/March 2005. The Congressional Research Service (CRS) estimates that most of the turnaround in the budget (surplus of 2.4% of GDP in FY 2000 to deficit of 3.6% of GDP in FY 2004) can be attributed to a fall in receipts from a historic high of 20.9% of GDP in 2000 to a 45-year low of 16.3% of GDP in 2004. According to CRS, 61% of changes in revenue are due to policy changes, and 39% are due to economic conditions. *Source*: Congressional Budget Office and Congressional Research Service of the Library of Congress.

gross domestic product (GDP) growth in the second half of that year. In their assessment, dated September 19, 2003 [Macroeconomic Advisers (2003)], they found that the tax cuts in the Jobs and Growth Tax Relief and Reconciliation Act of 2003 added another $101 billion to disposable personal income. The March 2005 projections for the fiscal deficit from the Congressional Budget Office (2005) indicate what may be in store for consumption spending, based on legislation to extend the expiring tax provisions—some $700 billion in additional potential consumption spending. All told, over the last 10 years, there has been a great deal of consumption spending supported, first, by stock-market wealth; then by home-equity wealth; and, finally, through deficit spending on the government accounts. More is slated for the future. What might be the implication of all that consumer spending on the trade balance?

The U.S. Bureau of Economic Analysis decomposes trade into end-use categories (Figure 7.12). The largest categories on both sides of the trade equation are capital goods and industrial supplies and materials (excluding energy), which together accounted for 45 percent of exports and 32 percent of imports in 2004. Until 1997, net trade in these goods cycled through larger and smaller surpluses, depending in large part on the U.S. and global business cycles. Since about that time, however, the trade balance in these goods has not recovered, even though global growth has revived. From a surplus of about $50 billion in 1997, this balance is now in deficit by some $30 billion. This change may reflect the initial and continued effects of the appreciation of the dollar. It may be a result of the relatively slow growth of investment in U.S. exporters' markets abroad, which has been masked by more robust aggregate measures of economic activity, such as GDP. Or, there may have been a permanent change in the international supply chain for production of capital goods, perhaps to center on China. And, finally, the fallout from the Asian financial crises may persist.

Although capital and industrial goods may be the largest category of trade flows, the largest component of the nonoil/nonagricultural trade deficit is consumer goods. Imports of consumer goods as a share of total merchandise imports rose dramatically in the last 25 years (from 14 to 25 percent), while consumer goods represent only a modest share of exports (12 percent in 2004). When added to the net deficit in autos,

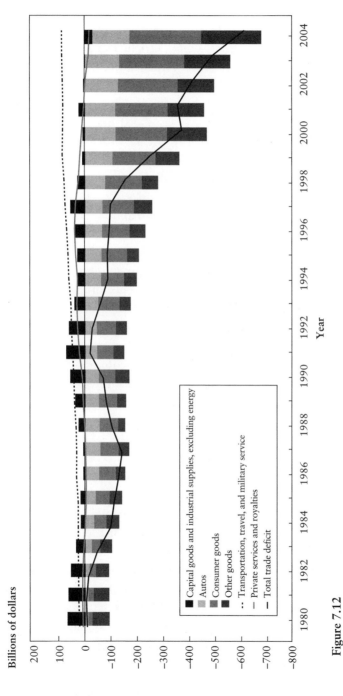

Figure 7.12
Disaggregated U.S. trade balance, 1980–2004. *Source:* U.S. Bureau of Economic Analysis, International Transactions Accounts.

nearly three-quarters of the increase in the nonoil/nonagricultural trade deficit since 1997 can be accounted for by these two categories of personal consumption expenditures. Only outright recession (in 1991 and 2001) stemmed the widening in these components of the trade deficit. For some goods (such as apparel, shoes, and computer peripherals), a story of lost comparative advantage resulting from the higher cost of U.S. labor is plausible. But, for the full range of consumer and automotive products, this explanation does not seem to square with the historical comparative advantage enjoyed by the United States in manufactured capital goods, which has held up remarkably well. It is likely that the very large structural imbalance in the consumer categories of trade is a reflection of extraordinarily robust domestic consumption and the declining trend in household savings in the United States.

In sum, the trends in the consumer goods deficit and in the trade deficit are not related directly to the fiscal position. But, to the extent that recent fiscal deficits are disproportionately a consequence of tax cuts that support consumption spending, to the extent that the pipeline of fiscal deficit contains another dose of tax cuts, and to the extent that the elasticity of import demand for consumer goods remains very high, the widening of the trade deficit in the past and likely into the future is, importantly, a consequence of the composition of the fiscal deficit toward revenue shortfalls due to tax cuts, rather than a consequence of the absolute magnitude of the fiscal deficit.

Asset flows offer the second perspective on the relationship between the fiscal and trade deficits. The magnitude and type of financial flow may increase the potential for a negative feedback loop between the two deficits, ultimately making them both unsustainable. Figure 7.13 details the inflows of financial capital. With respect to capital inflows, the $1.4 trillion inflow in 2004 was well more than we "needed" to finance the current account deficit of $670 billion or so. But, looking at the composition of the inflow, there is a rising share of interest-bearing financial assets in the foreign purchases of U.S. assets, in particular, of the form of official and private purchases of U.S. Treasury securities. This rising share of interest-bearing assets in capital inflows translates into a rising share of interest-bearing assets in the stock of the net international investment position (Figure 7.14).

Billions of dollars

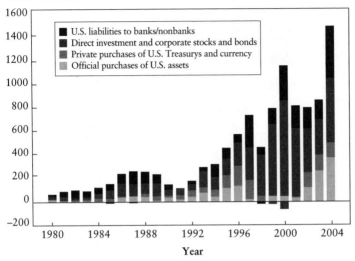

Figure 7.13
Foreign purchases of U.S. assets by asset type and purchaser. *Source:* U.S. Bureau of Economic Analysis, International Transactions Accounts.

The net international investment position (NIIP) of the United States turned negative in 1986, as the years of current account deficit translated into larger and larger foreign holdings of U.S. assets. From 1997 to 2003, the negative NIIP swelled from $0.8 trillion (about 7 percent of U.S. GDP) to $2.4 trillion (about 23 percent of GDP). Yet, net earnings throughout have been positive. How can the United States be a long-time borrower, yet still enjoy net positive investment earnings? Although this has been both a puzzle and a persistent feature of the data, a decomposition of the receipts and payments shows that the yield on U.S. foreign direct investment (FDI) abroad consistently exceeds that on FDI in the United States, although the yield differential has been narrowing (Figure 7.15). On the non-FDI portion of the stocks, the rates of return are quite similar. As the current account deficit has continued to widen, the share of the stock of U.S. assets in the form of financial instruments that yield interest receipts has shrunk. But, with global interest rates falling during the recent past, the overall payments on interest-bearing liabilities (including U.S. Treasury securities) have not risen very rapidly. So, the

Billions of dollars

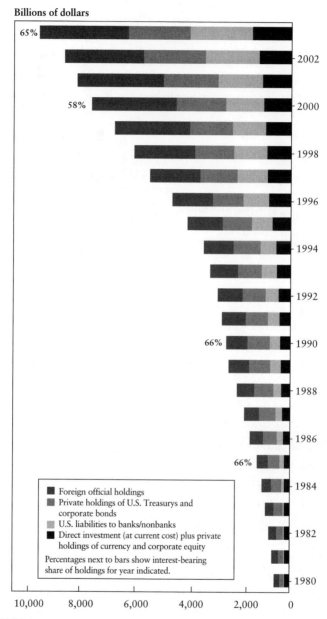

Figure 7.14 (a)
Foreign holdings of U.S. assets. *Source:* U.S. Bureau of Economic Analysis, Net International Investment Position of the United States.

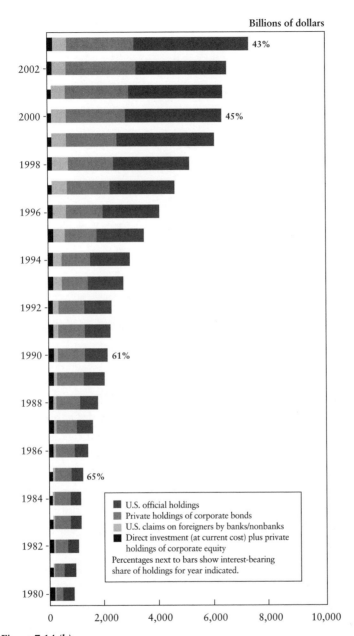

Figure 7.14 (b)
U.S. holdings of foreign assets. *Source:* U.S. Bureau of Economic Analysis, Net International Investment Position of the United States.

Percent

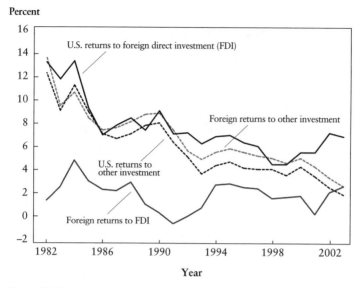

Figure 7.15
U.S. and foreign returns to investments abroad. *Source:* U.S. Bureau of Economic Analysis.

FDI net positive earnings have not yet been offset by the net interest payments on interest-bearing assets.

In the context of projected fiscal deficits, what does the nature of the disaggregated financial flows and stocks portend—both for fiscal balance and for the current account? Continued current account deficits suggest that the interest-bearing component of the stock of international investment liabilities may increase, and the interest-bearing component of the stock of international investment assets may shrink. As global interest rates start to climb, the ratio of payments due on interest-bearing liabilities relative to receipts from interest-bearing assets will turn against the United States, and the required net payments will erode the advantage on FDI returns. Overall, net investment payments (rather than the net receipts to which we have grown accustomed) will worsen the current account deficit.

Moreover, as the fiscal deficit widens, and as the share of U.S. Treasury securities held abroad increases (that share has already more than doubled in the last 10 years to over 50 percent), the interest paid on U.S. government debt will increasingly be paid to foreign holders, thereby augmenting the current account directly through the channel of interest payments on Treasury debt. Thus, there is an explicit negative feedback loop between the fiscal deficit and the current account deficit.

More generally, what does a larger current account deficit imply for foreign investors' portfolio decisions? *The Economist* magazine's Portfolio Poll surveys a number of investment houses on the composition of their global investment portfolios. Among the questions is one requesting information on the share of U.S. stocks in the equity portfolio of the firm. During the heyday of U.S. economic performance in the second half of the 1990s, the share of U.S. assets in these portfolios increased from about 30 to about 55 percent. That is where the share has remained since 2002. What will happen to that share going forward? With larger and larger current account deficits, the United States is offering more assets to the rest of the world. Will foreign investors buy those assets at the current interest rate and exchange rate? If not, one of the following will occur: Interest rates will rise, the dollar will fall, or some combination of the two.

In conclusion, what is today's relationship between the fiscal deficit and the trade deficit? The decomposition story implies that the tax-cut, consumption-spending channel has been key for getting the United States to where we are today, for both deficits. But tax cuts and trade in consumer goods have been important features of the economic landscape before. What makes this round of twin deficits different from earlier episodes, such as those of the Reagan era? There is more consumption spending in the fiscal-deficit pipeline, and the trade deficit in consumer goods and the consumption elasticity for imports are huge. Our net international investment position is much larger than before, and the interest-bearing component of it is higher. The foreign holding of U.S. Treasury securities is greater, and the U.S. investment share in global portfolios appears to have topped out. The external financing environment is more vulnerable, and the recipe for a negative feedback loop between the fiscal deficit and the trade deficit is in place. The important question is whether that vulnerability and negative feedback loop will be addressed.

References

Congressional Budget Office. 2005. An analysis of the president's budgetary proposals for fiscal year 2006. March.

Esenwein, Gregg, Marc Labonte, and Philip Winters. 2005. The federal budget deficit: A discussion of recent trends. Congressional Research Service. March 2.

Macroeconomic Advisers. 2002. *Economic Outlook* 20 (8) September.

Macroeconomic Advisers. 2003. *Economic Outlook* 21 (8) September.

What Can We Do About the "Twin" Deficits?

Alice M. Rivlin

I am delighted to be back at the Federal Reserve, especially at such a stimulating conference in such a beautiful place. Moreover, since I spent many more years of my life as a budget practitioner than as a central banker, I am particularly happy to be participating in a Fed conference on fiscal policy.

Truman, Frankel, and Mann have explained the twin deficit puzzle extremely well. I am going to concentrate on what we ought to do about it. I particularly want to focus on options for closing the fiscal deficit in the United States over the next decade. The two available options—cutting spending growth and raising tax rates—are both politically unattractive, but we do know they work. By contrast, there are no workable policies for closing the current account deficit directly. I doubt that anyone in this audience would endorse protectionism, manipulating the exchange rate, or deliberately creating a recession. Reducing the current account deficit is likely to be a byproduct of other policies—such as failure to address the fiscal deficit—that result in investors losing confidence in U.S. economic management and precipitating the corrective action of a falling dollar.

I confess that I was devoted to the twin deficit story in the 1980s. It certainly fit the facts of that decade, as Frankel points out. The Fed was focused on knocking out inflation and minimizing the risks of too much accommodation, so interest rates were high. The Reagan Administration cut tax rates, stepped up defense spending, and restrained domestic growth, but the restraint was not sufficient to offset the defense increases. Soaring deficits were exacerbated by recession and high debt service costs. National saving plummeted, but domestic investment did not take the whole hit. Capital flowed in from abroad, the dollar was strong, and the growing current account deficit seemed, indeed, to be a twin of the fiscal deficit.

The twin-deficit story was at least as important as were appeals to fiscal rectitude in building political support for the bipartisan actions that eventually tamed the budget deficit. Politicians from agricultural and industrial states saw the punishing effect of high interest rates and the high dollar on their constituents' export earnings. They bought into the idea that cutting the budget deficit would bring interest rates down, reduce the value of the dollar in international markets, and relieve the plight of farmers and industrial exporters.

A bipartisan consensus formed around the goal of deficit reduction, although not on how to achieve it. Democrats and Republicans worked together to create budget process rules that would force them to compromise their different priorities, while moving toward budget balance. Gramm–Rudman–Hollings was an ingenious attempt, but proved an unworkable process. The budget agreement of 1990, however, put caps on discretionary spending and adopted the so-called "PAYGO rules," which forbade entitlement increases or tax cuts without commensurate offsets. These decision rules created a self-disciplining process that worked reasonably effectively for close to a decade.

Debate on spending and tax policy was fiercely acrimonious and intensely partisan, but the consensus on the desirability of balance and the importance of budget rules held up. One result, which the end of the Cold War greatly facilitated, was slow growth in discretionary spending. Another was that significant tax cuts and entitlement increases were not enacted for a decade. There would have been plenty of political support for adding prescription drug coverage to Medicare, for example, but such a measure was too expensive to enact in the face of the PAYGO rules. Finally, of course, rapid growth in the economy and a booming stock market, combined with the small tax increases enacted in 1990 and 1993, produced a bonanza of federal revenues that moved the budget into unexpected surplus before the end of the decade. Some of the predicted benefits of lower deficits occurred, notably a reduction in interest rates. Fiscal restraint was certainly one of the factors, along with the acceleration of productivity growth and falling inflation, that encouraged the Fed not to tighten when unemployment rates plummeted in the second half of the decade. However, the promise of the twin-deficit story—that the current account deficit would follow the fiscal deficit down—definitely did not occur. Instead, when the current account deficit soared as the economy boomed, the story changed. The new story had to do with the high U.S. income-elasticity of imports, slower growth abroad, and the appeal of the United States to equity and direct investors. Our trading partners stopped lecturing us about fiscal irresponsibility and started fussing about our current account deficit. No one had an obvious remedy, however, other than slower growth of the U.S. economy, which was not an attractive prospect either for us or our trading partners.

Eventually, of course, the economy did slow. Recession, plus Reagan-like tax cuts and spending increases, turned huge actual and projected surpluses into huge actual and projected deficits early in the current decade. The current account deficit kept on growing, albeit at a somewhat slower rate. Now that the economy is recovering strongly, and the Fed is likely to become rapidly less accommodative, the specter of looming twin deficits similar to those of the 1980s has reappeared.

Since current fiscal deficits are unsustainable, one can hope that, once the election is over, there will be a new bipartisan consensus that the fiscal deficit threatens future prosperity and should be drastically reduced, if not eliminated. A new chapter of the twin-deficit story would bolster that consensus. From an economic perspective, the rationale for action relates to the dangers of the low U.S. national saving rate. The prospect of deficits putting upward pressure on interest rates becomes increasingly real as the economy approaches full capacity and the Fed focuses on the growing risk of inflation. But the prospect of higher interest rates slowing growth may not be enough to mobilize the political will to take the painful steps necessary to eliminate fiscal deficits. The connection between interest rates and deficits is perceived to be tenuous, and the magnitude of the effect, even at full employment, is not large enough to be perceived as a crisis. A rapid correction of the current account deficit, however, could produce an action-precipitating crisis. If failure to address the fiscal deficit leads international investors, perhaps especially Asian central banks, to conclude that the United States is not managing its fiscal affairs responsibly and that the dollar's prospects are poor, there could be a rush for the dollar exits. American investors could suddenly be dependent on domestic saving, without the cushion of inflowing foreign funds. The prospect of such an outcome could galvanize the financial community to press Washington for rapid fiscal deficit reduction before it is too late.

As the experience of the 1980s showed, it is easier for politicians to agree on a deficit reduction goal than on how to get there. Nevertheless, a group of us at the Brookings Institution recently decided to plunge ahead and try to answer the question: How would you balance the budget, if you decided to do so? We encapsulated our efforts in a slim volume edited by Isabel Sawhill and myself, called, *Restoring Fiscal Sanity: How to Balance the Budget* (Rivlin and Sawhill, 2004).

We started with the standard Congressional Budget Office projections, but adjusted them to make the recent tax cuts permanent (as the Bush Administration requests). We also assumed that the alternative minimum tax (AMT) would be reformed to keep the number of AMT payers from exploding, and that discretionary spending would grow with inflation and population. These assumptions implied that the deficit in the unified budget (which counts the surpluses in the retirement accounts as offsets to deficits in the rest of the budget) would remain at about 3.5 percent of the gross national product (GDP) for the next decade, and then rise rapidly as the baby boom generation begins to retire. Without counting those retirement surpluses—and one should remember that they will soon disappear—the deficit would be 5 to 6 percent of GDP over the decade.

We chose the fairly easy goal of moving to balance in the *unified* budget in 10 years. It would have been a lot harder to achieve balance without the retirement account offsets. We offered three plans, which we called the smaller government plan, the larger government plan, and the better government plan—all with the same goal of unified budget balance in 2014. In the smaller government plan we *tried* to achieve balance entirely by cutting spending. We reduced domestic discretionary spending below the projections for 2014 by $400 billion. That meant getting rid of commercial subsidies and agricultural price supports, privatizing air traffic control, eliminating the Export-Import Bank, and devolving *all* elementary and secondary education, housing, manpower training, environmental, and local law enforcement programs to states and localities without compensation. It also meant reducing NASA and the National Institutes of Health, eliminating highway earmarks, and reducing entitlement spending in Medicare, Social Security, and Medicaid. But despite these drastic actions, many of which shifted heavy burdens to state and local governments, we could not get the budget to balance in 2014. We had solved only about three-quarters of the problem. We had to find more revenues to achieve balance.

For the larger government plan, we looked at what the Democratic candidates were saying—there were multiple candidates at the time we started the project. We left projected domestic spending intact and added $185 billion by 2014 for education, health, and other new initiatives. We identified $90 billion in savings, $60 billion of it from defense. With these new initiatives, we needed over $600 billion in new taxes to make the budget balance in 2014. Just rolling back recent cuts fills less than half that gap, and one probably wouldn't want to roll them all back to 2001 rates. To make up the difference, we assumed a new value added tax (VAT).

Finally, we offered a "better" government plan, which included modest funding for new initiatives (far less than in the larger government plan). It also involved cutting back some existing programs (but less drastically than in the smaller government plan). Getting to balance still involved raising revenues in 2014 by $400 billion—more than the yield of rolling back the recent tax cuts for high-income people. We also increased the payroll tax slightly and raised the earnings ceiling on Social Security.

The authors didn't expect anyone to buy our particular solutions. We just wanted to get people thinking constructively about the problem. We believe the exercise illustrates several points:

• First, it *is* possible to get the unified budget back to balance over the next 10 years, although it will be very hard. Faster economic growth, of course, would make it easier.

• Second, budget balance is impossible to achieve entirely by cutting spending or entirely by increasing revenues. It will require making very difficult choices on both the spending side and the revenue side of the budget. Getting to balance will likely require cutting some current programs, paying for new initiatives, and increasing revenues in the fairest way possible.

• Restoring budget discipline requires reenacting the budget decision rules (or some version of them) that were so effective in the 1990s.

The United States was able to eliminate deficits in the 1990s because we had bipartisan consensus on the objective and the rules. There was no consensus on *how* to get there, or on how fast, but the decision rules forced the warring parties to make tradeoffs that would not otherwise have been made. Success in the next round will require both a consensus on the objective and restoration of the budget decision rules. We would suggest:

• new caps on discretionary spending, covering both defense and domestic programs;

• restoring PAYGO rules on both entitlements and taxes—meaning that new entitlements and tax cuts have to be offset;

• stricter definitions of emergency exceptions to make it harder to enact spending bills that do not count against the caps; and

• ruling out laws, especially tax laws, that sunset just to make their cost look smaller.

Much is at stake. The U.S. economy is flexible and productive. We can afford high-quality private and public services. We can afford to invest in the skills of the labor force, especially low-wage workers. We can have first-rate infrastructure and clean air and water, as well as strong military forces. It would be incredibly shortsighted to choose, instead, to run huge deficits that are debilitating, at best, and, at worst, risky. We should not let irresponsible policies jeopardize the strong economy that we need in order to make everything else possible.

References

Rivlin, Alice M., and Isabel Sawhill, eds. 2004. *Restoring fiscal sanity: How to balance the budget*. Washington, D.C.: Brookings Institution.

Contributing Authors

Alan J. Auerbach

Alan J. Auerbach is Robert D. Burch Professor of Economics and Law and director of the Burch Center for Tax Policy at the University of California, Berkeley. He is also a research associate at the National Bureau of Economic Research, a member of the advisory committee of the Bureau of Economic Analysis at the U.S. Department of Commerce, and a fellow of both the American Academy of Arts and Sciences and the Econometric Society. He has been a consultant to the U.S. Treasury, the OECD, the IMF, the World Bank, the Swedish Ministry of Finance, the City of San Francisco, and the New Zealand Treasury. Previously, Auerbach was deputy chief of staff at the U.S. Joint Committee on Taxation, and he held prior academic positions at the University of Pennsylvania and Harvard University. He has written and edited numerous books and articles, including "Fiscal Policy, Past and Present" in *Brookings Papers on Economic Activity*. Auerbach holds a B.A. from Yale University and a Ph.D. in economics from Harvard University.

Susanto Basu

Susanto Basu is Professor of Economics at Boston College and a visiting scholar at the Federal Reserve Bank of Boston. He is also a research associate at the National Bureau of Economic Research, a member of the executive committee of the Conference on Research in Income and Wealth, and associate editor of *QRJM*, an electronic journal of macroeconomics. He has been on the editorial board of the *American Economic Review* and has organized several conferences for the National Bureau of Economic Research. Basu is the author of numerous articles and has received many awards for excellence in teaching as well as the University of Michigan Faculty Recognition Award. He recently published "The Case of the Missing Productivity Growth," co-authored with J.G. Fernald, N. Outon, and S. Srinivasan, in the *NBER Macroeconomics Annual*. Basu holds an A.B. and a Ph.D. in economics from Harvard University.

Olivier J. Blanchard

Olivier J. Blanchard is Class of 1941 Professor of Economics at the Massachusetts Institute of Technology. He is also a fellow and council member of the Econometric Society, a member of the American Academy of Arts and Sciences, and a research associate at the National Bureau of Economic Research. He further serves as membre du Conseil d'Analyse Economique aupres du Premier Ministre, Paris, is a member of the Commission de la Nation, Paris, an adviser at the McKinsey Global Institute, and a member of advisory panels at the Federal Reserve Banks of New York and Boston. Blanchard chaired the economics department at MIT for a number of years and has held academic positions at Harvard University. He has been vice president of the American Economic Association and co-editor of the *Quarterly Journal of Economics*. He is the author of numerous books and articles, including, recently, "Fiscal Dominance and Inflation Targeting: Lessons from Brazil" in the MIT Press volume *Inflation Targeting, Debt, and the Brazilian Experience, 1999 to 2003*. He holds a Ph.D. in economics from MIT.

Alan S. Blinder

Alan S. Blinder is Gordon S. Rentschler Memorial Professor of Economics and director of the Center for Economic Policy Studies at Princeton University. He is also a partner in Promontory Financial Group, vice chairman of the Promontory Interfinancial Network, and vice chairman of the G7 Group. Blinder served as vice chairman of the Board of Governors of the Federal Reserve System from June 1994 until January 1996. He served as a member of President Clinton's first Council of Economic Advisers, as Al Gore's chief economic advisor during the 2000 Presidential campaign, and as deputy assistant director of the Congressional Budget Office when that agency started in 1975. A trustee of the Russell Sage Foundation and a former governor of the American Stock Exchange, he is the author or co-author of 16 books, including the textbook *Economics: Principles and Policy* (with William J. Baumol), and has written scores of scholarly articles. He holds an A.B. from Princeton University, an M.Sc. from the London School of Economics, and a Ph.D. from the Massachusetts Institute of Technology, all in economics.

Barry P. Bosworth

Barry P. Bosworth is Senior Fellow in the Economic Studies program at The Brookings Institution, where he holds the Robert V. Roosa Chair in International Economics. Previously, he was director of the President's Council on Wage and Price Stability under President Carter; visiting lecturer at the University of California, Berkeley; assistant professor at Harvard University; and staff economist at the Council of Economic Advisers. Bosworth's research has concentrated on issues of capital formation and saving behavior. His current projects include a study of the economic consequences of population aging, an examination of productivity growth in services, and an exploration of the determinants of economic growth in developing countries. Recent publications include *Services Productivity in the United States: New Sources of Growth*, co-authored with Jack Triplett; "The Empirics of Growth," co-authored with Susan Collins; and "Pension Reform and Saving," co-authored with Gary Burtless. Bosworth holds a B.A. and a Ph.D. in economics from the University of Michigan.

W. Elliot Brownlee

W. Elliot Brownlee is Professor Emeritus at the University of California, Santa Barbara. He joined the faculty of UCSB in 1967 and served there as professor of history from 1980 until his retirement in 2002, with a stint as a visiting professor at Princeton University. In addition, he served the University of California as faculty representative on the Board of Regents and as associate provost for the UC system. Brownlee's numerous books and published articles reflect his expertise in taxation, public finance, and American economic history. An article co-authored by Brownlee and C. Eugene Steuerle on Reagan administration tax policy appeared in

The Reagan Presidency: Pragmatic Conservatism and Its Legacies, which Brownlee co-edited with Hugh Davis Graham in 2003. Brownlee's most recent book is *Federal Taxation in America: A Short History* (second edition 2004, first edition, 1996). Brownlee earned an A.B. from Harvard University in 1963 and received his M.A. and Ph.D. degrees from the University of Wisconsin in 1965 and 1969, respectively.

Willem H. Buiter

Willem H. Buiter is Chief Economist and Special Counsellor to the President at the European Bank for Reconstruction and Development. He also holds a professorship in economics at the University of Amsterdam and serves as visiting professor at the London School of Economics and as a member of the editorial board of *International Economics and Economic Policy*. Previously, Buiter was professor of international macroeconomics and fellow of Trinity College at the University of Cambridge and a member of the monetary policy committee of the Bank of England. Earlier, he held academic posts at Yale University, the London School of Economics, Bristol University, and Princeton University. Buiter has consulted for the International Monetary Fund, the Inter-American Development Bank, the World Bank, the New Zealand Treasury, and the central bank of Peru. He is the author of numerous articles and books. He holds a B.A. in economics from Cambridge University and M.A., M.Phil., and Ph.D. degrees, all in economics, from Yale University.

Jean-Philippe Cotis

Jean-Philippe Cotis is Chief Economist and head of the economics department at the Organisation for Economic Cooperation and Development. Previously, he was director of the economics department at the French Ministry of Economy, Finance, and Industry. Cotis joined the Ministry in 1982 after graduating from the Ecole Supérieure des Sciences Economiques et Commerciales (ESSEC), the Ecole Nationale d'Administration (ENA), and Paris I Sorbonne. He was economic advisor to the minister in 1993 and 1994. Cotis was an economist at the International Monetary Fund from 1986 to 1988. During his career, Cotis has worked frequently with international institutions. He was formerly chair of the Economic Policy Committee of the European Union (2001–2002) and of OECD's Working Party No. 1. His research work has mainly concerned labor markets, macroeconomic policy, and taxation. Cotis has held various teaching assignments, including at the Ecole Nationale d'Administration, ESSEC, Ecole des Mines, and the Kennedy School of Government at Harvard University. His co-authors, **Jonathan Coppel** and **Luiz de Mello**, are senior economists within the economics department of the OECD.

James S. Duesenberry

James S. Duesenberry is Professor Emeritus in the economics department at Harvard University. Duesenberry is known for his policy work as an advisor to governments and policymakers worldwide, for his expertise in developing econometric models, and for his research into income, saving, and consumer behavior. He currently serves as a consultant to the Harvard Institute for International Development in Sri Lanka, Indonesia, and Gambia. He has been a visiting professor at the University of Kobe in Japan and at Southwest University of Finance and Economics, ChengDu, Sichuan, China. He was a member of the Council of Economic Advisers under President Johnson. He is the author of numerous articles and books about macroeconomics and central banking, including *Money, Banking, and the Economy*, which he co-authored with Thomas Mayer and Robert Z. Aliber. Duesenberry was chairman of the board of directors of the Federal Reserve Bank of Boston and currently serves on the Bank's academic advisory council. He received his A.B., A.M., and Ph.D. degrees in economics from the University of Michigan.

Douglas W. Elmendorf

Douglas W. Elmendorf is Assistant Director and Section Chief for Macroeconomic Analysis in the Division of Research and Statistics at the Federal Reserve Board. He joined the Federal Reserve Board as an economist in 1995, leaving in 1998 to become senior economist at the Council of Economic Advisers and then deputy assistant secretary at the U.S. Treasury. He rejoined the Federal Reserve Board in 2001. Prior to his career at the Board, Elmendorf served as an analyst at the Congressional Budget Office and as an assistant professor at Harvard University. Elmendorf's fields of interest include macroeconomics and public economics. His recent publications include "Short-Run Effects of

Fiscal Policy with Forward-Looking Financial Markets," co-authored with David L. Reifschneider, in the *National Tax Journal*, September 2002; and "Fiscal Policy and Social Security Policy During the 1990s," co-authored with Jeffrey B. Liebman and David W. Wilcox, in *American Economic Policy in the 1990s*. Elmendorf holds an A.B. in economics from Princeton University and a Ph.D. in economics from Harvard University.

Jeffrey A. Frankel

Jeffrey A. Frankel is James W. Harpel Professor of Capital Formation and Growth at Harvard University's Kennedy School of Government. He directs the program in international finance and macroeconomics at the National Bureau of Economic Research, where he is also a member of the business cycle dating committee. Frankel served on the Council of Economic Advisers from 1996 to 1999, where his responsibilities included international economics, macroeconomics, and the environment. Previously, he was professor of economics at the University of California, Berkeley. Other past affiliations include the Brookings Institution, Federal Reserve Board, Institute for International Economics, International Monetary Fund, University of Michigan, Yale University, and World Bank. Frankel's research interests include international finance, monetary policy, regional blocs, Asia, and global environmental issues. He has written, co-authored, or edited numerous articles and books, including the textbook *World Trade and Payments*, published in 2002. He holds a B.A. from Swarthmore College and a Ph.D. from MIT.

Benjamin M. Friedman

Benjamin M. Friedman is William Joseph Maier Professor of Political Economy and former chair of the department of economics at Harvard University. His research and writing focus primarily on economic policy and in particular on the role of financial markets in shaping how monetary and fiscal policies affect overall economic activity. Friedman's latest book is *The Moral Consequences of Economic Growth*. His earlier book, *Day of Reckoning: The Consequences of American Economic Growth Under Reagan and After*, received the George S. Eccles Prize.

Friedman is a director of the Private Export Funding Corporation and of the *Encyclopaedia Britannica*. He is a trustee of the Standish Mellon Investment Trust and a member of the Economic Advisory Council of the Federal Reserve Bank of New York, the Council on Foreign Relations, and the Brookings Panel on Economic Activity. Before joining the Harvard faculty, Friedman worked with Morgan Stanley. He received his A.B., A.M., and Ph.D. in economics from Harvard University and holds an M.Sc. in economics and politics from King's College, Cambridge, where he studied as a Marshall Scholar.

Richard W. Kopcke

Richard W. Kopcke currently is both Visiting Professor at Northeastern University's College of Business Administration and a visiting scholar in the Research Department of the Federal Reserve Bank of Boston, where he served as an economist for over 30 years and was most recently also a vice president. His recent articles have discussed such topics as inflation-indexed bonds, valuation of stocks, and issues related to mutual funds and financial stability. He has also worked intermittently as an advisor to the Bank of Zambia, the Bank of Lithuania, the Palestinian Monetary Authority, and the Central Bank of Iraq. Kopcke completed his bachelor's degree at the University of Michigan and received a Ph.D. from Harvard University.

Catherine L. Mann

Catherine L. Mann is Senior Fellow at the Institute for International Economics in Washington, D.C. Previously, she served as assistant director of the International Finance Division at the Federal Reserve Board, senior international economist on the President's Council of Economic Advisers, and adviser to the chief economist at the World Bank. Mann taught for 10 years as adjunct professor of management at the Owen School of Management at Vanderbilt University and for two years at The Johns Hopkins Nitze School for Advanced International Studies. She is the author or co-author of numerous books and articles, including *High-Tech and Globalization in America*. Her areas of research interest include economic and policy issues of global information, communications, and technology and broader issues of U.S. trade, the sustainability of the current account, and the exchange value of the dollar. She graduated from Harvard University and holds a Ph.D. from the Massachusetts Institute of Technology.

Van Doorn Ooms

Van Doorn Ooms is Senior Fellow and former senior vice president and director of research at the Committee for Economic Development. Previously, he was executive director for policy and chief economist of the Committee on the Budget, U.S. House of Representatives. He has also served as assistant director for economic policy (chief economist) at the Office of Management and Budget and as chief economist of the Committee on the Budget, U.S. Senate. Before entering public service, Ooms taught economics at Yale University and at Swarthmore College, where he was a professor of economics. His primary fields of interest are macroeconomics and fiscal policy, with special emphasis on the political economy of the U.S. budget. Ooms has recently supervised CED research projects in U.S. trade policy, education, urban development, labor markets, regulation, funding for basic research, Social Security, pension policy, welfare reform, and campaign finance. Ooms graduated *summa cum laude* from Amherst College, studied at Oxford University as a Rhodes Scholar, and received his Ph.D. in economics from Yale University.

Rudolph G. Penner

Rudolph G. Penner is Senior Fellow at the The Urban Institute, where he holds the Arjay and Frances Miller chair in public policy. Previously, he was a managing director of the Barents Group, a KPMG company. Penner has served as director of the Congressional Budget Office, assistant director for economic policy at the Office of Management and Budget, deputy assistant secretary for economic affairs at the Department of Housing and Urban Development, and senior staff economist at the Council of Economic Advisers. He has been a resident scholar at the American Enterprise Institute and a professor of economics at the University of Rochester. He is past president of the National Economists Club. The author of numerous books, pamphlets, and articles on tax and spending policy, Penner received the Abramson Prize for the best article published in 1988–89 in business economics. His most recent book, co-authored with Isabel Sawhill and Timothy Taylor, is *Updating America's Social Contract*. He holds an undergraduate degree from the University of Toronto and a Ph.D. in economics from The Johns Hopkins University.

Alice M. Rivlin

Alice M. Rivlin is Visiting Professor at the Public Policy Institute of Georgetown University and a Senior Fellow in the Economic Studies program at the The Brookings Institution, where she is director of the Greater Washington Research Program. She has served as vice chair of the Federal Reserve Board, director of the White House Office of Management and Budget, and chair of the District of Columbia Financial Management Assistance Authority. Rivlin was the founding director of the Congressional Budget Office. She was director of the economic studies program at Brookings for four years and also served at the U.S. Department of Health, Education, and Welfare as assistant secretary for planning and evaluation. The recipient of a MacArthur Foundation Prize Fellowship, Rivlin has taught at Harvard, George Mason, and the New School. She is a past president of the American Economic Association and has served on the boards of several corporations. She is currently a director of the Washington Post Company and BearingPoint. Rivlin holds a B.A. in economics from Bryn Mawr College and a Ph.D. in economics from Harvard University.

Christopher A. Sims

Christopher A. Sims is Professor of Economics at Princeton University. Previously, he was Henry Ford II Professor of Economics at Yale University. He has also taught at the University of Minnesota and Harvard University and has been a visiting scholar at the Federal Reserve Banks of New York and Philadelphia and a consultant to the Federal Reserve Bank of Minneapolis and the International Monetary Fund. Sims is a member of the National Academy of Sciences and the American Academy of Arts and Sciences and a fellow of the Econometric Society, where he served as president in 1995. His areas of research interest are econometric theory for dynamic models and macroeconomic theory and policy. He is the author of numerous articles, including "Implications of Rational Inattention" in the *Journal of Monetary Economics* (April 2003). Sims holds a B.A. in mathematics from Harvard College and a Ph.D. in economics from Harvard University.

C. Eugene Steuerle

C. Eugene Steuerle is a Senior Fellow at The Urban Institute, co-director of the Urban-Brookings Tax Policy Center, a columnist for *Tax Notes Magazine*, and the author or editor of numerous books, articles, reports, and columns. He serves on the National Committee on Vital and Health Statistics and on advisory panels or boards for the Congressional Budget Office, the Comptroller General of the United States, the Joint Committee on Taxation, the Independent Sector, and the *Journal of Economic Perspectives*. Previously, he has served as president of the National Tax Association, chair of the 1999 Technical Panel advising Social Security on its methods and assumptions, president of the National Economists Club Educational Foundation, deputy assistant secretary of the Treasury for tax analysis, and resident fellow at the American Enterprise Institute. Between 1984 and 1985, he served as economic coordinator and original organizer of the U.S. Treasury's tax reform effort. Steuerle's latest book is *Contemporary U.S. Tax Policy*. He received his Ph.D. from the University of Wisconsin.

Geoffrey M. B. Tootell

Geoffrey M. B. Tootell is Vice President and Economist at the Federal Reserve Bank of Boston, where he oversees the macroeconomics/open economy section of the Research Department. His primary responsibilities include providing economic analysis for the monetary policy deliberations of the bank president and its board of directors. Tootell's research focuses on monetary policy, with particular emphasis on the determinants of inflation and the decision-making of the Federal Open Market Committee. He has recently explored whether the Federal Reserve's economic forecasts might be improved by incorporating bank supervisory information and the role that asset markets play in monetary policy formation. He has also written a number of influential articles on racial patterns in mortgage lending. Tootell received his Ph.D. in economics from Harvard, where he also did his undergraduate work.

Robert K. Triest

Robert K. Triest is Senior Economist and Policy Advisor in the Research Department of the Federal Reserve Bank of Boston. Before joining the Bank in 1995, he was an assistant professor at The Johns Hopkins University and an associate professor at the University of California at Davis. Triest has also worked at the U.S. Bureau of the Census as a research associate and spent 2005 as a visiting scholar at the Center for Retirement Research at Boston College. His research has focused on topics in public finance and labor economics, such as the economic impacts of demographic change, Social Security reform, and the incentive effects of taxation. He has published articles in various professional journals and Boston Fed publications. He earned his bachelor's degree from Vassar College and his Ph.D. in economics from the University of Wisconsin.

Edwin M. Truman

Edwin M. Truman is Senior Fellow at the Institute for International Economics in Washington, D.C. Previously, he served as assistant secretary of the U.S. Treasury for international affairs. Before joining the U.S. Treasury, Truman was director and later staff director of the Division of International Finance at the Board of Governors of the Federal Reserve System and on the staff of the Federal Open Market Committee, having joined the Federal Reserve Board in 1972. Truman is the author of *Inflation Targeting in the World Economy* and co-author of *Chasing Dirty Money: The Fight Against Money Laundering*. He has published works on international monetary economics, international debt problems, economic development, and European economic integration. Truman is a former associate professor of economics at Yale University, where he received his M.A. and Ph.D. degrees. He holds a B.A. and an honorary L.L.D. from Amherst College.

Author Index

Subject Index